D1756030

The Architect of Modern Catalan

Pompeu Fabra (1868–1948)

UNIVERSITAT
POMPEU FABRA

Publication of this volume was planned as part of the programme of commemoration arranged by the Universitat Pompeu Fabra in 2006–2007, organised by the Presidency of the University. This initiative has been fully supported and sponsored by the University's Consell Social.

institut
ramon llull

Llengua i cultura catalanes

The translation of this work has received a grant from the Institut Ramon Llull.

The Architect of Modern Catalan

Pompeu Fabra (1868–1948)

Selected Writings

Selection and edition of texts and introduction by
Joan Costa Carreras

Translation by Alan Yates

Prologue by Georg Kremnitz

John Benjamins Publishing Company

Amsterdam / Philadelphia

The paper used in this publication meets the minimum requirements of
American National Standard for Information Sciences – Permanence of
Paper for Printed Library Materials, ANSI z39.48-1984.

Library of Congress Cataloging-in-Publication Data

Fabra, Pompeu, 1868-1948.
The architect of modern Catalan : selected writings / Pompeu Fabra (1868-1948) ;
     selection and edition of texts and introduction by Joan Costa Carreras ;
     translation by Alan Yates ; prologue by Georg Kremnitz.
    p. cm.
Includes bibliographical references and index.
1. Catalan language. I. Costa Carreras, J. (Joan) II. Yates, Alan, 1944- III. Title.
PC3809.F3A25   2009
409.2--dc22
[B]   2009017907
ISBN 978 90 272 3264 9 (HB; alk. paper)
ISBN 978 90 272 8924 7 (EB)

John Benjamins Publishing Co. · P.O. Box 36224 · 1020 ME Amsterdam · The Netherlands
John Benjamins North America · P.O. Box 27519 · Philadelphia PA 19118-0519 · USA

Table of contents

Acknowledgements   XI

The Pompeu Fabra University and the Architect of modern Catalan   XIII
  Joan Josep Moreso

Pompeu Fabra   XVII
  Salvador Giner

Pompeu Fabra: A universal linguist   XXI
  Joan Martí i Castells

Prologue   XXV
  Georg Kremnitz

1. **General presentation**   1
  Joan Costa Carreras

2. **The Catalan language**   3
  Joan Costa Carreras and Alan Yates
  2.1 The Catalan language domain 3
  2.2 The demography of Catalan 3
  2.3 The dialect divisions of Catalan 5
  2.4 The concept of a language community 5
  2.5 An outline of the social history of Catalan 6
    2.5.1 The origins and the Middle Ages 6
    2.5.2 Decadence 7
    2.5.3 The *Renaixença* 9
    2.5.4 *Modernisme* 11
    2.5.5 *Noucentisme* 14
    2.5.6 Developments through the twentieth century 18
      2.5.6.1 The Dictatorship of Miguel Primo de Rivera 18
      2.5.6.2 The Second Spanish Republic 20
      2.5.6.3 The Franco years 21
      2.5.6.4 The post-Franco era 23
  2.6 Bibliography and sources of information on Catalan 24
    2.6.1 Bibliography and materials for learning Catalan 24

2.6.1.1   Self-teaching methods   24

2.6.1.2   On-line multilingual dictionaries   25

2.6.1.3   Books for learning Catalan   25

2.6.1.4   On-line Catalan dictionaries   26

2.6.2   Other relevant source material   26

2.6.2.1   Useful web-sites   26

2.6.2.2   Works in English on the Catalan language   27

2.6.2.3   Works in Spanish on the Catalan language   27

2.6.2.4   Works in French on the Catalan language   27

2.6.2.5   Works in Catalan on the Catalan language   28

3.   **Pompeu Fabra: A life's work in applied linguistics**   **29**
   Joan Costa Carreras

3.1   Introduction   29

3.2   Pompeu Fabra: Biographical outline   30

3.3   Pompeu Fabra as theoretician of the literary language   37

3.3.1   An analysis of general reflections on literary language
explicit in Pompeu Fabra's writings   37

3.3.1.1   "On Various Unresolved Issues in Present-Day
Literary Catalan", 1907   38

3.3.1.2   Philological Conversation, 18/XI/1919   39

3.3.1.3   "The Task of Purifying Catalan", 1924   39

3 3.1.4   "A Conversation with Pompeu Fabra", May 1926   40

3.3.1.5   "On the Purification of the Literary Language", 1927   41

3.3.1.6   "On the Purification of the Literary Language", 1927   41

3.3.1.7   General Dictionary of the Catalan Language, 1932   42

3.3.1.8   "Deviations in the Concepts of Language
and Homeland", 1934   42

3.3.1.9   Catalan Grammar: Intermediate Course,
1935 edition   42

3.3.2   Criteria for syntactic codification   43

3.3.3   Relations between Fabra's conception of syntactical
codification and syntax   55

3.3.3.1   Fabra's conception of syntax   55

3.3.3.2   Relations between Fabra's conception
of syntactical codification and syntax   58

3.3.4   Relations between Fabra's conception of syntactical
codification and syntactical change   59

3.3.4.1   Fabra's conception of linguistic change   59

3.3.4.2   Relations between Fabra's conception
of syntactical codification and syntactical change   63
3.3.5   Relations between Fabra's conception of syntactical
codification and syntactical diversity   66
3.3.5.1   An analysis of general reflections on syntactical
diversity explicit in Pompeu Fabra's writings   66
3.3.5.2   Fabra's conception of linguistic diversity   67
3.3.5.3   Relations between Fabra's conception
of syntactical codification and syntactical diversity   70
3.3.6   Articulation of Fabra's principles for syntactical codification
and his ideas on syntax itself including syntactical change
and diversity   72
3.3.7   Normativisation in practice   74
3.4   Pompeu Fabra as grammarian   82
3.4.1   Grammars, addressed to a specialist readership,
with a basically descriptive objective   83
3.4.1.1   Ensayo de catalán moderno /
Essay on the Grammar of Modern Catalan (1891)   83
3.4.1.2   Contribució a la gramàtica catalana / *Contribution
to the Grammar of the Catalan Language* (1898)   83
3.4.1.3   Gramática de la lengua catalana /
Grammar of the Catalan Language (1912)   84
3.4.1.4   Gramàtica catalana: curs mitjà /
Catalan Grammar. Intermediate Course (1918)   84
3.4.1.5   Gramàtica francesa / *French Grammar* (1919)   84
3.4.1.6   Gramàtica anglesa / *English Grammar* (1924)   84
3.4.1.7   Gramàtica catalana / *Catalan Grammar* (1946)   85
3.4.1.8   Gramàtica catalana / *Catalan Grammar* (1956)   85
3.4.2   Grammars, addressed to a non-specialist public,
having a basically normative objective   85
3.4.2.1   Gramàtica catalana / *Catalan Grammar* (1918)   85
3.4.2.2   Abrégé de grammaire catalane /
Outline of French Grammar (1928)   86
3.4.2.3   Compendio de gramática catalana /
Compendium of Catalan Grammar (1929)   86
3.4.2.4   Grammaire catalane / *Catalan Grammar* (1941)   86
3.5   Pompeu Fabra as lexicographer   86
3.6   Pompeu Fabra as translator   89
3.7   Pompeu Fabra and toponymy   90
3.8   Pompeu Fabra as a manager of linguistic diversity   90

3.9 Texts by Pompeu Fabra   91
   3.9.1   Texts by Pompeu Fabra in Catalan   91
   3.9.2   Texts by Pompeu Fabra in Spanish   95
   3.9.3   Texts by Pompeu Fabra in French   95
3.10 Basic bibliography on Pompeu Fabra's work   96
   3.10.1 Introductory studies   96
      3.10.1.1 Basic bibliography on Pompeu Fabra's work in English   96
      3.10.1.2 Basic bibliography on Pompeu Fabra's work in Spanish   97
      3.10.1.3 Basic bibliography on Pompeu Fabra's work in Catalan   97
   3.10.2 Works consulted   97

4. **Presentation of the edition**   103
   4.1 The texts included in the anthology   103
      4.1.1   On the selection of texts translated   103
      4.1.2   List of texts translated   103
   4.2 About the translation   105
      4.2.1   Translation strategies   105
      4.2.2   Contextual information in the translation   106
         4.2.2.1   General remarks   106
         4.2.2.2   Footnotes   107
         4.2.2.3   Information supplied within each translated text   108
      4.2.3   Conventions used in the translations   111
         4.2.3.1   Italics   111
         4.2.3.2   Inverted commas   111
         4.2.3.3   Square brackets   111
      4.2.4   Abbreviations   112
      4.2.5   Sources of the texts translated   112

Selected writings of Pompeu Fabra   113
1. "Sobre la reforma lingüística y ortográfica" (*On Linguistic and Orthographical Reform*)   113
2. "Sobre diferents problemes pendents en l'actual català literari" (*On Various Unresolved Issues in Present-day Literary Catalan*)   118
3. "L'obra dels nostres descastellanitzants" (*Eradicating Castilian Influence: Our descastellanitzants*)   124
4. "Cal gramàtica als escriptors" (*Writers Need Grammar*)   126
5. "Literats i gramàtics" (*Writers and Grammarians*)   130

6. "Les normes de l'Institut" (*The Norms of the Institut d'Estudis Catalans*) **135**
7. "Castellanismes de la llengua escrita" (*Castilianisms in the Written Language*) **143**
8. "Filòlegs i poetes" (*Philologists and Poets*) **144**
9. "La tasca dels escriptors valencians i balears" (*The Task of the Valencian and Balearic Writers*) **147**
10. "Conversa filològica" (*Philological Conversation*) 18/XI/1919 **148**
11. " " " " 12/XII/1919 **149**
12. " " " " 7/I/1920 **150**
13. " " " " 15/V/1920 (1st para.) **151**
14. " " " " 25/V/1920 **151**
15. " " " " 10/VIII/1920 **152**
16. " " " " 30/VIII/1920 (1st para.) **152**
17. " " " " 9/X/1920 **153**
18. " " " " 3/XI/1920 **153**
19. " " " " 13/XII/1922 **154**
20. " " " " 30/XII/1922 **154**
21. " " " " 10/II/1923 **155**
22. " " " " 24/III/1923 (1st para.) **156**
23. " " " " 25/III/1923 (1st para.) **157**
24. " " " " 1/IV/1923 **157**
25. " " " " 13/IV/1923 **158**
26. " " " " 14/IV/1923 **159**
27. " " " " 16/IV/1923 **159**
28. " " " " 24/IV/1923 (2nd para.) **160**
29. " " " " 5/V/1923 (2nd para.) **161**
30. " " " " 13/V/1923 **161**
31. " " " " 19/V/1923 **162**
32. " " " " 10/VI/1923 **162**
33. " " " " 17/VI/1923 (2nd para.) **163**
34. " " " " 13/XII/1923 **163**
35. " " " " 16/I/1924 (1st para.) **164**
36. " " " " 26/I/1924 (1st para.) **164**
37. " " " " 30/I/1924 (1st para.) **164**
38. " " " " 2/II/1924 (1st para.) **165**
39. " " " " 5/II/1924 (1st para.) **165**
40. " " " " 15/II/1924 (1st para.) **166**
41. " " " " 26/III/1924 (1st para.) **166**
42. " " " " 4/V/1924 (1st para.) **167**

43.	"	"	"	"	10/VII/1924 (1st para.) **167**
44.	"	"	"	"	13/VII/1924 **167**
45.	"	"	"	"	5/VIII/1924 **168**
46.	"	"	"	"	26/VIII/1924 **169**
47.	"	"	"	"	10/IX/1924 **170**
48.	"	"	"	"	13/IX/1924 **171**

49. "L'obra de depuració del català" (*The Task of Purifying Catalan*)   **172**

50. "Conversa amb Pompeu Fabra" (*A Conversation with Pompeu Fabra*)   **187**

51. "Conversa filològica" (*Philological Conversation*)   17/VI/1926   **194**

52.   "   "   "   "   12/IX/1926   **194**

53.   "   "   "   "   17/VI/1927   **195**

54.   "   "   "   "   12/VI/1928   **196**

55. "De la depuració de la llengua literària" (*On the Purification of the Literary Language*)   **196**

56. "La normalització de la gramàtica" (*The Normalisation of Grammar*)   **204**

57. Pròleg al *Diccionari general de la llengua catalana* (Prologue to *Diccionari general de la llengua catalana*)   **206**

58. «Desviacions en els conceptes de llengua i Pàtria» (*Deviations in the Concepts of Language and Homeland*)   **208**

59. «Discurs del President» (*Presidential Address to the Barcelona Jocs Florals*)   **213**

Index of names and concepts   **221**

Acknowledgements

The editor and the Universitat Pompeu Fabra wish to acknowledge the authorisation generously granted by the Institut d'Estudis Catalans for the translation of Fabra's texts and their cooperation in bringing the publication project to fruition.

Grateful acknowledgement is also made of financial support received from the Institut Ramon Llull.

Personal thanks go to Carmen Pérez, delegate of the President of the Pompeu Fabra University for Linguistic Promotion, for her strong and efficient support from the beginning of this project; and to Anke de Looper, acquisition editor at John Benjamins Publishers, for her consideration, support and good advice.

The Pompeu Fabra University
and the Architect of modern Catalan

Pompeu Fabra is a key figure for the Catalan language and its culture. He is regarded as the *ordenador*, the person who put modern Catalan in order. His work on reconstructing the language – as a means of communication and also, especially, as a sign of identity – made him one of the outstanding personalities in the movement of *Noucentisme* which energised and defined the direction of Catalan nationalism from the beginning of the twentieth century.

President of the Institute of Catalan Studies and a founder member of its Philological Section; President of two of Barcelona's major cultural institutions, the Ateneu Barcelonès and the literary festival of the Jocs Florals; an assiduous contributor to numerous publications and editor-in-chief of the journal *Catalònia*; linguist, grammarian, lexicographer... a large part of this philologist's work was also connected with the University. Indeed, the figure of Pompeu Fabra personifies and exemplifies the Second Spanish Republic's commitment, in the 1930s, to educational reform. And, in Catalonia, this movement incorporated also the concept of Catalan national identity. During the period of the Republic (1931–1939), once autonomy was achieved for the University of Barcelona, Fabra presided over its independent board of trustees or *Patronat*. He was appointed directly to the Chair of Catalan Philology and he was in charge of the Department of Romance Languages and Literatures. His commitment to the University was absolute and, in collaboration with people like Jaume Serra Húnter and Pere Bosch-Gimpera – the two Presidents of the Republican period – and other fellow academics, he worked hard for the regeneration of the University in our country. Time was not on his side, however. The University Council, which had begun to operate in 1933, was disbanded in the wake of the political turbulence of October 1934. Fabra, on account of his official position, was held in prison for some weeks. During this period, as the object of great esteem and affection in the eyes of the Catalan people, he received time and again expressions of public homage. The University of Toulouse (Languedoc), for example awarded him an honorary Doctorate and the Societat Catalana d'Estudis Històrics made him their Honorary President.

At the Pompeu Fabra University (UPF) we resolved to dedicate the academic year 2006–2007 to specially commemorating the figure and the work of the philologist whom we honour everyday by officially bearing his name. And it was precisely through organising the Pompeu Fabra Year that we became aware of how, in one important respect, his production stood in a great void: there were no translations into English of any of his texts nor was there in that language any study of his work. The University's Department of Translation and Language Sciences had also realised that this was a major gap calling to be filled, as they had received requests for information on the subject from various specialists in language planning who were interested in the normalisation process of Catalan. All these enquirers expressed disappointment and perplexity about how academic bodies and publishers could allow such a lack to exist. It was something which showed up the contradiction between the admiration and recognition enjoyed by the figure of Pompeu Fabra throughout the Catalan-speaking domain and, by contrast, the fact of his being so unrecognised in Europe and in the rest of the world. Consequently, the University considered that steps should be taken to make Fabra's work known internationally – and, by extension, to promote international understanding about the Catalan language – through the first English-language edition of a selection of his texts, together with a biographical outline and an introductory study.

The appearance of the present publication is the gratifying outcome of close co-operation with the Institute of Catalan Studies. The University's *Consell Social* has from the outset wished to be involved in this project and to make its own contribution both to the spirit and the letter of the initiative. I wish also to acknowledge gratefully the grant received from the Institut Ramon Llull. The translation has been done by Dr. Alan Yates, Professor Emeritus of the University of Sheffield and Corresponding Member of the Philological Section of the Institute of Catalan Studies. His editorial advice has also been much appreciated. Preparation of the anthology of texts and of the introductory study are the work of Dr. Joan Costa Carreras, Lecturer in the Translation and Language Sciences Department of the UPF, who specialises in Fabra's ideas on normativisation.

The reader now has the book in his/her hands. Selection of the over fifty pieces that make up the compendium has been a complicated task, not just because of the sheer volume of Fabra's total output but also – above all – because of the quality and the importance of his writings. Pause for reflection is given by the fact that his Catalan Grammar, which he he was charged with composing for the Institute of Catalan Studies in 1918 – and which he continuously revised for its seven editions up to 1933 –, is still to this day (May 2009) the official Grammar of that academy. So too for the outstanding service performed by the General Dictionary of the Catalan Language, which Fabra published in 1932 and which became the normative dictionary of the Institute for more than sixty years.

Fabra's contributions to the Catalan language are beyond dispute. Nevertheless, the items selected for this edition display the multiple facets of an authority who did not restrict his work to dealing with *only* the linguistic, grammatical and lexical aspects of Catalan. His theoretical perspectives on the literary language, expounded in his newspaper articles and well represented in this volume, are memorable. For example, "On Linguistic and Orthographical Reform" (1892) "The Task of the Valencian and Balearic Writers" (1918), or his "Philological Conversations", a collection of articles published between 1919 and 1928, where he reflects on, among other issues, linguistic interference and the problems of the normative standard language. Meditations on the language and on its restoration to a fully normal condition are constant in Fabra's whole trajectory, and he took every opportunity to explain them also in speeches, lectures and, even, in the occasional interview that he granted, as in Tomàs Garcés's "Conversation with Pompeu Fabra" (1926). The format was not important. Everything he wrote was directed towards the same conclusion. Fabra's main achievement was not limited to regularising the Catalan language according to phonetic, morphological, syntactical or lexical criteria. That man who trained as an engineer decided one fine day, fortunately, that what he really wanted to *construct* was the grammar of Catalan, and his really great contribution was this: restoring to our own language the character of distinguishing symbol of the Catalan nation.

Pompeu Fabra is not only the man who fashioned the modern Catalan language: he himself is a symbol of our culture. For this reason the relevance of this book is undeniable. We should celebrate the opportunity we are now offered, both to bring the work and the figure of Fabra and of Catalan to the attention of the international public, and to facilitate study of them by specialists all over the world. Finally and in short, as President of the Universitat Pompeu Fabra, I am particularly gratified by the publication of this book, as a starting point for full justice to be done to the figure and the achievements of this Catalan philologist, giving to him the place he deserves in the international panorama.

Joan Josep Moreso
President
Universitat Pompeu Fabra

Pompeu Fabra

Most European tongues have found someone whose task was to establish their basic linguistic rules as well as the criteria whereby the language was to be used and consolidated. Substantial modern states and political units, particularly in Western Europe, found their canonical codifier and linguistic authority very early in their respective histories. They were often aided by the moral authority of a national writer – Dante, Shakespeare, Racine – including, in certain cases, that of a translator of Scripture, such as Melanchton or Luther. Their different contributions paved the way for the consolidation of what, in the course of time, would come to be known as the national language.

The history of the Catalan-speaking community in the modern era, however, meant that the emergence of a serious effort at the codification and modernisation of the language, entailing the establishment of grammatical rules and synctactic and other criteria, did not materialise until relatively recently. Attainment of this condition, common to most European languages, had to wait until a crucial modernising tendency within Catalan nationalism, the cultural movement called *Noucentisme*, took as one of its core tasks the "ordering", codifying and systematic study of the language. The process began towards the end of the nineteenth century and came to fruition during the first decades of the twentieth.

Catalonia was by then, within Spain, an industrial and forward-looking area, with a large cosmopolitan city, Barcelona, at its centre. For many of its citizens it looked as though the country, in sharp contrast with the Spain to which it politically belonged, had already achieved or was clearly on its way to achieving, the much longed-for effort to transform it into a really modern and advanced European society. The Catalan sense of a "national" identity, however, had been developed until then on the basis of Romantic visions of the country and of its language, all too often linked to nostalgic interpretations of a medieval past. The break with this outlook was being made already by the 1880s, and a key transitional figure here was the great poet Jacint Verdaguer. His masterpiece was the epic poem *Canigó* which powerfully sang the glories of the land, of its people and of the nation whose symbolic origins and ancient laws date back almost a hundred years before the English Magna Carta.

By the turn of the century the main dynamic of Catalan culture had shifted to an affirmation of modernity, with a distinctly nationalist emphasis. This was the significance of the cultural movement known as *Modernisme*. Its representative artistic products were exuberant, complex and spectacular, as is evidenced by the work of the celebrated architect Antoni Gaudí.

The *modernista* cycle overlapped with and was superseded by the movement of *Noucentisme* or "New-Centuryism". This was a reaction against its immediate intellectual and cultural precedents, both Romantic innocence and *Modernisme's* lack of a coherent political direction. Although Catalan society was being transformed, economically and politically, a concerted cultural effort was absolutely necessary to complete the process of modernisation. This is not the place to analyse the consequences, achievements or shortcomings of *Noucentisme*. Suffice it to say that one creation of the movement, the Institut d'Estudis Catalans, meant the establishment of a modern academy of the sciences and the humanities for the country. The year was 1907. The Institute immediately set to work in many fields. It began with the establishment of a national library, sent archaeological expeditions to until then neglected sites, set up new scientific and technological services and developed university-level courses in order to fill the many gaps from which the official University suffered. One of the *Institut's* main tasks was, soon after its foundation, the scientific study and thorough reform of the Catalan language itself.

The lexicographical labours and offices of the Institute were lucky to be able to count on some eminent linguists, among them Antoni Maria Alcover and Pompeu Fabra. There were differences between these two, though, on the criteria to be applied for the establishment of a common dictionary and grammar. In the end Fabra prevailed. In 1913 the Institute officially sanctioned the *Orthographical Norms* for the Catalan language. They were immediately applied by the then regional administration of the country, and were accepted by the vast majority of writers, publishers and the press. The *Norms* were then crowned by their recognition at the city of Castelló, in the Valencian region of the language, in 1932. In that same year a canonical dictionary of the Catalan language, produced under the direction of Fabra himself, became the standard reference for the language. Today, the latest edition of the official *Diccionari de la llengua catalana*, that of 2007, published by the Institute, is still inspired by and largely based on his work.

Not all European languages have had this much good fortune. Catalan indeed makes a very interesting case-study of "stateless languages" which have struggled successfully against degradation in the wake of the political development of modern Europe. Despite being historically the language of an outstanding culture, as well as the official language, nowadays, of relatively large territories – Catalonia itself, the old kingdom of Valencia, the Balearic Islands and some Mediterranean outposts of a medieval maritime empire – the Catalan language suffered since the sixteenth century the consequences of the endemic political fragmentation of its territories. Later, after 1714, it also suffered from defeat in war and, to this day, from political subordination.

The Catalan language, in all its remarkable unity and surprisingly minor varieties in its dialects, was lucky to find in Pompeu Fabra a man entirely equal to the task of endowing it with the formal characteristics of a modern language of culture. A chemical engineer by education, sober, rationalist, and serene in his passion, Fabra was one of the outstanding linguists of his age. We need to remind ourselves that, when the campaign for its formal normativisation and social normalisation was embarked upon, the language had been officially relegated entirely to its colloquial use and never taught in schools or used for official documents or in the press.

One is loath to admit to the view that a single man, no matter how extraordinary, can be a miraculous hero. Pompeu Fabra was not a miracle-maker: the simple fact is that he belonged to the crucial generation of cultural modernisers who founded the Institute and wholly situated Catalonia in the world of contemporary science, research and education. But he certainly was providential for the nation. And, indirectly, for the necessary recognition of the dignity of a language, any language, and its people in the modern world. We have only to think of what would have happened to the language and culture of the Catalan people today, had the grammatical, lexicographical and linguistic acumen of Fabra, let alone his civic dedication and his determination, not been put at their service.

The Institute is very happy to collaborate in this project with the University which bears the name of our great linguist Pompeu Fabra, in the publication of the present selection of his writings. I wish also to add a personal note to expression of the Institute's appreciation of the careful and accurate translations into English done by Professor Alan Yates, a good friend of many years' standing. He has performed here a valuable service to the Catalan language, by rendering in the *lingua franca* of our day some of the treasure of Fabra's work and making it accessible to the international community of linguists, by which it has to date remained too little known and too little acknowledged.

Salvador Giner
President
Institut d'Estudis Catalans

Pompeu Fabra: A universal linguist

It would be quite wrong to apply to Pompeu Fabra the cliché about the neglect or marginalisation frequently suffered by wise and committed people, which is what he was. Considered to be an indispensable authority both by his contemporaries and by those who continued his work through to our own time, he has been admired to the point of veneration. This is no wonder, because it is abundantly justified by the value of the research he carried out and, furthermore, by the fact that he laboured in the cause of a language threatened with disappearance, from which he successfully saved it. It is evident that, but for his intervention as a grammarian and as a codifier of Catalan, we would now no longer possess this birthright. Appreciation of how close to obliteration the language had come has not just arrived with the passing of the years: Fabra's own contemporaries were fully aware of this. Nevertheless, the fact that he devoted himself specifically to an impoverished language on the verge of extinction has probably prevented him from enjoying the international projection and recognition that his work deserves. His name ought to be mentioned in the roll-call of the most outstanding linguists, not only in the applied field but also in that of language theory. Pompeu Fabra never indulged in improvisation: quite the opposite, he based himself upon a solid general conception of linguistic science and upon an extraordinary knowledge of the history of Catalan and of all the other Romance languages. The specific weight of his contributions to grammar, lexicology and lexicography, phonology and phonetics, as well as to sociolinguistics, is as strong as that of the most eminent linguists.

We have, thus, a duty which cannot be shirked: to make those contributions accessible to all specialists in the field. Not just as an act of justice towards the person of Pompeu Fabra, but principally because of the ethical obligation to put into much wider service than hitherto the wisdom which characterised him.

It has been said that Fabra was the first Catalan linguist *stricto sensu*. This is true, but it is not the whole truth, since he was also one of the first linguists of modern times, anywhere. Without reference to individual special interests, the importance of his work can be compared, for example, with that of Ferdinand de Saussure, of Walther von Wartburg, of Wilhelm Meyer-Lübke, etc., even though it has not been as widely known as theirs. I want to stress that Pompeu Fabra, like them, did not restrict himself to applied linguistics in the context of a single language, but rather that he worked out and developed with great lucidity theoretical aspects that were far-reaching.

To create knowledge makes sense only if it is appropriately disseminated: such knowledge is useful only to the extent of its reaching the maximum possible number of people. If intellectual advances, in any area of knowledge, are restricted to a tight circle they may become sterile. Therefore, we must not fail to exploit adequately any means that can facilitate scientific progress, least of all nowadays when technology fortunately makes it possible for any frontier to be eliminated and for ideas to be put into limitless circulation.

* * *

The Philological Section of the Institute of Catalan Studies, of which Pompeu Fabra was President, applauds the initiative taken by the Universitat Pompeu Fabra to produce a select anthology in English of work by the man after whom that academic institution is named. Pleasure at this is increased by the fact that the project has been undertaken in co-operation with the Institute, a body to which Fabra, known as the Master, devoted his highest endeavours in research. His output is so vast that our present objective can be considered only as a first step in a process that demands continuation, hopefully to the extent of seeing his complete works translated into English and into other languages. This would be the most fitting homage to the conspicuous polyglot, a man who displayed the most delicate sensitivity towards all languages. Thus, in addition to his grammars *of* Catalan, *in* Catalan, he also wrote one *in* Spanish (*Ensayo de gramática de catalán moderno*: 1891) and two *in* French (*Abrégé de grammaire catalane*: 1928 and *Grammaire catalane*: 1941). Then there are his grammars *of* French *in* Catalan (*Gramàtica francesa*: 1919) and *of* English *in* Catalan (*Gramàtica anglesa*: 1924).

In all the diversity of Fabra's production, where his excellent work as a literary translator is to be included, there is one constant feature which does him the greatest possible credit: in whichever activity he was engaged, it was always with the will to be of service to society, to freedom, to democracy. Without disregarding universal relevance, his main preoccupation was with the needs of his own country.

Concerning the objectives of the present publication, a major problem to be overcome has been that of choosing the sample texts for inclusion in the anthology. It is no simple matter to decide which items call most strongly to be put together in this kind of introductory selection. The aim has been to offer a taste of writings of differing length, character and subject matter; some texts are highly specialised while others are more generally informative; items from books stand alongside articles published in newspapers and journals. Chronologically, the period covered goes from 1892 to 1934, that is to say, the most productive phase in the life of the Master.

Thematically what has been highlighted in the selection has been the process of normativisation of the Catalan language, because this was the issue which Fabra considered to be most urgent for social normalisation of its use. The need to unify lexis, grammar and spelling was the *sine qua non* condition for restoring the dignity and the efficacy of the language, with special attention paid to the literary register, without which Catalan could not be serviceable in works of advanced scholarship or in literary creation.

The anthology also underlines the importance attributed by Pomeu Fabra to variation across the full dialect range of Catalan, something which was always kept in view in the "compositional", inclusive methodology rigorously applied to establish the normative standard.

Bearing in mind the fact that reconstructing and ordering the Catalan language were aimed at consolidating the concept of "national language", the reader will find also in this anthology expositions of Fabra's position on the relationship between language and nation.

Prominence in the compilation, however, is given to the Philological Conversations, a labour to which the author himself gave preeminent attention from when the series was begun in 1919 in the pages of the newspaper *La Publicitat*. These articles constitute probably the best illustration of the admirable feeling for the language that Pompeu Fabra possessed. There is here a capacity for expounding arguments, themselves never arbitrary, based upon the consistency of linguistic knowledge and understanding: one sees very clearly that he was comfortable in defending his positions and in airing his doubts. Also in evidence are: his generosity in paying attention to problems which most troubled the users of the language; his didactic talents in the explanation of grammatical points and proposed solutions to problems; the well-reasoned flexibility applied to the appraisal of conflicting alternatives in grammatical suggestions. For all these reasons, the Philological Conversations are probably the best reflection of Fabra's exemplary endeavours as a grammarian and they constitute, without doubt, a singular and indispensable contribution to methodology and practice for codification of any language: a delight for the intellect, from which we should never cease to draw lessons.

* * *

We can take pleasure from having opened up this route which provides, for scholars around the world, access to Fabra's work. Another ambition to which we subscribe is that Fabra, the Master, should hereby enter the category of "universal Catalan", alongside so many others who have attained this condition. A decisive role in this project has been played by Alan Yates, of the University of Sheffield and also a Corresponding Member of the Philological Section. We are both pleased and grateful that such a prestigious scholar and colleague has been responsible for the English translation and for some editorial matters.

The Philological Section of the Institute of Catalan Studies is happy to be associated with a project which it sees as honouring Fabra the grammarian and which, above all, does justice to the scientific task that he carried out through a historical period that was crucial for the continuity of a language and of a people.

Joan Martí i Castells
President
Secció Filològica
Institut d'Estudis Catalans

Prologue

The name and the person of Pompeu Fabra are characterised by certain paradoxes: well known and highly esteemed in Catalonia and throughout the Catalan-speaking territories – his popular prestige among Catalans ranks indeed with the very highest – he is virtually unknown in the rest of Europe and world-wide. In general he does not figure in the major introductory works on Romance philology – with Tagliavini's *Le origini delle lingue neolatine* (1949) constituting the exception – and he is rarely given an entry in the great encyclopaedias from outside the Catalan domain. Being Catalan is his disadvantage: the big names of smaller national communities are not usually so well known outside their respective countries (or they are merely identified with the nation-state that governs their homeland). Fabra wrote in Catalan, with few exceptions, and he wrote on topics relating to Catalan language and grammar, subjects which do not translate easily into other languages and which do not necessarily interest even linguistic specialists from other societies.

The dates that mark out Fabra's biography also help to explain why he is ignored by the "great" European cultures. He was born in 1868, almost simultaneously with the institution of Spain's tumultuous First Republic, abundant in expectations so quickly dissolved, and he died on Christmas Day 1948, in Prada de Conflent, where he had been living in exile, affected by extreme hardship, after the traumatic end of the Spanish Civil War. His lifetime, then, coincides with a period of great agitation in the history of Spain and, especially, of the Catalan-speaking territories. At the time of his birth, the Romantic revival movement of the *Renaixença*[1] was gathering strong momentum; when he died Catalan culture found itself in the its most parlous situation since the time of the Nova Planta, the set of fundamental laws imposed by the first Bourbon king of Spain (Felipe/Felip V) after the War of Succession, in the early eighteenth century.

Fabra had witnessed the creation of the Institute of Catalan Studies (IEC), in 1907, which provided the necessary institutional support for his work on

---

1. See below, pp. 9–11. Other historical references in this Prologue can be followed up by use of the Index.

linguistic normativisation; he had had to endure the Dictatorship of Miguel Primo de Rivera; he had experienced the halcyon days of political autonomy under the Second Spanish Republic, in 1931–1932; and he had witnessed the disaster of that same Republic's collapse, when he was forced to take the road into exile, in 1939. None of this experience was conducive to his being recognised as an independent and often innovative linguist beyond the society into which he was born. Such "reparation" as could be made to his reputation by the new period of Catalan autonomy after 1979 could be effective within Catalan society, but it rarely went beyond these bounds. Moreover, linguistic science had moved on considerably in the four decades since Fabra's death.

Consequently, outside the Catalan-speaking domain, Fabra remains to this day a great but unacknowledged precursor. Certainly, it is understood that he is the spiritual father of the normative standard for the modern Catalan language, his one great concern which was already manifest before he became an adult. His model for this standard language took hold in Catalan society with surprising rapidity: the Orthographical Norms are promulgated in 1913, 1918 sees publication of the Catalan Grammar of the Institute of Catalan Studies, and in 1932 the *Diccionari general de la llengua catalana* appears. Within this period of just twenty years the victory of Fabra's idea of a modernised and standardised Norm for Catalan was almost total. 1932 also saw the formal promulgation of the *Normes de Castelló de la Plana*, signifying acceptance by the Valencian writers and intellectuals of Fabra's Norm. And, with this event, Fabra's work went out from Catalonia to conquer the whole space now designated as the *Països Catalans*, an entity which, although it had a virtual existence at that time, still did not have a generally accepted appellation. Even so, there was in those years opposition to what Fabra stood for. There was support for alternative referential regulation; there were people who would not accept Fabra's criteria, people who dreamed of a unity between Catalan and Occitan, people who disliked Fabra's *barcelonisme* or his deference towards the vernacular of the capital (explained by the fact that Barcelona was indubitably the major centre for the Catalan language), or people who simply wished to impose their own solution to the problem of normativisation of the language, without much reflection on the criteria to be applied. Certainly, Fabra could count on the support of such Catalan institutions as did exist at the time – especially the Institute of Catalan Studies, from 1907, and the semi-devolved administrative powers of the Mancomunitat, between 1914 and 1925[2] – but the essential element was without doubt the "professional" quality of the standard for modern Catalan that was shaped by Fabra, together with his own indefatigable efforts to promote this

---

2.   See below, p. 16.

referential model within Catalan society. Without general consent from the social milieu, it would have been impossible to drive forward claims for the official status of Catalan after the Dictatorship of Miguel Primo de Rivera (1923–1930) and, later, to activate the movement of "normalisation" after the death of Francisco Franco in 1975. (The Basques were disadvantaged in experiencing the same problem: in 1975 work towards establishing the *batua*, the unitary standard for *eusquera*, was still incomplete.) It must also be said that an integral component of Fabra's nature was his sense of civic engagement, the awareness that the success of his reforms depended on assent from the whole body of Catalan-speakers. Civic responsibility and scientific commitment were combined in him, in that familiar pairing of "science and passion" frequently evoked in our time by the linguist Antoni M. Badia i Margarit, one of Fabra's eminent successors.

But Fabra was not "just" the spiritual father of Catalan in its present-day standardised form. He was a linguist who was familiar with the most important aspects of contemporary linguistic studies. Reading his works, we see that he was abreast of developments world-wide. He was familiar with the best-known linguists of his day – at least with their published works – and he followed with critical interest the main developments in the discipline (as is demonstrated in the richly documented book by Xavier Lamuela and Josep Murgades: *Teoria de la llengua literària segons Fabra* [Barcelona, 1984]). He could read many different languages and so could consult these studies in the original. Moreover, he was in many respects a precursor of a line of reflection on human language which is nowadays well advanced but which in the first decades of the twentieth century was still not recognised by specialists: what we nowadays call sociolinguistics or sociology of language or other denominations. The conviction that linguistic phenomena are also social phenomena (as in the title of a well-known book by the socio-linguist Francesc Vallverdú: *El fet lingüístic com a fet social* [Barcelona, 1973]) was quite innovatory in the 1920s, at a time when the "neo-grammarians" with their positivist and mechanistic views on language still held maximum sway in the field of linguistics: Meyer-Lübke's book on Catalan (*Das Katalanische*) dates from 1925 and its scope is limited to examination of internal, formal linguistic features, accepting Catalan's status as an independent language by internal criteria alone. At this time too structuralism was only just beginning to make its mark: Saussure's *Cours de linguistique générale* had come out in 1916, in the middle of World War I. Although the *Cours* does contain some sociolinguistic reflections, the book's reception converted its author into the founder of structuralism. But, until the 1960s, this was a structuralism which concerned itself hardly at all with social phenomena. The people who did look in this particular direction stood on the edges of specialist linguistic studies: educators, some (very few) sociologists, some left-wing political militants.

Fabra, by contrast, was sensitive from the very start to the importance of social phenomena in linguistic behaviour. This is the reason why I believe that his
"Philological Conversations" were particularly effective in ensuring acceptance of
his proposals for the establishment of standard Catalan. These Conversations are
not exclusively philological: they constitute also a great pedagogical and socio-
linguistic endeavour to explain to people just why the establishment of a normative standard language was necessary – from the point of view of communication
within society – and also why this normative form had to be drawn up with the
strictest criteria. Many of Fabra's reflections would later become key elements in
sociolinguistics, although outside the Catalan-speaking domain his work as a great
precursor remained generally unacknowledged. (Certainly, he was not the only
one to see the relationship between language and society, before the specific discipline embraced this approach, but he was for sure one of the most interesting and
most modern of the pioneers.) Furthermore, reading the Philological Conversations is perhaps the best way to become familiar with Fabra's thinking, to see how
his mind worked and to understand the many facets integrated in his reflections.
This is why so much that is contained in these Conversations can be read, even today, with great interest and has lost none of its importance (being applicable still to
other situations of languages in contact and of languages in the phase of social reaf-
firmation). The distance between a sociolinguistic reflection *avant la lettre* and an
analysis of social communication is not very great, and Fabra sometimes exploited
this. Between a linguistics concerned merely with the production of utterances and
the study of reception – meaning also of communication – there is only a short
gap, and Fabra bridged this, well in advance of contemporaries working in related
fields. He saw, for example, the importance of the mass media of his day that were
beginning to play an increasingly significant role in social communication.

In another area, Fabra seems to uphold the view that the human being is naturally monolingual and that generally an option must be taken between one lan-

Pompeu Fabra was, certainly, a man of his times. When he speaks of the normative standard for Catalan he generally uses the term "literary language", revealing how the literary register was, according to the attitudes of those days, the most
prestigious form for any language. This translates a prejudice of the nineteenth-
century bourgeoisie, reflecting the contemporary reality that, before the invention
of modern modes of communication (wide-circulation press, radio, television,
etc.) literary language had indeed enjoyed this pre-eminent status. Any consideration of the relativity involved here was still extremely rare (and it would, perhaps,
have been more difficult in societies where orality and a still very limited written
production were the modes of communication). However, with a simple adjust-
ment of the terminology (understanding "literary language" to mean the normative standard), then Fabra's reflections on these matters maintain all their validity.

In another area, Fabra seems to uphold the view that the human being is naturally monolingual and that generally an option must be taken between one lan-

guage or another, that bi- or plurilingualism is not a long-term solution: such was the accepted wisdom of the last decades of the nineteenth century and the early twentieth century. This conviction in Fabra can no doubt be related to his Catalan nationalism, a dialectical product of the Spanish nationalism which, particularly over the turn of the century, was such a substantial presence. Nationalisms in this period are all exclusive, believing not just in the absolute perdurability of nations themselves but also in linguistic purity and even in the purity of the "blood". Nationalism, new-born in the nineteenth-century, claimed an existence outside time and, thus, a profound essentialism. The exclusivism of the dominant entity (through assimilation or exclusion) gives rise dialectically to the exclusivism of the dominated one. Play was made with elements like language/languages and culture without any account being taken of the fact that, throughout the whole history of the world as we know it, human groups have communicated in different tongues, switching between languages whenever this suited them. Naturally, the defensive nationalism of the dominated party, insofar as it comes as a response or an imitation, always has many more justifications than the aggressive nationalism of the dominating one, but then this can lead into a dialectic which can never be resolved. Generally, in his manuscripts, Fabra talks about "Spanish" and "Spaniards" (terms which are often changed, in the published texts, for "Castilian" and "Castilians"): through his use of this terminology he deliberately marks his distance from that Spain which had so many difficulties about admitting to its bosom cultural and linguistic pluralism. We all know that in this case the contradictions were reproduced in the Civil War, at such a high cost to the whole of Spain and all Spaniards. It must be hoped that a sense of respect for differences will never again allow a catastrophe of this kind to occur, and that Spain will continue along the road of recognising differences as the country's current Constitution ordains.

In another field, that of the delimitation of the linguistic boundaries of Catalan, Fabra also played an important role. We know that in the Middle Ages there arose the myth of a trans-Pyrenean *llengua llemosina*, an idealised concept in which the identities of Catalan and the *langue d'òc* or Provençal were (con)fused. The term was first mentioned in writing, in the early thirteenth century, by the Catalan Ramon Vidal de Besalú, the author of the *Razos de trobar* (a didactic treatise on the language of troubadour poetry), or perhaps his is just the first textual occurrence of which we have notice. Under this denomination were included all of the Occitanian and (perhaps?) the Catalan linguistic varieties. We must remember that in 1200 the Catalan domain stopped at Tortosa, at the mouth of the Ebro/Ebre river; the territory of Valencia was still under Islamic domination. The term *llemosí* (Limousin) continued to be used, as is well attested, especially in the south of the whole area concerned, but with the loosest of definitions (a historical process described by August Rafanell in *Un nom per a la llengua* [Vic, 1991]). In the modern era, the poet Bonaventura Carles Aribau renewed its use in a famous poem of 1833 which used to be conventionally taken as the starting-point and the rallying-cry of the Catalans' Romantic literary and cultural revival. Aribau, though, seems almost certainly to have exclusively in mind the Catalan domain and to ignore the Occitanian dimension. The *Renaixença* and the Occitanian *Félibrige*[3] converged in the 1870s, when the writer and historian Víctor Balaguer was living in exile in Provence, and from 1866, before the declaration of the First Spanish Republic, there were references to what the historian Rafanell calls the "Occitanian dream" (*La il·lusió occitana: la llengua dels catalans, entre Espanya i França* [Barcelona, 2006]). This ideal held that Catalan and Occitan were two geographical sides of a single language, the language which some had always designated as *llemosí*. From the linguistic point of view, the argument put forward was not absurd: if the treaty of 1204[4] had not foundered at the Battle of Muret (1213) and if the Occitanian and Catalan territories had come under a common government, then, as soon as a modern standard language became a necessity, the Occitan and the Catalan tongues might well have developed a common standard idiom. However, after defeat at Muret, the Catalan-Aragonese monarchs looked to the south rather than to the north, while relations between Catalonia and Occitania loosened and turned cold. After this there came the phase of integration of each domain into a different national state, Spain and France. And from the French Revolution onwards two very divergent histories began: the *Renaixença* was successful, at both the intellectual and the social level, whereas the Occitanian *Renaissènça*, while it did enjoy some achievements in the intellectual sphere (especially in literature), was a failure in social and political aspects (rather like what happened with the *Renaixença* in Catalan-speaking Valencia and the Balearic Islands). When this became more or less evident, it was (mainly) voices from Occitania and from Valencia which defended the old idea of the *llengua llemosina* or language unity between the two domains, hoping for aid from their Catalan brothers. This was something which placed at risk the success, always under threat, of Catalan in Catalonia itself. Fabra always understood this very clearly: he spoke out in favour of the unity among all the branches of the Catalan language: in Catalonia, in the Valencian lands, in the Balearic Islands, in Andorra, in the eastern fringe of Aragon, in northern Catalonia (French Roussillon) and

3.   Literary institution created by Frederic Mistral, J. Romilha and T. Aubanel in Avignon, 1854, to promote the use of Provençal/Occitan for modern poetry.

4.   The victory of Simon de Montfort, at the battle of Muret in 1213, in the "crusade" against the Albigensian heretics in the south of France, put an end to the politico-cultural momentum and the dynastic alliances that might have given viability to a unified feudal regime straddling the eastern Pyrenees.

in Alghero (Sardinia).[5] But he rejected the solution which would stretch from Guéret to Guardamar, from the northernmost extreme of Occitania to the southernmost point of the Catalan-speaking territories.[6] Thus he included in his work on the normative standard language all the aforementioned variants of Catalan, but he did not cover the Occitanian ones. And, when loud insistence for inclusion came from the latter quarter, Fabra was the leading signatory of a declaration by many leading Catalan intellectuals on "Deviations in the Concepts of Language and Homeland" (1934).[7] Those who signed this declaration aimed, on the one hand, to bring clarification (perhaps too forcefully) to a scientific debate and also, on the other hand, to avoid a situation in which the Catalan revival movement, by formulating unrealistic aspirations, might jettison its real potential. Naturally, Fabra and the Occitanian grammarian Loïs Alibèrt (1884–1959) agreed that the variants of the two languages were very close, in linguistic terms, and that there does exist a kind of continuum between the one and the other (Alibèrt always looked upon Catalan as a "branch of the common trunk"). Fabra, however, saw the need to mark out the limits of this proximity, which is why he put his name to the declaration. Throughout his life he pursued the ideal of making Catalan a ductile modern language that was equipped for each and every communicative function, but he was never seduced by impossible dreams: a posture in which there was perhaps an element of the good sense and discrimination denoted by the concept of the Catalans' stereotypical *seny*.[8] This was something else which was present in his personal make-up.

The image which we have today of Pompeu Fabra is one clearly influenced by recent history. His work suffered from the consequences of the Civil War: the years of exile were very hard; prohibition of the public use of the Catalan language brought to a halt and even put into reverse the process of normalisation which had begun propitiously during the Second Republic, and the ensuing interruption of almost forty years created new conditions which were altogether less positive for Catalan. After the defeat of the Republic (with which Catalan nationalism was by and large identified), a few people were able to carry the torch of the language –

---

5.   See map (p. 4) and pp. 5–6 below.

6.   Guéret is a town to the north-east of Limoges. The conventional delimitation of the *Països Catalans* is "from Salses (Roussillon) to Guardamar (Alacant), from Fraga (eastern Aragon) to Maó (Minorca)".

7.   Included in the selection of translated texts, below pp. 208–213.

8.   This concept, with its connotations of discrimination and good sense, is a positive aspect of the Catalan self-image. It is counterbalanced by the antithesis of *rauxa*, irrationality and impulsiveness.

precariously – inside the society of Catalonia. This was the case – to recall just one – of the philologist Ramon Aramon i Serra (1907–2000) who strove to ensure continuity for the Institute of Catalan Studies and to achieve international projection for that body throughout the Franco years. But in such a situation of oppression it was well-nigh impossible to continue the necessary work begun but not finished (the normativisation of Catalan was still not completed in 1939, it must be remembered) and it was even more difficult to engage in propaganda in favour of the language. This situation produced at the same time a withdrawal by the defenders of Catalan and a retrenchment into normativist positions that were taken as being set in stone. This resulted in an intellectual self-limitation that blocked the need to broaden standard Catalan in certain aspects, that is, quite simply, to face up to the new challenges confronting the language. There was, too, a "purist" reflex action which could sometimes put off even a favourably disposed public. I think that the Fabra of his own times was a more open-minded man than some who came after him, that he was more capable of responding to unexpected challenges. Fortunately, that instinctive retrenchment just referred to seems to me to be now a thing of the past. The importance of this cannot be overstated, because the new movements of migration and the successes of the Spanish/Castilian language that we have experienced in recent decades re-emphasise the precarious condition of the smaller languages with which it is in contact, Catalan included.

We are left with the image of a man who was able to exploit the linguistic tools of his own times and who, in relation to many aspects of the linguistic sciences, is a great but insufficiently recognised precursor. For this reason we should greet with much satisfaction the publication in English of a selected and annotated edition of his work. We hope that this volume will contribute to bringing the figure of Pompeu Fabra out of the situation of being unknown beyond the bounds of the Països Catalans, and to giving him the status that was always rightfully his.

Georg Kremnitz
University of Vienna

1. General presentation

The Universitat Pompeu Fabra (Pompeu Fabra University, Barcelona: UPF) resolved to dedicate the academic year 2006–2007 to specially commemorating the
figure and the work of the philologist whom it honours every day by officially
bearing his name. And it was precisely through organising the Pompeu Fabra
Year that the University became aware of how, in one important respect, his production stood in a great void: there were no translations into English of any of
his texts nor was there in that language any study of his work. The University's
Department of Translation and Language Sciences had also realised that this was
a major gap calling to be filled, as they had received requests for information on
the subject from various specialists in language planning who were interested in
the normalisation process of Catalan. All these enquirers expressed disappointment and perplexity about how academic bodies and publishers could allow such
a lack to exist. Consequently, the University considered that steps should be taken
to make Fabra's work known internationally through the first English-language
edition of a selection of his writings, together with a biographical outline and an
introductory study.

The appearance of the present volume is the gratifying outcome of close cooperation between the UPF and the Institute of Catalan Studies. The University's
Consell Social has from the outset wished to be involved in this project and to
make its own contribution both to the spirit and the letter of the initiative. Also to
be gratefully acknowledged is the grant towards publication costs received from
the Institut Ramon Llull.

The goal of the project is to put a representative selection of texts by Pompeu
Fabra at the disposal of international specialists, through the medium of English,
along with introductory studies on his contribution to reforming and fixing the
modern Catalan language.

The book now in the reader's hands is prefaced by a text from the heads of
each of the three institutions which have collaborated in bringing the project to
fruition: the President of the Institute of Catalan Studies (Institut d'Estudis Catalans: IEC), Dr. Salvador Giner; the President of the Philological Section of the
IEC, Dr. Joan Martí, and the President of the UPF, Dr. Joan Josep Moreso.

The main body of the book opens with a prologue by the renowned Romance philologist and expert in Fabra's work Dr. Georg Kremnitz (University of Vienna), who supplies a judicious appraisal of the Catalan linguist's importance in both the local and the European contexts. There follows an introductory study by Dr. Joan Costa Carreras (UPF), incorporating a number of suggestions made by the translator of all the Catalan materials, Dr. Alan Yates (University of Sheffield). This introduction begins with an outline survey of the social history of the Catalan language and the cultural conditions in which Fabra's work unfolded. Concluding with guidance on background reading and on up-to-date materials for learning Catalan. There follows a section on the contextualised biography of Fabra, and then a detailed discussion of the scientific bases of his work, of the criteria he followed and achievements made in the diverse areas of applied linguistics where his researches were influential, as a theoretician of the literary language, grammarian, lexicographer, translator, and authority on toponymy. To supply additional orientation and to facilitate further investigation on the part of the reader, this section ends with a list of texts by Fabra classified according to the languages in which they were published (Catalan, Spanish or French) and then a basic bibliography (similarly classified) on Fabra's work and on the normalisation of the modern Catalan language.

The selection of texts by Fabra given in English translation is preceded by an explanation of editorial principles and procedures: first, information on the 59 texts included in the anthology (justification of the selection, typology of texts translated, the list of the 59 texts and a list of the sources on which the translations are based); then a description of how the texts have been treated in a translation process designed to provide, unobtrusively, the linguistic and cultural information necessary to make Fabra's meaning as accessible as posssible for the 21st-century foreign reader.

A final global Index of names and concepts completes the editorial apparatus.

2. The Catalan language

2.1 The Catalan language domain

Catalan is a member of the family of Romance languages. It is the national language of Andorra, and a co-offcial language in the autonomous Spanish communities of the Balearic Islands, Catalonia and Valencia as well as in the city of Alghero (l'Alguer) on the Italian island of Sardinia. Within Spain Catalan is spoken also, although with no official status, in the eastern fringe of Aragon (known as La Franja de Ponent) and in the small enclave of El Carxe in the province of Murcia. In southern France it is the historic language of the Roussillon, corresponding roughly to the current *département* of the Pyrénées-Orientales, often referred to as Northern Catalonia. This distribution involves complex trans-state relationships and these continue to affect the complexities which arise when historico-political considerations are applied to past and present linguistic realities.

The linguistic domain of Catalan can be seen in the map on page 4, where the main dialect division (see §2.3) is also shown.

2.2 The demography of Catalan

The total extent of the all territories in which Catalan is spoken covers some 69,250 square kilometres. Reliable statistics for the number of speakers are not easy to come by. Overall, and conservatively, we can say that, of a total population of some eleven million people who live in the Catalan-speaking territories, the language is spoken by over seven million and is understood by nearly ten million. The "can understand" component of these figures represents a significant body of potential speakers.

Catalan has by far the largest number of speakers among all of Europe's "minority languages". It is also interesting to compare the basic demographic statistics with corresponding data for "national languages" in several recognised nation-states within Europe: there are more people who speak Catalan than those who speak, for example, Danish, Finnish, Albanian, Norwegian, Lithuanian, etc.

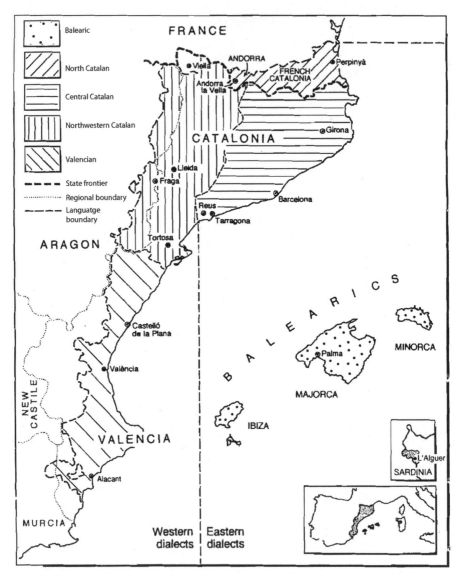

Map.   Catalan speaking areas and dialects
Reproduced with modifications from Max W. Wheeler, Alan Yates and Nicolau Dols, *Catalan: A Comprehensive Grammar* (London: Routledge, 1999), by courtesy of the publishers.

2.3   The dialect divisions of Catalan

Catalan is conventionally divided into two major dialect blocks, Eastern Catalan and Western Catalan, each of which encompasses several local varieties. The main Eastern-Western division is based on differences in phonology and features of verb morphology, together with some particular lexical differences. Across the whole range, however, there is a very high degree of mutual intelligibility between the dialects. The variety of Catalan spoken in Barcelona and the surrounding region is referred to as the Eastern Central dialect. Because of the demographic, administrative and cultural importance of the capital city this particular dialect has weighed heavily in the formation of normative standard Catalan in the contemporary era. This is an issue of which Pompeu Fabra was strongly aware, and which he addressed directly on numerous occasions.

2.4   The concept of a language community

Description of where Catalan is spoken leads to a necessary explanation of the concept of *Països Catalans* or Catalan Lands. The latter designation refers to "the group of territories whose language and culture are Catalan, situated along the western sea-board of the Mediterranean" (see the Map). This entity, defined basically by linguistic and cultural unity, can be identified in modern terms as a "stateless nation", a condition brought about by specific historical factors and the fragmented development of the individual compartments that occurred after a long phase of consolidation during the Middle Ages. (The process is outlined in §2.5 below.) When the idea of Catalan "nationhood" was revived, by the end of the nineteenth century, the need arose for an appropriate denomination to refer to the broad Catalan linguistico-cultural collectivity, stemming from the fact that the term "Catalonia" is ambiguous. It is the name of the old Principality of Catalonia and, metonymously, its linguistic and cultural entity, while in parallel the community name *català*/Catalan is used to designate both the populace of the Principality and that of all the associated territories. Several labels were proposed initially to denote the full geo-historical phenomenon, like *terres catalanes* (Catalan lands), *terres de llengua catalana* (Catalan-speaking lands), *Catalunya Gran* (Greater Catalonia) or *Catalònia* (Pompeu Fabra himself making use of these terms), but it was from the 1960s that the expression *Països Catalans* gained preference. In the process of transition to democracy in Spain (when a radical redrawing of the political map of that country seemed to be genuinely in prospect) the idea enjoyed success and the term *Països Catalans* entered the vocabulary of popular speech and even the vocabulary of certain political parties who utilised it to support nationalist claims. The present-day Constitution of Spain (1978), however, explicitly prevents any "mancommuning" of the autonomous Catalan-speaking regions, and this has meant that the concept of *Països Catalans* has lost some immediate momentum. It does remain alive, though, as a political ideal (still active in the dialectics and discourse of Catalanist politics) and, generally, as a way of referring to a sense of community identity, across administrative boundaries, based upon an historical and socio-linguistic reality.

2.5   An outline of the social history of Catalan

2.5.1   The origins and the Middle Ages

By the ninth century AD the Catalan language had evolved out of Vulgar Latin in a wide band straddling both sides of the eastern Pyrenees (the Counties of Rosselló, Empúries, Besalú, Cerdanya, Urgell, Pallars and Ribagorça) and, to the south, in the territories pertaining to the Roman province and later arch-diocese of La Tarraconense. While sharing features with both the Gallo-romance and Ibero-romance groups, Catalan could be said to have emerged, in its remote origins, as an eccentric dialect of Western Romance. The first complete texts recognisable as Catalan are juridical and religious and date from the twelfth century.

The spread of the language is associated with a process of political expansion, given definitive impetus with the separation of the County of Barcelona (988 AD) from the trunk of the Carolingian empire. From the eighth century onwards the Catalan Counts had headed a southwards and westwards wave of conquest, taking territories in the Iberian Peninsula. The northern parts of present-day Catalonia ("Old Catalonia") were held by the ninth century. "New Catalonia", north of the Ebre river, was progressively secured during the eleventh and twelfth centuries, and this was followed by expansion into the Valencian Land and across to the Balearic Islands and to Alghero in Sardinia (thirteenth century). The driving forces of this "foundational" process were Christianity and the dynamics of a feudal society. Both had profound effects in the make-up of Catalan civilisation.

By the 15th century, a period which saw the rise of Valencia as a centre of social and cultural dynamism, the Catalan presence had spread throughout the Mediterranean world. The correlation between political élan and linguistic (thence cultural and literary) consolidation was articulated through the Royal Chancelry, an institution responsible for the propagation of a highly standardised language. A golden age of medieval Catalan literature runs from the thirteenth-century Majorcan polymath Ramon Llull,[9] through the four great chronicles to the Valencian school of poetry culminating in Ausiàs March.[10] A transition from medieval to Renaissance values and tastes is discernible in the outstanding Valencian novel of chivalry *Tirant lo Blanc* and in aspects of the work of Bernat Metge[11] and Andreu Febrer.[12] Theirs was one of the "great languages" of medieval Europe. The spread of the printed word was a cardinal factor in the full flowering of the Renaissance, and the impact of the printing press, since its invention, was intimately associated with the emergence throughout Europe of the modern mind-set. Significantly, it was in Valencia in 1474 that *Trobes en llaors de la Verge Maria* (Poems in Praise of the Virgin Mary) appeared: the first book in the Iberian Peninsula to be produced with movable type.

Catalan, then, reached a peak of maturity and of cultural plenitude which would not be matched again until fully four centuries later. It was to these "glorious medieval authors" that Pompeu Fabra consistently referred, utilising them as a main pillar in his project to achieve "not the resurrection of a medieval language, but rather the formation of the modern language that would have emerged out of old Catalan were it not for the long centuries of literary decadence and of subordination to a foreign tongue." ("Philologists and Poets", 1918: included in the translated anthology).

2.5.2 Decadence

The "centuries of literary decadence" referred to by Fabra ensued upon the non-consummation of the full transition to Renaissance values that seemed to be

---

9. c. 1232 – c. 1315. Considered to be the founding father of Catalan literature. He was the first European author to use the vernacular for philosophical writing. His vast output (in Arabic and Latin as well as in Catalan) constructs a system of thought aimed at combating the influence of Islam. Narrative and poetic modes are integrated with his extensive philosophical, devotional and contemplative works.

10. c. 1397–1459. A highly original poet who transcended both the troubadour tradition and Italianate models in the exploration of subjective emotional moods, swerving between sensuality and idealism, with profound moral concerns. His writing is characterised by strict formal control, striking imagery and abrupt changes of tone and style.

11. c. 1340–1413. Courtier and writer. He absorbed humanist influences, visible in his poetry and his translations. His masterpiece is *Lo somni* (The Dream: 1399), an inventive piece of personal apologetics, embodying Renaissance values and ostensibly foreshadowing an evolution in Catalan prose-writing that did not come to general fruition.

12. c. 1377 – c. 1440. Poet, mainly noted for his verse translation of Dante's *Divina Commedia*.

heralded by Catalan authors like Joanot Martorell,[13] Metge and Febrer. The fact is that the effects of social and political crisis were already becoming visible at the moment of socio-cultural maturity and of the furthest spread of Catalan political dominion through the Mediterranean world. This conjuncture coincided too with the end of the Barcelona dynasty (1410), and the eventual union (1469) between Aragon and Castile. Economic and social decline affected the Catalan-speaking territories at the same time as Spain was becoming a major player on the world stage, especially with the opening-up of the Americas after 1492. From the Catalan perspective the sixteenth, seventeenth and eighteenth centuries were indeed a period of Decadence, in political and cultural terms and in terms of the standing of the language.

The unified Catalan koiné that had become well established by the fifteenth century suffered fragmentation, as awareness of its standardised conventions – and of the socio-cultural unity it reflected – was steadily eroded. By the end of the eighteenth century writers of Catalan had in mind only a regionally limited public for works in a local idiom. Generated by this situation was the emergence of the idea that the Valencian and Balearic varieties constituted distinct languages, an attitude that has been susceptible, particularly in recent times, to political manipulation, always to the advantage of the hegemony of Castilian and of Spanish centralism. Fabra's total project was based upon very coherent ideas regarding this subject (for example "The Task of the Valencian and Balearic writers", 1918: included in the translated anthology) and he contributed greatly to establishing the true boundaries of the Catalan language, as is emphasised by Georg Kremnitz in his prologue to this volume. A clear perspective on these matters was (and remains) indispensable, because the degrading and dispersion of the language were among the main negative legacies of the period of Decadence.

Under the Treaty of the Pyrenees (1659) the Roussillon was ceded by Felipe IV of Spain to Louis XIV of France, thus beginning the break-up of the integrity of the Catalan-speaking territories. By a royal decree of 1700 the French king prohibited all official use of the Catalan language, and since then the continued effects of a powerfully centralist state administration have all but reduced Catalan to the condition of a *patois* in Northern Catalonia. (Only very recently have token measures been taken, enshrined in an amendment (2008) to the French Constitution, to admit "regional languages" as part of the "patrimony" of the state, allowing them a presence in public life and education.)

---

13. c. 1414–1468. Author of *Tirant lo Blanc*, mentioned above. This important work is characterised by features which show an overlap between the conventions of chivalresque narratives and an embryonic modern realism. Cervantes praised it in these terms in *Don Quijote*.

To the south of the Pyrenees the low point of the Decadence is conventionally set at 1714, the end of the War of the Spanish Succession. The Bourbon Felipe V, newly installed on the Spanish throne issued a series of ordinances, known as the Decrees of the Nova Planta aimed at abolishing all Catalan political institutions and imposing Castilian laws and administrative structures. At a time when the other major languages of Europe were acquiring their dictionaries and their academies, the policy of the Nova Planta, imposed by right of conquest, had corresponding negative effects on the use of Catalan and on its capacity to evolve naturally as a fully-fledged modern language. Valencia was affected by such measures already from 1707: the decrees for Majorca and Catalonia were issued in 1715 and 1716 respectively. It was the relative inefficiency of Spanish centralism – handicapped by a weak economy and by the only partial evolution of Spain into a modern state on the European model – that prevented all the desired effects of this legislation from being achieved. Otherwise the social history of Catalan in the contemporary era might well have followed the same course on both sides of the Pyrenees.

An important factor that prevented this from happening was the notable demographic expansion of Catalonia dating from the eighteenth century. This was the basis for renewed economic momentum in the industrial age, bringing into relief the pre-existing material and cultural differences between Catalan society and the rest of Spain. The language, whose private and public use was still widespread especially at the popular level, was "rediscovered" as the embodiment and symbol of community identity. And this happened at a time when new ideas about nationhood were now percolating through Europe. In the early nineteenth century Catalan society was sufficiently modernised and coherent to be responsive to such ideas. And the language, although fragmented and enfeebled, still had the capacity both to fuel and to articulate them, becoming very quickly the central motive of collective self-affirmation.

The evolution of the modern Catalan revival movement falls into three overlapping phases, from early nineteenth-century beginnings to the emergence of an explicit and dynamic Catalan nationalism by the dawn of the twentieth century. These phases are referred to as *La Renaixença*, *Modernisme* and *Noucentisme*.

2.5.3 The *Renaixença*

The modern Catalan revival movement, known as the Renaixença, emerged under the sign of European Romanticism. The movement is conventionally, and very artificially, dated as beginning in 1833, with the publication of a celebrated ode (*La Pàtria* / The Homeland) by Bonaventura Carles Aribau.[14] He invoked the model of the troubadours in formulating a heartfelt plea for use of the native tongue in the expression of important thoughts and emotions. And his example fell on quite fertile ground, for reasons that have been mentioned above. A spate of "troubadouresque" poetry and some formal defences of Catalan as a language of culture ensued in the 1840s and 1850s. That Aribau himself referred to the language as *llemosí*, illustrates the strength of one particular current within Romanticism, that of a gaze turned nostalgically towards the Middle Ages. In the context of the Renaixença this had the effect of focusing its participants' attention on the Catalan golden age with all its political and cultural achievements. On the one hand this historical awareness sowed the seeds for recovery of a sense of collective identity, and for the earliest expressions of a will to assert it. On the other hand, though, the same Romantic historicism induced a mythification of the past and some major misconceptions about the true genealogy and linguistic relationships of Catalan, and also about its potential for the articulation of modern ideas. A high degree of bourgeois exclusivism (shunning the vulgar idiom of the majority of the population, either in the countryside or among the urban masses) was joined with the fashionable nostalgic cast of Romantic idealism. The combination explains why the principal cultural concerns and efforts of the early stage of the Renaixença were devoted to the restoration of the medieval Jocs Florals de la Gaia Ciència, the festival/competiton of troubadour poetry instituted in Barcelona in 1393 in imitation of models in Toulouse and Paris. 1859 saw the inauguration of the newly restored Jocs Florals de Barcelona (soon imitated in other centres of population), and for two decades the institution was the main focus for the energies of the Renaixença. The phenomenon certainly provided a new social prominence and respectability for cultural expression in Catalan. But a number of major contradictions were inherent in how the Jocs Florals engaged with the real forces at work in Catalan society. The Renaixença itself contained potential that went beyond "eistedfoddery" or the artificiality of a revived medievalism, and the movement was acquiring a cultural impetus and political overtones consonant with the social dynamic of the final decades of the nineteenth century. In literary terms, too, the limited scope of the Jocs Florals was soon naturally superseded by more ambitious products that articulated contemporary concerns in a more up-to-date deployment of Catalan as a literary vehicle. Significant, and internationally recognised, representatives of the major genres (in poetry, Jacint

---

14. 1798–1862. Poet, journalist, economist and politician. Imbued with the spirit of enlightened Liberalism, he was active in introducing Romantic ideas into Spain. His commitment to Catalan literature was not commensurate with the reverberations of *La Pàtria*, and the bulk of his output, literary and non-literary, was in Spanish.

Verdaguer (1845–1902); in the realist novel, Narcís Oller (1846–1930); in drama, Àngel Guimerà (1845–1924)) had appeared on the scene by the 1880s, all of them having made their debuts in the framework of the Jocs Florals. This development coincided with the emergence of political Catalanism in the 1890s.

Another symptomatic contradiction affected the activities of the Jocs Florals, one directly related to the condition of the Catalan language at the time. The institution undertook to publish the winning works of all the major classes in the competition. Year after year problems and disputes arose over questions of formal correctness, especially orthography, but there was neither the linguistic understanding, nor the discipline nor the authority necessary for adequate, unified solutions to be arrived at. A comparable experience was encountered also by the Reial Acadèmia de Bones Lletres de Barcelona, an eighteenth-century corporation that was reactivated in the spirit of the Renaixença, and which played (and still plays) an important role in Catalan intellectual life. But in this case too it was clear that sentiment and patriotic fervour could not meet the real needs of the Catalan language if it were ever to occupy its place, as a modern idiom, fully regularised and unified, among other languages of culture. The philological knowledge necessary to achieve this was still missing (understandably, given the ravages of the Decadence) as were the institutional authority and the administrative structures necessary to implement a complete reform. Awareness of this state of affairs comes through persistently in Fabra's writing (see particularly "Sobre la reforma ortográfica" (1892): included in the translated anthology) and it constitutes a major plank in his intellectual defence of the effective programme of modernisation and reform over which he came to preside.

The tensions between Renaixença conservatism and more dynamic or more popular manifestations of the Catalan revival were resolved over the turn of the nineteenth and twentieth centuries. The overlapping movements of *Modernisme* and *Noucentisme* brought to a head and in large measure gave consummation to the potential from the earlier phase.

2.5.4 *Modernisme*

This term (not to be confused with Modernism) has very particular connotations for the development of society and culture in modern Catalonia. It refers to a two-fold process occurring in the Principality (and secondarily in Valencia and the Balearic Islands) during the two crucial decades spanning the nineteenth and twentieth centuries. Within a continuing surge of social transformation (and against the background of political crisis in the Spanish state) there emerged together impulses for the explicit *modernisation* of a culture considered archaic, pedestrian and provincial – Catalan culture as it had taken shape during the Renaixença – and for the creation of specifically *national* modes of creativity, thought and expression. Both motives were intertwined, and related to a complex social ferment. Associated with the growth of political Catalanism, awareness increased that only by becoming cosmopolitan and abreast of the latest advances abroad would Catalan culture shake off its provincial complexion, thus to attain a higher degree of differentiation and independence from perceived deficiencies in the official Spanish-Castilian culture centred in Madrid. *Fin-de-siècle* Europe offered an apparently stable political model of bourgeois nationhood and, at the same time, a beguiling array of cultural options related to profound changes in taste, sensibility and fashion. Thus eclecticism was the watchword of Modernisme, and the spirit of the movement was enshrined in the stirring call made by the intellectual, Jaume Brossa:[15] *A èpoques noves, formes d'art noves*, each new era demands its own new forms of art.

The architecture of Antoni Gaudí[16] is Modernisme's most conspicuous, if not most representative, expression but a comparable exuberance is found across the whole range of cultural and intellectual manifestations: in all branches of literature (where the extremes of naturalism, symbolism, parnassianism, primitivism, decadentism, etc., could combine); in the pictorial, the plastic and the graphic arts (where, after post-impressionism, Art Nouveau and the Arts and Crafts movement were fully assimilated); in music, in an expanding interest in folk-lore, in sport, in new cultural media like photography and cinema, in any cultural activity that offered novelty and relevance. Catalan was taken for granted as the natural vehicle for this effervescence, but ideas about linguistic normalisation were generally subordinated to a total programme of "cultural revolution" that affirmed the timeless *Volkgeist* at the same time as it projected modernity and cosmopolitanism as essential features of Catalanness. The literature of Modernisme is impressive in its range and its quality, transcending spectacularly the impoverished or stilted idiom that was the vehicle for writing produced in the Renaixença. But the

---

15. 1869–1919. Critic and dramatist. He exemplified the revolutionary, even messianic, spirit within Modernisme, his ideas being influenced by Nietzsche and by contemporary anarchist writings. He championed the music of Wagner, and his own literary work was inspired by Zola and, especially, Ibsen.

16. 1852–1926. Architect. The expiatory temple of the Sagrada Família is his most ambitious and best known building: conceived in 1883, it occupied Gaudí exclusively in the last years of his life and is still in the process of construction. His religious devotion, combined with his bold aesthetic idiom and technical mastery, won him major clients in the highest echelons of Catalan society. The Parc Güell (1900–1914) and various domestic buildings by him are notable features of the Barcelona city-scape.

language still lacked formal consistency and uniformity. The more or less unspoken principle was that sincerity, enthusiasm and "genius" – legacies from late Romanticism – had priority and that "freedom of expression" could amply make up for discipline on any front. This common denominator attributed superiority to aesthetic emotion over analysis, to suggestion over statement. In such a vein two of the outstanding literary figures of *modernista* literature, the influential poet Joan Maragall[17] and the novelist Víctor Català[18] (pseudonym of Caterina Albert), produced work of the highest order. The former used an only slightly refined Barcelona vernacular, while the latter, among a loose assortment of contemporary "rural novelists", cultivated a "ruggedness" of expression bearing strong marks of a highly stylised hybrid rural dialect. Maragall, moreover, made some important doctrinal pronouncements on the "living word", defending the virtues of spontaneous utterance generated by simple souls or by poets in the ecstasy of inspiration. This aspect of Modernisme was far from conducive to linguistic reform, and it would be the target for virulent criticism when the more disciplined movement of Noucentisme gained ascendancy, placing the regularisation of Catalan and the creation of a normative standard at the head of its cultural priorities.

It was, nevertheless, the broad spirit of Modernisme, its innovatory even revolutionary emphasis, that enabled Pompeu Fabra to begin to put into practical effect his preoccupation with the regularisation and modernisation of Catalan. And the movement also provided him with his first base of operation. He collaborated with the energetic group of intellectuals, a spearhead of Modernisme, that was centred on the journal (1881–1884, 1889–1893) and publishing house of *L'Avenç*. One of its major priorities was promotion of a campaign for orthographical reform initiated by the publishers Jaume Massó i Torrents[19] and Joaquim Casas-Carbó.[20] During this period Fabra's ideas and proposals began to take definitive shape, and to receive publicity. But it was only when the movement

---

17. 1860–1911. Poet, journalist, intellectual. His poetry was influenced by the German tradition: Goethe, Novalis, Nietzsche. He wrote on subjects from nature and on civic themes, and he made modern interpretations of traditional Catalan legends. He engaged with major contemporary issues, and his writing overall exercised considerable moral authority among his contemporaries.

18. 1869–1966. Novelist and short-story writer. Her novel *Solitud* (Solitude: 1905) is internationally acclaimed. Here and in her stories she deals with intense, often violent, human conflict in stark rural settings. She also wrote poetry and plays.

19. 1863–1943. Publisher and scholar. He was a founder member of the Institute of Catalan Studies.

20. 1858–1943. Publisher and writer. His early writings on orthographical reform appeared in *L'Avenç* from 1890.

of Noucentisme gained the ascendancy that the political and institutional base for their full implementation came into being.

2.5.5 *Noucentisme*

The heyday of Modernisme contained already the forces which would bring about its crisis and demise. The extreme idealism of its cultural revolution was ultimately to prove unsusceptible to political channelling, and the movement of Noucentisme swiftly invoked the virtues of order, restraint and responsibility in the service of a national project whose socially conservative cast became clearer as its political achievements gained consistency. A new and most productive phase of cultural Catalanism gained ground at the turn of the century, taking over and monopolising the ambition to establish a modern national culture, appropriating some of Modernisme's means and forms of expression while vehemently repudiating others. The term Noucentisme was coined in 1906 by the movement's principal ideologue and publicist Eugeni d'Ors (pen-name *Xènius*),[21] invoking the Italian model of *Quattrocentismo*, *Cinquecentismo*, etc., and also playing on the ambiguity of the Catalan word *nou* meaning both "nine" and "new". Thus this New Centuryism carried strong implications of classical values and of going one better over Modernisme's aspirations for renovation. What should not be overlooked now, though, is that the latter claim masked essential continuities between the two movements. As has been mentioned, Fabra's work began under the *modernista* sign, and the same is true of Eugeni d'Ors and of Noucentisme's emblematic poet Josep Carner.[22]

These three were the key intellectuals in whom authority was invested on major fronts (language, ideas, literature) by the politican who orchestrated the tangible political gains of Catalanism in the first two decades of the twentieth

---

21. 1881–1954. Writer and intellectual. He promoted an ethics of art based on formal discipline and civic responsibility, effectively obedience to the "party line" of Prat de la Riba (see below, note 23 and pp. 16–17). His ideology was broadcast principally through a regular column, the *Glosari*, published in the newspaper *La Veu de Catalunya* between 1906 and 1923. General Secretary of the Institute of Catalan Studies from 1911, he moved to Madrid in 1923, where-after his writing was done in Castilian and he was detached from political and cultural Catalanism.

22. 1884–1970. Writer. His primary achievements were as a subtle, urbane poet who exemplified the literary temper of Noucentisme. He was also an accomplished short-story writer, essayist and translator. He collaborated closely with Prat de la Riba and with Fabra. His diplomatic career took him abroad in 1921, and this absence became exile after 1939.

century: Enric Prat de la Riba.[23] The blueprint for his national project was laid out in his influential book *La nacionalitat catalana* (1906). Historical, ethnographical and juridical arguments are combined in his extensive definition of nationhood, a definition that refers to the Enlightenment ideas of Leibnitz and the Romantic idealism of Herder to place language at the heart of community identity and aspirations.

1906 was manifestly the foundational year of Noucentisme, being marked by the debut of *Xènius*, by the publication of *La nacionalitat catalana* and also that of *Els fruits saborosos*, a book of poems by Josep Carner that struck the key-note of a new decorum in Catalan literature, a touch-stone of *noucentista* values. In that same year, moreover, the First International Congress on the Catalan Language was held in Barcelona. This clear example of what Joshua Fishman has characterised as the "First Congress phenomenon" was presided over by Antoni Maria Alcover,[24] on whose initiative it was convened. Divided into three sections (philologico-historical, literary and socio-juridical), the Congress brought together participants from all the Catalan-speaking areas and a few foreign delegates including Bernhard Schädel.[25] The topics covered related to various aspects of Catalan over its entire geo-historical spread, including fifteenth-century Greece. Seventeen plenary papers were presented together with sixty-one communications, including important contributions from Joan Maragall, Joaquim Ruyra,[26] Joseph Calmette from the Roussillon, the Spanish historian and philologist Ramón Menéndez Pidal, etc. Fabra was residing at the time in Bilbao

---

23. 1870–1917. Jurist and politician. Active in conservative Catalanist politics from the early 1890s, his party, the Lliga Regionalista was dominant in the first decades of the twentieth century. See also below, pp. 16–17.

24. 1862–1932. Priest, linguist and folklorist. A charismatic figure who made a major contribution to the scientific study and the formalisation of Catalan in the early twentieth century. He was first President of the Philological Section of the Institute of Catalan Studies. He clashed with Fabra and other members of the Institute, at a personal level and over linguistic issues, and from 1918 onwards worked in isolation, generally opposed to "official" policies for the reform of Catalan as they took shape. He continued working on his great ten-volume *Diccionari català-valencià-balear* (1926–1962) which was completed by Francesc de B. Moll (1903–1991). See below, p. 88.

25. 1878–1926. Philologist. He was a leading figure among the German scholars who laid the foundations of modern Romance Philology. He published studies on Catalan phonetics and dialectology, and collaborated with Alcover and others.

26. 1858–1939. Writer. Noted especially for his short narratives with a Mediterranean sea-board setting. His career began in the phase of Modernisme but he was adopted by the *noucentistes* as an exemplary writer, on account both of intellectual affinities and of his carefully crafted prose style. He worked with Fabra, through the IEC, and wrote on linguistic matters.

and his participation was limited to a relatively minor item on orthography and some comments on other contributions. Nonetheless, 1906 is seen as the point when his star rose into ascendancy and when his standing began to eclipse that of Alcover. The Congress, whose proceedings were published in 1908, had a considerable impact, both in its scientific aspect and in publicity it achieved, giving impetus to the revival movement throughout the *Països Catalans*. It prefigured in some ways the academic-*cum*-institutional base that the movement for language reform needed and that the political advances presided over by Prat de la Riba would put into place.

Fabra's early work drafted a design for the normativisation of modern Catalan, but this could only be fully articulated and extensively brought into play as part of a substantial and securely grounded political progress. Prat de la Riba was a politician of the first order, with a clearly formulated philosophy and programme that were associated with his high standing and influence in academic circles as a specialist in juridical theory. He played a large part in the conversion of the weekly organ *La Veu de Catalunya* into a daily newspaper that became, in 1899, the organ of the conservative Catalanist political party of the Lliga Regionalista. Prat himself had created this party, which he headed from 1901 until his death in 1917, and his role as editor-in-chief of *La Veu de Catalunya* was of a piece with his single-minded political activity. Against a background of unrest and agitation among the popular classes, Prat proposed a vision of a traditionalist and organicist Catalonia (as expounded in *La nacionalitat catalana*), a socially integrationalist and religious society, that would provide the fulfilment of Catalanist aspirations. His programme seemed to offer solutions both to violent social tensions in Catalonia and also to the crisis that the Spanish state was undergoing after the colonial crisis of 1898. Although he rejected the label of "federalist", he proposed the federation of an autonomous Principality of Catalonia with the other Iberian peoples, under a regime which could be either monarchical or republican. An integral part of this project was the aspiration of the Catalan bourgeoisie to work towards hegemony in the Peninsula, in defence of its own ideology and also of its markets.

In 1907 Prat was elected president of the Diputació (provincial government) of Barcelona, a position he occupied until his death. In 1914, as a consequence of persistent home-rule demands from the Catalan political classes, the Mancomunitat of Catalonia was set up. This was an amalgamation of the four provincial administrations (Barcelona, Girona, Tarragona and Lleida) which enjoyed limited (and poorly funded) devolved powers for internal affairs. Prat was elected as its first president, re-elected in 1917. Within this evolving framework, a local administrative infrastructure was created, largely due to Prat's dedication and to his ability to work with people of divergent intellectual tendencies. Prominent among these was Pompeu Fabra, a left-wing republican, whom he recalled to Barcelona from Bilbao in 1911 to occupy a newly created university chair of Catalan. Prior to this, also under the aegis of the Barcelona Diputació, Prat had overseen the foundation of the Institute of Catalan Studies in 1907. The Institute was divided in 1911 into three sections and Fabra was appointed as a founder member of the Philological Section, becoming its president in 1917 until his death in 1948.

All of these initiatives conformed to Prat de la Riba's clear perception of the primordial importance of a stable and normativised language in the organisation of a modern political entity, especially in public education and official use. The shortcomings of Catalan in this regard were all the more apparent at the time, as gains on the front of political autonomy were being achieved, including the formation of the very institutional bases from which language reform needed to be coordinated and implemented. After the watershed year of 1911 Fabra's ideas and his authority were able to be fully deployed. His work on the Institute's Orthographical Norms (1913) and Orthographical Dictionary (1917), the General Dictionary of the Catalan Language (1932), plus his Catalan Grammar of 1918, came out of his collaboration in the programme of Noucentisme, defined by the Valencian intellectual and writer Joan Fuster as "the biggest input of normalising effort ever received by the body of the country, since the time of Bishop Oliba [971–1046] at the very least".

A word is needed on Fabra's own use of cultural terminology, particularly that referring to the developmental phases outlined in this section which constituted the full context of his work. The Renaixença, Modernisme and Noucentisme were successive cycles with recognisable overlaps, particularly between the latter two. In Fabra's discourse the continuities are not at all perceptible (indeed, Renaixença is the only one of the three terms that he uses regularly, and with very particular connotations). In fact his strategy was consistently, even ruthlessly, to lump together the Renaixença and the *modernista* movement, tending to present them as a single cycle for which he uses a single term, predominantly Renaixença itself, signifying everything that went before the *Kulturkampf* of Noucentisme and its programme of language reform. "Chaos" and "anarchy" in the language are seen as what is being combated (a vision echoed on the ideological front by d'Ors/ *Xènius*). As has been suggested above, this strategy can be understood because of the *modernistes'* relaxed or "irresponsibly" variegated attitude to what Fabra and his supporters considered to be indispensable linguistic propriety. It is important to have this in mind when reading the texts presented in this volume: to recall that the *modernistes* saw themselves very much as heading a reaction against the culture of the Renaixença, and that the Noucentisme with which Fabra became fully identified derived important precedents and energies from Modernisme.

There are also a couple of related matters of semantics that can be mentioned here. Fabra himself repeatedly used a single word to express economically the full scope of the mission to which he was committed. This word is *redreçament*, whose dictionary rendering is "setting upright" and, figuratively, "reform", "recovery", "sorting out". His deployment of the term carries connotations of a total process begun in the nineteenth century, but its main emphasis (often associated with another word he favours, *tasca*, "task", "endeavour") is upon work in progress, difficulties to be overcome and a vision of the future. The translations in this volume systematically give, with occasional variations, "the restoration of Catalan to its rightful condition and status" as the semantic equivalent of *redreçament*. Finally in this context, Georg Kremnitz's remarks in the prologue are to be borne in mind regarding Fabra's systematic use of the term *llengua literària* (literary language), nowadays to be read as meaning "normativised standard" or "referential" language.

2.5.6 Developments through the twentieth century[27]

2.5.6.1 *The Dictatorship of Miguel Primo de Rivera*

In 1923 a coup led by General Primo de Rivera[28] placed the government of Spain in the hands of a Military Directorate, still under the monarchy of Alfonso XIII. Some conservative Catalanist sectors, including the Lliga Regionalista, had more or less connived at this, giving credit to the General's apparent pro-regionalist sympathies. Among the first measures announced by the Military Directorate were prohibition of the public use of Catalan and of Catalanist symbols, and also the closing down of a large number of nationalist organisations. Publications in Catalan were still allowed, but a rigid censorship of all expressions of dissident political opinion was applied. Josep Puig i Cadafalch,[29] Prat de la Riba's successor, against a background of mounting social tensions, resigned as President of the Mancomunitat in early 1924. Its administrative structures were already undermined, and in 1925 Primo de Rivera abolished it altogether. The General remained in power until 1930, but his Dictatorship collapsed when the King and the powerful sectors in

---

27. The following sections draw on Albert Balcells, *Catalan Nationalism, Past and Present* (Macmillan, London, 1996).

28. 1870–1930. Soldier and politician. As Captain General of Catalonia, he declared a military coup, in 1923, encouraged by the King and by important sectors of the Catalan bourgeoisie. His Military Directorate was effectively a dictatorship which implemented measures against all political expressions of Catalanism. His regime failed to resolve the crisis of Spanish government under the monarchy and ended in 1930. He died in exile in 1930.

29. 1867–1957. Architect, art historian and politician. President of the Mancomunitat after the death of Prat de la Riba in 1917.

Spanish society withdrew their support. Throughout the 1920s both working-class and left-wing Catalanist and Republican parties had been mobilising support and reorganising themselves. Together they had the momentum to win the municipal elections of April 1931 and this, reproduced in Republican successes throughout the whole of Spain, brought about the end the monarchy of Alfonso XIII and the swift declaration of the Second Spanish Republic.

Despite the anti-Catalanist ideology and behaviour of Primo de Rivera's regime, the period when he was in power saw positive gains for Catalan culture and, by extension, the cause of Catalan nationalism. This could occur because, while any overt political opposition was banned and the limited adminstrative powers of the Mancomunitat had been abolished, the Dictatorship did not prohibit what could pass as purely cultural activity carried out or published in the medium of Catalan. Such activity continued and, paradoxically, even prospered under the Military Directorate. The political arm of Catalanism was firmly bound, but energies were channelled into the surrogate of culture, as a sort of passive resistance that accumulated significant long-term gains. These were particularly robust on the language front. Private initiatives and finance moved in to loosen constraints on the Catalan cultural market (after a phase of establishment *dirigisme* during the period of the Mancomunitat) and publications in Catalan proliferated, tolerated by the regime subject to prior censorship. The readership in Catalan was growing and this went together with a corresponding increase in supply. The Spanish-language republican newspaper *La Publicidad* (where Fabra's Philological Conversations had begun to appear in 1919) was re-launched in Catalan as *La Publicitat* in 1922, ahead of the game, as it were. New daily newspapers followed, as did important magazines and journals, including the influential *Revista de Catalunya*. This expansion was reproduced on the book-publishing front. New publication houses were created and their lists included literary figures just beginning to make their mark as well as established authors. Two features of this panorama deserve comment. One is the sudden and substantial increase in the output of novels, from 1925, and the other is the dynamism of the artistic and literary vanguard: both symptomatic of cultural normality. To this must be added the significance of the collection *Els Nostres Clàssics* (Our Classics), initiated in 1924 and dedicated to providing accessible and reliable editions of texts from the Catalan golden age. Fabra makes special mention of the relevance of this event (in the 13/VII/1924 Philological Conversation, included in the present anthology), consonant with the importance he attached to study of the medieval authors as a crucial instrument for reform of the "literary language".

In 1924 the polyfacetic author Josep M. de Sagarra[30] observed with satisfaction that there obtained "a philological state of affairs where the [Catalan] writer finds that all the difficulties, primary and secondary, have been resolved, and that he can produce his work with a language that has been overhauled and perfected through use". From this time on the same sentiment will be repeated by other practising authors. With allowances made for a certain degree of wishful-thinking in Sagarra's assessment, it can certainly be interpreted as symptomatic. And it chimes in directly with Fabra's insistence on the important symbiosis between writers and grammarians.

2.5.6.2 *The Second Spanish Republic*
The advent of the Second Spanish Republic in 1931 gave a strong boost to the rising graph of progress for Catalanist aspirations. In the initial euphoria produced by the result of the municipal elections, the left-wing nationalist leader Francesc Macià[31] proclaimed an independent Catalan republic as a "member state of an Iberian federation". Negotiations with Madrid, however, quickly produced a back-pedalling and Macià renounced the initial position in exchange for a regional government within a unitary Spanish republican constitution. The historic name of the Generalitat[32] was adopted and the ensuing referendum on the Catalan Statute of Autonomy endorsed it by an overwhelming majority in a high turn-out of voters. Extended self-government; official status for the Catalan language in public administration, communications and education: these gains made the framework for a short but intense period of plenitude for Catalan culture in the 1930s.

The educational system did not become fully Catalanised during the brief period of the Republic, but considerable progress was made on this front, especially through the work of the Generalitat's Institut Escola, a centre for teacher training. Publication of the General Dictionary of the Catalan Language (1932)

---

30. 1894–1961. Writer. Prolific journalist and author of poetry, drama, narrative and memoirs. The quotation is from an article published in *La Publicitat*, 11/5/1924.

31. 1859–1933. Politician. First President of the autonomous Catalan government (1931–1933) under the Second Spanish Republic. Known as "the Grandfather", he enjoyed widespread popularity. He was succeeded as President of the Generalitat by Lluís Companys (1882–1940).

32. This was the permanent body representing the royal court in Catalonia and the kingdoms of Valencia and Aragon, from the end of the thirteenth century until the early eighteenth century. The institution enjoyed a high degree of regulatory and fiscal sovereignty, until abolition in all three areas under the decrees of the Nova Planta (1707–1716: see above p. 8). The term was revived as a convenient compromise in the delicate circumstances of 1931 and then again, as a historical continuation of that precedent, to designate the autonomous Catalan government of the post-Franco dispensation (see below p. 23).

was overseen by Fabra, on behalf of the Institute of Catalan Studies, with a sense of immediate urgency. There was also a corresponding surge in the press and in book-publishing. The ten Catalan-language dailies existing in 1927 had become twenty-five by 1933. Book production more than doubled between 1930 and 1936 (from 308 titles to 865). On the mass-communication front, Catalan radio programmes complemented these developments, indicating the movement towards a fully normalised situation for the language.

All of these developments, produced in a context of internal political conflict and growing international crisis, were violently truncated by the Spanish Civil War of 1936–1939. After a century of virtually constant progress, Catalan politics and the defence of the language were quickly brought very close to the point of extinction.

2.5.6.3 *The Franco years*

Catalan institutions and culture were major scapegoats of the vengeful repression that ensued upon General Franco's victory in the Civil War. In the immediate post-war aftermath (1939–1944) public use of the language was stamped upon and, before the defeat of fascism in Europe, a campaign of cultural genocide was in evidence. Catalan was replaced by Spanish in all the official and public spaces that it had come laboriously to occupy over the preceding years: in administration and politics; in education at every level; in publications and the media, where ruthless censorship was applied. Many Catalan politicians, public figures and intellectuals had been murdered; very many others were either exiled abroad or silenced in "internal exile". Although the use of Catalan was kept alive in private and family spheres, the imposed public monopoly of Castilian severely impacted on earlier advances made by the former. The desertion of Catalan, especially among the upper classes, was not uncommon and the linguistic integration of immigrants was impeded.

After the Allies' victory in 1945, the Franco regime had to loosen its stranglehold. Within the full international context of this, some relaxation of repressive measures that had driven Catalan underground began to be visible. The Institute of Catalan Studies had been clandestinely reorganised in 1942, and its operations were cautiously resumed on the two fronts where the Spanish state was most constrained from interfering: international academic relations and scholarly activity. A Catalan-language stage production was put on in 1948, and publication of books was resumed, hesitantly, in the late 1940s. The regime had a paternalistic attitude towards folkloric manifestations of "regionalism", and this resulted in authorisation of public participation in the *sardana*, the Catalans' national dance. Nervousness about being heard speaking the language in public started to decline, but the written presence of the language was still as exiguous as it had been since 1939. Explicit, organised opposition to the regime remained out of the question.

The late 1950s and the 1960s are recalled as a period of growing resistance in which defence of Catalan was popularly understood as a key force against an increasingly anachronistic political order in Spain. As the Franco regime began to lose its grip on affairs in a changing world, so the resilience and continuing cultural vitality of the Catalan language was exemplified in the emergence of impressive literary creations (primarily in poetry but also in narrative prose) and of an influential protest/popular song movement (known as *La Nova Cançó*, New Song). This was the first mass-culture manifestation to be articulated through Catalan, and it was a phenomenon that did much towards overcoming a serious impediment to eventual renewal of the normalisation process: the gap, magnified by repression, between the vernacular and the more formal levels of the language.[33]

The fact is that the ravages of the Civil War and of the Franco period had seriously set back what had been achieved in the first third of the twentieth century regarding progress towards recovery of Catalan's "proper condition and rightful status". Fabra, as we have remarked, viewed this as an on-going endeavour, with much still to be done on standardisation of the language as a prerequisite for its social normalisation. He declared his intention that the standard language, as a living organ, should be open to development and to further "innovation" (another word he used recurrently), including further incorporation of non-Barcelona usage. The long interlude of 1939–1975, with Fabra himself geographically isolated in the 1940s, had the effect of turning his works into a strict, unalterable orthodoxy, deviation from which was regarded by purists as unpatriotic. This attitude sat uncomfortably with observable realities: how the language had been steadily degraded in the Franco years, moving towards the condition of a *patois*, even on the way towards extinction; and how the literary idiom could appear to many Catalan-speakers to be an almost alien "moribund tongue" with "indigestible words…, almost unintelligible by now to many of us". The poet-dramatist Salvador Espriu[34] wrote these words in 1948, claiming that he was composing perhaps the last will and testament of his language. With hindsight, one can now appreciate that his jeremiad contributed to the underground chorus of resistance to annihilation.

---

33. This was a constant preoccupation of Fabra's: see particularly the final section, "The literary language and the spoken language' (in "The task of purifying Catalan'), and "On the purification of the literary language', reproduced in our anthology, pp. 185–187 and 196–197 and 202.

34. 1913–1985. Writer. The quotation is from his The Story of Esther (*Primera història d'Esther*: 1948), translated by Philip Polack (Sheffield: The Anglo-Catalan Society, 1989).

After 1962 relaxation of the state censorship (permitting, *inter alia*, publication of foreign literature in Catalan translation) and a new press law (1966) allowed further liberalisation. Throughout the 1960s gains for Catalan were registered in areas where public opinion, civic groups and nationalist cultural opposition could operate: pressure for education in Catalan at school and university level, the emergence of new and dynamic publishing concerns, new journals and even a short-lived weekly news magazine, a (very limited) presence on state radio and television channels, the inauguration of some local broadcasting stations, campaigns for municipal reform, etc. The panorama is balanced, however, by the fact that the number of new book titles published in Catalan in 1975 (611, this total having risen from the 270 recorded for 1962) was still short of the 865 new titles of 1936.[35]

2.5.6.4 *The post-Franco era*
The dictator Francisco Franco died in 1975, and Spain's difficult transition to democracy was expectantly observed from abroad, especially from the rest of Europe. In the post-Franco era the Catalan language enjoys special "respect" under the terms of the Spanish Constitution of 1978 and specific protection in the dispensations of the respective autonomy statutes of Catalonia (1979), Valencia (1982) and the Balearic Islands (1983). (As already explained, the term Generalitat, applied to the Catalan and the Valencian autonomous governments, corresponded to expediency as well as to historic legitimacy.[36]) In all three autonomous administrations the Catalan language is co-official with Spanish. Normalisation of Catalan's social use has been and continues to be an issue in each, even as the political conditions for this appear to be assured "on paper".

Regarding normativisation, it is only since the 1980s that the Institute of Catalan Studies and associated institutions have regained the authority to expand and modernise standard Catalan, introducing recommendations for terminology, for spoken language in the mass media, and for regional parastandards.

The pull of tendencies towards a fragmentation of Catalan has already been referred to above. Alongside the Barcelona-based norm which is used throughout Catalonia and to some extent elsewhere, de facto parastandards for Valencian and Balearic varieties had already grown up, becoming regularised in the late twentieth century largely through the practice of a few major publishers. These parastandards diverge from the Eastern Central norm only in retaining some

---

35. Data from Francesc Vallverdú, *L'ús del català: un futur controvertit* (Barcelona: Edicions 62, 1990), p. 32 and *passim*.

36. See above, p. 20.

regional differences of vocabulary and morphology. The differences are roughly comparable to those between Peninsular and American Spanish, or British and American English: one may easily read a page of text before encountering a feature which marks it as of one regional standard variety or of another. In recent years some authors and publishers in Catalonia have argued for, and practised, modifications of the standard language to reflect more popular usage, especially that of the Barcelona area, in vocabulary and syntax. The vehemence of polemics surrounding these deviations is out of proportion to the relatively modest scope of the innovations proposed. And it has to be said that the name of Fabra has been taken in vain on both sides.

A potentially much more serious trend, since the 1980s, has been one associated with claims that Valencian is not a Catalan regional variety but a separate language. (Similar claims have also been made in respect of the Balearic variety, but these have been more dilute, and exploited politically with less effect.) Anti-Catalan sentiment has been provoked and manipulated by (obviously centralist) political interests. In recent years there have been moves to overcome the conflict between "secessionists" and "unionists". A status quo for users of the Valencian variety is emerging, whereby a certain equilibrium exists between orthodoxies for the written language. The outcome is that users of this variety can favour formal expresssion that reflects features of the local spoken idiom or they can resort to the "common standard". And support for the official norms of the Institute of Catalan Studies continues to be generally given by educational institutions, publishers and most writers in Catalan. In such a situation, however, the purely philological reasoning of Fabra (see his address to the Valencian and Balearic writers, reproduced in this volume) still remains vulnerable to obfuscation by political vested interests.

2.6   Bibliography and sources of information on Catalan

2.6.1 Bibliography and materials for learning Catalan

2.6.1.1 *Self-teaching methods*

a. Intercat (http://intercat.gencat.cat/en/index.jsp): Intercat is a set of electronic resources for learning the Catalan language and for information about Catalan culture, aimed mainly at mobility students who visit Catalan universities.
b. Parla.cat (http://www.parla.cat): Parla.cat is a virtual learning space that offers every kind of educational material for learning the Catalan language. The course can be followed either through a self-managed learning method or with tutorial support.

c. The Servei d'autoformació en llengua catalana (SALC) is a self-training service for Catalan (http://salc.upf.edu/) offered by the Pompeu Fabra University, Barcelona. It incorporates self-teaching resources, from elementary to advanced levels, created by the Directorate General for Language Policy of the Generalitat of Catalonia.

2.6.1.2 *On-line multilingual dictionaries*
Diccionari de la llengua catalana multilingüe. At: http://www.grec.net.
Logos Dictionary. At: http://www.logos.it/dictionary/.

2.6.1.3 *Books for learning Catalan*
Clua, Esteve et al. 2003. *EuroComRom. Els set sedassos: aprendre a llegir les llengües romàniques simultàniament.* Aachen: Shaker. ISBN 3832206833.
Gèottsche, Katja et al. 2003. *EuroComRom – Os sete passadores: saber ler todas as linguas romanicas ja!.* Aachen: EuroCom. ISBN 3832208240.
Gili, Joan. 1993. *Introductory Catalan grammar: with a brief outline of the language and literature, a selection from Catalan writers, and a Catalan-English and English-Catalan vocabulary.* 5th ed. Oxford: The Dolphin Book. ISBN 0852150784.
Giudicetti, Gian Paolo et al. 2002. *EuroComRom: I setti setacci: impara a leggere le lingue romanze!.* Aachen: Shaker Verlag. ISBN 3826597427.
Ibarz, Alexander; Ibarz, Toni. 2005. *Colloquial Catalan.* London: Routledge. ISBN 978-0-415-23414-6.
Klein, Horst G.; Tilbert D. Stegmann. 2000. *EuroComROM, die sieben Siebe: Romanische Sprachen sofort lesen können.* Aachen: Shake Verlag. ISBN 3826569474.
Martín Peris, Ernesto et al. 2005. *EuroComRom – Los siete tamices: un fácil aprendizaje de la lectura en todas las lenguas románicas.* Aachen: Shaker. ISBN 3-8322-3303-2.
McCann, William J.; Horst G. Klein; Tilbert D. Stegmann. 2002. *EuroComROM, the seven sieves: how to read all the Romance languages right away.* Aachen: Shaker. ISBN 3832204377.
Meissner, Franz-Joseph et al. 2004. *EuroComRom – les sept tamis: lire les langues romanes dès le départ.* Aachen: Shaker. ISBN 3832212213.
Poch, Anna; Yates, Alan. 2004. *Teach Yourself Catalan* (with CD). London: Hodder & Stoughton. ISBN 0340870567.
Yates, Alan; Ibarz, Toni. 1992. *A Catalan Handbook: working with **Digui, digui**....* Sheffield: Botifarra Publications. ISBN 0-9520127-0-7. Also available as 1993 *A Catalan Handbook: Digui, digui...: Curs de català per a estrangers.* Barcelona: Generalitat de Catalunya. Departament de Cultura. ISBN 8439325797.

2.6.1.4 *On-line Catalan dictionaries*

Alcover, Antoni Maria; Moll, Francesc de B. 1932–1962. *Diccionari català-valencià-balear* (10 vols). Palma de Mallorca: Moll. Available at *http://dcvb.iecat.net/*.

Gran diccionari de la llengua catalana. Barcelona: Enciclopèdia Catalana, 1998. Available at *http://www.enciclopedia.cat/*.

Institut d'Estudis Catalans. 2007. *Diccionari de la llengua catalana*. 2a ed. Barcelona: Enciclopèdia Catalana / Ed. 62. Available at *http:/www.dlc.iec.cat/*.

2.6.2 Other relevant source material

2.6.2.1 *Useful web-sites*

a.   http://www.cpnl.cat: Consorci per a la Normalització Lingüística
     This Consortium was created through co-operation between the Catalan Generalitat and many municipalities, local councils and provincial governments, with the aim of facilitating the knowledge, use and dissemination of Catalonia's own language in all spheres of life.

b.   http://www.gencat.cat/index_eng.htm: Generalitat de Catalunya
     This site offers diverse information on all the areas for which powers of self-government reside in the Generalitat, the government of Catalonia which is responsible for, among many areas, language policy, culture, and education.

c.   http://www.gencat.cat/temes/eng/: Generalitat de Catalunya
     Catalan language web-site, specifically dedicated to the aspects of competence of the Generalitat in matters concerning the language.

d.   http://www.iec.cat: Institute of Catalan Studies
     This is the web-site of Catalonia's national academy which, through its Philological Section, officially regulates matters affecting the Catalan language, across all the territories in which it spoken.

e.   http://www.linguamon.cat: House of Languages
     This is the web-site of a body set up by the Generalitat de Catlunya with the aim of promoting the world's languages as:
         vehicles for communication, civilisation and dialogue,
         sources of personal development and human creativity, as well as repositories of mankind's heritage,
         embodiments of the rights of individuals and of linguistic communities.

f.   http://www.llull.cat/: Institut Ramon Llull
     The mission of the Institut Ramon Llull is official promotion of Catalan language and culture internationally, across all varieties and modes of expression.

2.6.2.2 *Works in English on the Catalan language*

Boix, Emili; Payrató, Lluís. 1997. "An Overview of Catalan Sociolinguistics and Pragmatics". *Catalan Review*, IX, 317–403.

Boix, Emili; Sanz, Cristina. 2008. "Language and Identity in Catalonia". *Bilingualism and Identity. Spanish at the crossroads with other languages*. Amsterdam: John Benjamins, 87–106.

Current Issues in Language and Society (1999), vol V, no. 3, a special isssue of this journal, devoted to various aspects of language-planning in Catalonia from the 1980s.

Gore, Sarah; John MacInnes. 1998. *The Politics of Language in Catalunya*. Edinburgh: University of Edinburgh. Department of Sociology. Edinburgh Working Papers in Sociology; 13. ISBN: 1-900522-60-8.

Hualde, José Ignacio. 1992. *Catalan: Descriptive grammar*. London: Routledge. ISBN 0415054982.

Martí i Castell, Joan. 1993. "The First International Catalan Language Congress, Barcelona, 13–18 October, 1906". In *The Earliest Stage of Language Planning: The 'First Congress' Phenomenon*, Joshua Fishman (ed.), 47–67. New York: Mouton de Gruyter. ISBN 3110135302.

Webber, Jude; Strubell i Trueta, Miquel. 1991. *The Catalan Language: Progress towards Normalisation*. Sheffield: The Anglo-Catalan Society. ISBN 0144-5863-7.

Wheeler, Max W.; Yates, Alan; Dols, Nicolau. 1999. *Catalan: A Comprehensive Grammar*. London: Routledge. ISBN 0-415-10342-8.

Wright, Sue (ed.). 1999. *Language, democracy and devolution in Catalonia*. Clevedon PA: Multilingual Matters.

2.6.2.3 *Works in Spanish on the Catalan language*

Badia i Margarit, Antoni M. 1985. *Gramática catalana*. 3rd reprint. Madrid: Gredos. (2 vols.) ISBN 8424911237.

Günter Holtus, Michael Metzeltin, Christian Schmitt (ed.). 1991. *Lexikon der Romanistischen Linguistik, LRL: Französisch, Okzitanisch, Katalanisch = Le français, L'occitan, Le catalan*. Vol. V, 2: *Okzitanisch, Katalanisch = L'occitan, Le catalan*. Tübingen: Max Niemeyer, 127–310. ISBN 3484502509.

Marí, Isidor. 1993. *Conocer la lengua y la cultura catalanas*. Palma de Mallorca: Llull, Federació d'Entitats Culturals dels Països Catalans. ISBN 84-604-7744-4.

Payrató, Lluís. 2006. "El catalán hoy. Rasgos lingüísticos, consideraciones sociolingüísticas y aspectos de política lingüística". In *Las lenguas españolas: un enfoque filológico*, Buitrago Gómez; María Cruz (eds.), 129–149. Madrid: Ministerio de Educación y Ciencia. ISBN 843694175.

2.6.2.4 Works in French on the Catalan language

Badia i Margarit, Antoni M. 2007. "L'Institut d'Estudis Catalans et les travaux de langue et civilisation catalanes." *Estudis Romànics*, XXIX: 7–42.

Badia i Margarit, Antoni M.; Straka, Georges (eds.). 1973. *La linguistique catalane. Colloque International organisé par le Centre de Philologie et Littératures Romanes de Strasbourg (1968)*. París: Klincksieck. ISBN 2252014806.

Boix, Emili; Payrató, Lluís; Vila, F. Xavier. 1997. "Espagnol-catalan". In: Goebl, H. et al. (eds.) *Kontaklinguistik = Contact Linguistics = Linguistique de contact*. Berlín: Walter de Gruyter, 2, 1296–1302. ISBN 3-11-015154-5.

Boix-Fuster, Emili; Milian-Massana, Antoni (eds.). 2002. *Aménagement linguistique dans les pays de langue catalane*. In: *Terminogramme: revue de recherche et d'information en aménagement linguistique et en terminologie* 103–104. Saint Laurent: Les Publications du Québec. ISSN 0225-3194.

Boyer, Henri; Christian Lagarde (dir.). 2002. *L'Espagne et ses langues: un modèle écolinguistique?* Paris; Budapest: L'Harmattan. ISBN 2-7475-2721-2.

Günter Holtus, Michael Metzeltin, Christian Schmitt (ed.). 1991. *Lexikon der Romanistischen Linguistik, LRL: Französisch, Okzitanisch, Katalanisch = Le français, L'occitan, Le catalan*. Vol. V, 2: *Okzitanisch, Katalanisch = L'occitan, Le catalan*. Tübingen: Max Niemeyer, 127–310. ISBN 3484503351.

Lamuela, Xavier. 1996. "La codification du catalan au XXe siècle". In: *Sociolinguistique: Territoire et objets*, Boyer, Henry (ed.), 159–177. Lausanne/Paris: Delachaux et Niestlé.

2.6.2.5 Works in Catalan on the Catalan language

Institut d'Estudis Catalans. Secció Filològica. 2009. *Gramàtica de la llengua catalana*. (Provisional version, available only on-line): *http://www.iecat.net/institucio/seccions/Filologica/gramatica/default.asp*].

Solà, Joan et al. (ed.). 2002. *Gramàtica del català contemporani*. (3 vols.) Barcelona: Empúries. ISBN 8475968694.

3. Pompeu Fabra:
A life's work in applied linguistics[37]

3.1 Introduction

In the preceding pages we have provided a short survey of the socio-linguistic history of Catalan which should enable the reader to position the figure and the work of Fabra in the context of his times. We proceed now to give a synthetic description of Pompeu Fabra's activity as a linguist *per se* and in particular of his work in applied linguistics (theoretician of standardisation, grammarian and lexicographer, including an account of his work on the normalisation of topography and as a literary translator). Looking at Fabra's total output, Joan Mascaró (2006) has recently made a distinction between his "*scientific work* [...] which belonged inside the linguistics of his day in the European academic world" and "the applied work of normativisation or of descriptive synthesis applied to diverse languages". He argues that this latter dimension, "although it is 'scientific' in the sense that it is rigorously competent and set upon previous scientific bases, is not scientific production in the strictest sense". Mascaró adds: "The scientific work of Fabra [...] that part of it which is totally detached from his work on normativisation, is constituted by no more than four articles [...] and three reviews [...]. Based on an approximate calculation of the number of pages, these amount to only 2.7% of his total written output." And he concludes that "Fabra felt no special interest in cultivating linguistics as a science in its own right, in other words, if it was not an auxiliary element in his normativising project." This is why we here devote more space and give first priority to explaining what has become generally known as the "theory of literary language according to Fabra".

Regarding his work as an applied linguistician, from the quantitative point of view (based on the number of his published pages in these areas), treatment of these aspects would demand a different order from that which we follow. His

37. We are grateful to Alan Yates, not only for his careful and intelligent translation of the following pages but also for his most helpful comments on the first draft of this text.

grammatical and lexicographical works are substantially longer than his texts containing socio-linguistic reflections. The order adopted here, however, is based upon the repercussion of Fabra's work in each of these activities. Georg Kremnitz's Prologue highlights the fact that Fabra was one of the first linguists or grammarians to attach importance to the social dimension of linguistic phenomena. As regards his conception of syntax and of linguistic change and diversity, these areas will be treated always in relation to Fabra's work on codification. Before proceeding to discuss Fabra's writings, though, we devote the next section to supplying biographical information which is essential for a full understanding of his life and work.

3.2   Pompeu Fabra: Biographical outline

Some biographical details are contained in Georg Kremnitz's text and in previous sections of this Introduction. Here we unify and supplement that information.

Pompeu Fabra i Poch was born in Barcelona in 1868 and he died, in exile, in Prada (the main town of the Conflent district, in the Catalan-speaking part of southern France) in 1948.

In an interview he gave in 1926, Fabra talked about how as an adolescent he became acutely aware of all the limitations, external and internal, affecting the contemporary written form(s) of the Catalan language. In the same interview, and in other texts reproduced in this volume, he explained the steps beyond this newly awakened linguistic consciousness, into study, with the detective materials available to him, and into the conviction that a root-and-branch reform of the language was an absolute cultural imperative. The intellectual atmosphere of the Catalonia in which the young Fabra developed (see above, especially §2.5.4) contained possibilities encouraging active dedication to this objective. His participation (1890–1892) in the campaign for orthographical reform conducted by the journal and publishing house L'Avenç clearly evinced his initial affiliation with the spirit of Modernisme, until the parameters of his ideas became increasingly and then fully aligned, in the first decade of the twentieth century, with the politico-cultural programme of Noucentisme. In the crucial year of 1911 he became fully integrated into the movement's key personnel. (On this phase, see §2.5.5, above.)

Despite his youthful vocation for the study of linguistics and Catalan grammar, Fabra bowed to his father's wish that he should do a degree course in industrial engineering at Barcelona university. Newly qualified, the need to make a living took him to a chair of chemistry at the School of Engineering in Bilbao. He resided in the Basque Country from 1902 until 1911, during which period he participated (1906) in the First International Congress on the Catalan Language.

Recalled in 1911 to Barcelona by Prat de la Riba, he was appointed to the newly created Chair of Catalan in the University, a position he occupied until it was abolished in 1924 by the dictatorship of Primo de Rivera. In the same year he became a founder member of the Philological Section of the Institute of Catalan Studies, set up by Prat de la Riba in 1907 and divided into three sections in 1911. He presided over the Philological Section from 1917 to 1948, and (between 1921 and 1939) he had several periods in the presidency of the IEC.

As already mentioned the landmarks of Fabra's activity on behalf of the IEC were the publication of the Orthographical Norms (1913); the Orthographical Dictionary (1917); the normative Catalan Grammar (first edition 1918, seventh and last edition 1933), and the General Dictionary of the Catalan Language (DGLC, 1932). (His prologues to the two dictionaries are included in our selection of texts in translation.) It must be recalled that the last phases of this work were carried out in conditions of considerable adversity, under the dictatorship, and of urgency with the advent of the Republic.

In 1932 Fabra regained his chair in the University of Barcelona, appointed directly to the position without having to go through the normally obligatory process of competitive examinations. A year later he became president of the University's governing council, after its being granted autonomous status under the Autonomy Statute for Catalonia (1932) within the Second Spanish Republic.

The official position that he held meant that Fabra was imprisoned after the turbulent episode of what is known as the "Events of October 6" in 1934. This was the name given to the insurrectional movement of that year presided over by the autonomous government of Catalonia. It was a response to the conservative involution of the Spanish Republican government, after a rightwards swing in the general election of November 1933. The Madrid government annulled recent Catalan legislation for improvement in the conditions of agricultural workers. This provoked a considerable exacerbation of anti-centralist feeling and led also to formation of a block of working class forces under the umbrella of the *Aliança Obrera*. A general strike was called in Barcelona and, on October 6, the President of the autonomous Catalan government, Lluís Companys,[38] proclaimed the establishment of a Catalan State as part of a Federal Spanish Republic. The senior military figure in Catalonia, under orders from Madrid, responded by imposing martial law and sending in troops to put down the rebellion. On October 7, in

---

38. 1882–1940. Politician. President of the Generalitat from 1934. Imprisoned for life after the events of that year, he returned to office in 1936 whereafter he headed the Catalan defence of the Spanish Republic. He fled to exile in France in 1939, from where he was returned by the Germans into the hands of the Franco regime and executed by firing squad, in the castle of Montjuic, Barcelona, on 15 October 1940.

view of the lack of popular support, Companys gave the order to surrender. President Companys and all the ministers in his government were imprisoned, tried and condemned to life imprisonment. Beyond these punishments, reprisals included the detention of hundreds of left-wing militants and leaders, closure of the headquarters of political parties, banning of culpable sectors of the press, eviction of tenant farmers and the de facto annulment of the Catalan Statute of Autonomy (a situation effectively maintained until the victory of the Popular Front in the elections of February 1936).

Fabra was able to resume his university position after those elections. It was a brief rehabilitation, however, and one lived out in ever-worsening adverse conditions. The Spanish Civil War had broken out in July 1936. With the occupation of Barcelona by Franco's troops in 1939, Fabra (along with many other Catalan intellectuals and politicians) was obliged to flee into exile. Until his death in 1948 he resided amid great privations in various towns in southern France. He went to Andorra in order to be able to make his will in a country where Catalan was the official language.

As regards the scholarly biography of Fabra, three stages can be identified in his trajectory:

a.   1883–1889, between the ages of 15 and 21. In this phase he is a complete and isolated autodidact (reading only the books, including dictionaries and grammars, found in his home or at the house of a friend).

b.   1890–1910: the period when he enters into contact with the Ateneu Barcelonès,[39] where he has access to the up-to-date bibliography of European linguistics, and with the editorial team of L'Avenç, with whom he sets in motion the campaign for linguistic reform. His prestige as a scholar is consolidated with his contributions to the First International Congress on the Catalan Language of 1906. His first works on grammar belong to this phase: Ensayo de catalán moderno (1891, in Castilian) and Contribució a la gramàtica catalana (1898, in Catalan). Each of these, unlike the other grammatical treatises available at the time, describes the contemporary oral language of Barcelona. Over this same period he is busy writing articles and giving lectures to expound his views. Significant among the published items are "On Linguistic and Orthographical Reform" (1892) and "On Various Unresolved Issues in Present-day Literary Catalan" (1907), both presented in this volume.

c.   1911–1948: called the "institutional" stage by Josep Murgades, initiated after Fabra becomes a member of the Philological Section of the IEC. This is the

---

39. Founded in 1860, the Ateneu is a private association, with an important library, which became (and still is nowadays) a major centre of Catalanist cultural and intellectual activities.

most productive period from every point of view, despite the difficulties encountered during Primo de Rivera's dictatorship and despite the tragic final phase (1939–1948) in exile.

Summing up and assessing the 55 years spent by Fabra in the study and the promotion of Catalan, his activity can be seen to have four aspects: his publications, his university teaching, the civic prestige he attained and utilised, and the lasting legacy of his work.

Well over a thousand texts authored by Fabra are extant. The present writer consulted 1,135 in the preparation of a doctoral dissertation (2004), and others have been discovered in the meantime. Their typology is as follows: articles, letters, dictionaries, speeches, interviews, "responses" to others' contributions to the 1906 Congress, grammars (see §3.4 below), manifestos, miscellanies on grammatical correctness, prologues, reviews of lectures, postcards and transcriptions of lecture courses given by him. It is an enormous and most heterogeneous corpus, from postcards to an entire dictionary. Discrimination must therefore be applied in evaluating the importance of each type of text, a criterion which we shall apply in the analysis to be made of the different facets of Fabra's linguistic and grammatical activities. One thing to which attention can be drawn, in general, is the polyglotism that he practised: he wrote in four languages (Catalan, Spanish, French and English) and, according to recent findings by specialists in his work, he dealt with phenomena in eighteen different languages other than Catalan itself (Spanish, French, Italian, Portuguese, Romanian, Latin, Classical Greek, English, German, Dano-Norwegian, Russian, Polish, Provençal, Sardinian, Arabic, Serbo-Croatian and Chinese), with different degrees of systemacity and exhaustiveness, ranging from an isolated or indirect reference, in one or more texts, through to the composition of a grammar of French and one of English.

Another notable feature of Fabra's written output is the concern he showed, from the very beginning, to utilise the daily press in order explain and give circulation to his ideas and decisions. Already in 1892, as we have seen, he published an article which can be characterised as programmatic. He never gave up this effort to spread his message. And, as has been emphasised in Georg Krenmitz's Prologue, this endeavour acquires an extraordinary dimension in the short articles which, under the heading Philological Conversations, he published, irregularly, over ten years (1919–1928) in *La Publicitat*, one of the major Catalan newspapers of the time. These pieces constitute a corpus of 842 texts which enable one to follow the trajectory of Fabra's thinking, and for this reason we include a good number in the selection of translated texts.

The circumstances associated with his tenure of a chair at Barcelona University have been mentioned already. (To those facts should be added the significant one that in 1945, in interminable exile and at the age of seventy-seven, he was invested with an honorary doctorate by the University of Toulouse.) Testimony to Fabra's dedication to his university teaching is to be found in the notes that have survived, taken by students of his. Some of these notes have been published (Lloret i Ramos 2006: 663–1098). We also have the testimony of a former pupil, Alfred Badia (1998: 206), who wrote: "Pompeu Fabra always spoke without any emphatic pomp at all, in an almost colloquial tone. His clarity of exposition was perfect and his scholarly rigour – peppered now and then with ironic remarks and even the occasional joke – was perfectly matched to his didactic intention. He was not there to show off: his desire was to communicate and to persuade. The teaching role disguised the presence of the wise researcher."

In the light of what has been said thus far, it is perfectly understandable how Pompeu Fabra became a civic figure beyond academic circles. The imposing writer and journalist Josep Pla (1897–1981) once affirmed: "Fabra was the most important Catalan of our day, because he is the only citizen of this country, in recent times, who, having set himself the aim of realising a specific public and general objective, achieved this with explicit and indisputable success. [...] Out of the indescribable, incredible disaster [the Civil War of 1936–1939], all that remains standing is a single body of work and a single figure: the figure and the work of Pompeu Fabra."

But the success achieved by Fabra was neither immediate nor easy. As a young man, when he was kicking over the traces, he faced up to the leading intellectual figures of the Renaixença, gathered around the Jocs Florals and the Reial Acadèmia de Bones Lletres, as his 1892 article testifies. The firm reliance he placed on the contemporary spoken language, his superior linguistic knowledge and the support of Prat de la Riba that he enjoyed after 1911 made many of the earlier generation of grammarians and writers adopt antagonistic positions regarding his proposals. Outstanding among these were Antoni Maria Alcover, Josep Calveras[40] and the institution of the Barcelona Jocs Florals which administered the most prestigious literary prizes then on offer and which until 1934 refused to accept the Orthographical Norms of the IEC.

Those who opposed Fabra's ideas for language reform and his influence were known as the *antinormistes*. Four basic objections converged in their reaction. Certain writers, some of the "old school" and some with *modernista* affiliations, held that the official Norms were an impediment to literary creativity. Alcover believed that the priority should be study of the language in general and not the achievement of a normative standard. Calveras argued that Fabra's proposals

---

40. 1890–1964. Grammarian and scholar, a member of the Jesuits. Author of a book on *The Reconstruction of the Catalan Literary Language* (1928).

made no allowances for different registers. And Ramon Miquel i Planes[41] asserted that any orthographical system differing radically from the Spanish one would entail difficulties for language teaching, because pupils would have to learn two different ways of spelling.

This notwithstanding, the young Fabra's reputation was spreading thanks to the reverberations of his lectures, classes and articles. With the publication of the Orthographical Norms, however, he became a figure of popular acclaim and by the 1930s he was regularly the object of homage celebrations. His popularity was something which meant that Spanish fascism could not overlook him. During the dictatorship of Primo de Rivera he was offered membership of the Real Academia Española (the academy which was the maximum authority in the regulation of the Spanish language). This honour, devised to dilute Fabra's Catalanist standing, was turned down. As he himself explained: "If I was considered to be a kind of symbol of the Catalan language it is quite clear to me that, if I were to show weakness, the language would be weakened. And I was sure that if the language was weakened, everything would collapse." In later years Fabra was converted into a sort of bogey-man by extreme elements on the militant Spanish right. During the Civil War the captain general of Franco's Army, Gonzalo Queipo de Llano, made repeated references to him, in radio broadcasts, as a declared enemy of Spain.

Other examples of Fabra's engagement with Catalanism and of his republican sympathies can be mentioned. In 1898 he was head of the editorial board of the journal *Catalònia* (a *modernista* publication which prefigured some of the spirit of Noucentisme), founded by the poet Joan Maragall. In 1913 he was persuaded to stand as a candidate for the left-wing Nationalist Federal Republican Union in the Barcelona municipal elections. From 1917 to 1936 he headed the pedagogical editorial committee of the Associació Protectora de l'Ensenyança Catalana. This was a private body, founded in 1899, committed to the cause of organising education in Catalan, which was finally closed down after the Civil War. He held the presidency of the Ateneu Barcelonès in 1924. The interview (included in our anthology) published by the writer Tomàs Garcés (1926) in the widely read and influential *Revista de Catalunya* appeared at a time when Fabra's involvement in public affairs was at its most active, with no sign of its diminishing. From 1930 to 1936 (with an interruption caused by the upheavals of 1934) he was the first president of Palestra, a patriotic, educational organisation for young people, along the lines of the Boy Scouts. In 1934 he accepted the presidency of the Jocs Florals, as a way of healing rifts and ending that institution's hostility to the Orthographical Norms. And even at the age of seventy-seven he became a minister of the

---

41. 1874–1950. Bibliophile, scholar and novelist.

government of the Generalitat in exile, joining the company of the most outstanding political figures of the post-war diaspora.

A supplementary piece of anecdotal information is worthy of note at this point. In 1938 the Linguaphone Institute, based in London, included in its Miniature Language Series a gramophone recording of a sample of the Catalan language, accompanied by a printed transcription of the recorded material. Linguaphone was a pioneer in the production of phonographic materials for language learning. The "two talks on the Catalan language" were recorded by Fabra and the educationalist the educationalist and philologist Delfí Dalmau (1891–1965; author of *Poliglotisme passiu*). Little is known about the circumstances of Fabra's presence in London in the troubled year of 1938, or about his contacts with Linguaphone. His collaboration with the company does, however, say much about his pragmatism and his interest in advanced ideas relating to applied linguistics. The item, presumably of his own choice, which he recorded was his "Address to the Valencian and Balearic Writers" (included in translation in the present volume). This detail adds to the poignancy of the episode, in view of the events which affected him soon after 1938.

Regarding the lasting legacy of Fabra's work, we have already reproduced the resonant judgement emitted by Josep Pla. Georg Kremnitz picks up the theme in his Prologue to this volume, stressing the importance (especially for education) of how, after the death of Franco in 1975, Catalan had at its disposal an already standardised lexicogrammar. Upon this basis the efforts of recovery and reconstruction on every level were more viable than they would have otherwise been. And this referential language was the product of Fabra's labours. The normative lexis is now fixed by the IEC's Dictionary of the Catalan Language (2007), but this work is considered to be an up-dating of Fabra's General Dictionary (DGLC) of 1932, in itself a model of lexicography.

Kremnitz adds: "Fabra could count on the support of such Catalan institutions as did exist at the time – especially the Institute of Catalan Studies, from 1907, and the semi-devolved administrative powers of the Mancomunitat, between 1914 and 1925 – but the essential element was without doubt the 'professional' quality of the standard for modern Catalan that was shaped by Fabra, together with his own indefatigable efforts to promote this referential model within Catalan society." If we look again at the basic division between "scientific" and "non-scientific" linguistic work, we find that the presence of Fabra is as visible in the normative terrain as in that of theory and description. Regarding his legacy for the former, only a few detailed aspects have had to be completed subsequently; and, in grammar and lexis, Fabra's work constituted the starting point for the IEC's Proposal for an Oral Standard (1990–2001) and for its Grammar of the Catalan Language, at present (May 2009) in the final stages of preparation. (This means, incidentally, that the official grammar is still Fabra's Catalan Grammar of 1918–1933.) As for the field of theory and description, it is sufficient to look at the bibliography cited in recent linguistic research on Catalan, where some work or other by Fabra will always figure, as a point of departure at least.

3.3   Pompeu Fabra as theoretician of the literary language

> "Fabra was also important for his studies, *avant la lettre*, of linguistic interference, understood to mean the process of influence exercised by a socio-politically dominating language upon a socio-politically dominated one."
>
> (Lamuela & Murgades 1984: 50–51)

The first thing to say is that Fabra did not publish any theoretical work on the fields in which he worked. Thus, in order to discover his objectives, the bases on which he operated, his methododology and his results, it has been necessary to read his texts carefully and to conduct two kinds of investigation on them: on the one hand, an analysis of his criteria for language codification based on a terminological trawl through his texts; on the other hand, an analysis of his principal ideas as they are disclosed in explicit general reflections upon these operations, ideas expressed in different texts of varying length.[42]

3.3.1   An analysis of general reflections on literary language explicit in Pompeu Fabra's writings

The most numerous group of texts containing general reflections[43] is formed by articles like *"On Linguistic and Orthographical Reform" (1892), "The Teaching of French in the Barcelona Institute" (1893), *"On Various Unresolved Issues in Present-Day Literary Catalan" (1907), *"The Task of the Valencian and Balearic Writers" (1918) and some of his Philological Conversations.

The second most numerous set of texts is made up of Fabra's speeches and lectures. Included among the former are *"The Task of Purifying Catalan" (1924), his Presidential address to the Ateneu Barcelonès, and his Presidential speech to the *Jocs Florals of Barcelona in 1934. Among the latter there is the lecture on "Catalan in Primary Schools" (1933) and the one he gave at the 1935 summer

---

42. The exposition here is based especially on Fabra's practice for syntactical codification. Codification of other aspects of language (phonetics, morphology, lexis and orthography) follows by and large the same criteria.

43. An asterisk (*) before a title indicates a text given in translation in this volume.

school of the Escola Normal de la Generalitat de Catalunya. Finally, we include here the *"Conversation with Pompeu Fabra" (1926).

The selection below – given, with accompanying commentary, in chronological order so that the evolution of Fabra's ideas can be followed – illustrates the main lines of Fabra's thinking on the Catalan language and on the process of *redreçament*.

3.3.1.1   *"On Various Unresolved Issues in Present-Day Literary Catalan", 1907*

> In reality, if every author were to write in his/her own Catalan – not in the language of the lowest strata of their region but in that of the most educated – the divergences that would appear in the literary language would perhaps not be, nowadays, as great as many people think. And one may believe, if favourable times for Catalan nationhood arrive, that these divergences would be steadily attenuated. There could come into effect a natural interpenetration between the literary language and the Catalan of the capital – not present-day Barcelonese but a quite different version of it, freed of Castilianisms, influenced by all the other dialects of our language, enriched, refined: the future tongue of the future capital of Greater Catalonia![44]

This fragment condenses some of Fabra's main ideas on *redreçament*:

– The monocentric conception of standardisation: Barcelona, ideally, should be the capital of all the territories where Catalan is spoken, the *Països Catalans* – that is, *Catalònia* as opposed to *Catalunya*/Catalonia – to become the centre where exchanges between the different dialects would take place, the dialects which would be orchestrated to enrich the dialect of Barcelona itself, the fundamental dialect which, itself, would have to be "de-Castilianised".

– The conception of a language as a pyramid, broad at its base, where the local varieties stand: codification and formal cultivation (Refinement) allows these dialects to move upwards towards a progressively more uniform formal variety.

– The identification between "nationality" ("homeland" in 1934) and linguistic domain, which returns, then, to Fabra's support for the idea of *Països Catalans*.

---

44. The original text has the single word *Catalònia* (italicised). Like some other contemporary intellectuals, Fabra used this term to differentiate between *Catalunya* (the Principality of Catalonia) and all of the Catalan-speaking territories. Later in the twentieth century, in political discourse, the term *Països Catalans* gained currency for the global demarcation (see Kremnitz, Prologue, pp. XXIX–XXX and §2.4).

3.3.1.2   *Philological Conversation, 18/XI/1919*

> IN PURSUIT OF PURITY IN THE LANGUAGE: CASTILIANISMS
>
> The work of restoring literary Catalan to its proper condition and status is above all one of removing the presence of Castilian influence. [...]
>
> [...] Castilian importations in modern Catalan are incalculably more numerous than a superficial examination of our language would disclose.
>
> In these daily notes we shall try to give an idea of how great is the number of Castilianisms in our present-day language, and thus to demonstrate the need for resorting abundantly to old Catalan forms, in the supposition that we are not to be satisfied with just a shallow clearing up of our language involving merely the extirpation of the most obvious imports from Castilian. [...]

This fragment belongs to the first of the Conversations and it has a programmatic spirit.

The first sentence contains one of Fabra's key concepts: that of "de-Castilianisation", alternating with "purification" (as found in the titles of several texts and *passim*). He creates a neological family with the words "to de-Castilianise", "de-Castilianisation" and "de-Castilianisers". He uses the last term very regularly (even in titles), with an ironic tone which is intensified in the syntagm "out-and-out de-Castilianiser", employed to refer to those dilettante grammarians or philologists who not only eliminate perfectly proper Catalan expressions (especially for learned words) but also introduce new alien ones.

This task of de-Castilianisation has to be so deep and systematic that the resulting gaps left by the elimination of so many non-Catalan expressions have to be filled with archaic forms that have fallen into disuse.

3.3.1.3   *"The Task of Purifying Catalan", 1924*

> Then, moreover, attention should be drawn to the discretionary, not obligatory character with which very many of the reforms affecting grammar are presented. [...] in the majority of cases, it is not prescribed to substitute a common construction with an archaic one. What is involved is the recovery of lost constructions or of grammatical words now no longer in common use, so that they, alongside existing options, increase the expressive resources of the language. [...]

This is an extract in which Fabra demonstrates the specificity of syntax. Just as in orthography, lexis and (albeit to a lesser degree) morphology what is proposed by the grammarian excludes other variants, for syntax Fabra puts into practice change which is planned "from above" and which anticipates a phase of competitive co-existence between the proposed innovation and the form to be proscribed, this being followed by a final phase: elimination of the latter or redistribution between the two forms, something by which the language is "enriched".

3.3.1.4   *"A Conversation with Pompeu Fabra", May 1926

The evolution of my own principles has settled and solidified, finally, in the present-day approach to problems of purifying our language: this is based on proper study of the living language [...]

The grammarian [...] has no individual authority to lay down the law *a priori*. From the study or the office it is impossible to anticipate and to cover every practical case. Sometimes the solution provided for a particular issue proves to be painfully uncomfortable in its application. When this occurs, the grammarian must not barricade himself tenaciously behind his theory, like some infallible superhuman authority. On the contrary, his duty is to attenuate any friction, looking to resolve conflict [between normative principles and colloquial usage] if this is necessary.

For my own part I could never lay down a norm before having submitted it to that test of efficacy mentioned earlier. I always leave it for our writers to try out and to decide, ultimately, on its viability. Not all writers, however, can help me in this. I find that they are divided into three groups, of which only the third can serve my needs. In the first group are those last remnants of nineteenth-century anarchy, who [...] passively obey the reflex action of jumping to the defence of their own defects. Then there is another group, perhaps more pernicious than the first one, containing those writers who espouse an expression or a word that they think improves the language, without stopping to consider whether or not it is viable [...]. Finally, in a third group [...] are those prudent writers, who are at the same time both creative and beneficially influential, always aware of their own responsibility. [...]

Now, the assay process, after four or five years of positive outcome, should result in a strict rule. Then we ought to be able to say that whoever does not do such and such a thing or whoever does not do something in this way or that, is quite simply committing a grammatical error. My ideal would be that, thanks to this mechanism, we could arrive at the position reached, without an Academy, by England. At least in this way we would be spared from and immune against the blunderings of would-be grammarians.

To summarise the preceding fragment it would suffice to reproduce literally the sub-heading placed by the interviewer above this section: "Democratic theory of the linguistic norm". The opening affirmation suggests the metaphor of the grammarian as a "notary" recording the facts: he has to study the language in order to see its characteristics. Thereafter the notary offers his proposal to those who use the language professionally (writers, journalists, proof-readers, etc.). The (patriotic) duty of those professionals is to try to put the proposal into practice. If it prospers among them it can become an "inflexible rule": whoever does not follow it is committing a "grammatical error". In this sense, it is a convention, but a convention arrived at through consensus, of a kind whose outstanding representation is the Norm for English, created by those who live professionally by their writing. If the proposal does not take on solid consistency then it is up to the grammarian either to come back with a new proposal or to accept the form that was to be replaced.

3.3.1.5   *"On the Purification of the Literary Language", 1927

> [...] The effort to reinstate the written language could not be limited now just to the literary domain – to the exclusion of technical registers, etc. – [...]
>
> If written Catalan had not moved outside of the area assigned to it by Milà i Fontanals[45] [...] it might then have been able to adopt more freely any innovatory reform, beyond all consideration of viability in common use of the language [...].

This fragment clearly exposes how Fabra's aim of *redreçament* fits perfectly with the classic schema of standardisation: the final phase is that of stylistic refinement (full recovery of "the technical registers").

3.3.1.6   *"On the Purification of the Literary Language", 1927

> We may come across a serious flaw in the modern language, and this is when, in order to be rid of it, we should resort to finding an alternative, be it an archaic or dialect form, or even a neologism [...] because what is most to be avoided is the creation of too big a schism between the written language and its spoken form.
>
> Acceptance of an innovatory reform by a large proportion of the Catalan-speaking public [...] can authenticate even a remedial change that is completely arbitrary. On the other hand, a venerable expression that has fallen into disuse and is then restored cannot strictly be considered as authentic if it does not have that acceptance.

The first paragraph here supplies the major pillars to support the remedying of deficiencies left behind by the first phase of de-Castilianisation: whether they be archaism, or dialectalism or neologism. The second paragraph is a fragment of the kind where Fabra – as a rhetorical device – indulges in the formulation of a more or less plausible hypothesis: the definitive criterion by which a proposal can be adopted as a formal rule is acceptance by "the Catalan-speaking public at large". (We should say in passing that this last term, often used by Fabra, is one among many pieces of evidence that Fabra had closely read the work of Ferdinand de Saussure, the phrase in question being characteristic of the author of the *Cours de linguistique générale*.)

---

45. See pp. 131 and 215, below.

3.3.1.7   *General Dictionary of the Catalan Language, 1932*

> **llenguatge** [language] Expression of thoughts by means of words; the totality of
> words and the means of combining them as used and understood by a human
> community, especially when fixed and fashioned by long use.

This definition makes clear Fabra's conception of language as a pyramid, implying a progression, from the base upwards – though habitual use, codification
and stylistic refinement – to the height of an apex, the higher and the narrower
the better.

3.3.1.8   **"Deviations in the Concepts of Language and Homeland", 1934*

> In order to make a comparison between any two languages, we must take par-
> ticularly into account the period from which compared texts come and the dia-
> lects to which these belong. The present-day versions of the two languages in
> question must, naturally, be referred to, and the terms of comparison should not
> be dialects from language-frontier zones but ones which have become consoli-
> dated as literary languages. (Two writers whose respective idioms could serve
> this purpose would be Frederic Mistral[46] and Jacint Verdaguer.) If we were to
> compare some early Catalan texts with contemporary Provençal ones, we would
> encounter instances of similarities in both sets shared with texts in other Ro-
> mance languages.

In this text Fabra defends the independence of Catalan in respect of Occitan, once
more with the vision of language as a pyramid: the terms of comparison must not
be the frontier dialects (the bases of the Catalan and the Occitanian pyramids are
contiguous) but rather the dialects that have become crystallised as literary languages (the modalities in each case that have become situated at the central core
of each pyramid and have become extended to occupy its highest part).

3.3.1.9   *Catalan Grammar: Intermediate Course, 1935 edition*

> [The fact of not including all the geographical variants] makes it essential to give
> teachers the following guidance for cases where the form set down in the book is
> not usual in the dialect of their pupils. When this is used […] to illustrate a defi-
> nition […], the teacher must replace it with the usual form in the students' dialect
> […]. At a later stage, though, he must always introduce them to the form given
> in the book […], and inform them that this is the one preferred in the literary
> language. Then he must teach them which of the dialect forms not registered in

---

46. 1830–1914. Writer and most prominent figure in the revival of nineteenth-century Occitanian language and culture, the Félibrige. He won the Nobel Prize in 1908. On Verdaguer, see
p. 150 below.

the book are tolerable in the literary language and which of them are completely inadmissible […]. A teacher in Barcelona will tell his pupils that they should write not *nosatros* but *nosaltres*, not *aquet* but *aquest*, not *capiguer* but *cabre*.

This fragment puts into practice Fabra's conception of the literary language as a continuum between the vernacular and the formal level: the pupils must gradually get used to working with a diglossia planned to bridge what can always be said and what must cease to be said as the language they use progresses up towards the apex of the pyramid. And he allows some flexibility between "form preferred by the literary language", "tolerable form" and "inadmissible form". The explicit reference, in the final sentence, to "inadmissible" forms in the language of Barcelona may seem to be just a detail or a comment with no great weight attached to it. Readers of Fabra's work know very well that he does not write anything which has not been fully thought out. So we wonder if using examples from vulgar Barcelonese – the base dialect for his codification – is not perhaps a means to pre-empt anti-centralist criticisms.

3.3.2 Criteria for syntactic codification

Having seen in Section 3.3.1 Fabra's basic principles on codification, we now move on to consider the specific criteria for syntactical codification that he observed. Our own research, following Lamuela (1995), shows that these criteria, as disclosed in the texts examined, are as follows:

1. Diasystemacity
2. Historicity
3. Regularity
   a. Distinctiveness
   b. Paradigmatic homogeneity
4. Etymological suitability
5. Structural appropriateness
   a. Grammatical appropriateness
6. Suitability to a linguistic conception
7. Suitability to a stylistic conception
8. Confirmed functionality
   a. Implantation
9. Prospective functionality
   a. Intelligibility
   b. Simplicity
   c. Acceptability
   d. Guarantee of pertinent use

10.   Autonomy
    a.   Genuineness
    b.   Specificity
11.   Analogy with other languages
12.   Evaluation of tests on usage
    a.   Evaluation of the implantation of an element
    b.   Evaluation of appropriate use

We proceed now to a presentation of how these criteria are defined or exemplified in a text or texts where Fabra makes a general reflection upon a particular criterion or where he has this criterion in mind.

1.   Diasystemacity
The complete range of all the dialects is considered in the operations of codification and completion.

Fabra takes account of this criterion in his article *"On Various Unresolved Issues in Present-day Literary Catalan" (1907):

> In reality, if every author were to write in *his/her own* Catalan – not in the language of the lowest strata of their region but in that of the most educated – the divergences that would appear in the literary language would perhaps not be, nowadays, as great as many people think.[47]

And in a fragment from his *presidential address to the Jocs Florals of 1934, referring to the need for familiarity with all the varieties of the language:

> [The systematic work of purifying and fixing Catalan] could be achieved only through knowledge [...] of all its modern spoken varieties.

2.   Historicity
The preferred forms are those which enjoy a longer tradition in literature:

> The work of restoring literary Catalan to its proper condition and status is above all one of removing the presence of Castilian influence. And in the majority of cases it is old Catalan which supplies us with the word or turn of phrase with which to replace ones brought in from the other language. [...]
>
> In these daily notes we shall try to give an idea of how great is the number of Castilianisms in our present-day language, and thus to demonstrate the need for resorting abundantly to old Catalan forms, in the supposition that we are not to be satisfied with just a shallow clearing up of our language involving merely the

---

47. As in this case, short quotations from texts translated for this volume are reproduced in our discussion. Where a long quotation from translated material is involved, some editing is done in this section, while location of the relevant passage in full is facilitated.

extirpation of the most obvious imports from Castilian. (*Philological Conversation, 18/XI/1919)

3. Regularity

3a. Distinctiveness. The preferred forms are those which avoid homonymy. In syntax encouragement is given to using functional oppositions or partially opposed structures. Also encouraged are diversity in means of avoiding ambiguity in a given construction, and providing the language with a bigger stock of expressive possibilities:

> When a word has undergone two different evolutions, the language sometimes takes possession of both resulting forms and, giving to each of them a separate sense, turns them in reality into two distinct words. This is to the language's advantage, since, instead of one word with two differentiated meanings, it possesses two words, one for each of these meanings. (*Philological Conversation, 13/XII/1923)

> A language like French which possesses a nominative *qui* and an accusative *que* has advantages on this point over another language (Spanish) which possesses only *que*, to refer both to a grammatical subject and to a direct object. (*Philological Conversation, 13/IX/1924)

> [...] The fact of having three or four words to express a single idea or a single thing represents richness in the language, but true richness consists, not precisely in having several words to express the same thing, but in being able to give a different shade of meaning to each of them. (Collected Lessons for the Higher Catalan Course (1933–1934): 103; see §3.9.1, 1933–1934)

3b. Paradigmatic homogeneity. The preferred forms are those which correspond to the most homogeneous paradigms:

> Everybody can perceive the difference between *Ens va posar els abrics* [= He put our coats on for us] and *Ens hi va posar els abrics* [= He put our coats on for us there]. The same difference exists between *Els va posar els abrics* [= He put their coats on for them] and *Els hi va posar els abrics* [= He put their coats on for them there], a distinction which disappears if in the first sentence we replace dative *els* by the combination *els hi* [...] (Philological Conversation, 8/XII/1922)

4. Etymological suitability

The preferred forms are those which preserve the meaning or the linguistic properties of their known etymons:

> But does it really mean nothing to them [...], in particular, that this meaning is one of the usual meanings of the Latin preposition *in*, which is the origin of our preposition *en*? (Philological Conversation, 23/I/1920)

[…] the inability to denote the end point of an act of going […] is not a common property of the Latin preposition *in* or of the Catalan one *en* (old Catalan, colloquial Catalan). Neither the etymology nor the history of our *en* can justify the exclusion of this word as a translation of the Castilian preposition *a* in cases like *Pujar en aquella ermita* [= to go up to that hermitage], *Anar en una altra part* [= to go somewhere else] (Philological Conversation 24/I/1920)

5. Structural appropriateness

To be rejected are changes in meaning or in properties of linguistic forms introduced without sufficient prior understanding. This also applies to innovatory procedures which infringe the particular rules of the language to be codified:

Our friend Josep Ferran i Mayoral[48] has said: "Obviously, in grammar as in everything else, habit – which can often be the perpetuation of a vice or simply of an act of negligence – is not sufficient to justify a rule. While it is right and necessary to pay Aristotelian attention to the facts, one should not forget the Platonic assessment, the possibility that *facts may be emended* in line with an ideal of perfection. Alongside the claims made on behalf of habit, it is also necessary in matters of grammar to pay attention to the claims of reason, of taste, of beauty, of culture."

Agreed. But the means of emending facts – and Ferran i Mayoral surely recognises this much – have to be supplied to us by the language itself. (*Philological Conversation, 10/IX/1924)

When a new word or a new turn of phrase appears in a writer's text, when some archaic form or neologism is recommended, it is curious how the innovation introduced or proposed finds proselytes immediately, whether or not it is appropriate. And it is curious too how people rush to use the novelty, even without having an exact idea of its meaning. It is a good thing that we are disposed to admit anything which tends to enrich and purify our language. But this should not mean accepting any novelty whatsoever. Beforehand we should make certain that what is involved is a real improvement (we should look carefully at exactly who is making the proposal!). And then we should not adopt anything until we have an exact idea of its true meaning and scope. We should remember, if nothing else, the case of causal *doncs*, of relative *quin*, of adversative *no res menys*.

It is better to renounce a word than to use it incorrectly. If the unfamiliar word comes in to substitute for a correct term habitually used, the best thing is to do without the former. If *desitjar, anhelar*, [= to want, desire] etc., are perfectly good, why use instead of them a new word: *freturar*? […] And in the event that replacement of a habitual word by a new one is unavoidable, because the former is absolutely inadmissible, then you must ascertain carefully what the substitute

---

48. 1883–1955. Essayist and translator. The first surname is usually written as Farran.

is to be *in each separate case*. If *recolzar* [= to lean, to prop up] can replace the Castilianism *apoiar* in one case or another, this does not mean that it can be so used in every context: *apoiar* meaning "to support, give support to", for instance, cannot be substituted by *recolzar*. (*Philological Conversation, 17/VI/1926)

5a. Grammatical appropriateness. To be rejected are changes made to the properties of linguistic forms introduced without sufficient prior understanding:

> We well know how dangerous it is to introduce into the literary language a word which is not the exact equivalent of the commonly used lexical item you are looking to displace. Time and again you will notice that the [proposed] innovation can replace the dubious item in one particular meaning only. But if, beyond this meaning A, the latter also has meanings B, C, etc., it will not be long before you find examples of the new word used to convey some of these senses as well. When [the third-person plural possessive] *llur* [= their] became fashionable, there soon appeared expressions like *l'home i llur fill* [= the man and his son, with *llur* instead of singular *el seu*]. When, more recently, [demonstrative pronoun] *ço* came into use we have suddenly started to find expressions like *ço útil, ço indispensable* [= the usefulness, the essentialness, where *ço* erroneously imitates the behaviour of Castilian neuter article *lo*]. (*Philological Conversation, 24/IV/1923)

> Something which occurs frequently, when an old conjunction is reintroduced into the language, is that many people give it a different value from the one it really used to have. (Philological Conversation, 4/X/1923)

6.   Suitability to a linguistic conception

To be rejected are forms considered aberrant according to the conception of linguistic behaviour held by the codifiers:

> In expressions of obligation [*has de mirar*] and in the periphrastic perfect [*vas mirar*] one can place the weak pronouns before the auxiliary [*ho has de mirar / ho vas mirar*] or attach them after the infinitive [*has de mirar-ho / vas mirar-ho*]. And it is well known that there are many people who do both the one thing and the other [*ho has de mirar-ho / ho vas mirar-ho*]. Obviously this latter construction, reduplicating the pronoun, must be carefully avoided in the written language. (Philological Conversation, 20/VII/1927)

7.   Suitability to a stylistic conception

It is held that codification concerns only certain registers, distinguished generally by a certain level of formality, and forms perceived as inadequate for the higher registers are relegated to non-codified ones:

> This repetition of one of the components of the sentence, expressed first by a relative [*que*] and then by a weak pronoun [*l'*] governed by the verb [*una solució que ells l'havien combatuda* [= a solution that they had discussed]], constitutes an

incorrect structure tolerable only in familiar style. Certainly, we do find examples of such repetition in other languages, but in all of these (except for Romanian, where it has become the normal structure) it is considered to be defective. Thus we, in our work of restoring Catalan to its proper condition, ought to be very careful to avoid this construction. (Philological Conversation, 31/XII/1919)

8.   Confirmed functionality

To be preferred are forms which have the greatest functional value, or which can achieve it easily.

8a.   Implantation. The preferred forms are those with the widest geographical and social distribution at the time of codification. This is because they have initially the greatest functional value of admissibility, regardless of whether they are traditional forms, innovations or interferences from other languages:

> **consagrar** *vt* [i.e. transitive verb] Fig. to endow with the quality of durability [...]
> *És una regla consagrada pel temps* [= It is a time-honoured rule]. (DGLC)

> In the very early stages of the Renaixença, the first form [al + infinitive], that is, the current Castilian form [for this temporal construction], was the one favoured, but later on the writers started to relegate al systematically in favour of *en*. It should be said, though, that the first of these forms is not to be condemned; but, since the recent tendency is to put en then it is advisable to follow it. (Collected Lessons for the Higher Catalan Course (1933–1934): 86; see §3.9.1, 1933–1934)

9.   Prospective functionality

To be preferred are those forms which can most easily acquire functional value.

9a.   Intelligibility. The preferred forms are those which, although not used by the people to whom they are being recommended, will nevertheless be understood and will be, thus, available for adoption:

> [...] it is clear that there will be nobody who will fail to understand the meaning of a sentence just because it is constructed with the aforementioned relative [*la qual cosa* = which thing]. (Philological Conversation, 30/XII/1919)

9b.   Simplicity. The preferred forms are those which are easiest to learn:

> [...] We believe, though, with everything taken into account, that of the two formulae *senyor En* [like Spanish *Señor Don*] and *Senyor* [= Mr.] the second is the only one which really thrives in the present-day language, and that it is obviously simpler, less forced than the first, while still being equally respectful. (Philological Conversation, 23/I/1923)

9c.   Acceptability. The preferred forms are those which are most easily acceptable:

P. 2 recto: In the old language *a ell* [= to him] is normal, while *ad ell* is exceedingly rare. And, anyway, I think it is more viable to replace *an ell* (which I consider inadmissible) with *a ell* rather than with *ad ell*. People will scarcely [? illegible word] notice the change of *an ell* for *a ell* [...], while, on the other hand, they will be not a little surprised by a new form *ad*! (Letter of 13/IX/1910)

9d. Guarantee of pertinent use. The preferred forms are those which are least likely to give rise to problems of structural suitability during the process of vehiculation:

[...] When an archaic word can replace one which is in currency in all its meanings [...] it cannot give rise to defective constructions. Such is the case with the substitution of [Castilian] *menos* [= less] by *menys* [...] But the same thing does not occur with [archaic third-person plural] possessive *llur*. *Llur* can replace *seu*, but not in every case. [...]

With the neuter pronoun *ço* something analogous occurs. With the adoption of the expression *ço que* to replace *lo que*, this *ço* has been found to be a replacement for the neuter article [...]. But then, on the basis of this substitution, many people have thought that they could replace *lo* by *ço* in each and every case, and they have begun to write *ço important* [= the importance] [...]. This use of the word *ço* is completely inadmisible: substitution of *lo* by *ço* is only licit when it is placed before the relative pronoun (*que, qui*) or before the preposition *de*. (Philological Conversation, 4/II/1920)

We have often pointed out the dangers implicit in the adoption of a word or phrase that is alien to the spoken language. [...] The correct construction *Mai no hi hem anat* [= We have never been there] sounds just as good to people as the incorrect one *No mai hi hem anat* [...]

Just let us consider what has happened with *llur*, used sometimes to refer to a singular possessor, or with *ço*, used by some to express the neuter category of the adjective (*ço important*), or with *no res menys* [= in addition], so often found employed as an adversative conjunction. And then, if the criterion of substituting every [relative] *que* as subject with *qui* were one day to triumph, we shudder to imagine the number of cases of *que* as complement or as conjunction that one would find being replaced by *qui*! Obviously this does not mean that one has to renounce the addition of the *no* omitted in the spoken idiom, nor the use of *llur* or of *ço*, nor that one ought to desist from changing every *que* into *qui* in the event of this innovation being judged appropriate. But we will be well advised to think very carefully before rushing into proposing any kind of syntactical innovation. (Philological Conversation, 25/II/1927)

10.   Autonomy

The preferred forms are those which favour the language being codified in relation to other languages.

10a. Genuineness. Endogenous forms are to be preferred over borrowings or calques.

> IN PURSUIT OF PURITY IN THE LANGUAGE: CASTILIANISMS
> The work of restoring literary Catalan to its proper condition and status is above all one of removing the presence of Castilian influence. [...]. (*Philological Conversation, 18/XI/1919)

10b. Specificity. Preferred forms are those which are specific to the language:

> It might perhaps be thought that it is not worth being concerned about an apparently insignificant detail like this [the use of *EL dilluns tindrà lloc* [= it will take place on Monday] instead of *Dilluns tindrà lloc*). But it is largely the sum of a whole assortment of small parts, seemingly unimportant, that makes the syntax of one language differentiated from that of another in the same family. [...] (*Philological Conversation, 13/XII/1922)

11.   Analogy with other languages
Preferred forms are those which coincide with those found in other languages:

> Whenever it is proposed that some imported mode of expression should be proscribed, people often complain about having to renounce it. They think it is almost impossible to do without it and its absence implies, so they hold, a grievous lacuna in the language, without considering that very often the expression in question is also quite alien to languages like Italian or French. On the other hand, we find many who will not make good use of expressive possibilities belonging to their own language when these are foreign to Spanish. Then they replace them almost systematically with the periphrases that Spanish is obliged to resort to for want of the same idioms. (*Philological Conversation, 17/VI/1927)

12.   Evaluation of tests on usage for codification proposals: in order to check the success of the codifiers' proposals during the experimentation period, the following criteria are applied.

12a. Evaluation of the implantation of an element. The forms adopted are those proposed by the codifiers which, during the period of experimentation, take root and acchieve effective use among speakers:

> The defects which coming generations will notice in present-day Catalan are of three kinds.
>   [...] But there are, unfortunately, defects of another kind, ones for which the remedy was found long ago but which continue to infest our written language: [...] *quin* used as a relative pronoun [instead of *qual*], *doncs* as a causal conjunction [instead of *puix* or *car*], *els hi* as third-person plural dative pronoun [instead

of *els*], [calqued on Castilian] constructions like *tenir que, a no ser que, per lo demés* [...] (*Philological Conversation, 30/XII/1922)

One can understand to some extent that the Catalan found in our publications should abound in errors of syntax and in Castilianisms. But what cannot be understood is that so many spelling mistakes should appear there and, even less, that they should contain so many erroneous verbal forms. (Philological Conversation, 24/V/1923)

Without doubt syntactical Castilianisms are among the most difficult ones to extirpate. If it is a matter of proscribing a single alien word for which an adequate substitute has been found, it is sufficient to denounce the offending item and to indicate what is to replace it. Then immediately one sees a reduction in the use of the alien word, often with it being soon expelled for good. Even in the case where substitution presents the difficulty of not being achievable through a single replacement word [...], not only is the intruder soon evicted but, after a certain period when erroneous substitutes are in play, the replacement words end up being correctly used.

But, when a syntactical Castilianism is involved, how very slowly does the process of elimination operate! And how frequent are the relapses it suffers! We must remember the cases of causal *doncs*, of the adjective *demés*, of the compound relative *el que*. [...] (*Philological Conversation, 12/VI/1928)

The evolution of my own principles has settled and solidified, finally, in the present-day approach to problems of purifying our language: this is based on proper study of the living language [...].

The grammarian has no individual authority to lay down the law *a priori*. From the study or the office it is impossible to anticipate and to cover every practical case. Sometimes the solution provided for a particular issue proves to be painfully uncomfortable in its application. When this occurs, the grammarian must not barricade himself tenaciously behind his theory, like some infallible superhuman authority. On the contrary, his duty is to attenuate any friction, looking to resolve conflict [between normative principles and colloquial usage] if this is necessary.

[...] For my own part I could never lay down a norm before having submitted it to that test of efficacy mentioned earlier. I always leave it for our writers to try out and to decide, ultimately, on its viability. Not all writers, however, can help me in this. I find that they are divided into three groups, of which only the third can serve my needs. In the first group are those last remnants of nineteenth-century anarchy, who [...] who passively obey the reflex action of jumping to the defence of their own defects. Then there is another group, perhaps more pernicious than the first one, containing those writers who espouse an expression or a word that they think improves the language, without stopping to consider whether or not it is viable [...]. Finally, in a third group [...] are those prudent writers, who are

at the same time both creative and beneficially influential, always aware of their own responsibility.

[...] Now, the assay process, after four or five years of positive outcome, should result in a strict rule. Then we ought to be able to say that whoever does not do such and such a thing or whoever does not do something in this way or that, is quite simply committing a grammatical error. My ideal would be that, thanks to this mechanism, we could arrive at the position reached, without an Academy, by England. At least in this way we would be spared from and immune against the blunderings of would-be grammarians. [...] (*Conversation with Pompeu Fabra (V/1926))

12b. Evaluation of appropriate use. Adopted are the forms proposed by the codifiers which have not given rise to problems of structural appropriateness during the process of vehiculation:

> Not so long ago we came across a *por lo delicado de la cuestión* translated by [the calque] *pel delicat de la qüestió* [= because of the delicacy of the matter]. A habitual word or turn of phrase has been deemed inaceptable, and a replacement or replacements have been found. But something else beyond this is required: knowing how to put the substitution into practice. In this final phase of innovation what is very important is to know whether the replacement is to be made by a single item or by more than one [...] You may propose proscription of the neuter article *lo*: but, as we have no single word which could serve for every case, elimination of *lo* proves to be extremely difficult. In this case there is a tendency for the same item to be used as a replacement for every instance. (Philological Conversation, 17/III/1927)

Of the twelve criteria above – some of which have more specific sub-divisions – those which Fabra took most into account are Autonomy (this above all), Historicity and Functionality, followed by Evaluation of tests on usage and Distinctiveness. From this it is clearly seen that his aim was that Catalan should be an autonomous language, clear and precise. To this end he placed reliance upon the oral variety of Barcelona, on the one hand, and upon the medieval repertoire on the other. This double focus corresponded to the concern to take into account the full range of stylistic diversity, from spontaneous oral registers through to the most carefully worked written ones. These objectives were seen as the culmination of a long process, during which the success of all relevant proposals had to be evaluated.

Also to be pointed out here is how the criterion of Analogy with other languages is particularly used by Fabra in order to demonstrate the autonomy of Catalan in relation to Spanish: Catalan as a distinct language which has had its own evolution, an evolution sometimes divergent from those of other languages, sometimes convergent with them, including – even – with that of Spanish.

As well as the criteria which are strictly to do with codification, we can observe in Fabra's texts the principle of completion, referred to here as a reflection on expressive needs.

Preference is given to forms which fill a gap in the language:

> Literary Catalan cannot renounce […] passive sentences […], sentences which do occur abundantly in our medieval language and which are likewise to be found in Spanish, Portuguese, French and Italian. And for as long as we do not renounce this type of sentence (something which would place Catalan in a position of inferiority in relation to the other literary languages), we are denied the option of forming the compound tenses of transitive verbs with the auxiliary *ésser*.
>
> (Philological Conversation, 17/XII/1922)

Then there is a criterion which has more to do with functional elaboration than with codification, a criterion to which we give the designation Stylistic distribution. It is a principle of functional formulation according to which certain synonymous or equivalent constructions can be distributed on a stylistic scale between greater or lesser formality:

> *El qual* is a relative that allows us to form quite complex relative sentences which would not be natural in the spoken language. […] When can these two forms [the simple and the compound relative] be used? It depends on the context. If the type of language is one which needs to strike a familiar note, the simple form is used; but in long sentences and if clarity of construction demands it, the compound form is to be preferred, as this is more fitted to styles where greater clarity is called for, and it is also more separated from the spoken language.
>
> (Higher Catalan Course, 1936–1937: 221–222; see §3.9.1, 1936–1937)

Also to be noted is the constant evaluation that Fabra applies to the tests on usage of his proposals.

As can be easily imagined, Fabra does not often utilise these criteria as single frames for focus, presenting them, rather, within reasoned discussions about syntactical codification. The great majority of these discussions are to be found in his Philological Conversations (1919–1928), texts which, on account of what they set out to achieve, could be expected to be the richest in this sense.

Regarding the complexity of the arguments themselves, what stands out is the feature that can be observed in the text "The word *qui*" (1930; see §3.9.1, 1930) where Fabra adduces seven different criteria and a reflection on expressive requirements: he rejects systematic distinction between *qui* as subject and *que* as direct object (grammatical appropriateness), despite all the following facts: that it was practised in old Catalan (historicity), that it would resolve confusion and that it represents an operative distinction (distinctiveness); that *que* as direct object had been considered a Castilianism (genuineness). His rejection is also made because the *qui/que* distinction has never been systematic as it is in French (analogy with other languages), because it is not practised by the majority of Catalan-speakers (implantation), because *qui* as subject produces a "strange effect" (acceptability and grammatical appropriateness) and because it offers no advantage (expressive requirement). Here is the text in question:

> Medieval Catalan did possess a weak *qui*. However, Catalan never established between weak *qui* and weak *que* the strict distinction which we observe in the French language, as is demonstrated by the numerous examples to be found of *que* as subject.
>
> [...] modern Catalan loses *qui* (totally or partially, depending on the dialect) which is replaced by the alternative *que* [...] The Renaixença reached the point, however, in order to reform the language of the Decadence, where the need was felt to open wide the gates to archaic forms. And so *qui* as subject was understandably taken up again by the literary language, on account of the suspicion that its loss might have been due to Castilian influence, and especially because cases of *qui* in the modern spoken language were encountered which seemed to them [the men of the Renaixença] to be survivors from our medieval language [...] But two divergent tendencies soon emerged: some accepted it only with reference to a personal subject, and even so there were those thus inclined who advised its use only in instances where it could serve to avoid ambiguity [...]; the others accepted it with its full value as found in old Catalan [...] making a rule which strictly followed the French distinction.
>
> [...] But then came a stage when viability, the probabilities of being reincorporated into the living language, was taken into account for the acceptance of innovations. At this point a strong reaction against weak *qui* came into effect.
>
> [...] we Catalans who in our normal speech never use nominative *qui* in truly adjectival relative constructions constitute a sizeable majority. We hear this word as a strong or accentuated one, and it cannot fail to create a strange effect for us, as though of an untimely emphasis, if we come across it at a place in a sentence where our linguistic sense made us expect a weak word.
>
> If we utter aloud a sentence such as *Això dóna-ho a l'home qui ha vingut aquest matí* [= Give this to the man who came this morning], does it not sound strange to our ears? And, if not, just consider the effect of using *que* [instead of *qui*] in this example. [...] The advantages that, in certain cases, might be offered by the use of *qui* as subject are illusory while ever the distinction between *qui* for the nominative and *que* as direct object is a mere convention, not something regularly heard [...] It does not seem likely that the word *qui*, as a distinctive signifier of a subject, could be put into people's mouths in specific cases [...] and so it could never give rise to sentences that offended our linguistic sense.

[…] The advantages of systematic use of *qui* as a subject […] would have to be very great for us to decide to make this kind of substitution.

There is one particular case […] where the spoken language still regularly uses the word *qui* […] This is when it serves to make a distinction […which is] important for the literary language […] We are talking about a *qui* which could be systematically adopted, as a real improvement for the literary language, without implying a distinction which would be alien to spoken Catalan. It would be simply the normalisation of a distinction which, established already in the Middle Ages, is still alive and which would thus not give rise to sentences that offended our linguistic sensitivity. But this distinction, if it were to be properly put into practice, necessitates abandonment of the other one (*qui* as subject – *que* as direct object).

The case in point makes clear the distinction between *el qui* and *el que*, which is losing ground to the advantage of the *el que/lo que* distinction. Both *el qui* [= the (masculine) person/one who] and neuter *el que* [= that which, what] are still very much alive. The literary language, which does not admit the neuter article *lo*, cannot, then, reasonably overlook the existence side by side of these two combinations. What it should do, rather, avoiding the vacillations of spoken Catalan, is make it a formal rule that *el qui* should be written systematically, when reference is to a person, and that *el que* should be used exclusively as a translation of Castilian *lo que* […]

This recalls Mascaró's affirmation that "Fabra's work applied to normativisation or on descriptive synthesis of diverse languages" is "scientific", in the sense that it is it is rigorously competent and set upon previous scientific bases. And some recent research has looked at Fabra's criteria for syntactical codification in relation to his thinking on both syntax itself and on syntactical change and diversity.

3.3.3 Relations between Fabra's conception of syntactical codification and syntax

3.3.3.1 *Fabra's conception of syntax*
As has been mentioned in the biographical outline, Fabra was an autodidact in his education in linguistics. It is known that he acquired a solid grounding in historical phonetics and morphology, from using the libraries of the Ateneu Barcelonès and the University of Barcelona, where he was able to study works by the major European researchers on historical grammar, comparativism and linguistics generally: among others Josep Maria d'Arteaga,[49] Charles Bally, Franz Bopp, Michel

---

49. 1846–1913. Composer and phonetician. From 1900 he was on the committee of the International Phonetic Association.

Bréal, Georg Curtius, Friedrich Christian Diez, Tomàs Forteza,[50] Jacob Grimm, Gustav Gröber, Otto Jespersen, Wilhelm Meyer-Lübke, Alfred Morel-Fatio, Paul Passy, Jean-Joseph Saroïhandy, Ferdinand de Saussure, Bernhard Schädel, Henry Sweet and Wilhelm Viëtor.

A product of this solid formation were articles he wrote like "Études de phonologie catalane" (1897), his reviews for *Revue Hispanique*[51] of "Remarques sur la conjugaison catalane" de Saroïhandy (1905), "Les *e* toniques du catalan" (1906), "Le Catalan dans la grammaire des langues romanes de W. Meyer-Lübke et dans le *Grundriss der rom. Philologie*" (1907). Demonstration of his excellent theoretical preparation is found in his interventions in the First International Congress on the Catalan Language (1906) and in works of his like the Grammar of the Catalan Language (1912), the Catalan Grammar: Intermediate Course (1918), his Catalan Grammar of 1946 and the one finally published in 1956. Other evidence of his sound formation is preserved in the notes taken by students of his at the University or elsewhere (as in a short course he gave on phonetics in 1935).

Fabra's scholarly activity – although not at all extensive, as has been pointed out – nevertheless covered all aspects of the language: phonetics, morphology, syntax and lexis, both from the synchronic point of view (taking linguistic diversity into account) and from the diachronic one.

Students of his work have given most prominence to the latter perspective, because, as stated, this was the terrain in which his early formation was grounded.

It has been noted how in phonetics, for example, he formulated what has become known as "Fabra's Law" of dialect distribution of tonic *e* in Catalan. But, beyond this his sound knowledge of diachronic phonetics and morphology enabled him to distinguish between the products of Catalan's own internal evolution and the outcome of interference.

Concerning his conception of syntax, it has been remarked that Fabra does not formulate explicitly any complete, systematic theory on the four big fields of phonetics, morphology, syntax and lexis. As for explicit definitions, we have found only those he gave for syntax itself, the most complete being the one in his General Dictionary: "**Syntax** […] Arrangement of words in discourse; the part of grammar which deals with this." This notwithstanding, careful and attentive reading of Fabra's work discloses much thinking centred on the complete nexus of

---

50. 1838–1898. Majorcan poet and philologist. His *Gramática catalana*, in Spanish, was eventually published in 1915 by Antoni Maria Alcover.

51. Journal founded (1894) and edited in Paris by R. Foulché-Delbosc. A total of 178 numbers (80 volumes) appeared until its closure in 1930. From 1905 it was published under the auspices of the Hispanic Society of America, New York, dedicated to studies on Hispanic philology, literature and history (Spanish, Catalan and Portuguese).

syntactical concerns. Regarding the relation between his conceptions of syntactical codification and syntax itself, we see immediately that it is neither his definition of syntax nor the conception implicit in a key term in Fabra's vocabulary, *redreçament* (discussed above), that enable us to see the relations between "syntax" and "codification" in Fabra's writings.

Moving into the conception of syntax as an aspect of language and as a discipline concerned with it, this can be summed up as follows. As mentioned, Fabra defines syntax explicitly as the field of functions and relationships of groups of words within the sentence. The term "relationships" covers three others, *lligam* [= bond, link], "order" and "structure", also basic according to Fabra. And these three terms are often made to work together with the lexical unit "construction" – defined in the DGLC as "syntactical arrangement" – the term that he most utilises.

If we observe an aspect of grammar as basic as the primordial one of syntactical description, the expression of a complete thought, it is seen how Fabra takes as his basic criterion for description of both the "sentence" and the "proposition" – the fundamental unit of syntax – not the functions and the relationships between (groups of) words, but rather the semantic criterion of "expression of a thought". This is because there is not one single canonical structure to express a thought (there are four of them, according to the Grammar of 1956). Moreover, fragments which express only an "idea" are, in certain communicative situations, taken positively as being a communication with a complete meaning, structures designated by Fabra (1956) as sentences, as "acts of verbalisation, expression or communication". Thus, in order to express a thought, the speakers of a language, according to the communicative situation, have available an extremely varied range of syntactical structures. It is deduced also that syntax alone is not sufficient to give full account of a language: one needs only to think of how Fabra distinguishes between "cases" or semantic roles and syntactical functions or "locations" in sentence structure.

A second criterion, necessary and sufficient – although not much used by Fabra – is that of the intonational unit. This takes Fabra to adduce structural, relational, modal, psychological and communicative criteria, using these to explain why certain non-canonical structures can function as communications with a complete meaning.

Analysis of the whole of Fabra's output has also made it possible to show how he had a very clear attitude – from his earliest works through to his last ones – regarding the nature of syntax.

3.3.3.2 *Relations between Fabra's conception of syntactical codification and syntax*

Mention has already been made of the prominence of the term *redreçament* (and of the root verb *redreçar*) in Fabra's vocabulary, and by extension its importance in his ideology. The least indirect formulation made by him of the concept is the example he supplies in the DGLC, in the entry *redreçar*: **Redreçar una llengua** *purificant-la, enriquint-la,* etc. [= to set a language to rights by purifying and enriching it, etc.]. In line with what Kremnitz says about Fabra's terminology and its more recent equivalences, this indirect formulation allows one to establish the following schema:

Fabra's terminology	Modern language-planning terminology
Redreçament	Corpus planning
Selection (Purification)	1st phase of codification
Refinement/Enrichment	Completion and cultivation
Fixation (Normalisation/	2nd phase of codification and cultivation
Grammaticalisation)	Successful vehiculation (Stabilisation)
Diffusion	Successful vehiculation (Stabilisation)

What enables one to see the link between this schema and Fabra's view of syntax is what we might call Fabra's "attitude". Fabra has a very clear attitude – from his earliest works through to his last ones – regarding the nature of syntax. He see it as the most important part of language and of grammar, but it is unfortunately the one which is most difficult to describe, to regulate, to teach, to learn and to practise properly. This is because syntax, unlike morphology or orthography, does not consist of discrete units but rather of the functions of units and the relations between them, something which makes these categories only minimally perceptible for the speaker. For this reason a circumspect attitude in approaching syntax is essential: to start from the established data of the language and to strive not to hem in phenomena which by their nature are superficially very varied. In many of his texts Fabra makes it clear that syntax is a system of possibilities, some of which have a real existence in the language while others do not.

One focus that appears frequently both in Fabra's description of and his prescriptions for syntax is that related to functionality. In his conception of syntax the definitive perspective for defining the expression of a complete thought was the semantic one ("the expression of a complete which can be made explicit in superficial structures which differ greatly according to the context in which the thought is formulated"). And among the criteria for codification most used by Fabra one finds that of confirmed functionality (implantation) and prospective functionality (intelligibility, simplicity, acceptability and guarantee of appropriate use). Beyond these, also relevant as quite regularly used criteria in the codification of syntax are historicity, autonomy, distinctiveness, structural appropriateness, suitability to a syntactical conception and the criterion known as stylistic distribution.

Also of note is the relationship between the two conceptions, of syntax and of codification, because of the fact that Fabra's attitude to syntax clearly demands empiricism in the description of it (syntax), a dependency which conforms to Fabra's acknowledgement of what Eugenio Coseriu has called "objective norm" and "system". Fabra requires that the means to modify observably defective features should be supplied by the language itself, the syntax of which is differentiated from that of any other language by structures effectively produced by its speakers, structures which must be the basis of codification (by virtue of the criterion of confirmed functionality). The conception of syntax, as a set of possibilities within the system, is present in many arguments put forward by Fabra in which he admits that constructions rejected by him as interferences could have been parallel developments in Catalan itself. This is also found in his frequent application of the criteria related to prospective functionality: Catalan-speakers may be able to internalise archaisms or structures from other dialects because they form(ed) part of the Catalan system.

3.3.4 Relations between Fabra's conception of syntactical codification and syntactical change

3.3.4.1 *Fabra's conception of linguistic change*
Fabra considers 102 different instances of syntactical change, basically in *"On Various Outstanding Issues in Present-day Literary Catalan" (1907), in the *Philological Conversations of 1919–1928, and in the Lessons from the Higher Catalan Course of 1933–1934.

The chronology of these texts enables us to see that linguistic change is a subject that runs continuously and systematically through Fabra's work. This impression is confirmed when we realise that he addresses the matter – with varying levels of depth, of course – from his lecture "Conjugation of the Catalan Verb. The Present Subjunctive and the Infinitive" of 1891, through to a letter of 15/VI/1942.

The first thing to have in mind is that, in the texts we analyse, Fabra does not present any complete theory or any explicit definition of linguistic change in general nor of syntactical change in particular. This notwithstanding, we have been able to deduce from a fragment of *"The Task of Purifying Catalan" (1924) a definition of a kind of syntactical Castilianism, a kind of calque: "Identification between the meanings of a Castilian grammatical word and those of a Catalan one, affecting the structure of the proposition in Catalan":

> This identification of meanings between Catalan and Spanish vocabulary is particularly deplorable when it affects words with grammatical functions. The word-for-word transfer often affects the way a clause is structured, constituting a syntactical Castilianism.

We have also identified the process of change which Fabra sets up as prototypical in the Conversation of 30/XII/1924:

> Even more than a single word, an alien construction can come into the language *without our realising it*. [...] Because our reading is every day and almost exclusively in a language (Spanish) which uses *se* for the third-person singular dative combined with a third-person direct object pronoun –*lo*, *la*, *los* or *las*–, the association in our mind between the word *se* and that [dative] meaning is established so firmly that, when translating from Spanish, we may not find it strange and thus inadvertently allow it to slip into our translation. Similarly we may well not be surprised to find it admitted into a text [composed] in Catalan. From this point on, there is the danger that *se* with the value of *li* or *hi* will be spontaneously produced. (Reproduced in Rafel 1984: 553)

The schema of Fabra's exposition is as follows:

a. There is a first phase of "exposure" to the new form ("reading every day, almost exclusively...").
b. There follows a phase of passive acceptance ("becoming established, unmodified, in our thoughts"), with these two successive stages:
   i. Translation from the Castilian ("translating out of that language it (the new form) may not appear alien to us and it may slip unnoticed into our translation").
   ii. Seeing it in Catalan texts ("and thus it might not strike us as odd when we find it accepted in a Catalan texts").
c. Finally, "the danger that it might be produced spontaneously".

In Fabra's view, change is inherent in languages, it occurs according to certain laws and each language has its own evolution. Catalan has evolved relatively little in comparison with the other Romance languages. His attitude as a researcher, when he is studying language change – unlike when he is working on codification – is neutral.

As regards the origins of syntactical change, it is necessary to use Labov's terminology: "change from above" and "change from below". Fabra gives it to be understood that syntax is a very malleable aspect of the language, especially because syntactical phenomena are not easily perceived. He describes in particular changes "from above" – understood to be changes consciously introduced generally by an elite – since there have been many more syntactical changes in the written language than in the spoken one in relation to the medieval written language.

To explain the causes of syntactical change, we find allusions in Fabra's texts first of all to interference – as a transference from the speaker of L1 of an L2 form when L1 is being written, and as a transfer from the speaker of L1 of an L1 form when L2 is being spoken. The term "interference" is used explicitly by Fabra in his lecture "Catalan in Primary School" (1933), a use from three years before the first recorded appearance of it in a European text (the communication on "Problèmes d'interférence linguistiques", by Kristian Sandfield, IV International Congress of Linguists, Copenhagen) or in a Catalan one (the work on *Passive Polyglotism*, by Delfí Dalmau), both from 1936. Despite this, his dictionary definition gives *interference* with a meaning only in the context of physics.

Then, in descending quantitative order, reference is made to internal analogy, analogy with Castilian, inappropriate derivation, natural evolution, crossing, the need for a particular form, the need for precision and superfluity.

Among the internal factors related to syntactical change, Fabra the researcher observes in the great majority of cases dealt with the interference of Castilian as the second language present in the Catalan-speaker's brain a first stage, direct – generating changes in the language –; and, in a second stage, indirect, making Catalans unable to recognise as authentic traditional forms in their own language. In descending quantitative order, Fabra mentions also the relative imperceptibility of syntactical phenomena; endogenous development of possibilities within the system; natural evolution; the permeability of the Catalan system relative to others; familiarity among Catalan-speakers, being bilingual, with the structures of Castilian; expressive economy; structural closeness between a given Catalan form and a Castilian one; the existence of certain linguistic contexts which favour the beginning of change.

Among factors which are both external and psycholinguistic, in descending quantitative order, Fabra mentions instinctive translation from Castilian, reading in Castilian, reading of Catalan-language newspapers, language learning and the need for a particular form.

Among strictly external factors, Fabra mentions cultural diversity, geographical diversity, cultural impoverishment, political boundaries and religious boundaries.

Change is systematically conceived by Fabra as a process having a phase of alternation between contending variants, one of which progressively prevails, although almost never absolutely.

For Fabra the researcher the consequences of changes studied are negative: disintegration of the language, ever more Castilianisms resulting from the increase in translation, changes in meaning of patrimonial words, and hypercorrections.

Among forces of resistance to change, he mentions particularly interference and ambiguity; secondarily, he refers to the "genius of the language", tradition, change of meaning in a living word and anacoluthon.

Regarding the direction of change, when a Castilian form and a Catalan one are competing, change favours the triumph of the former. Explicitly, according to Fabra, this happens when Catalan-speakers are writing their language. On the other hand – still according to Fabra's explicit mention – Catalan-speakers commit "Catalanisms" when they speak Castilian.

Regarding types of change, recent research has found in Fabra's texts, in descending quantitative order, overestimates of a distinction, substitutions, underestimates of a distinction, importations, losses, reinterpretations of a distinction, as well as additions, not always taken into account.

This classification, however, applied to changes as though they were processes affected by just a single one of the seven cases mentioned is insufficient. This shows up if we compare different readings of Fabra's interpretation of syntactical change between his Grammar of 1912 and the Philological Conversations. Comparison of the results shows that in the process of change there is an emergent variant and a traditional one: classification as one kind or the other depends on which of the two variants we have in view. Therefore, from a general perspective on the analysis of syntactical change, it seems that the conclusion must be drawn that, in order to give proper account of all the complexity of the process of change, it would be necessary to describe the situation at the starting point (a single form, two forms in a specific relationship, etc.), what is happening to the emergent variant (whether it is an interlinguistic or an intralinguistic importation, or whether it is a word with changing meaning or functions, etc), what is happening to the traditional variant (disappearing?, changing meaning or functions?, entering a new relationship with other forms, etc.), and then what is the final relationship between the two variants (the emergent one replacing the traditional one, the emerging one giving rise to a new relationship with the traditional one, etc.)

Finally, regarding the relationship between change and norm of habitual use, Fabra the researcher puts firmly in the foreground the cyclical nature of this: when a new form or a new distinction emerges, this can create a situation where rivalry between norms arises, leading to the triumph of a new norm. This idea is given very clear expression in the "Short-hand Notes from the Higher Course on Catalan (1934–1935), given by Pompeu Fabra at the Autonomous University of Barcelona" (Miravitlles 1971):

> Language is something which is continually evolving, undergoing certain changes of which we are unaware but which, in the long term, make that language significantly different. It is difficult to prevent this, and, if efforts at resistance fail

and a new form prevails, then it is accepted. All that the grammarians can say is: At the present time this is right and that other [competing] form is wrong. For this reason it has been said, very perspicaciously, that today's grammatical mistakes are the language of tomorrow.

This passage complements the one on the "Democratic Theory of the Norm" (§3.3.1.4): the norm is always an equilibrium which is unstable and flexible in the evolution of a language. And the grammarian must continually study this evolution in order not distort things. Fabra alludes perhaps to Charles Bally when he endorses the affirmation that "today's grammatical mistakes are the language of tomorrow".

3.3.4.2 *Relations between Fabra's conception of syntactical codification and syntactical change*

Regarding the relationship between Fabra's conceptions of "syntactical codification" and "syntactical change", it does not seem rash to affirm that he behaves like what we might call a "linguistic change manager". On the one hand, he responds to changes undergone by the language prior to the moment when he begins the operation of *redreçament*. On the other hand, one sees immediately that what he signifies by this term entails changes being made to the language as it is in the present moment.

With regard to the evolution undergone by Catalan up to the end of the nineteenth century, what stands out in first place is the activity which Fabra calls *depuració* (= purification) – in line with the criterion of autonomy –, entailing the rejection of changes produced by interference, even if these are well-rooted structures (thus contradicting the functional criterion of implantation). In this same area of interference, study of the syntax of other Romance languages – in line with the criterion of analogy with other languages – enables him to detect Castilian interferences, in cases like the relative combination *el que* (in sentences such as *el noi al que et refereixes* [= the boy you are referring to]): if this structure has not evolved in the other Romance languages and if it did not exist in medieval Catalan, it can only exist in present-day Catalan through the influence of Castilian, the only language to have developed this structure.

If we move on to the changes really introduced by the process of *redreçament*, it is immediately necessary to make a distinction between the changes promoted by Fabra and the ones which came about through the action of codification and which were neither anticipated nor desired. Since these are many, some more important than others, we shall address the latter in first place. Many forms and structures recovered out of the medieval language or from the dialects have resulted in certain speakers infringing what we call the grammatical appropriateness of such items. What come about are calques or hypercorrections as a consequence of deficient assimilation – perhaps because Fabra did not take sufficient account of the prospective functionality of these forms. Another undesired outcome of changes introduced by him is the negative reaction of many Catalan-speakers, for whom a particular change proposed by Fabra is felt to be ungrammatical – alien to the Catalan system – as a consequence of something we have called "secondary moment interference":

> A situation in which the speaker, in this case of Catalan, finds that he does not recognise the genuine forms as belonging to his own speech repertoire – this, according to Fabra, happens with the relative *qual* (*El noi al qual et refereixes ha sortit*) [= The boy you are talking about has left] or with use of the preposition *de* before an infinitive as subject (*M'agrada de treballar* [= I like working]) – preferring those forms which arise from interference – *el que* = *el qual* (*El noi al que et refereixes ha sortit*), the subject infinitive without preposition (*M'agrada Ø treballar*) – even though this is not their proper function: such is the case with possessive *quin* (*El noi quina mare* (*el mare de la qual*) *és sueca ha sortit* [= The boy whose mother is Swedish has left]). (Costa 2006: §3.3.1)

As for changes proposed by Fabra, we can say that these reproduce the process of spontaneous change, as a result of his deep knowledge of Catalan historical grammar. He declares from the start that he does not aim to restore the medieval language exactly as it used to be, but rather to attain the Catalan which would have emerged from the particular evolution of medieval Catalan but for the damaging effects of Spanish. Whence the importance, in Fabra's scheme of codification, which is attached to historical grammar and to the criterion of analogy with other languages.

It can be said that this application of William Labov's "change from above", as practised by Fabra, is a necessary consequence of rejection of changes produced by interference: if a long-accepted implantation is rejected, one or more genuine alternatives have to be offered that are acceptable as such to the speaker, accordingly in line with the effort to enrich the literary language. Fabra is confident that this would be possible, since the relative imperceptibility of syntactical phenomena would mean that the users of the language, with appropriate vehiculation, would adopt the normative proposals through imitation.

In order to make clear the relationships observable between Fabra's concepts of syntactical change and syntactical codification, we now review his main criteria of codification. First, a criterion with which the conception of change has an evident link is that of historicity. On the one hand, because sometimes – as in the case of a change of preposition before an infinitive complement – Fabra defends a genuine evolution rooted in the language (*pensar a fer ho* [= to think about doing it]) against a concurrent interference found in the written language (*pensar* en *fer-ho*). On the other hand, because, in order to fill a gap left by rejection of an interference, Fabra frequently proposes an archaic form, implantation of which he sees as feasible since he believes that the distance between modern Catalan and the medieval language is less than that found in other languages.

In the task of enriching expressive resources, it is essential to apply the criterion of prospective functionality: that is, to ensure that the change proposed will not bring problems along with it – at least not too many problems – as regards intelligibility, acceptability or the guarantee of appropriate use of the innovation. Application of this principle enables benefit to be gained from the fact that the same thing occurs with spontaneous change, which is itself the exploitation of possibilities within the system and which ensures that the proposed structure is absorbed in the way anticipated.

The last criterion with which connections can be established at this level is that of evaluation of tests on usage. With the strategy of leaving time for the normative proposal to co-exist with the structure to be substituted, until one or the other prevails, Fabra reproduces the change process that we can deduce from something he himself put forward. In his Philological Conversation of 30/XII/1924 he explains a particular change process. What is described here is a phase of exposure to the new form, followed by a phase of passive acceptance and then a final phase of spontaneous reproduction of the new form. If this change process – which Fabra always expounds as one of alternation between concurrent forms – ends in the success of the normative proposal after a reasonable time, then the structure which prevails becomes a "rule", and any concurrent form or forms become "mistakes".

Frequently, however, once the successful form is fixed, one finds that a discursive twist comes into Fabra's prescriptive texts: this is something which we cannot avoid mentioning, even though it means leaving the systematic analysis of his normative discourse in the terms proposed by Alain Berrendonner. The form in question, once adopted as normative, is presented as being principal or as having a longer tradition than the concurrent ones that were rejected, the latter being presented as deviations with respect to the former and, thus, as being later in appearing. Fabra often presents the criticised form as being a "substitution" of the one set up as a rule, even though the former may be older than the other or both may have co-existed.

3.3.5 Relations between Fabra's conception of syntactical codification and syntactical diversity

3.3.5.1 *An analysis of general reflections on syntactical diversity explicit in Pompeu Fabra's writings*

In parallel with what we have described in discussing Fabra as a theoretician of the literary language (§3.3.3.1), dealing with his conception of linguistic diversity, we can also cite fragments in which his basic ideas are expressed.

a. *Philological Conversation, 25/V/1920

> […] However, despite the strength of all these trends within the modern language, Catalan retains an essential distinctness in relation to Castilian. No educated person could ever look on it as a variant of Castilian, from which it differs profoundly in innumerable phonetic and morphological features, with comparable differences of syntax and lexis. […]. But, even if those alien traits were to persist, Catalan would still not be anything like, in relation to Castilian, the Andalusian dialect or even the *bable* of Asturias. Catalan is not one among so many Spanish dialects […] but rather a language that is perfectly distinct from Castilian.
>
> […] if we were to classify these [neo-Latin languages] according to their analogies and differences, Catalan would not go into the same group as Castilian, from which it is differentiated more than any other Romance language by certain really salient features.

The interest of this fragment lies in the fact that it reflects Fabra's conception of *language* and *dialect*. Catalan is independent from Castilian because of a criterion that is quantitative ("infinite number of features") and systematic. And the references to Andalusian and to Asturian *bable* as "Spanish dialects" disclose a double conception of "dialect": on the one hand, as a geographical variety (Andalusian) belonging to a language (Spanish); on the other hand, though, as a non-codified and non-refined language itself, without a pyramidal shape (*bable*), absorbed into a codified and refined language, with its own dialect continuum incorporated into the "pyramid" of another language (Spanish).

Also made clear is Fabra's position with respect to Catalan's grouping within the Romance family of languages, it being "differentiated more (from Spanish) than any other Romance language".

b. *Philological Conversation, 1/IV/1923

> One [writer] of them is satisfied with a provincial language, one which would be nothing more than a dialectal variant of Spanish, [superficially decked] with Catalan words and forms. The other's aspiration is that Catalonia should possess a veritable national language, the modern Catalan that would have emerged from our glorious medieval language were it not for the damaging effects of Spanish. […]

This fragment complements the previous one. Here the first affirmation expresses the possible situation of Catalan resembling that of Asturian *bable*, previously described as being "absorbed into a codified and refined language" (Spanish). The second one poses the alternative expressed in the syntagm "national language" ("national" being understood as being equivalent to the whole linguistic domain of Catalan), a codified and refined language in its own right. This double condition had been attained by Catalan in the fifteenth century – allowing for historical relativities and according to the particular circumstances of the Middle Ages. If it had continued to be fully used, codified and refined, it would have reached by its own natural evolution the stage into which Fabra now aims to lead it.

3.3.5.2 *Fabra's conception of linguistic diversity*

Regarding Fabra's synchronic perspective on linguistic phenomena, it is most evident in his treatment of lexis and syntax, always trying to have in mind – as Kremnitz points out – the social dimension of language. Joan Julià also talks about how "his production is framed within the neogrammatical current of his teacher Meyer-Lübke and of the first epoch of Saussure, Jespersen and the Prague School".

Much information on diversity in syntax is found in *"On Various Unresolved Issues in Present-day Literary Catalan" (1907), in the 1912 Grammar, in the *Philological Conversations, in the transcription of the Lessons from the Higher Catalan Course (1933–1934), with much more information on non-syntactical diversity supplied in the DGLC.

The chronology of these texts enables us to see that linguistic diversity is a subject that is continuously and systematically present in Fabra's work, an impression confirmed if we take into account that – with variable profundity, of course – Fabra discusses it from 1891 through to 1947.

On this subject there seems to be no clear distinction between Fabra as scholar and Fabra as codifier, since references to diversity are present in texts of all kinds, and the only difference is that he uses information on diversity to support proposals for normativisation or he occasionally censures certain groups for a particular socio-linguistic behaviour.

The first thing to say is that, in the analysed texts, Fabra does not present any complete theory or any explicit definition of linguistic diversity in general nor of syntactical diversity in particular. This notwithstanding, going carefully through his writings one can deduce clear positions on concrete aspects of the different types of diversity.

Thus, in the area of historical diversity – understood to be the succession of different stages in the history of Catalan – Fabra uses the lexical items *antic* [= ancient] and *arcaic* [= archaic] to refer to the Middle Ages and the term *modern* to refer general to his own times or to an immediately preceding past. This division into periods does not conform to the chronology used in general historiography: in the latter discipline the first two terms apply to classical antiquity prior to the fifth century, while "modern" designates the period between the fifteenth and the eighteenth centuries. Also of note, especially in contrast with present-day usage, is the fact that Fabra uses the terms Decadence and *renaixença* (generally with the lower-case initial letter) mainly as social phenomena or processes, very rarely to mean historical periods (and if he does do this, it is in a very vague way).

In the historical area, we need to note the distinction that Fabra marked out for the Middle Ages (*Philological Conversation, 12/IX/1926), between Catalan before the thirteenth century, with its "vacillating syntax", and the later stage, Catalan "in its period of maturity".

In the area of diatopy, to be particularly noted are the semantic relationships between different lexical units: use of the synonymous words *parlar* [= speech] and *llenguatge*, as hyperonyms of *idioma, llengua, dialecte* and *patuès*, given in the entry *parlar* of the DGLC, and the synonymy, in that dictionary and in other texts, between *idioma, parlar, llenguatge, llengua* and *dialecte*.

This last lexical unit, "dialect", has different meanings in Fabra's texts. The DGLC gives two definitions for it. First there is "Speech charcaterised by a set of local particularities"; and secondly, marked as "Esp(ecially)", there is "Regional variety of a language", with the example "The Attic dialect". Use of the terms "speech" and "local" in the first definition, and then of "variety" and "regional", with reference to one of the dialects of ancient Greece, gives one to believe that the lexical unit "dialect" covers a range of meaning from the geographically most reduced manners of speech – not of writing – through to regional varieties of a "literary language", a concept which Fabra himself defines as "more or less differentiated from the vernacular, used for writing by an educated people". In a lecture on "The Linguistic Unity of the Balearics, Catalonia, the Roussillon and Valencia" (1919) we find the passage in which Fabra affirms that Catalan, Valencian and Balearic are not dialects "in the modern, scientific sense", as differences between them are not great. This affirmation recalls the first definition of "dialect" included in the DGLC. It also accords with what Fabra says in his *Philological Conversation of 25/V/1920, where he gives as gradual criteria for linguistic autonomy between two linguistic entities the degree of distance, the quantity of different features and the systematicity of differences. Here, though, we must remember that the lexical unit "dialect", could be interpreted as meaning "geographical variety of a language" as well as "linguistic modality without a literary version and subordinated to another one" (see §3.3).

Regarding social diversity, what must first be remarked on is the large number of factors that we find in play, starting from a very broad concept of what might constitute a social factor. Thus we classify lexical units and fragments related to social diversity, to factors like professional activities or groups – in relief among these being various branches of publishing and translation –, the attitudes of certain social sectors towards language – the most commonly referred to being the "defenders of archaism" and the "de-Castilianisers" –, the degree of education or literacy in Catalan, weakly defined social groups – identified by terms like "many", "some", etc. –, a vertical organisation of society that is referred to vaguely and the habitual language of certain groups that are not defined at all.

In the functional field, the type of diversity that figures most in Fabra's work is, the factor of register that shows up as definitive is that of "mode". The distinction between oral mode and written mode is systematic in Fabra's work: many Castilianisms, for example, are present only in the written language; phenomena that are admissible in the spoken language are not allowed in the written one; etc. We find, sporadically, terms referring to the degree of specificity of a topic, to the degree of formality and to the degree of interaction between the emitter and the receptor in the communicative situation.

Finally, internal geographical diversity has a quantitatively anecdotal presence in Fabra's texts. This acquires – as we have said – special relevance since studies on his work have dealt particularly with diversity, especially with regard to its relationship with codification. An explanation of this fact could be that we have analysed texts in which Fabra is concerned with syntax, an aspect where diatopical diversity occurs less than in phonetics, morphology or lexis, or in codification, where there is less need to discuss it than in the establishment of orthography.

As regards inter-linguistic diversity, almost exclusively as found in the Romance family, does have a presence in Fabra's texts, since one of the tasks he took upon himself was that of determining what is authentically Catalan from what belongs to other languages.

The Conversation of 13/XII/1922 demands attention. Here there is a passage "it is largely the sum of a whole assortment of small parts, seemingly unimportant, that makes the syntax of one language differentiated from that of another in the same family" about which we have already pointed out that Fabra implicitly uses two criteria to evaluate the syntactical autonomy – the general autonomy too, we could say – of a particular linguistic modality. And in the *Conversation of 25/V/1920 (see §3.3.5.1), he applies as gradated defining criteria for this the degree (superficial or deep) of distance, the number of differential features (few, several, many or countless) and the systematicity of these differences (in phonetics, morphology, lexis and syntax, in all or in just one or some pf these aspects). Thus, in different texts, Fabra uses three criteria:

a. Quantitative: the sum of a series of small details.
b. Qualitative: small details, apparently insignificant.
c. Of degree: the greater or lesser distance between languages.

Regarding lexical units or fragments where more than one diversity is found to be present, the first thing to be said is that the large number of combinations disclosed gives an idea, first of all, of the difficulty of isolating different kinds of diversity, and, secondly, of the precision that Fabra can attain in expressions like "our medieval writers", where we find simultaneous reference to four types of diversity: inter-linguistic ("our"), social ("writers"), functional ("writers") and historical ("medieval").

As for the number of points for which Fabra's treatment explicitly incorporates some kind of diversity, these amount to 112. This alone gives an idea of the extent to which he includes the social dimension in his linguistic analysis.

3.3.5.3   *Relations between Fabra's conception of syntactical codification and syntactical diversity*

Looking at the relationship between Fabra's conceptions of syntactical codification and syntactical diversity, it does not seem to be going too far to say that his role might be seen as that of a "syntactical diversity manager". For one thing, he works on the diversity of the language at the time when he begins his work of reforming it. Then, it is immediately clear that this endeavour entails the introduction of variants that are in contention with others in the language as it then was.

Regarding the diversity within Catalan at the end of the nineteenth century, the first work to be done in Fabra's scheme of *redreçament* is that of selection; both for the choice of a dialect to form the basis of codification and also for evaluation of and selection between variants in specific cases. It must be borne in mind that, as for the base dialect, Fabra evolves from an early defence (1892) of the language of Barcelona as almost the exclusive basis, for reforming Catalan, through to an invitation to Valencians and Majorcans (1918) to purify their own variants as a way to construct the literary language.

Then there is the evaluation of and selection between variants in contention: it is first necessary to remember that this could affect every kind of diversity, except the historical category, and this aspect, in fact, only came into the frame if an archaic form had been reintroduced and Fabra was concerned in evaluating the need for it and its prospective functionality. So, if we begin with the most important kind of diversity affecting Fabra's work on codification, we should begin with functional diversity. First off, it is necessary to remember the definition given in the DGLC (under *literary*) for *literary language*: "*literary language*, more or less different from the vernacular, used by a community for writing; a language which possesses a literature". This concept establishes a continuum between extreme registers (literary and vernacular) and also that the formal register is associated with the written medium. Moreover, in other texts, speaking of the distinction between narration and dialogue, Fabra recognises that the language of literature possesses a diversity of registers.

Relevant to functional diversity are the criteria of Suitability to a stylistic conception – by which codification is concerned only with formal registers – and the compositional criterion concerned with stylistic distribution, by which the correct form is the one which is appropriate for the literary language while the ones to be discouraged may be suitable for colloquial registers. This consummates Fabra's affirmation that the richness of a language, as well as in offering a choice of synonymous structures, resides in its having them distributed over a range of stylistic possibilities. Then, linked to ideas of richness and enrichment, there is his reflection upon the expressive needs of a language: a true literary language has many of these, and they are to be satisfied by drawing upon the diverse varieties – historical, geographical and social – of that language.

A last important aspect of functional diversity for Fabra's codification is the factor of register. He considers that the starting point must be the contemporary oral language as it existed at the beginning of the twentieth century, often containing genuine evolutions not present in the written idiom, a medium that has been forged upon expressive and linguistic patterns from Spanish. One has only to recall how Fabra criticises the "bad Catalan that is currently written", in his Philological Conversation of 29/X/1925:

> [...] the wrongly used gerund, causal *doncs*, *el qual* or *el quin* translating [Spanish] *cuyo*, defects which are completely alien to the spoken language, where they have never managed to penetrate despite the double influence of Spanish and of the "bad Catalan that is currently written".
>
> This is a notable example of to what degree, when we are writing, we allow ourselves to be influenced by the language in which our reading is normally done. (SRomUB:785)

From the point of view of geographical diversity, the criterion which is manifestly relevant to it is that of diasystematicity, despite the fact that Fabra's earliest work was centred upon the Barcelona dialect. However, as the movement progresses for restoring Catalan to its proper condition and status, Fabra takes into account the whole diasystem, both to test the implantation of structures and, also, to draw upon the local dialects for alternatives to structures that have been rejected.

The third kind of diversity that is quantitatively pertinent for Fabra's codification is the social one, because his writings focus on quite a few sectors that are significant for particular socio-linguistic attitudes or modes of behaviour, even though these groups are characterised in a very loose fashion. We can think of the "out-and-out de-Castilianisers" or the "supporters of archaic forms", with whom he debates specific points: or those whom we now call "language professionals", such as writers, translators, proof-readers, journalists, to whom he constantly appeals to study his proposals and to adopt them, or to weigh up very carefully their own solutions. Then there are references to the indeterminate group of people who are literate in Catalan, potential agents for tests on evaluation of use.

As regards historical diversity, the criterion of Historicity is obviously related to this, both because a long tradition is an important condition for the defence of a particular structure, and also because of the fact that historical variety is a source of alternative solutions for rejected structures.

Inter-linguistic diversity is related to the criterion of Analogy with other languages – used, as we have seen, by Fabra to discover interferences from Spanish – but there is also a relationship here, foundational we might say, for the criterion of Autonomy. We need only recall how Fabra in the DGLC links *llenguatge* (a partial synonym of *llengua*; cf. French *langage* and *langue*) to the fact that it is fixed and refined by use, while the concepts of *patuès* [= *patois*] and *vernacle* are associated with the lack of literary cultivation. This is because the fixing and the refinement of a language variety contribute to making it autonomous with respect to other neighbouring varieties which have acquired their own personalities through similar processes that have been applied to them. These differing identities between neighbouring varieties are characterised by Fabra as follows: the distance between modalities is gradual (Degree as a criterion) and it is manifest in the sum (Quantitative criterion) of small features that are apparently insignificant (Qualitative criterion).

Finally, it should be said that structures proposed by Fabra for normative status frequently imply an increase in the existing range of diversity. This is because – as we have explained in discussing the relationships between conceptions of change and codification itself – he himself foresees, in the application of tests for use evaluation, a period of coexistence between his own proposal and the previously existing variants.

3.3.6 Articulation of Fabra's principles for syntactical codification and his ideas on syntax itself including syntactical change and diversity

Is there a coherent articulation between, on the one hand, Fabra's ideas on syntactical codification and, on the other, his ideas on syntax itself as well as on syntactical change and diversity? We think the answer is affirmative, and that it can be summarised by saying that Fabra's syntactical codification consists of prudent and efficient procedures applied to syntactical change and diversity. The prudence is constantly manifest in his treating syntax as the most important part of the language and – because it is the part of the language where the object of analysis are not discrete units but relations between sets of them – the most difficult one to describe and to prescribe for, since it would be absurd to try to impose rigid norms upon it (unlike in orthography, for example). Prudence is manifest also in the long, meticulous process of establishment of rules by means of the criterion of evaluation of usage testing, following the process of development between spontaneous change and an open-ended period when variants are in play together.

Efficiency is demonstrated by Fabra on two fronts: both in the treatment of the linguistic changes, endogenous and exogenous, which led to the diversified reality of Catalan at the end of the nineteenth century, and in the application "from above" of changes that he sees as being feasible because of the characteristics of syntax – malleability, near-imperceptibility – despite the fact that in some cases undesirable secondary effects may be produced, such as infringements of appropriate use (hypercorrections or calques).

From the point of view of the general process of *redreçament*, Fabra analyses which of the existing variants are the product of endogenous changes and which are not, selecting genuine variants whenever he can. If he detects an expressive need brought about by rejection of a borrowed form or by Catalan's access to new registers, he looks to find the desideratum in the old language or in synchronic varieties, after assessing the prospective functionality of the various possibilities.

From the point of view of his full range of criteria, mention has already been made of the interaction between the conceptions of syntax, of linguistic change and diversity, and of codification in the evaluation of tests on usage. Allusion to the Historicity criterion has already been made: the evolution of the language may have allowed an interference to occur; this is rejected, to be substituted by an archaic form; this constitutes a change – made from above – and it increases the existing range of diversity until such time as it can be made fixed in the referential language; the interference then becomes a "mistake".

But the criteria in which the relationships between these conceptions are richest are those associated with functionality. We have seen the importance attached by Fabra to the availability of a fixed and perfected modality – that is, the fruit of interventions by grammarians and lexicographers, deployed then by competent editors – in order for a particular linguistic modality to be as autonomous as possible in respect of neighbouring modalities. In Coseriu's terms, we deduce that for Fabra "language" and "dialect" are objective norms, but the language is a language largely – or mostly – because it can call upon a prescriptive Norm. Without this, what obtains is a series of contiguous geographical varieties, side by side, having diffuse boundaries with neighbouring dialectal continuums. With the establishment of the norm, the dialectal aggregation becomes a pyramid where these components are bound together in a single language.

For this to be achieved in the case of Catalan, it has been necessary to differentiate internal evolutions from exogenous ones, and to substitute the latter exogenous evolutions. It has also been necessary to foster and boost as much as possible those structures which are characteristic of Catalan, in line with the criterion of Specificity. Such substitution has been possible only if the proposed replacement structure has fulfilled the requirements – or enough of them – of prospective functionality: to be intelligible, simple and acceptable, and to present guarantees of appropriate use.

This whole conception of syntax, of change and diversity and of codification presupposes the conviction that a language is a system of possibilities upon which its speakers have an effect, but in which the grammarian can also intervene to accept or to reject certain of its internal evolutions and certain variants, as well as to foster particular evolutions and variants.

Regarding description of and prescription for phonetics and morphology (on lexis, see §3.6, below), a *tour d'horizons* shows in first place that Fabra was the first Catalan phonetician to devote systematic and exhaustive attention to the subject, arising out of his grounding in comparativism and neo-grammatical studies. This feature is exemplified both in his grammars and in his technical articles. In the former, of course, his fundamental interest is of an applied nature – to fix orthoepy in Catalan – while in the latter his objective is description of phonetics and study of evolution there. In morphology also this perspective shows Fabra's activity to be "really revolutionary". To this field he applies criteria of modernisation, unification, autonomy and acceptance of the spoken language. But what really stands out here is the decision not to accept analogical forms if they had not been firmly integrated. This meant that the difficulties to be overcome involved geographical variety of forms, Castilianisation and analogy.

3.3.7 Normativisation in practice

A simple "before-and-after" comparison is a very convenient way to illustrate the effects of Fabra's normativisation programme for the modern Catalan language. Here, to this end, we present fragments from a short narrative by the novelist Narcís Oller,[52] exactly as the text appeared in its original nineteenth-century edi-

---

52. See above, §2.5.3.

tion, contrasted with the corrected version that was published in the late 1920s in the author's Complete Works.

The selection of this particular sample was not made at random. Oller was the writer who introduced modern narrative realism into Catalan literature from the late 1870s. His major novels, published between 1882 and 1906 gained him success both locally and internationally, establishing his reputation as the founding father of the genre in Catalan. With the advent of Noucentisme he became side-lined and his work neglected, especially because of his identification with the "old school" of writers and because of his declared opposition to the spirit and the practise of the normativisation programme headed by Pompeu Fabra. He maintained his *antinormista* stance until well into the 1920s. By then a new surge in demand for full-scale narrative fiction in Catalan was apparent, and Oller's literary reputation enjoyed a revival. In this context, he bowed gracefully to the inevitable and authorised the publication of his Complete Works (1928–1930) in a fully corrected and modernised edition. It was published in the life-time both of Oller and of Fabra, and it would have been read by each of the two men, from different perpectives, obviously.

The task of adapting Oller's language to the normative standard was assigned to Emili Guanyavents,[53] a pupil and collaborator of Fabra himself. Guanyavents's meticulous approach to this task assimilated the *noucentistes'* harsh criticisms of the defectiveness of Oller's writing, and a number of stylistic "improvements" accompanied the purely linguistic revision. In the original (1879) version of fragments from Oller's first published book, we see direct exemplification of written Catalan as it was inherited from the period of Decadence and perpetuated during the Renaixença: "impoverished", "corrupt", "unstable", riddled with Castilianisms at every level (orthographical, lexical, morphological and syntactical) as Fabra so insistently described it in his writings.

From the revised version (1929) of the same text, set alongside the original, we can identify the practical effects of a systematic correction carried out according to all the principles and criteria of the model for modern standard Catalan, established by then as fully orthodox. The differences give the measure of the achievement in establishing what recent generations can take for granted as their cultural birthright.

The brief extract chosen for this exercise is taken from a text entitled "Dos mesos de món" (Two Months in Society), included in the volume *Croquis del natural* (Life Sketches). It is a short epistolary narrative, exchanges between two well-educated young Barcelona women of relatively high bourgeois status. As well as mirroring the literary language as used by Oller and his contemporaries, our

---

53. See below, note 110 to [56] "The Normalisation of Grammar' in the anthology of translated texts.

sample has an added value of socio-linguistic interest, in two particular details. First: private correspondence belongs at the interface of spoken/informal language use (intimacy) and the written/formal level (culture). Maria's arguments prefigure, interestingly, Fabra's own experience and his account of the circumstances in which he himself, in his youth, had his eyes opened to major linguistic issues as they affected the contemporary status and condition of Catalan.[54] Secondly, the case she makes for the "dignification" of Catalan reflects ideas on language and identity which are clearly those which were gathering consistency during the Renaixença, filtered in the narrative through the mind of a young female representative of the late-nineteenth-century Barcelona bourgeoisie. These ideas are framed by Maria in historical and socio-linguistic terms very close to those which go into the composition of Fabra's total concept of *redreçament*.

***

We present the two editions side by side in order to make comparison easy. We then point out the principal and most representative effects of the modernisation of Catalan as exemplified in this sample.

1879[55]	1929[56]
1 de Octubre.	1 d'octubre de 1870.
Estimada María: Sols pera darte gust t' escrich en catalá, y pots ben creure que casibe estich empenedida d' haver convingut en ferho, perque lluny de trobar aquella facilitat que 'm prometia, sento lligada ma ploma com si escrigués en francés, que ja sabs lo que 'm costava.	Estimada Maria: Sols per donar-te gust t'escric en català, i pots ben creure que quasi estic penedida d'haver convingut a fer-ho, perquè, lluny de trobar aquella facilitat que em prometia, sento lligada ma ploma com si escrigués en francès, que ja saps el que em costava.
Quan més penso en nostre conveni, menos me l'esplico, y al veure ton entussiasme per nostra llengua t' atmiro com á un sér extraordinari: perqué ¿qué té de bonich lo catalá ni quina aplicació pot tenir pera nosaltres que, modestia apart, som fillas de familias distingidas y relacionadas, per lo tant, ab personas que posseheixen l'hermosa llengua de Cervantes? Nostres papás han escrit sempre en castellá y, en nostres familias, escriure catalá es retrocedir á l'època dels avis ó besavis.	Com més penso en el nostre conveni, menys me l'explico, i, en veure ton entusiasme per la nostra llengua, t'admiro com a un ésser extraordinari. Perquè ¿què té de bonic el català, ni quina aplicació pot tenir per a nosaltres, que, modèstia a part, som filles de famílies distingides i relacionades, per tant, amb persones que posseeixen la bella llengua de Cervantes? Els nostres papàs han escrit sempre en castellà, i, en les nostres famílies, escriure en català és retrocedir a l'època dels avis o dels besavis.

54. See the "Conversation with Pompeu Fabra", reproduced in the anthology of texts.

55. Narcís Oller, "Tres mesos de mon", *Cróquis del natural*, Barcelona: Imprenta de la Renaixensa, 1879.

56. "Tres mesos de món", *Croquis de natural* in *Obres completes de Narcís Oller*, Vol. VII, Barcelona: Gustau Gili, 1929.

Comprench que tú, entussiasta per la llengua catalana y per las costums sencillas del camp, cregas útil y agradable retrocedirhi; mes jo que no penso com tú, si penso alguna cosa, jo que sóls visch de sentiments y no puch expressar més qu' aquestos, may podré avenirme sens gran esfors (com m' obligas á fer llegint llibres que no sé llegir y fullejant á cada pas lo diccionari per no causarte un disgust), á escriure una llengua que, si be parlo, no m' agrada ni la considero necessaria per a res. […]

Pel prompte dech dirte, qu' al arrivar aquí, varem trobar á mama, bona y plorosa de goig de poderme abrassar despres de ma llarga estada en lo col·legi. Mos germanets molt crescuts, y 'ls dos petits, tan monos com nos los habia pintat lo papá. […]

Tinch un quarto qu' es una joya; nó encatifat com lo teu, perque aquí 's guardan les catifas sóls per a las pessas bonas; mes, está estorat, té dos parells de cortinas ab son transparent á la moderna... […]

Adeu.

Adela.

P.D. He mostrat aquesta carta als papás y al véurela en catalá han esclafit á riure y diuhen que tú i jo nos hem tornat bojas.

[Maria to Adela]

3 de Octubre.

Bé, molt bé, ma mellor amiga. No m' importen tos planys, res me fan tas queixas: si vols que 't contesti, has d' escriurem en català. […]

¡Que dins de nostras familias escriure en català es retrocedir! ¿Per qué? Tindrias rahó si jo 't diguès: no aprengas lo castellá; no aprengas may aquesta llengua que no coneixian nostres avis. Pero jo no dich tal cosa ni la proposaré may. Pretench tan sóls qu' á mi m'escrigas en la llengua que parlém quan estém juntas.

¿A qué amagarme la veritat? Tot alló de mon entussiasme per la llengua y per las costums senzillas, com lo de que tú sents y no pensas, no 't pót valdre. Es un pretest ab lo qual vols disfressar una veritat que veig bellugar entre tas lletras.

Comprenc que tu, entusiasta per la llengua catalana i pels costums senzills del camp, creguis útil i agradable retrocedir-hi; però jo, que no penso com tu (si quelcom penso), jo, que sols visc de sentiments i no puc expressar altra cosa que aquests, mai no podré avenir-me sense gran esforç (com el que m'obligues a fer llegint llibres que no sé llegir i fullejant a cada pas el diccionari, per no causar-te un disgust) a escriure una llengua que, si bé parlo, no m'agrada ni considero necessària per a res. […]

Mentrestant he de dir-te que en arribar ací vàrem trobar la mama bona i plorosa de goig de poder-me abraçar després de ma llarga estada en el col·legi. Mos germanets molt crescuts, i els dos petits tan bufons com ens els havia pintat el papà.

Tinc una cambra que és una joia: no encatifada, com la teva (perquè ací es guarden les catifes sols per a les peces bones), però és estorada, té dos parells de cortines i un transparent a la moderna... […]

Adéu.

ADELA.

P.D. He mostrat aquesta carta als papàs, i en veure-la en català han esclafit a riure i diuen que tu i jo ens hem tornat boges.

[Maria to Adela]

3 d'octubre.

Bé, molt bé, ma millor amiga. No m'importen tos planys, res no em fan tes queixes: si vols que et contesti has d'escriure'm en català. […]

¡Que dins les nostres famílies escriure en català és retrocedir! Per què? Tindries raó si jo et digués: "No aprenguis el castellà; no aprenguis mai aquesta llengua que no coneixien els nostres avis." Però jo no dic tal cosa ni la proposaré mai: pretenc tan sols que a mi m'escriguis en la llengua que parlem quan estem juntes.

Per què amagar-me la veritat? Tot allò de mon entusiasme per la llengua i pels costums senzills, com allò altre que dius, que tu sents i no penses, no et pot valer: és un pretext amb el qual vols disfressar una veritat que veig bellugar entre tes lletres.

A mesura qu 'ls anys esmortuiren lo resentiment natural del vensut contra 'l vensedor, s'esmortuí la resistencia a l'assimilació y, per tant, á apendre la llengua castellana. Essent aquesta tan diferenta de la nostra com la francesa, no ha pogut encara passar á las classes mes baixas ni ha lograt sisquera, en altres provincias ahont se parlan dialectes del castellá ó fa més segles qu' aquest hi domina, esser lo llenguatje comú de las classes altas. Aixó no obstant, aquestas, en nostra terra, lo posseheixen, si pot dirse possehirlo com lo saben certs catalans y sobre tot las catalanas; y ab l'afany de mostrarnos á certa altura d' educació superior á la del poble, hem acabat per desdenyar l' escriure en catalá y fins saberlo llegir, sens pararnos en l' efecte estrany que ha de causar á tot esperit serio veure tal desdeny, mentres en familia y en els actes més íntims de la vida no parlém altra llengua. [...]
Maria.

A mesura que els anys esmorteïren el ressentiment natural del vençut contra el vencedor, s'esmorteí la resistència a l'assimilació i, per tant, a aprendre la llengua castellana. Essent aquesta tan diferent de la nostra com la francesa, no ha pogut encara passar a les classes més baixes, ni ha aconseguit solament, com en altres províncies on es parlen dialectes del castellà o fa més segles que aquest hi domina, ésser el llenguatge comú de les classes altes. Això no obstant, aquestes, a la nostra terra, el posseeixen, si pot dir-se posseir-lo saber-lo com el saben certs catalans i sobretot les catalanes; i amb l'afany de mostrar-nos a certa altura d'educació superior a la del poble, hem acabat per desdenyar-nos d'escriure en català, i fins de saber-lo llegir, sense parar-nos en l'efecte estrany que ha de causar a tot esperit seriós veure tal desdeny, mentre en família i en els actes més íntims de la vida no parlem altre llengua. [...]
MARIA.

Below we indicate schematically changes introduced into the 1929 corrected version which are representative of major points at issue during the process of reforming modern written Catalan. All of these are recurrent concerns addressed by Fabra throughout the sequence of his writings reproduced in our translated anthology.

a. Spelling

Description	1879	1929
Written accents: de-Castilianisation and consistency.	*María, prometia,* etc. *modestia, familias,* etc. *sols/sóls, ó,* etc. *y*	*Maria, prometia modèstia, famílies sols, o i*
Written accents: use of the grave accent (`) to mark open vowels. Formal consistency corresponding to phonology.	*catalá, época, francés*	*català, època, francès*
Elimination of non-etymological *h*.	*escrich, posseheixen*	*escric, posseeixen*
Feminine plural forms in *-es*	*fillas, familias,* etc.	*filles, famílies*
Recovery of *ç*.	*esfors, [pessa]/pessas, vensut*	*esforç, [peça]/peces, vençut*
Establishment of the digraph *l·l*.	*col-legi*	*col·legi*

Regularisation of use of the apostrophe.	t' escrich, etc. que 'm, y'ls, contra'l, etc. qu' al, etc. escriurem, etc.	t'escric que em, i els, contra el que en escriure'm
Use of the hyphen to attach clitics to the verb.	ferho, véurela, possehirlo, etc.	fer-ho, veure-la, posseir-lo
Elimination of forms derived from Castilian pronunciation.	[s]: entussiasme, entussiasta	[z]: entusiasme, entusiasta

b. Morphology

Description	1879	1929
Nominal morphology: substitution of forms considered to be archaic.	lo catalá, nos los, etc.	el català, ens els
Nominal morphology: recovery of the true Catalan gender: de-Castilianisation.	las costums (f.)	els costums (m.)
Nominal morphology: substitution of colloquial forms.	aquestos, diferenta	aquests, diferent
Verbal morphology: substitution of forms considered to be archaic.	cregas, aprengas, escrigas	creguis, aprenguis, escriguis
Verbal morphology: substitution of colloquial forms.	valdre	valer

c. Syntax

Description	1879	1929
Substitution of Castilian-based constructions.	Sols **pera** darte gust t' escrich haver convingut **en** ferho **lo** que 'm costava trobar **á** [la] mama	Sols **per** donar-te gust t'escric haver convingut **a** fer-ho **el** que em costava trobar la mama
Recovery of constructions considered to be both more authentic and clearer.	may podré avenirme	mai **no** podré avenir-me

d. Vocabulary

Description	1879	1929
Substitution of Castilianisms.	menos, hermosa, monos, quarto, lograt, sisquera, etc.	menys, bella, bufons, cambra, aconseguit, solament
Substitution of archaic forms.	mellor, ab, sens	millor, amb, sense

Some final observations on the corrector's "stylistic improvement" are worth making. One can detect here the conscientious motive of eradicating blatantly inauthentic constructions, calqued on Castilian, as in:

> Tot alló de mon entussiasme per la llengua y per las costums senzillas, *com lo de que tú sents y no pensas*, no 't pót valdre. (1879)

> Tot allò de mon entusiasme per la llengua i pels costums senzills, *com allò altre que dius, que tu sents i no penses*, no et pot valer. (1929)

Here the corrector has elegantly resolved the double Castilianism of *lo de que* (*lo* as neuter pronoun, preposition *de* introducing *que*) by recasting the clause as a natural and authentic construction in Catalan.

Also visible in the 1929 version is evidence of "purism" and the promotion of "innovations", both deriving from the linguistic experimentation described at various points by Fabra. This phenomenon belongs to the stage when the reform of Catalan was well advanced and very widely accepted, enabling its proponents and exponents to push the limits of the purification process. We observe this in two cases present in our sample. First, *alguna cosa* (1879) becomes *quelcom* (1929), the former being perfectly natural and authentic, the latter being an archaic form which the *fabristes* promoted, largely to combat the prevalence of the Castilianism *algo* [= something]. Similarly for *aquí* (1879) which becomes *ací* (1929): here again an alternative from old Catalan is favoured over a perfectly correct and current form which happens to coincide with its Castilian equivalent. Fabra's own justifications of this particular method of "innovation" (in, for example, several "Philological Conversations") are exemplified in the details just discussed. Nowadays both *quelcom* and *ací* have their place in the Catalan lexicon, typical though of a very high and cultured register.

Translation:

> 1 October [1870]
> Dear Maria: Just to give you pleasure I am writing to you in Catalan, and I want you to know that I am almost repenting that I ever agreed to do this, because, far from finding that it would be as easy as promised, my pen seems not to move at all freely, as if I were writing in French, and you know how difficult I used to find that.
>
> The more I think about our agreement, the less I understand it, and, seeing your enthusiasm for our language, I admire you as being someone quite extraordinary. What is so attractive about Catalan, I ask you, and what useful application can it have for us who are, without undue modesty, daughters of distinguished families with our ties to people who possess the beautiful language of Cervantes?

Our parents have always written in Castilian and, in our families, to write in Catalan is to go back to the times of our grandparents or great-grandparents.

I can understand that you, with your enthusiasm for the Catalan language and for the simple ways of country living, should think that it is useful and pleasant to go back there; but I, who live only through my feelings and can express nothing other than these, shall never adapt except without great effort (like that which you oblige me to make in reading books I cannot read and in endlessly turning the pages of the dictionary, just to avoid upsetting you) to writing in a language which, although I speak it, I dislike and do not consider necessary for anything. [...]

Meanwhile I must tell you that on arriving here we found Mummy in good health and tearful with joy at being able to embrace me after my long stay away at school. My little brothers have grown up a lot, and the two little ones are just as cute as Daddy had described them.

My room is delightful: it is not carpeted, unlike yours (because here carpets go only in the best rooms), but it does have rugs, and two pairs of curtains with a modern-style lace to the window.

Good-bye for now.

ADELA.

PS. I have shown this letter to Mummy and Daddy, and seeing it written in Catalan has made them burst out laughing and they say that you and I have gone mad.

[Maria to Adela]

3 October.

Very well, very well, best friend of mine. Your laments have no effect on me, and your complaints bother me not at all: if you want me to reply to you then you must write to me in Catalan. [...]

To say that in our families writing in Catalan is a backwards step! You would be right if I were to say to you: "Do not learn Castilian: never learn that language which our grandparents did not know." But I am saying nothing of the sort, nor shall I ever propose such a thing: all I ask for is that you should write to me in the language which we speak when we are together.

Why hide the truth from me? The whole question of my enthusiasm for the language and for the simple ways of life, like the other things you say, about feeling rather than thinking: these are not real arguments, just a pretext with which you are trying to disguise a truth which I can see moving between the words you write.

As the passing of the years dampened the natural resentment felt by the vanquished against the victor, so resistance to assimilation was dampened and, with it, resistance to learning the Castilian language. Being as different from our language as is French, Castilian still has not permeated down to the lower classes, nor has it even managed to become the common language of the upper classes, which has happened in other provinces where dialects of Castilian are spoken or where this language has been dominant for more centuries. Nevertheless, these upper classes, in our country, do have a command of Castilian, if we can use this expression to apply to the knowledge of it displayed by certain Catalans, especially Catalan women. And with the urge to show that we occupy a level of education above that of the common people, we have become contemptuous about writing in Catalan, and even about being able to read it, without stopping to observe the strange effect that such contempt must create now on any serious-minded person, when at the same time we speak only this language among the family and in our most private behaviour. [...]

MARIA.

3.4   Pompeu Fabra as grammarian

It is an established fact in linguistics that there are theoretical grammars, descriptive grammars, pedagogical grammars and normative grammars. We have seen that Fabra did not write a theoretical one; and we have also seen that the grammars he did write can be called descriptive, pedagogical or normative. Another established fact is that his Catalan Grammar first published in 1918 and revised in seven editions up to 1933 has received unanimous consideration as being normative, both because of its perceptive intention and because of the moral and official authority invested in it from the beginning by the IEC.

Does this mean that this work does not include description and that pedagogy does not enter into it? Hardly. The question itself has to do with the objectives that lay behind Fabra's texts.[57] *Grosso modo*, there are three that can be distinguished: the descriptive objective, theoretical; the normative one, concerned with codification; and the pedagogical one, concerned with spreading the results of the preceding two. The distinction is clear enough, but one must bear in mind that very few of Fabra's texts conform to just one of the three objectives (something which is inherent to grammatical texts generally).

It is relevant also to take into account the readership of these works. Explicitly or implicitly Fabra addresses, in different texts, various types of reader. Among these is a specialist public, starting with his colleagues in the enterprise of language reform, Massó i Torrents and Casas-Carbó, as recipients of letters on lin-

---

57. On Fabra's awareness of this issue, the following affirmations are sufficiently revealing: "We are beginning at the end, and we are already happily composing didactical grammars (...) Will they just teach you general grammar?' (Questions of Catalan Grammar (1911)) or "Heeding the suggestions of some teachers, we have suppressed (...) definition of the active and passive voices (...). The essential thing is not that the young pupil should learn the definitions of the parts of speech, but that he should be able to distinguish between them (...)'. (Preliminary Note to the second edition of the Intermediate Course of 1923.)

guistic topics, or the readers of articles published in specialised journals. We go on to classify, in descending order of specialisation, the composition of his whole readership:

a. undergraduates of courses at the Autonomous University;
b. school-teachers, to whom he addressed articles in specialist journals, his lectures at training colleges, as well as the Catalan Grammar: Intermediate Course and the "posthumous" Grammar of 1956;
c. writers and "people who write for a general public", a collective addressed as such in many of his articles;
d. non-university students on general educational courses, and
e. the "Catalan-speaking public at large", the readership of his numerous press articles published over many years and the users of the Institute's Dictionary itself.

With the two criteria (objectives and readership) in mind, the following classification of Fabra's grammars can be made.[58]

3.4.1 Grammars, addressed to a specialist readership, with a basically descriptive objective

3.4.1.1 Ensayo de catalán moderno /
Essay on the Grammar of Modern Catalan (1891)
Written in Castilian. This is a work which signified a radical innovation, not just becase it describes the oral Catalan of Barcelona, but also because it corresponds to a new conception of grammar: the grammatical system of the language is to be found in the spoken language and this must be faithfully described. Fabra here basically deals with questions of phonetics and morphology and analyses the normative scheme currently in force.

3.4.1.2 Contribució a la gramàtica catalana /
Contribution to the Grammar of the Catalan Language (1898)
This work can be seen to display already the influence of the major neo-grammarians and comparativists. It comprises four monographic studies on "applied linguistics": orthography, nominal morphology, verbal morphology and the order of weak pronouns.

---

58. We do not include here the advertised *Catalan grammar* (Coromines (1956: VI)) the manuscript of which was lost, nor a Grammar of Romanian of which none of the contents have survived.

3.4.1.3   Gramática de la lengua catalana /
Grammar of the Catalan Language (1912)

Written in Castilian. Scholars concur that this is the "principal grammatical treatise written by Fabra", on account both of its erudition and of the huge amount
of diachronic and synchronic information that it contains. It describes modern Eastern Catalan, following the lines laid down in the great syntheses of the
comparativists and the neo-grammarians: phonetics, morphology, syntax and
word-formation, with references when appropriate to other languages (Castilian,
French, Italian and English), to historical grammar and to the other dialects of
Catalan. It is addressed to Spanish intellectuals wishing to learn Catalan, and is
accordingly written in Castilian. It ends with a selection of extracts from Catalan
literature of every period.

3.4.1.4   Gramàtica catalana: curs mitjà /
Catalan Grammar. Intermediate Course (1918)

This book is considered important, on the one hand, because it aims at covering
particular needs in the pedagogical field, and also, on the other hand, because it is
a grammatical work with a more marked didactic orientation. Prominent among
these – although exercises are not provided – are Fabra's trade-mark empiricism
and the organisation of the material around the noun and the verb, an approach
previously unknown in the Spanish state. It enjoyed great success: five editions up
to 1935, in which Fabra regularly adjusted the contents and the exposition on the
basis of comments received from teachers. The book was aimed at pupils over 11,
with the input of a teacher always assumed (especially regarding the relationship
between dialects and the standard language; see §3.3.1.9, above). Its objective was
declared to be "a descriptive grammar based on a functional conception of language", consonant with the ideas of linguists like Jespersen.

3.4.1.5   Gramàtica francesa / *French Grammar (1919)*

Written in Catalan, this work – together with the English Grammar of 1924 – was
designed by Fabra to make Catalan a normal educational medium and to assist
teachers of French and English. It is a "descriptive (and contrastive) grammar
with a clear didactic intention" applying aspects of linguistic structuralism, of
articulatory and descriptive phonetics, and of the "direct method" in language
teaching. It is divided into two parts, covering first phonetics and then morphology and syntax.

3.4.1.6   Gramàtica anglesa / *English Grammar (1924)*

This has the same structure as the French Grammar. As well as sharing the objectives of the latter, it also has the declared aim of promoting the Reform Movement

in the teaching of second languages initiated by Wilhelm Viëtor in 1882 and supported by John Storm, Paul Hassy, Henry Sweet and Otto Jespersen.

3.4.1.7 Gramàtica catalana / *Catalan Grammar (1946)*
This is the first version, published in Paris, of the work discussed next.

3.4.1.8 Gramàtica catalana / *Catalan Grammar (1956)*
Edited posthumously by Joan Coromines,[59] whose prologue highlights the innovation and the profundity with which Fabra treats aspects of syntax and lexis. He recalls how the author himself used to refer to this work as his "Grammar for teachers", because it was conceived as a primary tool for the teacher of Catalan.

Obviously, it is debatable whether all the above Grammars share the same profile of the specialised reader and the same version of the descriptive objective. A broad overview, however, enables us to group them together. It must be said that the Grammars of 1918, 1946 and 1956 are aimed at a specialist readership constituted by school-teachers, and so description in them is accompanied by a pedagogical approach.

3.4.2 Grammars, addressed to a non-specialist public, having a basically normative objective

3.4.2.1 Gramàtica catalana / *Catalan Grammar (1918)*
This work is still recognised as giving the official normative model, until such time as the Grammar of the Catalan Language is published by the IEC.[60] According to Joan Solà, this Grammar aimed at "fixing clearly and concisely and in a non-argumentative style a set of questions of Catalan grammar which writers and the general public of that time were in urgent need of and which were then mature enough in formulation to be put together for publication". What this meant, at the time, was "basically orthographical and morphological problems". The book went through seven editions until 1933, and Fabra – as with the Catalan Grammar. Intermediate Course – made regular amendments to it based on reactions from users.

---

59. 1905–1997. Linguist educated in various major universities world-wide and pupil of Fabra. Professor in the University of Barcelona until 1939 and afterwards in Argentina and the USA. His immense and internationally renowned scholarly output is crowned by his etymological dictionaries of Spanish and Catalan.

60. The provisional version can be consulted on-line at http:www.iecat.net/institució/seccions/ Filològica/default.asp.

3.4.2.2 Abrégé de grammaire catalane / *Outline of French Grammar (1928)*
The aim of this work, as of its Castilian counterpart listed next, has been summarised as "to ensure that a non-Catalan reader can have a good description of the basic characteristics of what could be called the literary model of the Catalan language." Both works follow almost exactly the structure of the official Catalan Grammar of 1918.

3.4.2.3 Compendio de gramática catalana /
           Compendium of Catalan Grammar (1929)
See above.

3.4.2.4 Grammaire catalane / *Catalan Grammar (1941)*
Published in exile. It is an expanded version of the *Abrégé* and it was well received, going into a second edition in 1946 (in Fabra's lifetime) and then, posthumously, four further editions, the last one in 1984.

This second group, then, is made up of the official normative grammar and versions of it in French (two) and in Castilian.

Classifying Fabra's grammatical works in this way is further justified by the treatment of syntax which Fabra gives in each of the two groups. We can observe that, in the descriptive works – except in the Grammar of 1912, where this is at least not so clear – in the Intermediate Course (1918–1935), the 1946 Grammar and the 1956 one, relationships between groups of words are ordered hierarchically upon the noun and the verb, the nuclei of the subject and the predicate which constitute the terms of most sentences (except those which do not have an explicit logical subject). In the other works, the explanation of syntax is developed upon the traditional parts of the sentence. This duality, alongside distinctions like those found between "general grammar" and "didactic grammar", and alongside exclusive use of the terms "sentence" and "proposition" in the specialised texts, confirms that there is a descriptive Fabra (who can, if necessary, give advice to language teachers) and a prescriptive, didactic Fabra who addresses directly the Catalan-speaking public at large.

3.5   Pompeu Fabra as lexicographer

> [...] the whole of his [Fabra's] work as a grammarian and a lexicographer is a grand, detailed and well-reasoned proposal to the writers and, along with them, to the educated Catalan-speaking public as a whole: these are the people – the writers, the public – who have the last word. But only for as long as the writers

properly exercise their craft and the public at large possess the necessary enlightenment, it must be added.

> (Carles Riba (1954). "Preface to the second edition". Fabra, Pompeu.
> *Diccionari general de la llengua catalana*. Barcelona: EDHASA.)

In the field of lexis, the first thing of note is the treatment given to it by Fabra in his 1912 Grammar (in Castilian). He devotes 50 pages to Catalan neology (the first grammarian to address the subject). Moreover, he provides a two-column bilingual Catalan-Castilian vocabulary, showing pronunciation. This treatment of neology is completed in his posthumously published Grammar of 1956.

The most important work done by Fabra in lexicography was, according to Joan Solà, that of ordering, completing and preparing for publication the lexicographical material collected by Marià Aguiló i Fuster[61] – a task brought to completion in collaboration with Manuel de Montoliu[62] – comprising the eight volumes of the Aguiló Dictionary (1914–1934).

The second landmark in this domain was, in 1917, the Orthographical Dictionary, which served – until the publication of the dictionary containing definitions – to fix the spelling of Catalan according to the Orthographical Norms (1913) of the IEC. The Orthographical Dictionary, considered by Germà Colón to be the "macrostructure" of the DGLC of 1932, went into four editions up to 1937.[63] Its 423 double-column pages contain entries for over 40,000 words.

And the DGLC is, it goes without saying, the really major landmark. This is not just because it was the official dictionary of the IEC for over sixty years, from its publication in 1932 until 1995, when the Institute published its new normative Dictionary of the Catalan Language. It is an emblematic work also because of the conditions in which it was put together, under the harsh dictatorship of Primo de Rivera (1923–1930), against adversities of every kind.

In describing the different aspects of the DGLC (popularly known as the "Fabra dictionary"), Colón begins by examining its *raison d'être*, which he relates to the expectations created by the big developments in socio-linguistics of the first third of the twentieth century: the First International Congress on the Catalan Language of 1906; the creation of the IEC's Philological Section in 1911; publication of the Institute's Orthographical Dictionary (1917) and Orthographical Norms (1918), and of the normative Catalan Grammar in 1918 (with six revised

---

61. 1825–1897. Majorcan writer, lexicographer and bibliographer, active and influential in the nineteenth-century linguistic and literary revival of Catalan. His first name is also recorded as *Marian*.

62. 1877–1961. Literary historian and critic.

63. The translation of Fabra's prologue to the DGLC is given in the present volume.

editions up to 1932). The DGLC represented the consummation of the normative proposals offered by Fabra to the educated "Catalan-speaking public at large". Colón then proceeds to characterise five major features which account for the magnitude of this Dictionary's importance.

Regarding the "lexicographical precedents of Fabra", the only really substantial one was Labèrnia's Dictionary of the Catalan Language with Castilian and Latin Correspondences of 1839. Fabra could not avail himself of the first fascicules of what would become the ten-volume *Diccionari català-valencià-balear*, publication of which was begun by Antoni Maria Alcover in 1926.[64] The Aguiló Dictionary, referred to above, which Fabra had been engaged in publishing, was merely "an index of words".

Analysis of the macrostructure (criteria for the selection of words) of the DGLC, covers six aspects, the first of which is the degree of originality of Fabra's work on it. This centres on the fact that it is the first monolingual dictionary in the entire history of Catalan, with foreign models in the *Diccionario de la Real Academia Española* (DRAE, 1925), *Webster's New International Dictionary* of 1911 and the *Dictionnaire général de la langue française* (1890–1902). The DGLC follows these in the completing of definitions with *ad hoc* definitions. The degree of synchrony in the lexical items included presents certain incoherencies, as many archaic forms are incorporated while many words in circulation at the time do not appear. Issues are raised by the fact that the Fabra dictionary was conceived as being normative, entailing reticence about non-Barcelonese dialectal forms, exclusion of technical terms or extremely colloquial ones, exclusion of probable Castilianisms and a tendency towards Gallicism. Then there is the issue of the "level of language": any word suspected of vulgarism is rejected by Fabra, but not always consistently. The geographical range of the vocabulary admitted likewise raises questions, mainly because Fabra restricts coverage to Eastern Catalan, the dialects of the Barcelona and Girona regions, with scant attention to varieties from further afield. Colón goes as far as to say that "without exaggeration [...] Valencia and Majorca barely get a look-in". Also commented on is some incoherence in the use of chronological indicators in the definitions.

The DGLC's microstructure (information supplied in the entries) also deserves comment. The individual entries are extremely clear and well written, noticeably superior, even, to those of the DRAE of 1925. Intellectual rigour and

---

64. Published between 1926 and 1962. After the death in 1932 of Alcover (see above, note 24), work on this dictionary was completed by his collaborator, the Majorcan philologist and publisher Francesc de Borja Moll (1903–1991) who adapted its spelling to the Norms of the IEC. It is referred to as the DCVB or "the Alcover-Moll". This dictionary can be consulted at http://dcvb.iecat.net/.

precision of definitions, syntagmatic information appropriately supplied and the presentation of scientific names of animals and plants: these are distinct virtues of Fabra's dictionary. To be criticised, from a modern-day perspective, certainly is the artificiality of some of the examples, and also certain inconsistencies. The latter are particularly visible in indications of usage, in the treatment of homonyms and in the reflection of a prevailing ideology, especially in religious subjects. Reliance on the *Dictionnaire général* of Hatzfeld, Darmesteter and Thomas is transparent, basically in the imitation of definitions and examples given in that work, sometimes literally translated, sometimes adapted to Catalan reality.

Such "criticism", however, must be understood in the full context of the preparation and the publication of the DGLC. Fabra's work was still on-going and incomplete in the 1930s, and the Spanish Civil War imposed an interruption, followed by a dangerous stasis, from the effects of which Catalan has only recently, over the last three decades, dynamically renewed the normalisation process from a basis of relative institutional autonomy. It is significant that Fabra himself, right up to the time of his death in 1948, continued work on improving and completing the DGLC, maintaining contact with exiled and "home-based" members of the IEC. The "Fabra dictionary" did a great service to the community and the language it was designed for.

3.6   Pompeu Fabra as translator

Fabra's translations of foreign literary works into Catalan will form a separate volume of his Complete Works, at present in the course of publication. The editor of the volume in question, Enric Gallèn, has remarked that Fabra's activity in this sphere coincides with the period (1893–1898) of his early association with the *modernista* group of *L'Avenç*. (discussed in §2.5.4, above). His main motive for involvement in literary translation was ostensibly to use this as a way of testing and putting into practice his developing ideas for orthographical and grammatical reform. That theatre was his preferred genre for this end is quite consistent with Fabra's thinking on language, given the primacy in drama of the spoken word. Also to be noted is the fact that the works he translated reflect very clearly some of the new aesthetic preferences (Symbolism in particular) and the ideological trends (Nietzschean vitalism) brought into fashion by Catalan Modernisme. His translations that have been conserved are: Maurice Maeterlinck's *L'Intruse* (1893) and *Intérieur* (1898), and Henrik Ibsen's *Ghosts* (1894, in collaboration with Casas-Carbó). His versions of the two works by Maeterlinck were publicly staged in 1893 and 1899, respectively.

Fabra's polyglotism has been mentioned in our biographical section (3.2). His activity as a translator adds qualitatively (but not quantitatively) to this dimension in him. But it should also be kept in perspective. No doubt he did translate Maeterlinck directly from the French. However it is known that the version of *Ghosts* was done not from the original Norwegian but rather from one or more French translations of the work that were in circulation. That his range for translation was confined to works in French is rather typical of what occurred in many (almost certainly most) other cases figuring in the spate of literary translations of key modern works into Catalan, a wave that was encouraged by the cultural programmes of both Modernisme and Noucentisme.

There are references to other literary translations done by Fabra: texts by Ibsen (*Rosmerholm*), Baudelaire (*Petits poèmes en prose*) and E. A. Poe (*The Gold Bug* and *Ulalume*). If these were in fact completed, they were certainly not published, and no surviving manuscripts have been discovered to date.

3.7   Pompeu Fabra and toponymy

Among the duties covered by the Philological Section of the IEC, Fabra and his collaborators had to deal with the matter of normalising the official toponymy (place names) of the Principality of Catalonia. The outcome of this work were the documents "Report on the preparation of the Dictionary of Catalan toponymy and onomastics [proper names] presented by the Institute of Catalan Studies to the President of the Mancomunitat de Catalunya" (1924) and the "List of names of the Municipalities of Catalonia drawn up by the Philological Section of the Institute of Catalan Studies, with the collaboration of the (government) Commission on Territorial Division". This activity can be seen, of course, as an extension of the lexicographical work of the Philological Section. Its context (as reflected clearly in the titles quoted above) was that of twentieth-century gains in administrative autonomy, within newly formed institutional frameworks, acquired in the unfolding process of Catalan self-affirmation. It was an integral dimension, then, of language policy associated with "linguistic nationalism".

3.8   Pompeu Fabra as a manager of linguistic diversity

Everything that has been explained above about Fabra's work is summed up in the title given to this Section 3. Determined from a very early age to turn Catalan into the language of culture that would have taken shape out of a full and uninterrupted cultural activity from the fifteenth century onwards, he put his outstanding aptitudes as linguist and grammarian at the service of establishing a normative orthography, grammar and lexis. As has been stressed already, this objective entailed close attention to the social and historical dimensions of the language, with a sharp focus on its diverse and changing reality. The success of his proposals was not achieved without a struggle, because from his first publication in 1891, quite revolutionary in its content, his views met with incomprehension among Catalan intellectuals. Later, when he had become part of the institutional establishment, with misunderstanding still continuing, he was confronted by dissensions of the kind arising quite normally in a pluralistic society. He had also to contend with the hostility of the Spanish government, and finally with military defeat and exile. But the body of his Complete Works (currently in the course of publication) has an enduring importance on two fronts: as an abundant source of valuable perspectives on grammatical description, and as the bed-rock of Catalan's survival as a fully-fledged language of culture.

3.9   Texts by Pompeu Fabra

A complete critical edition of Pompeu Fabra's works is in progress (volumes 1–3 and 5 having been already published). Its publication data are: Mir, Jordi; Solà, Joan (eds) 2005– . *Pompeu Fabra: Obres completes*. Barcelona: Proa.

Listed here are texts by Fabra that are cited in the foregoing presentation of his work. For ease of consultation, they are classified according to the language in which they were originally written.

Within each language grouping references are ordered chronologically. Alongside the items written in languages other than Catalan some titles not cited are included, in order to provide a fuller idea of the scope of Fabra's work. Texts given in translation in the present volume are marked with an asterisk. References to works which reproduce texts by Fabra are given in §3.10.2.

3.9.1 Texts by Pompeu Fabra in Catalan

1891
"Conjugació del verb català. Present de subjuntiu y infinitiu". *L'Avenç* (31/12), 381–385.
1893
Arnau, Esteve (pseudonym of Fabra.). "L'ensenyança de la llengua francesa a l'Institut de Barcelona". *L'Avenç*, 2nd series, V, no. 1 (15/I/1893), 5–7.

—. "L'ensenyança de la llengua francesa a l'Institut de Barcelona". *L'Avenç*, 2nd series, V, no. 2 (31/I/1893), 24–28.

—. "L'ensenyança de la llengua francesa a l'Institut de Barcelona". *L'Avenç*, 2nd series, V, no. 3 (15/II/1893), 40–43.

—. "L'ensenyança de la llengua francesa a l'Institut de Barcelona". *L'Avenç*, (28/II/1893), 58–62. 2nd series, V, no. 4, (28/II/1893), 58–62.

—. "L'ensenyança de la llengua francesa a l'Institut de Barcelona". *L'Avenç*, 2nd series, V, no. 8 (31/IV/1893), 122–126.

Translation of *L'intrusa (L'intruse)*, by Maurice Maeterlinck. *L'Avenç*, 2nd series, V?, no. ?? (15–31/VIII/1894), 225–240.

1894

Translation (in collaboration with Joaquim Casas-Carbó) of *Espectres: drama de família en tres actes (Gengangere)*, by Henrik Ibsen. Barcelona: L'Avenç.

1898

Contribució a la gramàtica catalana. 2005. *Pompeu Fabra: Obres completes. Volum 1: Gramàtiques de 1891, 1898, 1912*, Mir, Jordi; Solà, Joan (eds.), 331–439. Barcelona: Proa.

Translation of *Interior (Intérieur)*, by Maurice Maeterlinck. *Catalonia*, 25–33.

1906

"Qüestions d'ortografia catalana". *Primer Congrés Internacional de la Llengua Catalana. Barcelona, octubre de 1906.* 2nd. ed. Barcelona: Vicens-Vives, 1986.

1907

*"Sobre diferents problemes pendents en l'actual català literari". *Pompeu Fabra: Obres completes. Volum 3: Articles erudits. Gramàtiques francesa i anglesa.*, Mir, Jordi; Solà, Joan (eds.), 2006, 202–228. Barcelona: Proa.

1910

Letter dated 13/9. Archive of the Ateneu Barcelonès. (Reprint in Lamuela & Murgades (1984: 239–240) and by Marquet (2002: 94–96).)

1911

Qüestions de gramàtica catalana. Barcelona: L'Avenç.

1913

Normes ortogràfiques. (Barcelona): Institut d'Estudis Catalans.

1913–1914

"Els mots àtons en el parlar de Barcelona". *Pompeu Fabra: Obres completes. Volum 3: Articles erudits. Gramàtiques francesa i anglesa*, Mir, Jordi; Solà, Joan (eds.), 2006, 229–248. Barcelona: Proa.

1917

Diccionari ortogràfic. [Barcelona]: Institut d'Estudis Catalans.

1918

Gramàtica catalana. Barcelona: Institut d'Estudis Catalans, 1995. (Biblioteca Filològica; XII.) (2nd reprint of the 7th edition, 1933.)

Gramàtica catalana: curs mitjà. Pompeu Fabra: Obres completes. Volum 2: Sil·labari. Gramàtiques de 1918 (curs mitjà), 1928, 1929, 1941. Cursos orals. Mir, Jordi; Solà, Joan (eds.), 2006, 223–327. Barcelona: Proa. (Reprint of the 5th. edition, 1935.)

*"La tasca dels escriptors valencians i balears". *Nostra Parla*, ?, ?. (Reprint in Vallverdú (1980: 147–148).)

1919

"L'unitat llinguistica de Balears, Catalunya, Rosselló i València". *Butlletí de Nostra Parla (Secció catalana)*, no. ? (july–august), 9–10.

Gramàtica francesa. Pompeu Fabra: Obres completes. Volum 3: Articles erudits. Gramàtiques francesa i anglesa, Mir, Jordi; Solà, Joan (eds.), 2006, 339–640. Barcelona: Proa.

1919–1928

*Converses filològiques.[65] Rafel i Fontanals, Joaquim (ed.). 1983. *Converses filològiques I. Edició crítica a cura de Joaquim Rafel i Fontanals* and Rafel i Fontanals, Joaquim (ed.). 1984. *Converses filològiques II. Edició crítica a cura de Joaquim Rafel i Fontanals* Barcelona: Edhasa.

*SRomUB: "Fabra / Converses filològiques" (without catalogue details). (Box with this label held in the library of the Seminari de Romàniques of the University of Barcelona. The contents comprise 881 sheets, loosely assembled and undated, numbered, with individual Conversations cut and pasted or in typescript. Another folder, ascribed to Artur Martorell, contains 263 Conversations, numbered in pencil, cut and pasted, not in the original chronological order. These were probably publishers' copy for the Barcino edition of the *Converses filològiques*.)

1923

"Advertiment". *Gramàtica catalana. Curs mitjà*. 2nd ed. Barcelona: Associació Protectora de l'Ensenyança Catalana. (Reprint in Lamuela & Murgades, 1984: 186–187).

1924

*L'obra de depuració del català. (Reprint in Vallverdú (1980: 149–165).)

---

65. Only a selection of these articles is given in translation in the present volume. Not all of them are currently available in book form. A complete critical edition is at present in preparation to appear in Mir/Solà (2005–).

Gramàtica anglesa. Pompeu Fabra: Obres completes. Volum 3: Articles erudits. Gramàtiques francesa i anglesa, Mir, Jordi; Solà, Joan (eds.), 2006, 665–983. Barcelona: Proa.

1926

*"Conversa amb Pompeu Fabra". *Revista de Catalunya*, no. 23(?) (May), 485–494.

"La coordinació i la subordinació en els documents de la cancilleria catalana durant el segle XIVè". *Pompeu Fabra: Obres completes. Volum 3: Articles erudits. Gramàtiques francesa i anglesa*, Mir, Jordi; Solà, Joan (eds.), 2006, 257–288. Barcelona: Proa.

1927

*De la depuració de la llengua literària. (Reprint in Vallverdú (1980: 167–176).)

1930

"El mot *qui*". *Mirador,* no. 53 (30/1), 5.

1932

Diccionari general de la llengua catalana. Barcelona: Llibreria Catalònia. (Reprint in Mir, Jordi; Solà, Joan (eds.). 2007. *Pompeu Fabra: Obres completes. Volum 5: Diccionari general de la llengua catalana*. Barcelona: Proa.

1933

"El català a l'escola primària". Manuscript 2804 of the Biblioteca de Catalunya.

1933–1934

Galtés i Torres, Pere. 1988. *Recull de les lliçons del curs de català superior 1933–1934 pel mestre En Pompeu Fabra*. Barcelona: Impremta Guinart.

1934

*"Desviacions en els conceptes de llengua i Pàtria". *Oc,* 16–17 (January–April), 76–80. (Reprint in Lamuela & Murgades (1984: pp. 283–289).)

*"Discurs del President". *Jocs Florals de Barcelona.* (no publication details), 19–29. (Reprint in Lamuela & Murgades (1984: pp. 199–206).)

1934–1935

Miravitlles, Joan. 1971. *Apunts taquigràfics del Curs superior de català (1934–1935) professat per Pompeu Fabra a la Universitat Autònoma de Barcelona*. Andorra la Vella: EROSA. (Reprint in Mir, Jordi; Solà, Joan (eds.). 2006. *Pompeu Fabra: Obres completes. Volum 2: Sil·labari. Gramàtiques de 1918 (curs mitjà), 1928, 1929, 1941. Cursos orals*. Barcelona: Proa, 813–972.)

1935

"Escola Normal de la Generalitat de Catalunya. Escola d'estiu del 1935. Conferència d'en Pompeu Fabra. 2 de setembre. Tema: Llengua Catalana". (Reprint in Marcet/Solà (1998: 194).)

1936–1937

Curs superior de català professat pel mestre Pompeu Fabra a la Universitat Autònoma de Barcelona. (Typewritten notes taken by Anna Pi i Sousa, with manuscript corrections by Joan Coromines and an unfinished index prepared by Gabriel Ferrater. Manuscript 2372, Biblioteca de Catalunya.)

1937

Les principals faltes de gramàtica. 2nd. ed. Barcelona: Barcino.

1942

Letter dated 15/6. Manent/Manent (1998).

1946

Gramàtica catalana. París: Edicions de Cultura Catalana.

1956

Gramàtica catalana. 19th ed. Barcelona: Teide, 2007.

3.9.2 Texts by Pompeu Fabra in Spanish

1891

Ensayo de catalán moderno. Pompeu Fabra: Obres completes. Volum 1: Gramà-tiques de 1891, 1898, 1912, Mir, Jordi; Solà, Joan (eds.), 2005, 205–329. Barcelona: Proa.

1892

"Sobre la reforma ortográfica". La Vanguardia (22/3), 4. (Reprint in Lamuela & Murgades (1984:164–169).)

1912

Gramática de la lengua catalana. Pompeu Fabra: Obres completes. Volum 1: Gramàtiques de 1891, 1898, 1912, Mir, Jordi; Solà, Joan (eds.). 2005, 441–946. Barcelona: Proa.

1923?

"El catalán y sus análogos". *Enciclopedia universal ilustrada Espasa-Calpe,* vol. XXI, 444–450. Reprint in Ferrer/Gómez-Ten (2007:27–37).

1929

Compendio de gramática catalana. Pompeu Fabra: Obres completes. Volum 2: Sil·labari. Gramàtiques de 1918 (curs mitjà), 1928, 1929, 1941. Cursos orals, Mir, Jordi; Solà, Joan (eds.), 2006, 431–516. Barcelona: Proa.

3.9.3 Texts by Pompeu Fabra in French

1897

"Études de phonologie catalane". *Pompeu Fabra: Obres completes. Volum 3: Arti-cles erudits. Gramàtiques francesa i anglesa,* Mir, Jordi; Solà, Joan (eds.), 2006, 55–84. Barcelona: Proa.

1905

"Remarques sur la conjugaison catalane". *Pompeu Fabra: Obres completes. Volum 3: Articles erudits. Gramàtiques francesa i anglesa*, Mir, Jordi; Solà, Joan (eds.), 2006, 95–104. Barcelona: Proa.

1906

"Les *e* toniques du catalan". *Pompeu Fabra: Obres completes. Volum 3: Articles erudits. Gramàtiques francesa i anglesa*, Mir, Jordi; Solà, Joan (eds.), 2006, 141–158. Barcelona: Proa.

1907

"Le Catalan dans la grammaire des langues romanes de W. Meyer-Lübke et dans le *Grundriss der rom. Philologie*". *Pompeu Fabra: Obres completes. Volum 3: Articles erudits. Gramàtiques francesa i anglesa*, Mir, Jordi; Solà, Joan (eds.). 2006, 159–206. Barcelona: Proa.

1928

Abrégé de grammaire catalane. Pompeu Fabra: Obres completes. Volum 2: Sil·labari. Gramàtiques de 1918 (curs mitjà), 1928, 1929, 1941, Cursos orals, Mir, Jordi; Solà, Joan (eds.). 2006, 333–430. Barcelona: Proa.

1941

Grammaire catalane. Pompeu Fabra: Obres completes. Volum 2: Sil·labari. Gramàtiques de 1918 (curs mitjà), 1928, 1929, 1941. Cursos orals, Mir, Jordi; Solà, Joan (eds.). 2006, 517–661. Barcelona: Proa.

3.10   Basic bibliography on Pompeu Fabra's work

3.10.1   Introductory studies

3.10.1.1   *Basic bibliography on Pompeu Fabra's work in English*

Costa, Joan

2006   "Criteria for linguistic codification and completion". *ALPES EUROPA – Soziolinguistica y language planning. Atti del convegno = Ac dl convegn = Akten des Symposiums Alpes Europa, Urtijëi/Sankt Ulrich/Ortisei (12–14.12.2002)*, Dell'Aquila, Vittorio; Iannàcaro, Gabriele; Stuflesser, Mathias (ed.), 43–52. (S. l.): Regione Autonoma Trentino Alto-Adige: Autonome Region Trentino-Südtirol: istitut Cultural Ladin Majon di Fascegn: Centre d'Études Linguistiques pour l'Europe.

Universitat Pompeu Fabra

2008   *Homenatge a Pompeu Fabra: exposició bibliogràfica.* http://www.upf.edu/ expo_pompeufabra/english/ (Last consulted 21 May 2009.)

3.10.1.2 *Basic bibliography on Pompeu Fabra's work in Spanish*

Universitat Pompeu Fabra
2008   *Homenatge a Pompeu Fabra: exposició bibliogràfica.* http://www.upf.edu/
expo_pompeufabra/cast/ (Last consulted 21 May 2009.)
Torrent-Lenzen, Aina (1997). *Pompeu Fabra y la configuración del catalán moderno.* Bonn: Romanistischer Verlag. (Abhandlungen zur Sprache und Lit-
eratur; 104.)

3.10.1.3 *Basic bibliography on Pompeu Fabra's work in Catalan*

Badia i Margarit, Antoni M.
1977   "Gramàtica normativa enfront gramàtica descriptiva en català modern".
Treballs de Sociolingüística Catalana, 1, 37–54.
Costa, Joan
2005   *Norma i variació sintàctiques: la concepció de Pompeu Fabra (1891–1948).*
http://www.tdx.cesca.es/TDX-0116106-120523. ISBN: 84-689-6585-5.
Dipòsit legal: GI-1560-2005. (Published 16 January 2006.)
At press. *La norma sintàctica del català segons Pompeu Fabra.* Berlin: Peniope.
(Études linguistiques = Linguistische Studien Band; 2). ISBN 978-3-936609-
30-1.
Ginebra, Jordi; Solà, Joan
2007   *La vida i l'obra de Pompeu Fabra.* Barcelona: Teide.
Mir, Jordi; Solà, Joan (eds.).
2005–   *Pompeu Fabra. Obres completes:* Barcelona Enciclopèdia Catalana. (Volumes 1–3 and 5 published as at November 2008.)
Solà, Joan
2006   *Pompeu Fabra i Poch.* http://www.iec.cat/gc/digitalAssets/6275_PFabra.
pdf. (Last consulted 21 May 2009.)
Universitat Pompeu Fabra
2008   *Homenatge a Pompeu Fabra: exposició bibliogràfica.* http://www.upf.edu/
homenatge_pompeu/ (Last consulted 21 May 2009.)
Vallverdú, Francesc (ed.)
1980   *Pompeu Fabra. La llengua catalana i la seva normalització.* Barcelona: Edicions 62. (Les Millors Obres de la Literatura Catalana; 28.)

3.10.2   Works consulted

Balcells, Albert
1996   *Catalan nationalism, Past and Present.* London: Macmillan.

Badia, Alfred
1998   Mir, Jordi. *Memòria de Pompeu Fabra. 50 testimonis contemporanis*, 206.
        Barcelona: Proa.
Bally, Charles
1935   *Le langage et la vie*. 3rd. ed. 1st reprint. Geneva: Droz, 1977.
Berrendonner, Alain
1982   *L'éternel grammairien*. Geneva: Peter Lang.
Bibiloni, Gabriel
1997   *Llengua estàndard i variació lingüística*. València: Eliseu Climent.
Bonet, Sebastià
1989   "Els manuals de gramàtica i la llengua normativa". *Actes de les Terceres
        Jornades d'Estudi de la Llengua Normativa. Departament de Filologia Cata-
        lana de la Universitat de Barcelona. 17 i 18 de desembre de 1987*, Martí, Joan;
        Pons, Lídia; Solà, Joan (ed.), 11–73. Barcelona: Abadia de Montserrat. (Milà
        i Fontanals; 12).
1991   *Els manuals gramaticals i la llengua normativa. Estudis de gramatografia
        catalana*. (Doctoral thesis presented in 1991 at the University of Barcelona.)
1993a   "L'*Ensayo de gramática de catalán moderno*". Fabra (1891).
1993b   II. "La *Contribució a la gramàtica de la llengua catalana*". Fabra (1898
        (1993)).
2000   "Fabra: sintaxi diferencial i interferència". *La lingüística de Pompeu Fab-
        ra*, Ginebra, Martínez Gili, Raül-David; Pradilla, Miquel Àngel (ed.), 49–80.
        Alacant: Institut Interuniversitari de Filologia Valenciana; Universitat Rovira
        i Virgili. 2 volumes.
2005   "Algunes observacions sobre la terminologia gramatical fabriana". *Pompeu
        Fabra: Obres completes. Volum 1: Gramàtiques de 1891, 1898, 1912*, Mir, Jordi;
        Solà, Joan (eds.). 2005, 164–166. Barcelona: Proa.
Castanyer, M. Teresa
2006   Introduction to Fabra's *Gramàtica francesa. Pompeu Fabra: Obres com-
        pletes. Volum 3: Articles erudits. Gramàtiques francesa i anglesa*, Mir, Jordi;
        Solà, Joan (eds.). 2006, 289–338. Barcelona: Proa.
Colón, Germà
2007   Introduction to *Diccionari general de la llengua catalana. Pompeu Fabra:
        Obres completes. Volum 5: Diccionari general de la llengua catalana*, Mir, Jordi;
        Solà, Joan (eds.), 15–40. Barcelona: Proa.
Coseriu, Eugenio
1988   *Competencia lingüística. Elementos de la teoría del hablar*. Madrid: Gredos,
        1992.

Costa, Joan
2006   *Norma i variació sintàctiques: la concepció de Pompeu Fabra (1891–1948).*
        http://www.tdx.cesca.es/TDX-0116106-120523. ISBN: 84-689-6585-5. (Doc-
        toral thesis published January 2006.)
At press.   *La norma sintàctica del català segons Pompeu Fabra.* Berlin: Peniope.
        (Études linguistiques = Linguistische Studien Band; 2). ISBN 978-3-936609-
        30-1.
Ferrater, Gabriel
1968   "Les gramàtiques de Pompeu Fabra". *Sobre el llenguatge*, 3–12. Barcelona:
        Quaderns Crema, 1990.
Ferrer, Joan; Gómez-Ten, R.
2007   "Un estudi no conegut de Pompeu Fabra". *Llengua Nacional*, 59.
Fishman, Joshua A. (ed.).
1993   *The Earliest Stage of Language Planning: The "First Congress' Phenomenon.*
        New York: Mouton de Gruyter.
Frei, H.
1929   *Grammaire des fautes.* París/Geneva: Slaktin, 1982.
Enric Gallén
2007   "Traducció, literatura i compromís en Fabra". *La figura i l'obra de Pompeu
        Fabra*, 67–85. Barcelona; Universitat Pompeu Fabra.
Ginebra, Jordi; Solà, Joan
2007   *La vida i l'obra de Pompeu Fabra.* Barcelona: Teide.
Iglésias, Narcís
2004   *Una revisió de Fabra, una crítica a la norma. L'obra lingüística de Josep
        Calveras.* Girona: CCG / Universitat de Girona.
Institut d'Estudis Catalans
2007   *Diccionari de la llengua catalana.* 2nd ed. Barcelona: Enciclopèdia Cata-
        lana; Edicions 62. Consultable on-line: *http://dlc.iec.cat/.*
Julià, Joan
2005   "Introducció general a l'època i a la lingüística catalana". *Pompeu Fabra:
        Obres completes. Volum 1: Gramàtiques de 1891, 1898, 1912*, Mir, Jordi; Solà,
        Joan (eds.). 2005, 93–156. Barcelona: Proa.
Labov, William
1983   *Modelos sociolingüísticos.* Madrid: Cátedra. Translation of *Sociolinguistic
        Patterns.* Oxford: Basil Blackwell, 1972.
Lamuela, Xavier
1995   "Criteris de codificació i de compleció lingüístiques". *Els Marges*, 53
        (setembre), 15–30.

Lamuela, Xavier; Costa, Joan

2002　Adaptation to syntax of criteria discussed by Lamuela (1995). (Manuscript.)

Lamuela, Xavier; Murgades, Josep

1984　*Teoria de la llengua literària segons Fabra*. Barcelona: Quaderns Crema.

Lloret, Maria-Rosa; Ramos, Joan-Rafael

2006　"La *Gramàtica catalana. Curs mitjà* (1918) de Pompeu Fabra", "Les gramàtiques de Pompeu Fabra destinades a un públic no català" and "Els cursos orals de Pompeu Fabra". *Pompeu Fabra: Obres completes. Volum 2: Sil·labari. Gramàtiques de 1918 (curs mitjà), 1928, 1929, 1941. Cursos orals*, Mir, Jordi; Solà, Joan (eds.), 2006, 207–220, 321–332 and 663–706. Barcelona: Proa.

Manent, Albert; Manent, Jordi (eds.)

1998　"Cartes de Pompeu Fabra a Josep Pous i Pagès, edited by Albert Manent i Segimon and Jordi Manent i Tomàs". *Els Marges*, 61 (setembre), 41–63.

Marcet, Josep; Solà, Joan

1998　"Bibliografia de Pompeu Fabra". *Homenatge a Pompeu Fabra 1868–1948. Fidelitat a la llengua nacional. Biografia. Antologia. Bibliografia*, 127–225. Barcelona: Generalitat de Catalunya; Institut d'Estudis Catalans.

Marquet, Lluís (ed.).

2002　*Fabra abans de Fabra. Correspondència amb Joaquim Casas Carbó*. Vic: Girona: Eumo; Universitat de Girona.

Martí i Castell, Joan

1993　"The First International Catalan Language Congress, Barcelona, 13–18 October, 1906". Fishman (1993), p. 47–67.

Mascaró, Joan

2006　"L'obra científica de Pompeu Fabra. Articles majors". *Pompeu Fabra: Obres completes. Volum 3: Articles erudits. Gramàtiques francesa i anglesa*, Mir, Jordi; Solà, Joan (eds.), 2006, 13–54. Barcelona: Proa.

Mir, Jordi; Solà, Joan (eds.)

2005–　*Pompeu Fabra. Obres completes*. Barcelona: Proa. (Volumes 1–3 and 5 published.)

Payrató, Lluís

1985　*La interferència lingüística. Comentaris i exemples català-castellà*. Barcelona: Curial / Abadia de Montserrat.

Pla, Josep

1984　"Pompeu Fabra (1868–1948)". *Uns homenots: Prat de la Riba – Pompeu Fabra – Joaquim Ruyra – Ramon Turró*, 61–96. Barcelona: Destino.

Rafel i Fontanals, Joaquim (ed.)

1983　*Converses filològiques I. Edició crítica a cura de Joaquim Rafel i Fontanals*. Barcelona: Edhasa.

1984   *Converses filològiques II. Edició crítica a cura de Joaquim Rafel i Fontanals* Barcelona: Edhasa.

Riba, Carles

1954   "Prefaci a la segona edició". *Diccionari general de la llengua catalana,* Pompeu Fabra, XI–XVIII. Barcelona: Edhasa.

Saragossà, Abelard

1999   "Els criteris de la norma a partir de textos de Fabra". *Bescanvi i identitat: Interculturalitat i construcció de la llengua,* Cano, M. Antònia (et al.), 201–242. Alacant: Institut Interuniversitari de Filologia valenciana / Universitat d'Alacant / Departament de Filologia Catalana / Ajuntament de la Nucia.

Segarra, Mila

1984   "Reflexions sobre la normativa sintàctica actual". *Problemàtica de la normativa del català. Actes de les Primeres Jornades d'Estudi de la Llengua Normativa,* Cabré, M. Teresa; Martí, Joan; Pons, Lídia (eds.), 13–36. Barcelona: Abadia de Montserrat.

2000   "La codificació fabriana i els altres parlars". *Simposi Pompeu Fabra: Jornades científiques de l'Institut d'Estudis Catalans,* Argenter, Joan Albert (ed.), 199–226. Barcelona: Institut d'Estudis Catalans.

Solà, Joan

1977   *Del català incorrecte al català correcte. Història dels criteris de correcció lingüística.* Barcelona: Edicions 62.

1981   "Prefaci". *Pompeu Fabra. Gramàtica catalana.* Barcelona: Aqua.

1987   *L'obra de Pompeu Fabra.* Barcelona: Teide.

1988   (Without title.) *Diccionari Aguiló: Materials lexicogràfics aplegats per Marià Aguiló i Fuster: Revisats i publicats sota la cura de Pompeu Fabra i Manuel de Montoliu,* (5). Barcelona: Alta Fulla. (Facsimile edition.)

2006   *Pompeu Fabra i Poch.* http://www.iec.cat/gc/digitalAssets/6275_PFabra. pdf. (Last consulted 21 May 2009.)

Vallverdú, Francesc (ed.)

1980   *Pompeu Fabra. La llengua catalana i la seva normalització.* Barcelona: Edicions 62. (Les Millors Obres de la Literatura Catalana; 28.)

1990   *L'ús del català: un futur controvertit.* Barcelona: Edicions 62.

Wheeler, Max

2006   Introduction to Fabra's *Gramàtica anglesa. Pompeu Fabra: Obres completes. Volum 3: Articles erudits. Gramàtiques francesa i anglesa,* Mir, Jordi; Solà, Joan (eds.), 2006, 641–664. Barcelona: Proa.

4. Presentation of the edition

4.1 The texts included in the anthology

4.1.1 On the selection of texts translated

The 59 texts included in the anthology have been selected with the primary aim of reflecting the principal ideas of Pompeu Fabra on the normalisation of the Catalan language. Not all of these published items have been translated in their entirety. This decision was taken for two reasons: on the one hand, there are some texts in which Fabra goes into fine detail and into a level of casuistry which are difficult even for the Catalan reader to follow, and which contribute nothing that is absolutely essential for understanding the main ideas he is expounding. On the other hand, he inevitably repeats his ideas in different texts: where this occurs, we have chosen for translation individual texts which best suit the objective of our anthology and, when material from these recurs in other selected pieces, such segments have been omitted. Clear indication is given of where this has been done in the translation (see §4.2.3.3).

4.1.2 List of texts translated

1. "Sobre la reforma lingüística y ortográfica" (*On Linguistic and Orthographical Reform*).
2. "Sobre diferents problemes pendents en l'actual català literari" (*On Various Unresolved Issues in Present-day Literary Catalan*).
3. "L'obra dels nostres descastellanitzants" (*Eradicating Castilian Influence: Our descastellanitzants*).
4. "Cal gramàtica als escriptors" (*Writers Need Grammar*).
5. "Literats i gramàtics" (*Writers and Grammarians*).
6. "Les normes de l'Institut" (*The Norms of the Institut d'Estudis Catalans*).
7. "Castellanismes de la llengua escrita" (*Castilianisms in the Written Language*).
8. "Filòlegs i poetes" (*Philologists and Poets*).

9. "La tasca dels escriptors valencians i balears" (*The Task of the Valencian and Balearic Writers*)

10. "Conversa filològica" (*Philological Conversation*)   18/XI/1919

11.	”	”	”	”	12/XII/1919
12.	”	”	”	”	7/I/1920
13.	”	”	”	”	15/V/1920 (1st para.)
14.	”	”	”	”	25/V/1920
15.	”	”	”	”	10/VIII/1920
16.	”	”	”	”	30/VIII/1920 (1st para.)
17.	”	”	”	”	9/X/1920
18.	”	”	”	”	3/XI/1920
19.	”	”	”	”	13/XII/1922
20.	”	”	”	”	30/XII/1922
21.	”	”	”	”	10/II/1923
22.	”	”	”	”	24/III/1923 (1st para.)
23.	”	”	”	”	25/III/1923 (1st para.)
24.	”	”	”	”	1/IV/1923
25.	”	”	”	”	13/IV/1923
26.	”	”	”	”	14/IV/1923
27.	”	”	”	”	16/IV/1923
28.	”	”	”	”	24/IV/1923 (2nd para.)
29.	”	”	”	”	5/V/1923 (2nd para.)
30.	”	”	”	”	13/V/1923
31.	”	”	”	”	19/V/1923
32.	”	”	”	”	10/VI/1923
33.	”	”	”	”	17/VI/1923 (2nd para.)
34.	”	”	”	”	13/XII/1923
35.	”	”	”	”	16/I/1924 (1st para.)
36.	”	”	”	”	26/I/1924 (1st para.)
37.	”	”	”	”	30/I/1924 (1st para.)
38.	”	”	”	”	2/II/1924 (1st para.)
39.	”	”	”	”	5/II/1924 (1st para.)
40.	”	”	”	”	15/II/1924 (1st para.)
41.	”	”	”	”	26/III/1924 (1st para.)
42.	”	”	”	”	4/V/1924 (1st para.)
43.	”	”	”	”	10/VII/1924 (1st para.)
44.	”	”	”	”	13/VII/1924
45.	”	”	”	”	5/VIII/1924
46.	”	”	”	”	26/VIII/1924
47.	”	”	”	”	10/IX/1924

48.   ”   ”   ”   ”   13/IX/1924
49. "L'obra de depuració del català" (*The Task of Purifying Catalan*)
50. "Conversa amb Pompeu Fabra" (*A Conversation with Pompeu Fabra*)
51. "Conversa filològica" (*Philological Conversation*)   17/VI/1926
52.   ”   ”   ”   ”   12/IX/1926
53.   ”   ”   ”   ”   17/VI/1927
54.   ”   ”   ”   ”   12/VI/1928
55. "De la depuració de la llengua literària" (*On the Purification of the Literary Language*).
56. "La normalització de la gramàtica" (*The Normalisation of Grammar*).
57. Pròleg al *Diccionari general de la llengua catalana* (Prologue to *Diccionari general de la llengua catalana* [1932]).
58. «Desviacions en els conceptes de llengua i Pàtria» (*Deviations in the Concepts of Language and Homeland*).
59. «Discurs del President» (*Presidential Address to the Barcelona Jocs Florals*)

4.2   About the translation

4.2.1 Translation strategies

The sentence structure of Fabra's prose has quite frequently been modified in the translation process. For example: he often used strings of short propositions separated by colons or semi-colons; this feature of Fabra's style has been adjusted; the main consequences are punctuation changes and expedients to indicate connections between ideas. On the other hand, the complexity of a few passages has demanded the splitting and redistribution of sentences. Some long paragraphs in the original have been divided into shorter ones.

Fabra's motives were "scientific" and didactic; he was also concerned to eliminate any possibility of ambiguity; his writing, thus, shows little cosmetic effort to avoid repetition. The translated versions of his texts reflect, partly, this characteristic of the prose, while some repetitions have been eliminated in order to facilitate reading.

The recognised translation procedure of *explicitation* has been systematically followed in order to incorporate into the English versions certain contextual and cultural information that would be taken for granted in a Catalan reader. This policy has been adopted on account of the denotative character of the original texts, and also in order to avoid cluttering the translation with an excess of square brackets containing clarifications (see below, §4.2.2.1 and §4.2.3.3). For example:

the insertion without square brackets of the terms "palatal" and "palatalised" in the following segment,

> ...palatal *l* as in Castilian, *ll*, and yet we pronounce as double *ll* a good number of words like *collegi* and *carretella* which ought to be written *col-legi* and *carretel-la*, as the spelling here represents a sound distinct from palatalised *ll*.

Fabra made scant use of abbreviations formed with initial capital letters. The editor and the translator have applied discretion in resorting to these, in order to preserve agility in the English versions, in line with the following principle. The first appearance of the item in question is given a functional translation, followed by square brackets containing the original Catalan title or term and its standard abbreviation, as in, for example, "Institute of Catalan Studies [Institut d'Estudis Catalans; IEC]". The abbreviation with capital letters is regularly used in subsequent appearances. A list of recurrent abbreviations is supplied in §4.2.4.

4.2.2 Contextual information in the translation

4.2.2.1 *General remarks*

A guiding principle of the translation is that the reader will be aware at all times of what material belongs to Fabra's exposition in the original and what are supplementary interventions made by the translator for the sake of clarity. Except where simple explicitation is involved (§4.2.1, above), all necessary interventions made by the editor or the translator are indicated by square brackets (§4.2.3.3).

Relevant information for interpretation of the original is supplied within each individual text in the anthology, treated as though it were the first one to be encountered by the reader. However, the functional translations of certain basic concepts are clarified where necessary (in the text or in footnotes: §4.2.2.2) at their first appearance, either in the introductory study or in Fabra's writings. Subsequent appearances of such terms can clarified by use of the Index of names and concepts, where bold type indicates the main explanatory reference for a particular item.

When comprehension of a text seems to call for it, discretion has occasionally been applied in supplying brief summaries of material in the original not given in translation. The most substantial instances of this, indicated by square brackets, are to be found in "The Norms of the Institut d'Estudis Catalans" (pp. 139–140). This procedure is consistent with what is explained above and also in §4.2.2.3, below.

The items most reiterated throughout the whole corpus of Fabra's writings are certain key words and concepts related to the context and objectives of his work. One such is *tasca* (= task, work). Again, for ease of reading the translations, repetitions are not systematically reproduced, and synonymous equivalents are resorted to judiciously. Cases in point are: *depuració*, not always rendered literally as "purification", and *innovació*, often used by Fabra to mean an old word or form restored to the modern language. Attention is paid in our Introduction to the connotations of other frequently used terms like *redreçament*, or Decadence, and the Renaixença (frequently paraphrased as "the nineteenth-century [linguistic and cultural] revival movement"). Italics are not used for Renaixença or for some other key words reproduced in Catalan in the translations. *Institute of Catalan Studies* is generally the form given for Institut d'Estudis Catalans (IEC).

As with examples mentioned in the previous paragraph, a number of key phenomena and concepts in Fabra's writing are referred to in our introductory study (§3) according to solutions applied in translation of the original texts. Another representative instance of this is our treatment of the concept of "Greater Catalonia" or *Països Catalans*, as discussed in the preliminary pages and as it occurs in the texts "On various unresolved issues in present-day literary Catalan" and "Deviations in the concepts of language and homeland". These cultural and contextual lexical units (referring to publications, movements, events, institutions, etc.) are generally dealt with, in the translations of Fabra's writings, as follows: on their first appearance in a given text, they are rendered with a literal or functional translation, followed in square brackets by what appears in the original, thus enabling the reader to become familiarised with this form. Subsequent use of the Catalan form alone should thus be readily understandable. The first mention is also, usually, where any necessary complementary information about a concept is supplied.

4.2.2.2 *Footnotes*

Where Fabra refers to a work in a general or a generic way, without bibliographical detail, the exact title of the work in question is given in a footnote. So, for example, reference in the original to "Bofarull and Blanch in their 1867 grammar" is complemented in a note giving details of their *Gramática de la lengua catalana*; so to for a list of dictionaries given with abbreviated references by Fabra himself, where a note is supplied providing the full title and details of each one.

Where Fabra introduces a local toponym, this is explained in a footnote if proper comprehension of the text calls for it. This is the case with the historico-cultural connotations of the Empordà region to which Fabra alludes in "The task of purifying Catalan". For individual people, mentioned either in the introductory texts or in Fabra's own, these are presented, at the first mention, with the family name preceded by the given name. Subsequent references to the same figure are with the family name only. This system is applied to principal names appearing in each text, regardless of whether the same name has already appeared in a previous one. This has meant that baptismal names have been introduced into texts which do not give them in the original. The first reference to an individual about whom the reader, unfamiliar with the Catalan context, will probably know nothing is amplified with essential biographical information, usually in a footnote, occasionally in the text: basically a brief indication of that person's relevance to Fabra's interests. The basic format for the treatment of this kind of information is illustrated, for example, by the reference in the text to Bulbena ("On various unresolved issues..."), amplified in the footnote which reads "Antoni Bulbena i Tusell (1854–1946): philologist. He opposed many of Fabra's proposals for the modernisation of Catalan." More complete bio-bibliographical details are supplied for major historical, intellectual and artistic figures, especially where this is essential to understanding Fabra's argument and its setting.

It is to be remarked that Fabra himself made very sparing use of footnotes. Where a note is given in the original text, this is indicated by the use of an asterisk. An asterisk is also used, after the title of each individual pieces, to indicate publication details of the original and also, where relevant, the edition used as the source for translation.

Thus all the numbered footnotes in this volume are provided by the translator or the editor. The system for giving bio-bibliographical details, as described above, is complemented by information provided for references made to events, cultural movements, institutions, etc., essential backgound for understanding Fabra's work and its context. The first main appearance of the name or term in question is usually where the relevant footnote is inserted. Subsequent occurrences are referred back to the initial annotation, to facilitate recovery of necessary information. As already mentioned, the Index of names and concepts also indicates (by the use of bold type) where first main references and the corresponding notes are located.

4.2.2.3 *Information supplied within each translated text*

Preliminary to each of the of the 59 items translated, details of the original on which the English version is based are given in a footnote, referenced in each case with a single asterisk after the title: original title, abbreviated source publication, date of publication and original source language if this was Castilian. Complete source publication data are provided at §4.2.5.

Many of the illustrative examples contained in Fabra's discourse will not be easily intelligible to the non-Catalan reader. For this reason, when an English translation or gloss of these examples has seemed essential, this is given between square brackets. Where the need for this is most obvious is in examples constituted by full sentences, as for example in:

the use of the preposition *a* to introduce a personal direct object (*Veig A la Maria* instead of *Veig la Maria* [= I see Maria]), the invariable past participle in compound tenses (*He LLEGIT la carta* instead of *He LLEGIDA la carta* [= I have read the letter]) and the use of the one auxiliary verb to form these compound tenses (*HAVIA vingut* instead of *ERA vingut* [= I/he/she had come]). [...] causal use of *doncs* (*estarà malalt, DONCS no m'escriu* [= he must be ill, because he hasn't written to me])

On the other hand, there are points in his writing where Fabra can be sure that his reasoning is clear for his original readers and that examples are not required. In such cases, where their presence for the foreign reader seems indispensable, illustrative examples have been added in the translation, as in:

In order to establish a sound rule [for example, in the case of the *b*/*v* vacillation] it was necessary to study the correspondence between the Latin and the Catalan labials: Latin *p* does not always correspond to Catalan *p*, a Latin *b* does not always give rise to Catalan *b*

or

The main cases in point here are *ct, pt, bs, gn, mpt*, etc., and Catalan is more conservative than Castilian in this feature. [c.f., Cast./Cat.: *escritor*/*escriptor*, *objeto*/*objecte*, *cautivo*/*captiu*, *redentor*/*redemptor*, etc. [...]

In some cases it has been felt necessary to clarify similarly the Catalan or Castilian identity of certain lexical items, as in:

Plasso [from *plazo*] is quite obviously an embarrassing intromission from Castilian, but if we just knock off the -*o* it becomes transformed into what passes wrongly for a Catalan word [*plaç*]."

This system is also occasionally applied to elucidate the degree of correctness implied in certain examples adduced by Fabra:

This is the case when an unauthentic word like *lograr* or a misused one (*brostar* instead of *brotar*) is pointed out, or when a replacement is sought for some Castilianism or other (*permanèixer* [Cat. *romandre, restar*] or *floreixent* [Cat. *florint*]).

and to indicate where Catalan forms coincide with equivalents in Castilian (or other languages):

... words like *gràcies* or *venir* [in Spanish, *gracias* or *venir*], carefully replacing them with *mercès* and *vindre*.

Complementary information of other kinds is also sparingly supplied between square brackets, in order to facilitate understanding of Fabra's reasoning. This may involve grammatical identification of items in an example:

> ... that *mía, tua, sua* could be used for *meva, teva, seva* [posessives], but never *em, et, ens* [weak pronouns] for *me, te, nos*; that instead of *parlem, parleu, parlés* we should write *parlam, parlau, parlás*; that the subjunctive mode of first-conjugation verbs ended [not in *i* but] in *e* just as in Castilian.

Elsewhere it may be a case of introducing a piece of linguistic, comparative or explicatory information, not explicit in the original text, that makes the intended meaning clearer for a foreign reader, as in cases like:

> the Castilian distinction between *ave* [zoological genus] and *pájaro* [zoological species].
> I never wrote *ñ* [for *ny*].
> There were the supporters of [feminine] plurals in *-es*"
> ...kill off the [impersonal] verb *caldre*
> ... keeping geminate *ll* [*l·l* in the modern language]
> ... the verb *haver* used impersonally is now always accompanied by adverbial *hi*, in the language of the principality of Catalonia [*hi ha* = there is/are: cf. French *il y a*]

Finally there are a few cases where important implicit connotations in the original are parenthetically made explicit or where natural expression in English is accounted for:

> ... any important [natural] feature of the language
> ... grammarians and [modern] writers drew models for their reforms
> ... what anyone does when they want to know something: they [make an effort to] learn.

In the texts selected for the anthology Fabra did not deploy any symbolic system of phonetic transcription. At certain points in our translations, however, it has been felt necessary to make the author's meaning clear and accessible by giving transcriptions in the International Phonetic Alphabet. In order to differentiate between this Alphabet's use of square brackets and how such parentheses are employed generally in our edition, each of the relatively few phonetic transcriptions supplied is set in the text, accompanied by a numbered footnote which explains "Phonetic transcription given by the translator".

4.2.3 Conventions used in the translations

4.2.3.1 *Italics*
The original texts favour italic script where present-day English usage would prefer inverted commas, to show, as well as emphasis, sometimes quotation or ironic tone. This feature is preserved in the translations (alongside standard use of italics for all quotations in Catalan and in languages other than English). Example:

> ... about the *horrible* Catalan spoken nowadays. It would be a good idea for us to begin to concentrate on the *horrible* Catalan that is written these days.

Titles and proper names (in the broad sense) are not italicised in Catalan typography, and this feature is carried over into our English versions: thus, Institut d'Estudis Catalans, Secció Filològica, Ateneu Barcelonès, etc. The principle is then extended to apply to major cultural phenomena, for which (usually after first appearances in italicised form) normal type is used for these names too: Renaixença, Modernisme, Noucentisme, etc., while italics are used for adjectival derivations like *modernista*, *noucentista*, etc.

4.2.3.2 *Inverted commas*
The house style of double inverted commas is followed throughout, with single inverted commas used for embedded quotation marks. When it does not contradict what is said above about retention of italics as used in the source texts, the translation occasionally applies inverted commas to indicate unusual or ironic use of a term, or a word that appears in normal type in the original but which constitutes an unfamiliar neologism in English, as in "to de-Castilianise", "de-Castilianiser", etc.

4.2.3.3 *Square brackets*
As explained above, square brackets are used systematically to indicate all of the translator's interventions in the English versions (see §4.2.2.1 and §4.2.2.3). This constitutes a major functional procedure in our rendering into English of Fabra's writings, and, for convenience, we can summarise its application as follows. Square brackets appearing in the main text contain:

a. English versions of examples used by Fabra: shown thus [=]. Translations are given only when the meaning of examples is crucial to Fabra's argument.
b. Minimal explanation of grammatical function when this seems necessary; equivalences in other languages (mainly Castilian); other concise information necessary for the English reader to follow the argument of the original.

c. Indication that a segment of the original text has not been translated: shown thus [...].
d. Brief summary, occasionally, of the content of a suppressed segment, especially when Fabra makes reference to it in the translated text.
e. Phonetic transcriptions. All transcriptions in the International Phonetic Alphabet, if supplied for clarity by the translator, are incorporated in the main text, with a numbered footnote to indicate this.

4.2.4 Abbreviations

The only abbreviations used, throughout the volume, are the following:

Cast.   Castilian
Cat.   Catalan
DGLC   Diccionari General de la Llengua Catalana/General Dictionary of the Catalan Language
IEC   Institut d'Estudis Catalans/Institute of Catalan Studies

4.2.5 Sources of the texts translated

Fabra, Pompeu. 1911. *Qüestions de gramàtica catalana*. Barcelona: L'Avenç.
—. 1932. *El català literari*. Barcelona: Barcino.
—. 1919–1928. "Fabra / Converses filològiques" [without catalogue details]. [Box with this label held in the library of the Seminari de Romàniques of the University of Barcelona. The contents comprise 881 sheets, loosely assembled and undated, numbered, with individual Conversations cut and pasted or in typescript. Another folder, ascribed to Artur Martorell, contains 263 Conversations, numbered in pencil, cut and pasted, not in the original chronological order. These were probably publishers' copy for the Barcino edition of the *Converses Filològiques*.]. Fabra, Pompeu (1919–1928).
Lamuela, Xavier; Murgades, Josep. 1984. *Teoria de la llengua literària segons Fabra*. Barcelona: Quaderns Crema.
Rafel i Fontanals, Joaquim (ed.). 1983. *Converses filològiques I. Edició crítica a cura de Joaquim Rafel i Fontanals*. Barcelona: Edhasa.
Rafel i Fontanals, Joaquim (ed.). 1984. *Converses filològiques II. Edició crítica a cura de Joaquim Rafel i Fontanals*. Barcelona: Edhasa.
Vallverdú, Francesc (ed.). 1980. *Pompeu Fabra. La llengua catalana i la seva normalització*. Barcelona: Edicions 62. (Les Millors Obres de la Literatura Catalana; 28.)

Selected writings of Pompeu Fabra

[1]   On linguistic and orthographical reform*

At school I was taught, very badly, a language which I have never managed to speak well and which I shall never be able to write with any fluency. On the other hand, I was never taught either to read or to write my own language. On leaving school, I could write out dictation in Castilian while being quite unable ever to compose two lines in the language, and yet I could not write the words of the language in which I spoke. From my reading of Catalan newspapers and journals I knew the pronunciation of the groups *ny* [ɲ], *ch* [k] and *ig* [tʃ] in final position, of *tx* [tʃ][66] and of certain consonants. But, ignorant about the Catalan vowel system and also about Catalan having more silent consonants than just the silent *h* of Castilian, I was poor at reading the language, as are the majority of ordinary Catalans and quite a few Catalanist partisans. I could not even spell the words which make up the language. If I was ever going to write Catalan properly, then, I would have to study it. At every step I encountered orthographical difficulties, and I could not rely entirely on a procedure which enabled me to resolve many of these. I never wrote *ñ* [for *ny*], nor *ch* for *tx* or *ig*, and always put *h* after a final *c*, but beyond these instances I wrote Catalan with the orthographical system of the Spanish language. For example, I always wrote *caball* instead of *cavall* because *caballo* is how this word is written in Castilian. Then, analogously, I used a *v* in the adjective *immobil* [modern spelling *immòbil*], which I would write *inmóvil*, with *v*, *n* and the acute accent [ó], exactly how nowadays most of our authors

---

* "Sobre la reforma lingüística y ortográfica". *La Vanguardia* (22/III/1892), 4. Reprinted in: Lamuela & Murgades (1984: 164–169). The early date of this text explains the fact that some examples given by Fabra reflect the "unreformed' spelling of Catalan prior to the *Normes ortogràfiques*.

66. Phonetic transcriptions given by the translator.

write this word. I studied Catalan using the grammar of Antoni de Bofarull and Adolf Blanch.[67]

I learned then that in the literary language the masculine definite article should always be *lo*; that *mía, tua, sua* could be used for *meva, teva, seva* [possessives], but never *em, et, ens* [weak pronouns] for *me, te, nos*; that instead of *parlem, parleu, parlés* we should write *parlam, parlau, parlás*; that the subjunctive mode of first-conjugation verbs ended [not in *i* but] in *e* just as in Castilian, etcetera, etc. As for orthography, the comfortable procedure described above served conveniently: I could continue to write *caball* and *inmóvil*.

It did not take me long to realise that the rules given by Bofarull and Blanch were not universally followed: in books and journals I came across countless words written differently from how they appeared in the Pere Labernia [*sic*] dictionary.[68] [...] I continued for a long time to write according to Bofarull's system, the one I had learned, out of routine. I did not understand how anyone could write an infinitive without final *r*, or words like *cavall* (Spanish, *caballo*; Latin *caballus*) with a *v*.

And I wondered why some people wrote *les, cases*, instead of *las, casas*, giving plural forms in *es* for nouns ending in *a* in the singular. Nor was there any uniformity in morphology. Everybody conjugated verbs as they saw fit: you could find [imperfect subjunctive] *parlassen* or *parlessen* and *parlessin*; [present indicative] *parlam* and *parlem*; [present subjunctive] *parle, dorma, servesca* and *parli, dormi, serveixi*. And in verb conjugation I saw many writers using forms common in the spoken language, the living forms that I had used before studying the grammar of Bofarull and Blanch. So, almost without being aware of doing it, in a natural way, I gave up following their rules and I myself went back to writing those forms which I had stopped using only because I believed them to be excluded from the literary language. Why had these grammarians excluded them? Had they got their conjugation system right? Had they been right about everything else? I read through their grammar thoroughly and carefully, and my disillusionment was complete.

---

67. Antoni de Bofarull (1821–1892): historian and author. He was influential in the restoration of the Jocs Florals (1859) and produced the first Romantic novel in Catalan. Adolf Blanch (1832–1887): poet, grammarian, historian and journalist. Together they produced in 1867 a *Gramática de la lengua catalana* (written in Spanish) which remained influential until the early years of the twentieth century.

68. Labernia is the Castilian spelling of the first surname of Pere Labèrnia i Esteller (1802–1860): philologist and lexicographer who published a two-volume dictionary of Catalan in 1839–1840. The work was expanded by a group of contributors after his death, entitled *Diccionari de la llengua catalana ab la correspondencia castellana i llatina* (Dictionary of the Catalan Language with Castilian and Latin correspondences: 1864–1865 and 1888).

The authors themselves condemned their own scheme of conjugation in a "rule" which went as follows: "In the event of coming across a word which according to the rule would appear strange or antiquated, one should always prefer – as can be well determined by individual good sense – the form which is in common use, even when this contravenes the rule itself." Until this moment I had written exclusively following Bofarull's orthographic system. Henceforth I could no longer keep rejecting one spelling or another merely because it did not conform to the prescriptions of this grammarian, now no longer for me an indisputable authority. I wondered if those who wrote *cavall* with a *v* and certain infinitives like *veure, prendre*, etc., without a final *r* might not be right. And at the same time as Bofarull's authority was waning for me, the Castilian influence became weaker as I studied other Romance languages. In French there were a vast number of infinitives not ending in *r*; *caballo* was *cheval* in French, *cavallo* in Italian; both French and Portuguese use the *ç* cedilla… Castilian could no longer serve me as a guide in the future.

There was no orthographical system that everyone followed, so in each case of doubt over the spelling of a word a decision had to be taken in favour of one form or another: one could not alternate between *creure* and *créure*, *mateix* and *meteix*, *casas* and *cases*. [...] In order to establish a sound rule [for example, in the case of the *b*/*v* vacillation] it was necessary to study the correspondence between the Latin and the Catalan labials: Latin *p* does not always correspond to Catalan *p*, a Latin *b* does not always give rise to Catalan *b*. Only by dint of serious study would it perhaps be possible for rules of spelling to be established that could be admitted by all. Was not study a way of working towards orthographical uniformity? It appears not, according to some. This uniformity would only be achieved, they alleged, through a kind of casting of votes among the principal writers, putting up for resolution questions like "How should *meteix* be spelled?" There could be no other way to do it: study is not a means to achieving the desired uniformity: on the contrary, [it was alleged,] by studying one comes to see that much of what is generally accepted, much where there is precisely uniformity, is bad and unacceptable; and this leads to the proposal of reforms like that put forward by *L'Avenç*, radical reforms that are quite counterproductive, when everything could be sorted out by a simple casting of votes. This is basically what we were told quite recently by a well-known Catalan author. The truth is that through study it would very soon become apparent that modern Catalan orthography follows too slavishly the Castilian model. We have the same system of syllable stress as the Castilian language; we use written accents in the same way as do the Castilians, in exactly the same cases. When the Spanish Academy introduces a modification to the system, this is forthwith introduced into Catalan: so the Academia de Buenas

Letras[69] supresses the grave accent; [like the Spaniards] we put an accent on the preposition *a*, despite it being unstressed. We represent [palatal] *l* as in Castilian, *ll*, and yet we pronounce as double *ll* a good number of words like *collegi* and *carretella* which ought to be written *col·legi* and *carretel·la*, as the spelling here represents a sound distinct from [palatalised] *ll*. In Catalan we pronounce *immortal*, *commoure*, etc., with a double *m* sound. In Latin these words have double *m* and it was natural to write them in this way, as happens in French, Italian, Portuguese and even English. Yet most of our authors write them with *nm*, as in Castilian, following Bofarull's rule which states "The letter *m* cannot be doubled; only when demanded by pronunciation (*sic*), an *n* will precede it, e.g. *inmens*, *inmóvil*".

This is the state our spelling system is in: it is the Castilian one with a handful of inopportune conventions and a system for use of the apostrophe which, by marking impossible elisions, makes it awkward to read our language. And still some people believe that all that needs to be done for the good of our literature is "to reach an agreement on how to spell *les* or *las*, *vaig* or *vatx*, *meteix* or *mateix*, *baixo* or *baxo* and other such trifles where there are discrepancies"! As if the only disagreements we have are about matters of orthography. Are there not major differences between us on something more important? Are we all in agreement about the essentials of modern literary Catalan? Looking just at verb conjugation, we observe discrepancies like those I have pointed out above: some people take to be extremely vulgar forms admired by others as literary. Just as for orthography it was necessary to decide upon one spelling or another, so too here decisions had to be taken between one particular form or another. Morphology joined orthography as an object of my studies, as would syntax shortly afterwards.

My researches in morphology and syntax also gave extremely negative results. This was because a true understanding of Catalan made it impossible to continue banishing from the written language many forms and constructions deemed by all our writers to be vulgar or defective. My studies were directed from the start to producing a grammar of Catalan in Spanish, a grammar like those used to learn French, Italian, etc. It would begin with an explanation of Catalan pronunciation and would give a presentation of its grammatical system, omitting explanation of syntactical rules common to both languages and any definitions that were out of place in a comparative grammar. I produced a grammar of the literary Catalan in most general use. Once I had completed it, though, I was satisfied with only two

---

69. Known in Catalan as the Reial Acadèmia de Bones Lletres de Barcelona. See Introductory study, §2.5.3, p. 9. Founded in 1729, in the spirit of the Enlightenment, the Academy cultivated historical and literary studies. Its conservative tendencies have been generally outweighed by its function as a forum for affirmation of Catalan cultural identity from the nineteenth century onwards.

of its chapters, the one on nouns and the one on the verb, in which I kept strictly to how the spoken language behaves. French grammars taught me the language spoken by the French, whereas my grammar did not fully do this for Catalan. So gradually I substituted arbitrary rules with ones based on the spoken language throughout, rejecting none of its forms or particles, to end up with a grammatical description of this modality. A digest is contained in my *Ensayo de Gramática de Catalán Moderno*, a work whose principal objective is exposition of the grammatical system of Eastern Catalan. Understanding the structures of this particular dialect, how could I possibly prefer, to the language spoken by the majority of Catalans, that *academic* Catalan so much in use, some of whose forms are simply unpronounceable?

I have tried to explain how I came to be in favour of a linguistic and orthographical reform. Disagreement among our authors led me to study our language and its orthography, with the ambition of adopting the best system and of contributing to the unification that was so to be desired. Careful investigation in these areas made me realise how defective is our spelling system, and yet how regular is the grammatical system of our particular dialect. For this reason I advocate orthographical reform, believing that modern literary Catalan can be nothing other than the spoken language, once its vocabulary and syntax have been thoroughly expurgated.

Some people cannot see that discrepancies go deeper than how certain words should be spelled and they are unwilling to recognise that some features on which there is no discrepancy are in fact defective and unacceptable, like the use of certain orthographical conventions imported from Castilian. Such people believe that the most positive and patriotic behaviour is to reach agreement on whether to write *les* or *las*, *meteix* or *mateix*. For me and for my companions in *L'Avenç*, it is more positive and much more patriotic not to spurn the language which we use in everyday speech, and to study it with affection; to try to disclose the integral regularity of its grammatical system; to prevent substitution of its forms, based on coherent and characteristic norms, by others which are archaic, some of them unpronounceable; to strive to purify and enrich its vocabulary and syntax, to provide it with a spelling system of its own, less indebted to Castilian, more in harmony with the essential personality of our language.

[2]   On various unresolved issues in present-day literary Catalan*

Everyone is well aware that there are very few questions of orthography, morphology or syntax upon which our writers are in complete agreement.

When the nineteenth-century literary revival [Renaixença] began, spoken Catalan displayed too many damaging effects of Castilian influence for it to be integrally adoptable as a written idiom. Thus there began immediately the task of cleansing and polishing it, with the object of replacing words and constructions deemed to be unauthentic with alternatives culled from the language of our early classics or from rural varieties of the spoken language. It was necessary moreover to stabilise the use of many individual letters, of written accents and of the apostrophe. The task undertaken was huge and difficult. It entailed the sorting out of innumerable issues, deciding in every case between different solutions put forward. As there was no unanimously acknowledged authority, all kinds of divergences inevitably emerged.

The number of these divergences has been steadily increasing as new questions have arisen. Only a few of the earliest issues, like that of the feminine plural forms, have been definitively resolved, when at last it proved possible to raise the matter and to discuss it reasonably, after passions subsided among those who created difficulties. However, the vast majority of the big issues that have been continually arising are still today in a state comparable to that of the famous question of [feminine plural forms] -*as* versus -*es* thirty years ago. And they are likely to be without a generally accepted solution for quite some time.

The present study, intended as a sort of inventory of such questions, has no claims to completeness. It would, indeed, be an interminable task to examine one by one all the issues which today divide opinion and practice among our authors. Thus, while trying not to overlook any of the most important questions, we have deliberately left aside many secondary concerns, coverage of which would have made this study excessively long.

[Controversial linguistic issues]

In the first period of our renaixença, the questions which provoked most argument and a great many divergences concerned mainly orthographical and morphological topics. Some writers on these subjects proscribed use of the ç, others stood firmly against rejecting it. The latter faction, following a strictly etymologi-

---

* "Sobre diferents problemes pendents en l'actual català literari". *Anuari de l'Institut d'Estudis Catalans* (1907), pp. 352–369. Reprinted in Vallverdú (1980: 83–106).

cal criterion, favoured the spelling *caball*, *gobern*, etc., while the others defended *cavall*, *govern*, etc., based on tradition. There were the supporters of [mainly feminine] plurals in *-es*, and those who supported plurals in *-as*. Nobody could agree over which verbal desinences should be given preference. Gradually, however, the orthographical and morphological system devised by Bofarull gained ever more general acceptance. The point was reached where one might have thought that everybody would eventually accept it. And perhaps this might have been the case, had it not been for the campaign of opposition conducted by the men of *L'Avenç*.

This group took the side of Marià Aguiló,[70] supporting traditionalist criteria in orthography, against Antoni de Bofarull's fanciful interpretations of etymology, and demonstrating irrefutably the validity of plurals in *-es* (Joaquim Cases-Carbó). The "linguistic campaign" of *L'Avenç* offered two other key features: first, prestige given to the verbal desinences and certain other morphological traits of the central dialect – from the desire to make the written language more nimble – and then the tendency to simplify the spelling system by shaking out unhelpful complications, such as purely etymological diacritical marks or the *y* [instead of *i*] in diphthongs.

When *L'Avenç* ceased publication efforts continued to infiltrate the specific reforms advocated through the journal. Hostilities are declared between Bofarull's system and the system of *L'Avenç*. For some time the whole issue is reduced to this two-sided conflict, without any new questions being raised. But this period, which we can say is one of simple rallying of support on one side and the other, soon comes to an end. While the old subjects continue to be worked over, new ones come successively into the frame: suppression of the preposed apostrophe (Fabra), use of the grave accent on open *e* and *o* (Jaume Nonell),[71] use of the hyphen before contracted forms of pronouns *m*, *t*, etc. (Antoni Bulbena),[72] adoption

---

70. 1825–1897. Writer, lexicographer and bibliographer, a major figure in the nineteenth-century linguistic and literary revival of Catalan.

71. Jaume Nonell i Mas (1844–1922): author of a Catalan Grammar (1898) and other linguistic studies.

72. Antoni Bulbena i Tusell (1854–1946): philologist. He opposed many of Fabra's proposals for the modernisation of Catalan.

of new symbols for representation of palatal *l* (Melcior Cases,[73] Fabra), substitution of acute and grave accents by subscript diacritical marks (Fabra).[74]

While this is happening in the field of orthography, there continues to be discussion in the field of morphology over the old questions of subjunctive forms in *-i*, and over the desinences *-ám, -áu, -ás*, etc. At this same time, the task of purging our dictionary of Castilian influences, work in progress since the very origins of the Renaixença, an extremely important problem arises: that of determining the correct Catalan forms of Latinisms that our language had taken preformed out of Castilian. In the earliest stage words like *centro, fecundo, método, opúsculo* were accepted without scruple (Pere Labèrnia, Pau Estorch),[75] but a campaign soon began against these embarrassing Castilianisms, and some specific rules were established for creating authentic Catalan versions of such Latinisms. This then gives rise to a new series of morphological questions, the cause, in their turn, of fresh disputes and divergences.

Then finally, syntactical questions, the object of little study at first, have acquired great importance of late. Attention to these matters has been aroused particularly by the campaign led by Antoni M. Alcover in favour of eliminating from Catalan syntax the Castilian imprint, a campaign begun some seven years ago in a lecture given at the Ateneu Barcelonès, pointing out at the time three major syntactical Castilianisms, among others: the use of the preposition *a* to introduce a personal direct object (*Veig A la Maria* instead of *Veig la Maria* [= I see Maria]), the invariable past participle in compound tenses (*He LLEGIT la carta* instead of *He LLEGIDA la carta* [= I have read the letter]) and the use of the one auxiliary verb to form these compound tenses (*HAVIA vingut* instead of *ERA vingut* [= I/he/she had come]). Nowadays syntactical questions enjoy a preferential ranking, and some people are as concerned about clearing out Castilian influences from our grammar as much as from our vocabulary. We register here as important syntactical questions, as well as the three just mentioned, those affecting certain verbal tenses (*si demanés...* or *si demanava...*[= if I were to ask...]), the use of some prepositions (*a* and *en, per* and *per a*), the use of words with conjunctive functions (*qui* and *que, quin* and *qual, puix* and *doncs*), negative particles (*mai no*

---

73. Melcior Cases i Rubiol (dates of birth and death not known): author of a study (1903) on palatal and double *l* in Catalan, translator from French and contributor to several journals. Enquiries among colleagues have failed to produce more detail about this figure.

74. This radical proposal (expounded in Fabra's work before 1912) was abandoned because of practical difficulties and because it ran counter to conventions of accentuation shared by the other Romance languages.

75. Pau Estorch i Siqués (1805–1870): Romantic poet and amateur philologist, the author of a treatise (1852) on poetics and rhyme and also of a Catalan Grammar (1857).

ve and *mai ve, no* and *no... pas*), the correct order of collocation of weak object pronouns (Alcover), the neuter article (Bulbena), the suppression of unstressed prepositions before the conjunction *que* (Fabra).

[Orthography]

From the beginnings of the Renaixença until the present moment, there has been frequent discussion of the importance to be ascribed to Latin etymology in the fixing of our orthography. The different issues in which etymology has been invoked can be divided under three headings: (1) correct spelling of two related letters like *b* and *v*, representing two phonemes originally differentiated but subsequently confused, although still kept distinct in certain major dialects, (2) correct spelling of two letters like *ç* (sometimes *c*) and *s* (sometimes *ss*), representing two phonemes originally differentiated but now identical, and (3) spelling for letters whose presence is purely etymological, like the *h* of *home*.
[...]

[Morphology]

The most important morphological questions are those relating to the conjugation of verbs. While some authors accept all the verbal desinences of the central dialect, others admit only verb-endings present in the older language, and between these two positions a whole range of intermediate systems can be found.
[...]

[Learned words]

Work on Catalanising the numerous learned words introduced into our language directly from Castilian is confronted by various problem issues, the main ones relating to post-tonic vowels, especially final *-o* and *-e*.
[...]
    Finally to be noted is a certain aversion to Latinisms on the part of those who compile dictionaries and corrective lists of corrupt vocabulary, and also, in general, on the part of the out-and-out *descastellanitzants*.[76] We have no need to put up here a defence of Latinisms: our sister languages are full of them, and it is not

---

76. Fabra regularly drew attention to confusion created by extreme "de-Castilianisers", those who were concerned exclusively with eradicating Castilianisms, real or supposed, from modern Catalan. He focuses on this issue in items 3 and 49 of the translated texts.

for us Catalans, with an impoverished and damaged vocabulary in serious need of repair, to look disdainfully on words from the mother language which have been gracefully welcomed by the French, the Spaniards, the Portuguese, the Italians and the Romanians. We can only understand the antipathy towards Latinisms if it is seen as arising from the observation that such words appear to have too close a resemblance to their counterparts in Castilian. And nowadays it seems that the priority is not exactly to remove Castilian influences from our own language but, rather, to distance Catalan as much as possible from its neighbour. One example: formation of the Latinism *elevar* (Italian *elevare*, French *élever*, Portuguese *elevar*), which, because it is guilty of being identical to Castilian *elevar*, is systematically replaced, opportunely or not, by the dyed-in-the-wool Catalan verb *enlairar*. To this obsession with Castilian we are indebted for *etat, ambent, essença, greuíssim* and innumerable other botch-jobs which infest modern-day written Catalan.

[Syntax]

[...]
A large number of the divergences that are observable in syntactical matters are due to real syntactical errors committed by some people which others quite simply avoid. These are errors which are often the product of the writer's inattention to detail (*els hi* instead of dative *els*) or of Castilian influence (pleonastic *en ell* [= in it] combined with adverbial pronoun *hi* referring to a thing, instead of *hi* alone). But they are also frequently errors committed quite deliberately in the mistaken belief that they are elegant solutions to some flaw or other, real or imaginary, in the spoken language. Examples of this are: causal use of *doncs* (*estarà malalt, DONCS no m'escriu* [= he must be ill, because he hasn't written to me]), invented to correct the Castilianism *pues*; the relative *el quin*, with which many people avoid *el qual*, felt to be too close to Castilian *el cual*; the pleonasms *en el qual HI...*, *del qual EN...*, etc.

[Conclusion]

The definitive solution to most of the morphological and syntactical questions we have examined depends on how we are to resolve a cardinal issue which has been debated on several occasions (latterly in the Congrés de la Llengua Catalana). We are talking about the relationship there should be between the literary Catalan of the future and the language as it is spoken. Should we repudiate absolutely the changes that the language has undergone, changes which have broken the unity attained in earlier times? Or should we make the literary language rest upon the spoken language, purifying and refining it, while avoiding all those adjustments which might make it appear stilted? Should we allow, as has been proposed from time to time, the existence of two languages between which there is virtually no percolation: one which is purely literary, archaic and immobilized, and the other, familiar, vulgar, condemned to perpetual degradation? Or is this dualism to be rejected, in favour of the will for the two levels of language to be so close to one another that the spoken version can infuse all its vitality into the literary one, while, at the same time, absorbing all the improvements and refinements that come into the latter?

If the first of these options is taken up, then almost all the current morphological and syntactical disputes just disappear: the old literary language provides ready-made solutions. There would be no doubt, in such a case, that the subjunctive forms in –*i* are to be rejected in favour of adopting those in -*e* and -*a*, although these are incompatible with the central dialect. Likewise, we should repudiate substitution of the desinences -*àm*, -*àu*, -*às* by -*èm*, -*èu*, -*és*, and we should adopt use of both auxiliaries *haver* and *ésser* in compound tenses. There would, then, be no problem about proscribing the ending -*o* for the first-person present indicative, or about reviving use of the demonstrative pronoun *ço*. For the indicative preterite there would be nothing to prevent adoption of the classical paradigm, nowadays completely abandoned: *temí, temist, temé, temem, temés, temeren*. And, regarding combinations of weak object pronouns, we could even allow ourselves the pleasure of separating ourselves from all the other Romance languages, by placing the accusative before the dative (*lo 'm, la 'm*, etc.).

If it is the second solution which is accepted, then all the complications re-emerge and present very great difficulties, even if the criterion is unanimously adopted of staying as close as possible to the older language. For the fact is that, in every instance, even where the superiority of the archaic solution is indisputable, we shall still have to assess the probabilities of being able to revive it. And, moreover, how would it then be possible to ensure that the literary language can faithfully reflect the dialect varieties of the spoken language? If the old language were not adopted as model, there would be only one means of achieving this last effect. It would entail adoption of one of the present-day dialects as the basis for the future literary language, and this dialect could be none other than that of the capital. Obviously, while ever there are many who believe that the language of Barcelona is the worst Catalan of all, there is little chance we will decide to give it this preference, even though it is the only candidate.

A lot of people, however, do not consider it a great disadvantage that the literary language should reflect the dialectal differences of the spoken idiom (Joan Maragall). And it is to be observed that some hold out against this precisely because they fear that the language would in this way incline towards a uniformity imposed by the growing preponderance of the Barcelona dialect (Francesc Carreras).[77] In reality, if every author were to write in *his/her own* Catalan – not in the language of the lowest strata of their region but in that of the most educated – the divergences that would appear in the literary language would perhaps not be, nowadays, as great as many people think. And one may believe, if favourable times for Catalan nationhood arrive, that these divergences would be steadily attenuated. There could come into effect a natural interpenetration between the literary language and the Catalan of the capital – not present-day Barcelonese but a quite different version of it, freed of Castilianisms, influenced by all the other dialects of our language, enriched, refined: the future tongue of the future capital of *Greater Catalonia*![78]

[3]   Eradicating Castilian influence: our *descastellanitzants**

Our language has not suffered just a single misfortune. After it was reborn as a literary language, when the work began to purge it of Castilian influence and to polish it, a new scourge beset Catalan: the philological and grammatical ignorance of many of those who cultivate it.

We pretend to free our language from the imperfections it presents due to Castilian influence, and what we do is to introduce other ones in extraordinary measure.

You will often hear people talk disparagingly about "Catalan as she is spoken", about the *horrible* Catalan spoken nowadays. It would be a good idea for us to begin to concentrate on the *horrible* Catalan that is written these days.

To "de-Castilianise" has become synonymous in our time with a distancing from Castilian, and to achieve this we frequently reject or disfigure words and constructions for the simple reason that they resemble too closely the corresponding forms in Castilian. On the other hand, we use Castilian-based forms which are quite unknown in spoken Catalan, and we think we have struck a blow for purity by simply eliminating the final -*o* of a word which is Castilian through-and-

---

77. Francesc Carreras Candi (1862–1937): lawyer, historian and politician.

78. The original text has the single word *Catalònia* (italicised). Like some other contemporary intellectuals, Fabra used this term to differentiate between Catalunya (the Principality of Catalonia) and all of the Catalan-speaking territories. Later in the twentieth century, in political discourse, the term *Països Catalans* gained currency for the global demarcation (see Kremnitz, Prologue pp. XXIX–XXX and Introductory study, §2.4, pp. 5–6).

*   "L'obra dels nostres descastellanitzants". Fabra (1911: 7–13).

through, or by putting *hi* after an *en ell*, itself a servile calque of *en él*. Sometimes, attempting to avoid a Castilianism, we commit an even worse one. At other times we flee from an imaginary Castilianism only to fall into a real one.

We believe we can see such unwelcome presences here, there and everywhere. In *edat* or *castedat*, is not the *d* attributable to Castilian influence? Does not *ambient* owe its *i* to the same source, and so too for words ending in *-ància* and *-ència*? So we must write *etat, castetat, ambent, essença, ignorança*... Meanwhile nobody stops to examine whether the word under suspicion is really attributable to Castilian influence. *Edat* is as Catalan as can be, *ambient* gets its *i* direct from Latin (*ambiens*), our old texts are full of words ending in *-ància* and *-ència*. But *edat, ambient, essència*, while not alien imports, have every appearance of being just this when compared with the words made up by our de-Castilianisers, and this is sufficient reason for them to be rejected as Castilianisms. Between two words or two forms, it is enough for one of them to bear less resemblance to its Castilian equivalent for it to be systematically preferred. I know people who, for this very reason, prefer *vindre* to *venir, valdre* to *valer, poguer* to *poder*... And while we are distracted by changing *edat* into *etat, ambient* into *ambent, gravíssim* into *greuíssim, xoc* into *topada, gràcies* into *mercès*, we overlook so very many items which are truly Castilianisms! One half of the energy consumed by this present-day phobia about Castilian, if it were properly channelled, would be enough to cleanse our language of all trace of Castilian influence. The obvious fact is that our present-day written language is at least as marred by Castilian as is the *horrible* spoken Catalan we hear all the time. Its vocabulary is, indeed, calqued upon Castilian, its construction is purely Castilian, its very spelling is subordinated to the official language [of the Spanish state]. We even copy its mistakes: take, for example, the word *automòbil*, which we write incorrectly (*automòvil*) for the simple reason that the Castilians also spell it erroneously.

If we have a poor eye for spotting Castilian imports, we have possibly an even poorer hand when it comes to emending them. When we discover a Castilianism, real or imaginary, there is a favourite quick fix. It is often just a matter of suppressing or changing some single letter or other. *Plasso* [from *plazo*] is quite obviously an embarrassing intromission from Castilian, but if we just knock off the *-o* it becomes transformed into what passes wrongly for a Catalan word [*plaç*]. [...]

As can be seen, we tinker and meddle at will: anyone at all has the right to disfigure or invent words, or to change their meaning. One grammarian recently wanted to introduce into Catalan the Castilian distinction between *ave* [zoological genus] and *pájaro* [zoological species], by making our *ocell* equivalent to only the latter of these. The single remedy against the arbitrary procedures of these *descastellanitzants* would be careful study of our classic writers. This would teach us that *ocell* (equivalent of French *oiseau*) translates *ave* as well as *pájaro*.* It would show likewise that *edat, ambient, gràcies*, are perfectly good Catalan words, and that *doncs* cannot be used always where Castilian *pues* occurs. It would teach us to construct relative clauses properly, to push aside forms like *volguer, sapiguer, sigués, vegés*, and to use in moderation the weak adverbial pronouns *hi* and *en*. But we should not be too optimistic on this score: if those who set themselves up as our defenders against Castilian intrusions do occasionally read our medieval authors, it tends to be so that they can draw our attention to some precious archaism or other that is utterly useless. [...]

Nothing is more advisable and necessary than the study of our older language. For this to be really profitable, however, we should need a grounding in philological scholarship which at the present time we are completely lacking. It is unimaginable, for example, how much benefit would come from the creation in Catalonia of a university chair of Romance languages. This would be to begin at the proper beginning. What we are doing, though, is beginning at the end, and, full of self-satisfaction, we set about writing didactic grammar books. Circumstances drive us to this, and the grammars which come out are received most enthusiastically. For my own part, every time I hear of the appearance of one of these works, I shudder to think what they must teach our young people. [...] The truth is that we are far from being able to say that our books for the teaching of Catalan are better than the worst ones available for Castilian.

[4]   **Writers need grammar****

There are still many writers who show disdain for the grammarian's task. The allegation is that this figure would oblige the writer to make use of use certain verbal forms, would prevent him from using this or that habitually recurrent construction or prohibit him, in his poetry, from recourse to the synaloephas that are enshrined in the prosodic tradition of the Jocs Florals. The writer cannot be

---

* "...cervos, lleons, *falcons, àguiles, perdius, faisans* e altres moltes bèsties e *ocells*...' [= ...deer, lions, *falcons, eagles, partridges, pheasants* and many other beasts and *birds*] (Bernat Metge); "...e un *colom* ama més son par *colom* que no fa cavall ne *altre aucell*' [= ...and a *dove* loves its fellow *dove* more than does a horse or any other *bird* among their own kind] (Ramon Llull); "...voltors, corbs e altres *aucells* de rapina' [= vultures, crows and other *birds* of prey] (*Tirant lo Blanc*). [Footnote by Fabra in the original text].

** "Cal gramàtica als escriptors". *La Revista*, I, 2 (10/VI/1915), 1–3. Reprinted in: Lamuela & Murgades (1984: 179–183).

subjected to all of this. It would kill his spontaneity, and, as has been very frequently repeated, the writer must sacrifice everything to spontaneity.[79]

But let us take a closer look. This spontaneity question, does it mean that the writer has to write the same way as he usually speaks? Does it mean that if in ordinary conversation he says *puesto* and *hasta*, he is obliged to use in his literary products these words which issue spontaneously from his lips? Oh, no, you will say: everyone knows perfectly well that these words are Castilian and that when he is writing the author will seek to replace them with Catalan words. So far, so good: but this is already a constraining corrective, a limitation of that sovereign spontaneity.

One might say without thinking *puesto* or *hasta* or *sin embargo*, but one knows really that these words are Castilian and, in writing, one avoids them. It might entail perhaps the rejection of a line of verse, the refashioning of a whole clause, but one believes that this is unavoidable. No one would nowadays dare to write those words invoking the ancient privileges of spontaneity. And, moreover, everybody would adjudge that a writer's inspiration was meagre and his creative power quite impoverished, if these faculties did not withstand the test of the unavoidable effort to purify our vocabulary. The person who has fine things to say will not fail to say them because he has to subject himself to this effort. He will say them, rather, in an even finer form. The work of art will lose nothing by it, rather will it gain.

Nowadays, when a writer knows that a word is alien, he rejects it, trying to replace it with an authentically Catalan one. If he occasionally omits to do this, it is because of an oversight, or through ignorance, and he will not attempt a defence in the name of spontaneity. This is the general behaviour as regards lexical Castilianisms, with no thought that the work of art can be at all adversely affected by it. Why then should we not behave the same as regards all the other effects of Castilian that disfigure our language? Everyone agrees that we must eject from it Castilian words. Why then should we not combat in the same way Castilian constructions, Castilian rhythms, all of the perturbations suffered by Catalan under the influence of the other language?

[...] If in Catalan publications we observe at present many more syntactical and prosodic Castilianisms than lexical ones, it is surely to be attributed to nothing other than the fact that the former are harder to detect than the latter.

---

79. Spontaneity, identified with sincerity, was a highly prized virtue in the literature of Catalan Modernisme, with its neo-Romantic ideology (see Introductory study §2.5.4, pp. 11). The movement overlapped with the cycle of cultural advances of which linguistic normalisation (with associated virtues of order and control) was a dominant feature. This explains the emphasis of Fabra's argument here.

It cannot be knowingly, in conformity with a specific theory of artistic creation, that many writers still commit these solecisms. They simply do not know that this is what they are. Otherwise one could not explain why they are perpetrated by authors who perhaps do not dare to use [good Catalan] words like *gràcies* or *venir*, carefully replacing them with *mercès* and *vindre*. Therefore it would seem that these authors ought to feel infinite gratitude to the person who might help them to uncover Castilianisms and who might indicate the way to remedy them: the grammarian. But these authors are precisely the ones who despise the job of the grammarian.

And yet this is an indispensable labour in the undertaking of recovery, reform and stabilisation of our literary language. It has suffered innumerable deformations, many of them difficult to recognise. Only meticulous examination of every word, of every form, of every construction can lead us to the disclosure of all the Castilian features that infest modern Catalan. Only profound study of the early language and perfect knowledge of the present-day dialects can provide us with the means of rectification, guiding us at the same time in the delicate work of discriminating among the multiplicity of living forms and constructions.

There are innumerable instances that one could adduce to demonstrate the usefulness of grammatical studies in the current circumstances of our language. We shall restrict ourselves to two instances, taken virtually at random.[80]

Modern Catalan presents, side by side and with identical meaning, the two constructions *amb la condició que ho facis de seguida* and *amb la condició de que ho facis de seguida* [= on condition that you do it straight away]. The second one is nowadays looked on as a Castilianism. Who could ever have suspected, at first sight, that such a common construction, the one perhaps preferred by our nineteenth-century writers, could be attributed as well, just like *puesto* or *sin embargo*, to the perturbing action of Castilian? How did this come to be understood? Studying a chapter dealing with complementisation in the comparative grammar of neo-Latin languages, it was noticed that Castilian differed from French, Italian and Romanian in that it admitted the preposition *de* before the conjunction *que*. Knowledge of this fact alone created doubt about the legitimacy of the second of the two Catalan constructions, identical to a *characteristic* construction of Castilian. Then the following question was posed: how did our ancient writers deal with complement clauses? And then these writers were read with special attention being paid to this aspect of grammar. And it became convincingly clear that they always, without exception, introduced the complement clause by means of the conjunction *que* standing alone: "...*ells li liuraríen la vida ab la condició* **que**

---

80. Only the first of the two examples mentioned by Fabra is given in translation. The second one concerns a detailed point of verbal morphology, explained in historical terms.

aquells qui anar-se'n volrìen se n'anassen la on se volguessen" [= ...they would spare his life on condition that those who wished to depart could go where-ever they wished] (Chronicle of Pere III); *"...tramés la coloma, qui aportá per senyal un ram d'olivera en significança* **que** *la mar era baixada"* [= ... the dove was released, and it carried as a token a twig from an olive tree signifying that the tide had gone down] (Ramon Llull); *"E lo Emperador mostrava tenir gran desig* **que** *lo seu capital fos en lo camp"* [= And the Emperor showed his strong desire that his worth should be demonstrated on the battle-field] (*Tirant lo Blanc*); *"e donassen ocasió* **que** *fossen be coneguts en lurs costums e maneres"* [= and they provided the opportunity to be easily recognised by their habits and their behaviour] (Bernat Metge). Of the two constructions referred to, the first one was, thus, indubitably, the one to be preferred, the only correct one.

[...]

Scientific study of the evolution of Latin sounds and forms in Catalan, full understanding of the morphology of the early language, scrupulous comparison of the syntactical rules of the different Romance languages: only these things can guide us safely in the endeavour to stabilise our syllable system, our orthography, our morphology and our syntax, all of them damaged, together with our vocabulary, by the pernicious double action of a long period of literary decline and the weight of a strong Castilian influence.

Much has been achieved in the task of restoring our language to its authentic condition and its true national status. It is to be regretted, though, that the results obtained are not exploited by everyone, and that many writers continue to commit errors induced by Castilian influence which have for many years been denounced. In syntax, for example, we still encounter solecisms as serious as would be the use of lexical items like *puesto* and *sin embargo*.

An author of fifty years ago has to be read with a great indulgence towards his almost bilingual vocabulary, and towards his syntax and prosody deeply imbued with the presence of the other language. His generation encountered a Catalan which was thoroughly damaged, and recovery of our own syllabication, syntax and lexis was not going to be achieved overnight. Many things which today, after a long labour of purification, we know to be unhealthy deviations in the language were at that time considered perfectly acceptable: illustrious authors wrote quite naturally *hermós* [Cast. *hermoso*], made *suau* a monosyllable or translated *quienes* by *quins*. Nowadays none of these defects are any longer tolerable.

And yet they still occur very frequently. The fact is that there are very few writers who are ready and willing to take advantage of the discoveries and findings made by those who strive to enrich and purify our language. Certain things which have been *mathematically* demonstrated to be quite absurd can still be found at every end and turn within the majority of our publications. *Doncs* instead of *puix*, *quin* for *qual*, *el que* for *el qual*, *els demés* for *els altres*, *per a* when *per* is required, *els hi* instead of *els* alone, *aparescut* for *aparegut*, *pretenir* instead of *pretendre*: no excuse is available to the writer who nowadays goes on writing such things, as if no one had alerted that they are nonsensical. This disdain for the labours of the grammarian means that there can be a writer, with appreciable qualities in other respects, a man of letters, whose Catalan is inferior to that of the shop assistant or student with no literary pretensions. The latter, however, desiring to write adequately his own language, does what anyone does when they want to know something: they make an effort to learn.

The writer who spurns or ignores the task of the grammarian is an inadequate writer and an inadequate patriot. Instead of contributing to the endeavour of putting our language in perfect condition, he sets up obstacles in the way of this, collaborating in the perpetuation of embarrassing blemishes from which the literary language ought to have been freed long ago.

[5]   Writers and grammarians*

When they offered me the presidency of this year's Jocs Florals, the organisers explained that they had been influenced to do this through consideration of my standing as a linguist. The work of the grammarian has been so often slighted, it has been so frequently said that grammar was if anything dangerous for literary creation, that it must have surprised many people that I, as a person with no other distinction except that attaching to my grammatical studies, should have been designated to preside over this annual festival of the art of the troubadours. I too have been surprised, because this reveals the existence of a now powerful reaction against a prejudice which did untold harm to the efforts to restore definitively our literary language to its rightful condition and status. I refer to the belief that writers could and even should manage without the work of the grammarians.

Writers as grammarians

There was a quite absurd animadversion shown by men of letters towards the grammarian in the early periods of our literary Renaixença. Remember that Catalan writers, at the beginning of this revival, found themselves with a language which was impoverished, disfigured, damaged by innumerable Castilianisms, a

---

* "Literats i gramàtics". Presidential address delivered at the Jocs Florals in Lleida, 1915. Reprinted in Vallverdú (1980: 135–140).

language which they could not adopt for literary use without trying to cleanse, enrich and elevate it. And this could not be achieved without a perfect knowledge of old Catalan and of modern dialects, to guide us in the challenging task of discovering and setting straight the aberrations affecting the language. Nor could it be achieved without an exact understanding of the laws of linguistic evolution and of the history of other literary languages. Our writers, then, surely felt an urgent need for the appearance of a linguist-grammarian to come to their aid in the patriotic endeavour of rebuilding a language which, through centuries of neglect for formal use and of subjugation to Castilian, had come down to us in a sickly and impoverished state, and for which everybody's ambition was to see it restored to its rightful standing in the family of Latin languages.

From the beginning of the nineteenth-century Renaixença this need to refashion the language was felt so keenly that every individual writer became a grammarian: every one of them was concerned to banish from the language they wrote anything which looked as though it came in due to Castilian influence. They resorted either to archaic solutions, to neologisms or to rural-dialect forms, in order to regulate the choice of grammatical forms and of spellings, and in order to reshape their vocabulary. In this way, all of them, in varying degrees, and with varying degrees of effectiveness, performed the task of the grammarian. This notwithstanding, they all shared a mistrust of grammar itself, as of something dangerous, not just for literary creation but even for the health of the language itself.

We had our Manuel Milà i Fontanals,[81] and we had our Marià Aguiló. Did they exert much influence on how their contemporaries wrote? One was an illustrious philologist; the other, a tireless scrutiniser of old Catalan and of living dialects. It is obvious that not even to men of this calibre was the capacity given to carry out the total mission of restoring the language to its proper condition and standing. We do owe to them, however, eternal gratitude, since it was they who opened up and smoothed for us the challenging route which was the correct one. Nowadays, all those who labour to good effect on the purification and the stabilisation of literary Catalan, can consider themselves to be their successors. And each new step forward redounds to new honour for the two Masters. But we must ask: did these two men really see their teachings followed and their doctrines adopted? No: because every individual writer went his own way; nobody was prepared to recognise the authority of a master; everybody was a master himself;

81. (1810–1884). Philologist and writer. From 1845 professor of literature at Barcelona University. His publications on traditional Catalan poetry were very influential in the Romantic literary revival and he was himself a notable poet. He participated in the Jocs Florals and was president (1861–1878?) of the Reial Acadèmia de Bones Lletres de Barcelona, from which platforms his proposals for orthographical reform were promulgated. On Aguiló, see pp. 87 and 119.

everybody had made up, whether appropriately or erroneously, their own way of doing things. It was at this time that the deplorable dispute over [feminine plural endings in] -*as* and -*es* came about, and that the members of a certain academy were unable to reach an agreement about whether the correct word was *alfabet* or *beceroles* [each of them perfectly authentic and acceptable].[82]

Literary indiscipline

That reluctance to recognise any authority, that mistrust of work done by others, that obstinate resistance to being convinced have all diminished considerably. But we are still a long way from seeing their total disappearance among our literary practitioners. While those attitudes are weaker, they still constitute the greatest obstacle in the way of the work of clarifying and fixing literary Catalan. In innumerable issues, we still see how progress towards acceptance is much hindered for the correct solution aimed at remedying a Castilianism or any other defect in the language. And thus some major defects, having been clearly denounced, and the proper way of avoiding them having been found, continue to be committed by a large number of writers, because the solution proposed has been unfortunate enough to displease them, or perhaps because information about it has not even reached them.

In the early stages of our literary Renaixença, while writers felt the need to refashion the language, there was in this matter no authority that was generally recognised. Each one of them resolved in his own particular way the multiple problems of lexis and of grammar that kept cropping up. What they achieved was necessarily fragmentary and lacking unity, corrupted by innumerable errors. To the blemishes acquired by the language over centuries of literary decline were added other new ones, more embarrassing because they were deliberately introduced. The language was choked with stubborn archaisms and badly contrived neologisms, while it was encased in a system of metrics and of grammatical construction, Castilian in everything but name, which everyone accepted as authentic.

Orthographical anarchy

The major cause of amazement, however, is the multiformity that came to be displayed by the written language. Rare was the contentious detail that did not receive two or three different solutions, and it would have been hard to find two writers absolutely agreed upon every question. Those who supported a particular

---

82. *Beceroles*: a chart for teaching recognition and pronunciation of written letters.

approach to one problem were irreconcilably at odds regarding another one. [...] There was an infinite list of words that appeared with two, three, four and even more different spellings. In one period of time eight different ways of writing the adverb *on* have been in use all together.

On occasions attempts were made to unify the spelling system. In the early years of the Jocs Florals, Milà i Fontanals drew up a set of orthographical norms. Later, the [Reial] Acadèmia de Bones Lletres charged Josep Balari i Jovany[83] with devising a pattern for spelling. All these efforts were in vain. Everybody stayed attached to their own system, quite unwilling to sacrifice a single one of the habits they followed when writing. But that is not the whole of it. The chaos was not thought to be undesirable; on the contrary, people justified it, claiming that for everybody to write how they saw fit was something which accorded marvellously with our collective character, opposed to any kind of imposition. They argued that perhaps with time a way of unifying orthography and fixing the written language might be arrived at, but this would be a gradual process. There was no urgency; it was a matter of secondary importance, since the highly admirable masterpieces of our nineteenth-century renaissance had been produced without any such support. They were unwilling to understand that while ever Catalan was a language without a unified spelling system, without a stabilised lexis and grammar, it could not be implanted in schools, nor could it aspire to being used in official administration, and it suffered conditions of overwhelming inferiority in its competition with Castilian. At the present time, after half a century of literary revival, it is a question of elevating Catalan to its rightful status within Catalonia, with the majority of our people welcoming enthusiastically the publication of the Orthographical Norms of the Institute of Catalan Studies,[84] seen as a great forwards step in the move to stabilise our language and affirm its authentically national category. In these circumstances the survivors from the old undisciplined generations rise up against the Norms, not because they offer one particular solution or another, but simply because they are norms, and these people declare that they do not want orthographical unification and that they are unwilling to make any effort to attain it.

---

83. 1844–1904. Philologist and scholar. Professor of Greek at the University of Barcelona (1881–1901). His spelling system for Catalan (1883) was widely followed until Fabra's reforms gained general acceptance. See below (pp. 135–142).

84. See item 6 of the translated texts.

The reaction in favour of normalisation

We must feel infinitely grateful to the writers of our renaixença, to whom we are indebted for the recovery of Catalan as a literary language. But we cannot imitate them in their spirit of indiscipline, or in their disdain for grammatical studies. This is something which is being progressively understood by the new generations, as is proved by the success of the Orthographical Norms of the Institute of Catalan Studies and by the ever increasing attention paid by young writers to the grammarian's work. This person is now beginning to be seen as an indispensable collaborator in the task of setting our language back on its feet. There is a reaction against previous prejudices, and this will move us along more safely and swiftly in the work of stabilising and expurgating the written language. And when the palpable results of the linguists' spirit of discipline and cooperation are felt, then we can expect to see the decrease or the complete ending of hostility from the older cohort towards the new generations' endeavours. The lie will then be given to the belief that the said hostile attitude is due to their resentment at feeling outclassed and superseded by youth.

Obviously they have been superseded as regards the language itself. It would be sad if it had been otherwise, and they would have been the first to deplore it. This is because, with Catalan reduced to the state of decadence and disarray in which they found it, a complete restoration could not have been the work of a single generation. The task to be carried through was so vast that they, those who initiated it, could not have harboured the aspiration of bringing it to completion. We all have to resign ourselves to being overtaken by those coming along behind. The achievements of today will be added to those from yesterday, as those from tomorrow will come to be added to today's. Let us strive to ensure that the work of recovery is not held up at the point which it has reached through our efforts. Let us put our wills, rather, to ensuring that the process continues uninterrupted, until our beloved native language is completely reformed, with its lexical treasure-store rediscovered, along with its own syllabication and its own syntax, after expulsion of all the Castilian intrusions that disfigure and demean it.

[6]   The norms of the Institut d'Estudis Catalans*

Orthography in the period of Decadence

In the epoch when the other neo-Latin languages were stabilising and modernising their orthographies, Catalan was going through the period of literary decadence which continued until the mid-nineteenth century. Thus we find perpetuated in its written form at that stage a certain number of medieval conventions which imposed gross disfigurements in words of erudite origin, as, for instance, the practice of putting *y* for *i* in diphthongs that made people write *heroych, inroyt, ovoyde,* etcetera. Written Catalan, without prospects of renewal, clung on to those conventions, which were quite unsuitable for a modern language. And at the same time it was infiltrated by a host of erroneous spellings which originated in servile imitation of Castilian orthography: *e* was replaced by *a* in the plurals of words whose singular ended in *-a;* Catalan *v* was replaced by Castilian *b* in such words as *cavall, govern, cascavell,* while [vice-versa] the Catalan *b* in cases like *rebentar, baró, biga* became Castilian *v.* When the literary revival movement began, Catalan thus displayed an anachronous spelling system with innumerable blemishes from the effects of Castilian influence. This would have to be the object of a double operation of modernisation and purification, as part of the total struggle for recovery that lay ahead.

Orthographical anarchy, orthographical unification

One of the effects of the enterprise was the emergence of a prodigious diversity of orthographical systems. All of those who, since the restoration [in 1859] of the Jocs Florals, had attempted to introduce improvements to the written language as it was carried through from the period of decadence – the orthography that was defended by the likes of Antoni de Bofarull and Adolf Blanch – had aroused irate protestation from the writers of the day. Those who perceived, for example, the grave error of writing *a* instead of *e* in the plural forms of nouns ending in *-a,* proposing the restoration of *-es,* waited for years and years to see this applied, although even today we could find some ancient master in all branches of the art of the troubadours still supporting *-as.* Nonetheless, each of the viable reforms successively proposed had begun to make headway. A period of renewal begins with a background of discordance coming from Marià Aguiló, Manuel Milà i

---

* "Les normes de l'Institut". Prologue to the first edition of the *Diccionari ortogràfic* of the IEC (1917). Reprinted in Vallverdú (1980: 107–128).

Fontanals and company. And it is during this period that – with no universally recognised authority to impose appropriate innovations – there arises the state of anarchy we have all witnessed, where each author used his own way of spelling, according to whichever of the reforms he had seen fit to adopt.

The orthographical chaos reached such a pitch that many people would have preferred a voluntary return to the shrivelled and provincial written language that prevailed in the closing stages of the period of decadence. It was a state of affairs which clearly called for remedial action. But this could not be based upon a return to how things used to be: the innovations proposed by Aguiló and by those who continued his line had already made too many inroads. Remedy for the affliction had to be sought through progressive extension of the ground being gained by those reforms which comprised authentic improvement. And, indeed, as time went on, the orthographical disorder had diminished considerably, with the majority of contemporary writers coinciding in the acceptance of an ever increasing number of innovations. There were, however, still those who were disinclined to modify their own peculiar way of writing, being especially intransigent towards reforms which tended to modernise or to simplify Catalan spelling, reforms which they condemned as being contrary to tradition.

With the creation of the Institute of Catalan Studies (IEC), this corporation realised that its publications carried Catalan abroad, to be read by scholars of every country. This was attended by awareness of the strong desirability that the published material should appear with uniform spelling. Thus the Institute decided to draw up its own orthographical norms, to be followed by its members and contributors. A commission was appointed to study thoroughly the various issues to be resolved, and then to propose for each one a solution that would express a majority of favourable opinions. A set of rules would thereby be obtained and these, once sanctioned by a plenary assembly of the IEC, would be adopted for all its publications.

Policy on *a/e* and *v/b*

The first questions examined by the commission were those relating to pairs of letters which have an identical pronunciation in the central dialect but which are still differentiated in other local speech varieties, like unstressed *a* and *e*, or *b* and *v*.

On this subject what prevailed was the criterion upheld previously by Aguiló, entailing – ahead of any consideration determined by etymology, over and above the habits contracted through Castilian influence in the period of decadence – observance of the spelling in medieval texts and of the pronunciation found in those dialects which preserve the old distinctions. [...]

Words of learned origin

In second place study and discussion were focused at length on questions relating to the spelling of words borrowed from the classical languages or formed with Greek or Latin elements. One such was representation of dental and velar occlusives at the end of words, represented constantly by some writers with -*t* and -*ch*, while others wrote either -*t* and -*c* or -*d* and -*g*. The first of these systems, faithful to tradition in the matter, led us into excessive disfigurement of a large number of Latinisms and Hellenisms, originally in -*d* or -*g* and written with these final consonants in the other modern languages [i.e., erroneous preference for *àcit* over *àcid, exerc(h)* over *exerg*].[85]

If Catalan stuck in such cases to the spellings – qualified by some, not without reason, as barbarous – other than -*d*/-*g*, then ours constituted an irritating exception among the languages with a scholarly Greco-Latin vocabulary, all of which stay as close as possible to the original forms of their learned words. At the point when Catalan was entering decisively into the concert of languages of culture, when thousands of scholarly words were going to find their place therein, it was natural that the Institute should favour adoption of the system which enabled it to keep -*d* and -*g* in such Latinisms and Hellenisms [despite the fact that these final phonemes are pronounced unvoiced, as is also the case with final -*b* pronounced as -*p*: e.g., *verb, hidròfob*].

[...]

Final -*d* and -*g*; asyllabic *i*

Those who favoured acceptance of final -*d* and -*g*, as well as of asyllabic *i* [instead of *y*], did not, however, limit use of these letters to only words of erudite origin. And the Institute saw fit to imitate them in this as well. A natural consequence of the admission of final final -*d* and -*g* in learned words like *àcid* and *diftong* was that these letters should be admitted as well in words of popular origin like *sord* and *sang*, when *d* and *g* are present in their etymons (*surdus, sanguis*). This allowed a very simple rule to be established on the use of the final -*b*, -*d* and –*g*: these letters would be written in all words having *b*, *d* or *g* in the original words from which they are derived, without it being necessary to determine in

---

85. This and the following explanations given between square brackets summarise points made in detail in the original text. The translator's glosses are supplied to clarify and illustrate Fabra's argument.

every single case if the item in question is a loan-word or an endogenous one (Norm 14). [...]

[Norm 5 establishes use of *i* instead of *y* in the diphthongs *ai, ei, oi* and *ui*, and Fabra in this section justifies, historically and comparatively, restriction of *y* in the modern language to its integration in the digraph *ny*.]

Greco-Latin combinations of letters

In Catalan, as in Castilian and the other neo-Latin languages, borrowings from Latin and Greek introduce certain combinations of consonants which are not found in words of popular origin. The main cases in point here are *ct, pt, bs, gn, mpt*, etc., and Catalan is more conservative than Castilian in this feature. [c.f., Cast./Cat.: *escritor/escriptor, objeto/objecte, cautivo/captiu, redentor/redemptor*, etc. Related considerations lead Fabra here to justify use of the suspended point in *l·l*, retaining representation of the double *ll* sound of Latin, while the digraph *ll* represents palatal *l* [ʎ] as in Castilian. (Norm 7)] [...]

Other letters

Still concerning the spelling of learned words, the Institute established that for the correct spelling of the voiced and unvoiced sibilant (intervocalic *s/ss*) the guide should be not modern pronunciation, often defective, but etymology, which should always govern orthography [in this detail]. And, according to the same Norm 11, the orthography should govern pronunciation: the words *adhesió* and *centèsim*, for example, should be written with a single *s* because this is how they appear in Latin; in no way should habitual pronunciation with unvoiced *s* be allowed to justify their being spelled *adhessió, centèssim*, forms to be repudiated as erroneous. [...]

[Other details discussed in this section, in line with the above criterion, include treatment of: *c/q* before *ua, ue, ui, uo; s/z; h* (see below); *ç/s; g/j; tx/tj*.]

Intervocalic *h*

[...] It was only recently that some people, attempting to normalise use of non-etymological intervocalic *h*, used it to indicate the disappearance of an original Latin consonant, whereas others proposed its complete suppression. Those holding the first position accused the others of going against tradition, of showing thus no respect for the old spellings *rahó, plaher, agrahir*, etc., to be replaced by the modernisers with *raó*, *plaer*, a*grair*, etc. But those traditionalists failed to see that they too changed the established spelling of countless words by writing *tihó*, *fihar*, *cruhel*, etc., instead of *tió*, *fiar*, *cruel*, etc. Both systems, then, were equally guilty of changing accustomed spellings; one side was as disrespectful of *tradition* as the other. There was no doubt, though, that the position of those favouring the suppression of *h* was to be preferred, since it entailed a notable orthographical simplification. It also showed the pointlessness of indicating with *h* the dropping of a Latin consonant, a function which had in any case to be relinquished in cases like *reina* (from *regina*), *beina* (from *vagina*), *cuina* (from **cocina*), *cuidar* (from *cogitare*), *remei* (from *remedium*).

The four linguodentals

The letter *ç* had fallen into such disuse that Bofarull and Blanch, in their 1867 grammar [*Gramática de la lengua catalana*], deemed it to have been eliminated completely. Aguiló and others, however, opposing general use and practice, got it reinstated, and latterly it has been commonly accepted, although writers have shown discrepancy about the words in which it should figure. Catalan formerly used to possess, just like Castilian, four linguodentals, represented respectively by *s* [...], by *ss* or *s* [...], by *z* [...] and by *ç* or *c* [...]. The Institute readily adopted a system which, at the same time as it highlighted a characteristic feature of Catalan, greatly simplified our spelling, freeing it in fact from subservience to Castilian orthography. This is because, as is well known, the allegedly traditional system in Catalan boils down basically to representing unvoiced *s* with either *ç* or *s*, depending on whether its Castilian counterpart is *z* or *s*.

Written accents [and other conventional signs]

Also to be resolved were questions relating to written signs: accents, the dieresis, the hyphen and the apostrophe [the latter two in clitic clusters]. Regarding accents (acute and grave), the Institute restricted itself to adopting the system in most widespread use (Norm 16), leaving for later – when the present Orthographical Dictionary was to be put together – full study of the modifications called for in order for it to be better adapted to the phonological particularities of Catalan. On the other hand, the other orthographical signs were the object, on the part of the commission, of much careful inquiry, as questions were involved here concerning whose solutions there were deep divergences among writers.

[...]

Reinforced forms of pronouns

[...] In Catalan the asyllabic forms tend to eliminate the syllabic ones (it is not *no m veu* that is replaced by *no me veu*, but *me veu* which becomes *m veu*). The asyllabic forms cannot be pronounced without the support of a preceding vowel, and so unstressed *e* is heard before the consonant (*em veu*), giving the set of reinforced forms (*em, et, el*, etc.).

These are, then, products of a process of uniformisation of the weak pronouns, a process observable in all the other [Romance] languages but which in Catalan has moved in the opposite direction. The reinforced forms have spread and taken root in the spoken language almost totally eliminating the corresponding full forms (*me, lo*, etc.), to the extent that not to admit them in written Catalan would produce a serious separation between the two modes, while also disguising a characteristic feature of Catalan morphology. In Romanian the weak pronouns have undergone an analogous evolution, and that language has readily admitted its own reinforced forms (made up of the neuter vowel *î* before asyllabic *l, mi*, etc, giving *îl, îmi*, etc.) [...]

Medieval orthography

The Institute accepted, then, a large number of the innovations introduced by different authors into Catalan orthography in the early stages of the nineteenth-century literary renaissance. This accounts for the opposition that its spelling system has encountered on the part of some writers, who dub it *anti-traditional* and reproach it for not always respecting the medieval model that they themselves regard as untouchable. Contrary to what these people would believe, the Institute has taken medieval spellings very much into account, while combating systematically every distortion introduced over time by etymological and grammatical preoccupations, and especially by the imitation of Castilian. But this respect for medieval orthography had to avoid the extreme of rejecting innovations that comprised indisputable improvement in how Catalan should be written. Not a single neo-Latin language maintains its medieval orthographical system intact: every one of them has undergone the kinds of modification that have been accepted by the Institute. [...] If in the modern language some specific phonological or morphological changes had occurred that medieval spelling did not reflect, or that were incompatible with the old written forms, then it was perfectly reasonable for modifications to be made in line with the effects of evolution. This was particularly the case if the development in question constituted a characteristic trait of Catalan and therefore highlighted the language's unique personality. At the same time, we had not to allow an exaggerated respect for certain medieval spellings to make us disfigure loan-words from Latin or Greek to the extent of making them difficult to recognise properly, to distinguish, for example, whether *sòlit* was from *solidus* or *solitus*. Nor was it right for us to perpetuate stubbornly or even to systematise certain written forms that were characteristic of the manuscript tradition but are nowadays completely inappropriate. It would have been as ill-advised as resisting the implantation of innovations which, with only the slightest change to the appearance of words, make them easier to read or contribute to greater clarity in the written language.

It must be said that some of the most disputed of the IEC's orthographical norms do not contradict medieval spelling, or contradict it no more than solutions advocated by the champions of the old orthography. The form *'m* following a pause is as distant from old *me* as is the reinforced form *em*; the solution *examecsamen* (Antoni Bulbena) is as non-traditional as *eixam-examen* proposed by the Institute; no more respect is shown towards old spelling by those who use the non-etymological intervocalic *h* to represent a dropped Latin consonant than by those who suppress this feature altogether; *i* is certainly not how the copulative conjunction is represented in old Catalan, but nor is *y*, which only appears sporadically (as does *hi* also) for *e*, with *y* in this function becoming generalised only relatively late, when Catalan literature is in advanced decadence, and it constitutes yet another case of Catalan orthography moving ever closer to Castilian; *per a*, such a bone of contention, is a medieval form.

The Orthographical Norms

Detractors notwithstanding, very shortly after their publication the *Normes ortogràfiques* had been adopted by the great majority of present-day writers and Catalan-language publications, a success which was decisive in encouraging the Institute to pursue its endeavour of fixing Catalan orthography. This body had been well aware, from the very start, that its task should be not just that of compiling a set of norms. The proper scope, after all the issues had been studied and appropriate solutions adopted for each one, was to establish correct spelling, word by word, in line with the norms established. Their application was, indeed, going to present numerous difficulties: any given word could raise questions like the following – was it to be written with *b* or *v*?, with *ç* or *s*?; was it learned or popular in origin?; was it or was it not a true derivation from another particular word? The responsibility of the Institute was to resolve such difficulties, necessarily complementing the work done by the commission on spelling. This complementary function was entrusted to the IEC's Philological Section [instituted in 1911], and it would be translated into the compilation of a full orthographical word-list, to contain every Catalan word (duly indexed) in its spelled form as ordained by the Institute's *Normes ortogràfiques*.

The offices of the Philological Section have been working on this enterprise for a long time. The alphabetical list was assembled of words that make up this Dictionary, in the compilation of which Pere Labèrnia's dictionary (1864 edition) had served as basic support, with the very important lexicographical gatherings done by Aguiló and Antoni M. Alcover also being used. After this came the study of words of doubtful spelling, seeking out their origins, their histories, dialect pronunciations, all the circumstances, in short, that could lead us to knowledge of the correct written forms. This research led us frequently to reject what were habitual spellings: just as, for example, the erroneousness of *caball*, *gobern*, etc., had once been recognised, now it was seen that in many other words it was necessary to replace the *b*, brought in through imitation of Castilian, with the *v* demanded by old Catalan and by the pronunciation of Majorca and other regions where the *b/v* distinction is maintained. It may well be that some habitual forms admitted under this heading, without demonstration of their authenticity, will be shown by further research to be erroneous. In order for them to be corrected in subsequent editions of the Orthographical Dictionary, the Institute relies not only on the results of its own dialect inquiries and its scrutiny of manuscripts, but also on the suggestions made by anyone who might notice errors of any kind in the current edition.

Revision and completion of the Norms

The compiling of the Orthographical Dictionary made it necessary for the Norms to be kept under review in the progress towards completion. Having drawn up special lists of the words affected by each single Norm, it became apparent that the contents of some of them were in need of modification, in order to bring them into full accordance with the criteria that inspired them. In addition, the orthographical commission had already postponed revision of the system of written accents, along with the establishment of some supplementary rules such as the ones relating to the spelling of homonyms, to use of the preposed apostrophe, etc. A result of the work performed by the Philological Section to revise and complete the Norms has been the admission here of some emendations and additions, affecting principally the use of accents, of the dieresis, of *ç* and of final occlusives. [...]

[7]   Castilianisms in the written language*

In the written language many Castilianisms from spoken Catalan are avoided. On the other hand, however, written Catalan has its own repertoire of such defects. In writing we produce, in fact, a great number of syntactical faults rooted in Castilian which would just not occur in speech. There has arisen, then, the curious circumstance whereby, at a time when the removal of Castilian influences from our language is proceeding apace, this alien factor imposes on our writers constructions that convert their Catalan into a language syntactically even closer to Castilian than is the Catalan routinely spoken.

In the first phase of the Renaixença (and even nowadays occasionally) the fact that Castilian says *Viven en Gerona* [= They live in Girona] made us write *Viuen en Girona*, while everybody says *Viuen a Girona*. On the other hand, no one dares to write *Pujaren en aquella muntanya* [= They climbed that mountain], normal in proper Catalan, preferring *a aquella muntanya* or *an aquella muntanya*, on account of the distaste for using *en* where Castilian uses *a*. Thus we see written Catalan being infiltrated by the Castilian rule by which *en* is used to introduce indication of where something is or something happens (*Viven en Gerona. Nevó en Puigcerdà* [= It snowed in Puigcerdà]), while *a* indicates the place towards which movement is made (*Fueron a París* [= They went to Paris]), a rule which Catalan has never observed. And this prescription weighs so heavily upon our writers that many of them, even when they are advised that it is a rule which does not apply nor has ever applied in Catalan, will insist on believing it and on continuing to see as a grammatical error the use in certain cases of a preposition different from the one required by the Castilian rule.

Then, if they find in old Catalan a construction like *Eren en Itàlia* [= They were in Italy] they think they are correct in writing *Viuen en Girona*, in line with the aforementioned Castilian rule. What they fail to see, though, is that in old Catalan *Anaren en Itàlia* [= They went to Italy] was also commonly written, and that, before geographical names, if both prepositions *a* and *en* were used, this was not because of the Castilian rule. Thus to write *Eren en Itàlia* and *Anaren a Itàlia* constitutes a Castilianism in [modern] Catalan. [...]

---

* "Castellanismes de la llengua escrita". *La Revista* (1917), XLVI, 312. Reprinted in Vallverdú (1980: 129–134).

[8] Philologists and poets*

In the arduous task of refashioning our literary language, it is encouraging to observe the enormous advances already achieved, the high degree of purification and flexibility that Catalan has attained. But it is especially heartening to see how present-day writers are collaborating so effectively in this undertaking, in their readiness to welcome all the improvements that are being constantly suggested by an ever deeper knowledge of the spoken language and of old Catalan.

The initiators of the Renaixença

The initiators of our nineteenth-century literary renaissance understood from the very start that the written language had to be the object of a labour of purification and enrichment. But it is certain that none of them had an exact idea of the magnitude of what was being undertaken. Right at the beginning of the laborious restoration of Catalan to its rightful condition and status, they were not in a position to perceive the state of degradation into which the language had fallen. And, moreover, their moderate aspirations regarding the use of Catalan as a literary language called for only a partial elimination of the Castilian imprint. (We must recall that Manuel Milà i Fontanals saw Catalan as being excluded from every field except that of lyrical poetry or comic poetry of a popular cast.) Those who, like Milà, thought that Catalan was prohibited in perpetuity from being a vehicle of expression for "philosophical, cosmopolitan and universal thought" could not imagine that one day it would claim to be elevated to the condition of national language of Catalonia, with the corollary that we would wish to see it totally freed from servitude to Castilian, in possession of its full lexical treasure-store, no longer vitiated and half perished. The work to be done was, then, much greater than could have been suspected by the worthy people who initiated it, as Catalan had fallen much lower than they believed, and it had to be lifted much higher than they would have ever dared to hope.

They courageously began, however, the task of setting aright the written language, basically a task of de-Castilianisation: to discover the words, constructions and pronunciations from the other language that had progressively displaced authentic Catalan ones, and to retrieve the latter through study of the living language and, above all, of medieval Catalan. But this agenda of expurgation remained for a long time exclusively limited to the area of vocabulary, where Castilian influence

---

* "Filòlegs i poetes". Fragment of the presidential address delivered at the Jocs Florals in Mataró, 1918. Reprinted in Vallverdú (1980: 141–146).

was most apparent. And, even so, in this very area, how very far were the earliest writers of the Renaixença from recognising the extent of the affliction that they were proposing to remedy! Only as the work of sieving out alien intromissions progressed has it been seen to what great extent our vocabulary had been damaged by Castilian influence. For, while there were Castilianisms that were obvious at first sight, words that in their form show up immediately as being Castilian, there were others that required a profound knowledge of linguistic evolution for them to be identified. And amongst the most difficult to recognise were, precisely, the most embarrassing ones, involving semantic misrepresentation: [polysemous] *remetre*, for example, equated with Castilian *remitir* [= to send], *gosar* [= to dare] given the meaning of Castilian *gozar* [= to enjoy]. On top of this there were derivative suffixes, differences in the gender of nouns...

It is sufficient to realise how far Castilianisation had progressed in our language in order to understand that the task of recovery could not be completed by a single generation. But we must further be aware that it was just as necessary to purge Catalan syntax, metrics, orthography and even pronunciation, and that these matters had not even had attention drawn to them. We can take any piece of nineteenth-century poetry from the Jocs Florals and find evinced there a concern about the lexis: a dialectal or archaic word replacing some Castilian form from everyday Catalan. But what we also find there, on the other hand, is a thoroughly Castilianised system of syllable counting – *suau* treated as a monosyllable, *comiat* as bisyllabic –, a Castilian pronunciation of contiguous vowels infiltrating our language. And this, far from being reacted against in that poetry, is seen to be favoured, to the extent that the language there admits contractions that spoken Catalan has never made. And, in the same way, certain Castilian constructions are used there more abundantly than in our language as it is commonly spoken. No: although some very beautiful poems might have been produced using that vehicle, present-day Catalan authors, while feeling deep gratitude towards those first writers in our modern renaissance, could not accept their Catalan as a model. Their language was in the very earliest stages of being purified, and the best way of being worthy successors to them was, without doubt, to continue with their task of sifting out Castilian influences.

Our contemporary writers and the purification of Catalan

Present-day writers, fortunately, far from being satisfied with the results obtained by their predecessors, are endeavouring to write in a Catalan that is ever more pure and perfect. To disclose one by one the Castilianisms which infest our language, to attain both a perfect knowledge of the living idiom, with all its dialectal varieties, and a perfect knowledge of old Catalan, these are the responsibilities of the philologist. But afterwards there still has to come the job of remedying the alien forms identified and of enriching the language by deploying the materials contributed by the philologist. And this is the task of the man of letters. It entails a most delicate labour of discriminate selection, for not every form taken from old Catalan is acceptable, and even less so all the words and expressions supplied to us by the dialects. And in this work of selection our present-day writers excel, cognisant of the philologists' discoveries and encouraged by a spirit of collaboration and discipline unprecedented in [the history of] our literature.

Archaic and dialectal forms

Two dangers were entailed in the aim of curing the defects of modern Catalan by means of the broad admission of archaisms and dialectal importations: we all know that there are those who pretend that we should write Catalan as it was in the fifteenth century, and then those who desire the written language to display all the dialect varieties of the spoken one. These two dangers will be avoided through the wise example and the good taste of our present-day writers.

It is indisputable that we needed to make modern Catalan move back closer towards the medieval language: lost words and forgotten constructions had to be recovered. This obviously had to be done with good sense and discretion, gradually, with great care that the outcome did not appear in any way stilted, not trying out more old forms until the previous ones had been assimilated, incorporated once more into the living language. We find ourselves today well advanced along this route: words and constructions that only yesterday were seen as very bold archaisms are now encountered even in the spoken language, and old features are now generally accepted that only yesterday everybody would have rejected. We must not seek, however, to make this alignment of the modern with the ancient a blanket identification, something which anyway would be impossible. The ideal which we are pursuing is not the resurrection of a medieval language, but rather the formation of the modern language that would have emerged out of old Catalan were it not for the long centuries of literary decadence and of subordination to a foreign tongue.

It is also indisputable that it was right and proper to enrich and invigorate written Catalan with valuable inputs from the dialects. Thus it was a reason for rejoicing to see how every writer used as readily and as freely as possible words and expressions characteristic of his own regional speech. This could be no handicap at all for the unity of the written language, as long as it was practised by people of true literary calibre, those with a proper understanding of what constitutes a literary language. By this we mean that each one of them, within a single morphology and a single syntax, would present words and expressions gleaned from their own dialect, combining the desire to see them incorporated into the literary language with the will to accept into their own idiom words and expressions offered by writers from other Catalan-speaking parts. This, however, is completely different from what some people advocate when they urge everybody to write in the Catalan of their own region, with all of its morphological and syntactical peculiarities: a strange way to work for the restoration of our literary language. In every part of the world, when a literature has been created in a particular linguistic domain, we see, supreme over the multiform variety of the spoken language, how a literary language takes shape issuing from a long and most careful labour of selection and fixation. And this did indeed happen in the Catalan-speaking lands, we Catalans did have our own national language in which dialect differences barely showed through. We are now in a position where we can repair the process of debasement and disintegration of centuries of decadence, and we will neither welcome nor perpetuate the old state of affairs by indiscriminate acceptance of forms and constructions that have no literary tradition, lumping together the basest and the coarsest of them with forms and constructions consecrated by our glorious medieval writers.

[9]   The task of the Valencian and Balearic writers*

I once remarked to a Valencian writer: "We Catalans would wish only that you and your colleagues might undertake a concerted purification of the language that you use, without worrying in the least about coming nearer to how we speak it in Catalonia. The aim would be to rid Valencian of Castilian influences, to set it back on its own feet and to enrich it, restoring it to a proper relationship with the language of your own great medieval writers. In this way, while serving purely Valencian interests, you would in fact have contributed to the greater good of Catalan, moving towards the common ground. By elevating your written language above ways of speaking that prevail in present-day Valencia, by basing it on the language used there in the fifteenth century, you would produce a Valencian that would not be a distinct language from our Catalan, but rather the true Valencian modality of the Catalan language, standing side-by-side with its Catalonian and Balearic counterparts."

Most Valencian and Balearic speakers of Catalan still believe that the task of unifying the written language would mean subordinating their dialectal varieties

---

* "La tasca dels escriptors valencians i balears". *Nostra Parla* (1918), 7, 4–5. Reprinted in Vallverdú (1980: 147–148).

to the Catalan of Catalonia. This is not so: there is no intention of subordinating one variety to another; the objective is simply to put into effect, within the three main Catalan-speaking regions, a process of purification and recovery of the language. Each of these regions has its own classics among the great works our old literature. Let each of them take these as models for purification and recovery of the respective dialect varieties. This alone would ensure that, without any of us moving away from our own Catalan, we would be writing barely differentiated modalities of a single literary language.

With the elimination, in each variety, of lexical and syntactical Castilianisms, when the written language has restored to it words and constructions lost through centuries of literary decadence, when this language has been enriched with words and expressions that are provided by present-day variants in the spoken language, banishing the corruptions that abound and avoiding spellings that perpetuate merely dialectal pronunciations, once these conditions were achieved, the remaining differences to be found between the Catalan of Catalonia, the Catalan of Valencia and the Catalan of the Balearic Islands would be reduced to a few morphological divergences which, by their number and their importance, would in no way justify anyone in talking about, as some still do, a Valencian language and a Majorcan language set apart from a Catalan language.

(Philological Conversations 1919)*

[10]   In pursuit of purity in the language: Castilianisms (18/XI/1919)

The work of restoring literary Catalan to its proper condition and status is above all one of removing the presence of Castilian influence. And in the majority of cases it is old Catalan which supplies us with the word or turn of phrase with which to replace ones brought in from the other language. This explains the growing number of archaic forms found in the present-day literary language.

Many people may deem to be excessively numerous the borrowings from medieval Catalan. But this attitude is due to the fact that they have no precise idea of the level of Castilianisation reached by our language during the centuries when it was subordinated to its neighbour. Castilian importations in modern Catalan are incalculably more numerous than a superficial examination of our language would disclose.

---

* "Converses filològiques" (1919). Rafel (1983). See note to the sequence Philological Conversations 1922, below p. 154 and Introduction, p. 19. Individual Conversations did not generally have an independent title, and henceforth we supply as a heading the date of publication of each piece.

Some of these are quite easy to recognise, like for example *puesto, cuento, ruedo*, words whose form alone betrays them immediately as foreign. More difficult to discover, however, are those with a form which could equally be Catalan or Castilian, like *tonelada*, or words which have been invested with a Catalan form, such as *estribació* [< *estribación*].

In the cases of *tonelada* and *estribació*, for us to be able to brand them as imports from Castilian, we need to be aware that they are derived from *tonel* and *estribo* [whose Catalan synonyms are distinct and do not give rise to the same suffixation]. Similarly, in the case of a word like *hermós*, we need to appreciate that loss of initial Latin *f* is a phonetic transformation alien to Catalan, so that a word like *formosus* could give in our language *formós* or *fermós*, but never *hermós*, the latter being a Catalan shape given to the Castilian word *hermoso*. Even beyond this, though, there are Castilianisms, like *enterar*, which are only revealed to us as such by their absence from our old texts, where the ideas they denote nowadays are constantly conveyed by other words: Castilianisms, then, the discovery of which demands deep study of the language.

Furthermore, and without leaving the lexical field, there is a class of such words which are even harder to detect and which are possibly the most humiliating. These are the ones which consist, not of a foreign borrowing, but of the change in meaning of a Catalan word under the influence of a Castilian one. We have given to the verb *lliurar*, for example, the meaning of *deslliurar* [= to deliver, to free] belonging to the Castilian verb *librar*; *remetre* has acquired the meaning of *trametre*, which is that of the Castilian verb *remitir* [= to send].

In these daily notes we shall try to give an idea of how great is the number of Castilianisms in our present-day language, and thus to demonstrate the need for resorting abundantly to old Catalan forms, in the supposition that we are not to be satisfied with just a shallow clearing up of our language involving merely the extirpation of the most obvious imports from Castilian.

∗∗∗

[11]   12/XII/1919

In order to remedy Castilianisms, we need not resort exclusively to old Catalan. By looking to dialectal behaviour, we are supplied with valuable materials with which to refashion the vocabulary of the literary language. And then also one can have recourse to borrowings from Latin, something which our medieval writers practised abundantly. After this there is the possibility of resorting to derivation, a procedure which has the special advantage that a derived form, appropriately made, is immediately understood by everybody. At the same time as we are scanning the old language and modes of speaking from beyond the metropolis, without neglecting classical loan-words, we must seek to vivify our own suffixes and make them fit to produce new derivatives.

In the central dialect of Catalan the majority of derivative suffixes had become petrified, as it were, incapable of engendering new formations. For example, with only a very limited number of adjectives formed with the suffix -ívol, time was that these did not seem to have the strength to provide a model for generation of new adjectives in -ívol. That was until Jacint Verdaguer[86] introduced into the literary language a host of such adjectives, and then -ívol became a productive suffix, making possible the creation of new adjectives with this ending.

In rural speech and in old Catalan we find a great number of derivatives that are unknown in the modern written language. Let us welcome them attentively, thereby enriching our lexis not only with words recovered in this way, but also with ones which the suffixes, reinvigorated, can give rise to.

***

(Philological Conversations 1920)*

[12]   7/I/1920

Our modern writers, when they put into use an archaic word, do not always give to it the meaning which it had in old Catalan. This is sometimes perhaps out of ignorance, but often it is done deliberately, with the aim of remedying a deficiency in the modern language.

When a word from the old language has come into present-day Catalan after having undergone over time a change of meaning, the modern literary language can perfectly well admit this change in the majority of cases. Acceptance of the new meaning is then nothing but the recognition of an evident reality.

---

86. 1845–1902. Celebrated as the national poet of Catalonia. Trained as a priest, his literary talents were recognised while he was still a seminarist. Illness and personal crises deeply affected his life, which was marked by conflict with both his patrons (the aristocratic-industrialist Güell family) and the ecclesiastical authorities. His exceptional creative talent was supported by a great linguistic richness based in the living idiom of his native region of Vic and reinforced through contacts with the main linguistic scholars of the Renaixença. His status as a writer is complemented by that of major contributor to the consolidation of modern literary Catalan. He exploited popular materials in his writing and published several collections of basically religious poems, with an ascetic or mystical character. Another aspect of his work were poems on civic or patriotic subjects. He is most celebrated, including at the international level, for his major epic poems L'Atlàntida (1877) and Canigó (1886). His writings in prose (travelogues, folk tales, journalism and private polemics) further contribute to his pre-eminent standing in the Catalan literary canon.

*   "Converses filològiques" (1920). Rafel (1983).

However, when we reintroduce into the written language an ancient word that had fallen into disuse, we are not entitled to give to it a meaning or a value different from the one it had in old Catalan. Once the archaism has become a living form again, then the evolution of the language can bring it to acquire a new meaning which we generally should admit. At the point of taking it from the old language, however, we should obviously give it the original meaning. If this were not done, we should be arbitrarily establishing a divorce between the ancient vocabulary and the modern one.

* * *

[13]   15/V/1920

It is often the case that two forms of pronunciation or two constructions, one Catalan and the other Castilian, are equally familiar to us and we use them without differentiation, unaware that one belongs properly to Catalan and the other to Castilian. We speak, thus, in a Castilianised Catalan and vice-versa, out of sheer ignorance on our part of what belongs to one language and what to the other. [...]

* * *

[14]   25/V/1920

Regular readers of these Conversations may have formed an idea of the Castilianised state that our language has reached, a state from which it is only now beginning to emerge. If we look at its vocabulary we see there an enormous number of words taken from Castilian and of semantic dislocations caused by the same influence. Also numerous are the constructions that we have borrowed from the official language of Spain. If we study the language used by the poets of the Renaixença, we find there a thoroughly Castilian pronunciation of vowel combinations. The spelling system inherited from the earlier period of decadence gives us a lot of rules and countless individual spellings taken from the hegemonic language.

However, despite the strength of all these trends within the modern language, Catalan retains an essential distinctness in relation to Castilian. No educated person could ever look on it as a variant of Castilian, from which it differs profoundly in innumerable phonetic and morphological features, with comparable differences of syntax and lexis. Obviously we cannot be happy about the disfigurements of every kind that our language has suffered under Castilian influence, and we must fight them at all costs. But, even if those alien traits were to persist, Catalan would still not be anything like, in relation to Castilian, the Andalusian dialect or even the *bable* of Asturias. Catalan is not one among so many *Spanish dialects*, as some would have it, but rather a language that is perfectly distinct from Castilian.

Our belief is that all Catalans should be made aware of the main traits that set our language apart from Castilian. This is so that they could respond properly to claims that Catalan and Castilian are not even sisters but twins within in the family of neo-Latin languages, when in reality, if we were to classify these according to their analogies and differences, Catalan would not go into the same group as Castilian, from which it is differentiated more than any other Romance language by certain really salient features. Because of this we shall devote some of these Conversations to pointing out certain essential differences that separate Catalan from the Spanish language.

***

[15]   10/VIII/1920

People want to hear you say that such and such a word, such and such a turn of phrase must be replaced by some other "in each and every case": instead of "menos", for example, what should be said is "menys". In cases like this, substitution is a relatively easy matter: *menys* has been rapidly generalised in written Catalan and has now penetrated even into the spoken language.

But people have become accustomed to matching up every Castilian word or expression with a single Catalan one, the same one in all instances. If you tell them that instead of *pues* they must say *doncs*, except when the former is a causal conjunction, people will still tend to replace *pues* with *doncs* in every case, writing sentences like the following [ungrammatical one]: *No va venir, doncs està malalt*, when what they mean is *No va venir, perquè està malalt* [= He did not come, because he is ill]. In a prologue signed by an "academician" we have recently come across a causal *doncs*!

Not very long ago it was recommended that *reial* should be used instead of *real* when the meaning is "pertaining to royalty" (in French, *royal*). And soon afterwards one could see *reial* written in place of *real* meaning "real", "actually existing as a thing or occurring in fact" (in French, *réel*). A few days ago we found examples of this in a local newspaper.

***

[16]   30/VIII/1920

We frequently receive letters from readers asking for clarification on a subject, giving us a suggestion or objecting to something we have said. We are unable to respond to these individually because we are not supplied with an address. In future,

when we think that the reply to certain letters of this kind may be of some interest to most readers of these Conversations, we shall give a response in these columns. It will be a way of establishing a correspondence with our readers, and we shall be most pleased to provide answers to their queries insofar as we are able.
[…]

***

[17]   9/X/1920

It will be impossible to ensure that people write Catalan correctly while ever the majority of Catalan publications abound in spelling mistakes. People will for sure not make mistakes with a word whose spelling is difficult if, in what they read, they have constantly encountered it properly spelled. Otherwise, the memory of an erroneous spelling can easily make them write it incorrectly.

For this reason it is so regrettable that the employees of our printing houses, with very few exceptions, do not possess a perfect knowledge of Catalan rules of spelling. If an author does not deliver to the printers copy that is already orthographically correct, he can have little expectation, in most cases, that what he has written will come out free from spelling mistakes. On the contrary, it sometimes happens that new errors are added to ones in the original material not properly corrected at the printers, as we ourselves have more than once observed.

It is only through reading that one would come to have a command of Catalan orthography, on condition, of course, that Catalan publications came out with faultless spelling. Nowadays, the opposite happens: someone who has studied and learned the rules of spelling is in danger of unlearning them by reading our publications, littered with all kinds of orthographical errors.

***

[18]   3/XI/1920

When there is a Catalan word which has no exactly corresponding term in Castilian, we frequently observe, in the written language, so deeply affected by Castilian, a sort of tendency to by-pass the authentic item. Thus it is that some fine Catalan words are in danger of falling into disuse, to be replaced by items in their stead which translate literally those used in Castilian and which fail to translate exactly the Catalan ones in question.

This happens, as we have pointed out previously, with the [impersonal] verb *caldre* [= to be necessary], which we find systematically replaced by *ésser precís*, *ésser necessari*, *fer falta*, [or even the blatant calque] *haver-hi que*. The same happens with the adverb *sovint* [= often], for which people regularly prefer *moltes vegades* [Cast. *muchas veces*], *amb freqüència* [Cast. *con frecuencia*] or even [another gross calque] *a menut* [Cast. *a menudo*] [...]

(Philological Conversations 1922)*

[19]   13/XII/1922

Another case where Catalan draws too close to Spanish is in the use of the article before the names of the days of the week. At every end and turn we find in Catalan texts phrases like *EL dilluns tindrà lloc* [= it will take place on Monday], or *això s'esdevingué EL dimarts passat* [= that happened last Tuesday].

It might perhaps be thought that it is not worth being concerned about an apparently insignificant detail like this. But it is largely the sum of a whole assortment of small parts, seemingly unimportant, that makes the syntax of one language differentiated from that of another in the same family. Today we allow *el dilluns* for *dilluns* to become widespread, tomorrow we shall see the same thing happening with *pel matí* instead of *al matí* [= in the morning: cf. Cast. *por la mañana*] then later on with *ahir tarda* instead of *ahir a la tarda* [= yesterday afternoon] and gradually we shall reach the point where adverbial expressions of time in the two languages have become [structurally] identical, to the detriment, naturally, of Catalan. Indeed, we have recently noticed in use such un-Catalan expressions as *demà per la tarda* and *ahir tarda*!

∗∗∗

[20]   30/XII/1922

The defects which coming generations will notice in present-day Catalan are of three kinds.

There are no doubt some which are still unsuspected. As the work of purification of our language progressed, we discovered time and again imperfections that we all fell into ever since the earliest stages of our nineteenth-century cultural revival. In this same way, as we continue to move forward in the process of recovery, it is to be expected that forms and constructions today considered authentic will in future be seen as defective and will be proscribed from the language.

Another class of imperfections are those with which we are already acquainted but which still await the necessary solution to remedy them. Our intention was to deal exclusively with such questions in these Conversations, either by report-

---

* "Converses filològiques" (1922). Rafel (1984). The Philological Conversations given in translation in the following pages (from the years 1922, 1923, 1924, 1926, 1927 and 1928) appeared

ing on recently discovered solutions or by explaining to our writers matters still unresolved and thus encouraging their collaboration.

But there are, unfortunately, defects of another kind, ones for which the remedy was found long ago but which continue to infest our written language: spellings like *reventar* and *varó* (for *rebentar* and *baró*), forms like *mantinguent* and *diguent* (for *mantenint* and *dient*), or *complascut* and *aparescut* (for *complagut* and *aparegut*), *quin* used as a relative pronoun (instead of *qual*), *doncs* as a causal conjunction (instead of *puix* or *car*), *els hi* as third-person plural dative pronoun (instead of *els*), *baix* as a proposition (instead of *sota*), constructions like *tenir que, a no ser que, per lo demés*, and so many Castilian or hybrid words, like *entregar, enterar, averiguar, lograr, alentar, recaudar, plaç, aclaració, estribació*.

And for as long as these embarrassing mistakes remain so common, the struggle against them must go on, even at the risk of causing annoyance to those people, fortunately more numerous by the day, for whom this kind of advice is no longer necessary.

∗∗∗

(Philological Conversations 1923)*

[21]   10/II/1923

After we restarted publication of our Philological Conversations in the pages of the *La Publicitat,* since its re-launch as a Catalan newspaper, we have received numerous letters. Some of these asked for clarification on certain topics we had covered. Others pointed out errors of grammar or vocabulary committed by one writer or another, while yet others suggested solutions to some of the multiple problems still pending in the task of purifying and stabilising literary Catalan. The answers to a large number of these letters are to be found in previously published Conversations. If others are still awaiting reply, the reason is (as their authors are entitled to know) that response to an enquiry on a single point is not sufficient subject matter for a whole article in this series. This is the case when an unauthentic word like *lograr* or a misused one (*brostar* instead of *brotar*) is pointed out, or when a replacement is sought for some Castilianism or other (*permanèixer*

---

originally in the newspaper *La Publicitat*. In 1922 the political party Acció Catalana acquired the Spanish-language paper *La Publicidad* and converted it successfully into the organ of radical Catalanism, incorporating the signatures of many leading figures of the contemporary intelligentsia. The paper flourished especially during the 1920s and then through to the Civil War. It was finally shut down by the Franco regime in 1939. See Introduction, p. 19.

* "Converses filològiques" (1923). Rafel (1984).

[*romandre, restar*] or *floreixent* [*florint*]). We shall reply to detailed queries of this kind when we have assembled a batch of analogous errors or Castilianisms.

One type of question, however, will only exceptionally receive a response: those concerning orthography. For example, one gentleman has asked us which of the three spellings – *janer, jener* or *gener* – is the proper one and why. The answer to the first question will be found by him in the Orthographical Dictionary of the Institute of Catalan Studies, and we are unable to offer him any other one. As for the second question, we can direct him back to one of our Conversations of two or three years ago, where he will find the reasons for preferring *gener* to *janer*. (He will not find there, for sure, reference to English *January*, which he cites, as an apparent supporter of *janer*. What he will find is Italian *gennaio* and Spanish *enero*, continuations, like Catalan *gener*, of a *genuarium* from vulgar Latin.) Our regular readers will doubtless be grateful to us for not being distracted by questions, like the last ones, which are already resolved, when there are so many others, syntactical and lexicographical, still requiring a satisfactory answer.

***

[22]   24/III/1923

It is necessary to pay attention not just to single words in isolation, but to phrases or combinations of words. A given phrase may be made up entirely of perfectly proper Catalan words and still be as un-admissible as the single word *apoio* or *seguro*.

Present-day Catalan abounds in phrases that are Spanish through and through. Expressions like *venir actuando, seguir registrándose, ha quedado restablecido* are quite commonly translated, word for word, as *venir actuant, seguir registrant-se, ha quedat restablert*.

And, similarly, there is no set phrase in Spanish that Catalan does not accept, resulting in the freezing out of the authentic Catalan equivalent. Thus we see how our *no s'ho val* started to give way to *no hi ha de què* [from Castilian *no hay de qué*], and now, recently, how our *no s'hi val* is being pushed out by *no hi ha dret* [from Castilian *no hay derecho*].

And then, beyond this, if we move from the phrase to the proposition and from there to the clause, we find the whole pattern deeply marked by Spanish: word order, verb tenses, the linking of propositions. This happens to such an extent that quite frequently a text in Catalan can be clear of any Spanish words as such and even correct as regards use of prepositions and other grammatical features, but it is still totally Spanish in structure and in the arrangement of clauses. And there is no way of making this kind of sentence more Catalan by overloading it with pleonastic adverbials *hi* and *en*, nor by resorting to archaic or dialect words when our one big concern is for each of these to be the exact translation of a Spanish word.

***

[23]   25/III/1923

When two words, one of them Spanish and the other Catalan, have a common meaning, we tend in such cases to attribute to the Catalan word all the other connotations conveyed by the Spanish one. And this happens even with words in the most common use. Our *res* translates *nada* to mean "nothing", but because *nada* also has the meaning of *cap mica*, that is of *gens* [= not at all], we thus tend to apply this sense to the word *res*. It is no longer unusual to hear, among speakers from Barcelona, expressions like *No ha plogut res*, instead of *No ha plogut gens* [= It has not rained at all]. [...]

***

[24]   1/IV/1923

Within a short space of time we have received two letters, one from a Catalan writer and the other from his son, which disclose two sharply differentiated criteria regarding the purification of Catalan. The former expresses regret about the ditching of a particular Spanish construction, as recommended long ago by me and nowadays put into practice by most young writers. The latter, on the other hand, is impatient because we still cannot make up our minds to adopt an innovation which presents almost insuperable difficulties.

We can describe in the following way the first of these positions regarding the problem of clearing the Spanish influence out of Catalan. This correspondent surely approves of our repudiation of a word like *apoio*, but he would be quite content if we were to substitute it with *apoi*. If *apoi* were still not admitted, he would perhaps get used to the idea of renouncing it too, but only on the condition that we found a perfectly synonymous word for *apoyo*. He is all in favour of replacing Spanish words with Catalan ones, but only provided that the latter have exactly the same meaning as the former. Otherwise, this person, who on subjects of many kinds employs a completely Spanish[-derived] vocabulary, would have to perform the tiresome job of translating his own thoughts whenever he writes in Catalan. Often he would even find that he cannot express himself at all faithfully, just as if he were writing in a foreign language. And in the same way that he cannot willingly accept a vocabulary that is semantically too far removed from Spanish, he is also going baulk at adopting a syntax that is one hundred per cent Catalan. Doing this would force him to renounce countless Spanish constructions which he thinks are indispensable, being as deeply rooted as they are in our impoverished provincial Catalan.

What this man would like is a Catalan which is semantically and syntactically stencilled directly from Spanish. His son, on the other hand, is anxious to see our language completely freed from every trace of Spanish influence. One of them is satisfied with a provincial language, one which would be nothing more than a dialectal variant of Spanish, [superficially decked] with Catalan words and forms. The other's aspiration is that Catalonia should possess a veritable national language, the modern Catalan that would have emerged from our glorious medieval language were it not for the damaging effects of Spanish.

To write in the sort of Catalan that is extolled by the advocates of its total purification is in truth a difficult endeavour. It requires everybody to be, in varying degrees, constantly engaged in an effort [akin to that] of translation. How much easier it would be for us to make do with a Catalan which has been slightly tidied up, but which is semantically and syntactically identical to Spanish!

However difficult it might be for us to write in a language that obliges us to renounce an infinite number of words and constructions, there are nevertheless many, and there will be more by the day, who think that it is worthwhile to make this effort, in order to possess a language that can be called truly national, and of which it cannot be said, as one Spanish writer has declared, that Catalan is nothing more than Castilian with Catalan words.

✳✳✳

[25]   13/IV/1923

We have in general circulation some English words which have not have not found their Catalan translation but which can be considered to be positive acquisitions for our language. Such imports should be given a Catalan spelling, always provided that how they are pronounced is not too far removed from how they sound in the original language. Thus the word *football*, pronounced [in English approximately like] *futbol*, is nowadays admitted by everybody, written *futbol*, a spelling with the advantage of pointing away from the pronunciation *fotball* [fod·baʎ][87] which the English spelling might indicate [for us].

A word like *hands*, however, has been given an extravagant pronunciation by those who have learned this word just from hearing it. It comes out like *jems* (with the Castilian *jota* [χ] sound), but it cannot be written according to this pronuncia-

---

87. Phonetic transcriptions supplied by the translator. See also the Conversation of 16/IV/1923, below.

tion, although we have seen it set down thus in certain sports journals. To this we must add that *g* in Catalan represents a quite different sound [3] from the one we give to it in ['χεms] *gems* [if this spelling is opted for].

In the case of a word like *hands* it is obviously better not to try to modify the spelling. This is if we choose not to translate it, which is what people sometimes do spontaneously by shouting *mans!* when a player commits hand-ball.

***

[26]   14/1V/1923

What does it benefit us that Castilianisms and other defects of modern Catalan are being arduously rectified, if the majority of those who write Catalan are not ready and willing to take advantage of the results coming from that labour of purification? The number of Castilianisms and defective constructions which are still to be satisfactorily cleared up is getting smaller by the day, thanks to the efforts of literary people and philologists. No one would suspect this to be the case, however, if they were to base their judgement on the Catalan that habitually appears in our publications, full of grammatical errors and embarrassing Castilianisms.

The Catalan that we see in print is, if anything, getting worse. This is explained by the fact that many of the present-day contributors to our publications have suddenly taken to writing in Catalan with very little or no knowledge at all of Catalan grammar, and almost completely ignorant about all that has been achieved in recent years to purify the language. Since it cannot be expected that they will all of a sudden learn to write Catalan correctly, it thus becomes imperative that our publishing houses should be seriously concerned about the correctness of material submitted to them. It ought no longer to be possible for a Barcelona newspaper to print at every end and turn constructions like *hi ha que haver vist, trobar-se front a un públic, amb dir que…, ignorar el paradero, alentar a prosseguir*, etc. [all of them calqued upon Castilian expressions for which Catalan has its own natural and authentic equivalents].

It is undeniable that one of the principal causes of the Castilianisation of ordinary Catalan is reading newspapers written in Spanish. But we have to ask if reading Catalan newspapers is any less harmful while ever these are written in a Catalan which vouchsafes acceptability for the worst Castilianisms.

***

[27]   16/IV/1923

There is an obvious danger in being slow to provide a Catalan spelling for a [loan-]word from French or English. The danger is that people who learn such words, not aurally but from seeing them in writing, give them an erroneous pronunciation, too far removed from how they sound in their original languages. Before we decided to write *futbol*, there were many who saw the word written *foot ball* and pronounced it *fut·ball* [fud·baʎ]. Sporting terms, thanks to the wide diffusion of the sporting press, are in more danger than others of receiving an erroneous pronunciation. We need only to observe how the words *referee, linesman, penalty* (whose correct pronunciation is *riferí* [rifə·ri], *láinsman* ['lɛjnsmən], *pénlty* ['pɛnəlti]) are regularly pronounced *réferi* ['rɛfəri], *linésman* [li·nɛzmən], *penálti* [pə·nalti].[88]

But does this mean that we must urgently find a Catalan way of spelling these words, as we have done with *foot ball* [*futbol*] or *goal* [*gol*]? They are, we believe, terms which we should try to replace with Catalan denominations, and so it is preferable, for as long as we are using them only provisionally, to preserve their exotic appearance rather than to dress them up in Catalan garb, thereby making it more difficult to expel them.

Already, in our view, we could do without *referee* and *linesman*, replaced by *àrbitre* and *jutge de línia* (just as *porter* has taken perfectly well the place of *goalkeeper*). As for *penalty*, could we not find a substitute for that curious *penal*, where the stress is placed on a vowel which in the original word is precisely... silent?

***

[28] 24/IV/1923

We well know how dangerous it is to introduce into the literary language a word which is not the exact equivalent of the commonly used lexical item you are looking to displace. Time and again you will notice that the [proposed] innovation can replace the dubious item in one particular meaning only. But if, beyond this meaning A, the latter also has meanings B, C, etc., it will not be long before you find examples of the new word used to convey some of these senses as well. When [the third-person plural possessive] *llur* [= their] became fashionable, there soon appeared expressions like *l'home i llur fill* [with *llur* instead of singular *el seu*]. When, more recently, [demonstrative pronoun] *ço* came into use we have suddenly started to find expressions like *ço útil, ço indispensable* [where *ço* erroneously imitates the behaviour of Castilian neuter article *lo*].
[...]

***

---

88. All phonetic transcriptions in this passage supplied by the translator.

[29]   5/V/1923

In the Castilianised guise our language has taken on, Catalan words which do not
have an exact [cognate] equivalent in Spanish tend to display a relatively enfeebled resilience, being generally replaced by locutions or periphrases that translate
them in Spanish.

One such word is *sovint* [= often: cf. French *souvent*], scarcely used by some
writers, who almost systematically replace it with *amb freqüència, moltes vegades* and even *a menut* [the first two being mere correspondences with Castilian *con frecuencia* and *muchas veces*, while *a menut* is a crude calque on Castilian
a menudo].

With *sovint*, though, an even stranger thing has happened. As though this
word had disappeared from all memory, one may find a writer, wishing to employ
an adverb to express the frequency of an action, who writes *sovintment* instead of
sovint. And *sovint* has found yet another substitute (this time a really knotty one):
sovintejadament.

We can see no useful point in inventing words like *sovintment* and *sovintejadament*, having as we do *sovint*.

***

[30]   13/V/1923

Great care must be taken not to allow Catalan to become pointlessly overfilled with
archaic words. When the word in common use is proper and correct, this must
in general be the one to be preferred. All too often, in the enterprise of purifying
our vocabulary, we have to resort to centuries-old expressions, and so we should
avoid the self-indulgence of unnecessarily recovering lost words. There is nowadays, unfortunately, this strong tendency to avoid the regular word when this has,
or seems to have, an archaic synonym. Many people, by systematically favouring
the latter over the former, deceive themselves into thinking they are writing better
Catalan. What they fail to realise is that a Castilian construction becomes no less
Castilian, and a corrupt construction does not become correct, just through the
wedging in of the occasional word not found in everyday Catalan. And, with the
presence of these accessories, our language loses in naturalness without gaining in
purity. It even perhaps loses in correctness, as archaic words are much more prone
to being used inappropriately than are ones which are familiar to us.

Time and again we find in modern prose archaic words deployed with a meaning which does not rightly belong to them, or which gives rise to erroneous constructions. Before using a word which does not form part of our habitual idiom,
we need to know its exact meaning, and we need to understand precisely what its

grammatical category is. And even when we are certain about being able to use it properly, we still must examine whether using it confers any real advantage.

***

[31]   19/V/1923

Much progress has been made in the task of stabilising literary Catalan. Our spelling system is now settled and, despite the propaganda efforts of its few adversaries, it is accepted by the immense majority of those who write Catalan. Our morphology is also close to being completely stable. New advances are made daily in the fixing of our lexis. What is lagging behind is the matter of syntax. But even in this most delicate area, where the effort of purification is beset by really tenacious resistance, much progress has been made, and today a set of well-founded rules can be supplied which no good writer should stand against or fail to follow rigorously.

To date, however, in the majority of syntactical matters, the grammarians limit themselves to pointing out correct solutions without imposing them. They leave to the free discretion of the writer whether to employ the proposed improvement or what is encountered in common use, which they, the linguists, judge to be defective but which they are not bold enough to proscribe. In many cases, though, the time has perhaps come for optional innovations to be made obligatory. Is it not now time, for example, to make quite inadmissible the use of weak prepositions before the conjunction *que*, or to prescribe obligatory use of the preposition *de* before an infinitive when this infinitive is the subject of a verb which precedes it [e.g. *és curios d'observar que...* = it is curious to observe that...]?

***

[32]   10/VI/1923

Everybody is aware of how, throughout the modern literary revival of Catalan, we have been preoccupied with orthographical questions. On the other hand, there has been very little attention paid to matters of orthoepy or correct pronunciation. This has been perhaps no bad thing because, without a stabilised spelling system, we would merely have engendered a large number of erroneous pronunciations. If it were considered advisable and feasible, we could now attempt to reinstate the *v* sound, bearing in mind that only ten years ago this move would have given rise to mistakes of pronunciation, as it would have been applied to words like *rebentar, biga, buidar, bolcar* that were incorrectly written with *v* through the influence of Spanish.

These days, thanks to having an established orthography, we can begin to pay attention to orthoepy. [This said], it is perhaps too early, while we still do not have public education in Catalan, to attempt to get the *v* sound restored…

[…]

***

[33] 17/VI/1923

These days there are, unfortunately, many people who, faced with two synonymous words or two words which they think are synonyms, systematically prefer the one which is not usual in spoken Catalan. There is, widespread among us, a kind of aversion towards habitual words. Our language is thought to be better if it is littered with a certain number of unusual words.

This predilection for out-of-the-way vocabulary – reprehensible enough when equivalent meanings are conveyed by an habitual word and its [potential] substitute – is the cause of a large number of imperfections to be found in written Catalan. This is because cases abound where the substitute for the habitual word does not have the same meaning as the one it replaces.

[…] Why say *adés* instead of *ara* [= now]? Is *ara* wrong? [Obviously not.] Aversion to the usual word, in this case, has made us use *adés* with a meaning which it does not possess. *Adés* denotes a past or future time which is very close to the present, but not the present moment itself. *Ara* can substituted by *adés* only in exceptional cases.

***

[34] 13/XII/1923

When a word has undergone two different evolutions, the language sometimes takes possession of both resulting forms and, giving to each of them a separate sense, turns them in reality into two distinct words. This is to the language's advantage, since, instead of one word with two differentiated meanings, it possesses two words, one for each of these meanings. This is the case with the two French verbs *ployer* and *plier*, each derived from *plicare*. Spanish has made a new word from *varón*, which was merely a written variant of *barón*.

In central Catalan we encounter quite a few instances where a single old word nowadays appears in two different guises. And we note that, in many such cases, the two forms are not interchangeable. This occurs, for example with *jau* [= lie down] and *jeu* [= lie, sleep], with *llança* [= throw] and *llença* [= throw away], *avança* [= advance] and *avença* [= progress, save]. In such cases we think that it would be wrong to repudiate one of these forms as inferior, or to accept both of them with an identical meaning. Rather, it would be better to accept both forms, as French has done with *ployer* and *plier*, while giving exclusively or at least preferentially to each of them just one of the two meanings conveyed by the primitive word.

***

(Philological Conversations 1924)*

[35]   16/I/1924

There are certain forms which at one time were in fashion and which were then abandoned as being incorrect or not recommendable. It is curious to find them coming back into circulation as new personnel arrives on the scene to swell the numbers of people who write in Catalan.
[...]
    Careful checking of copy for the printers is the only way to avoid the revival or the persistence of certain linguistic defects, since people here take such a long time to inform themselves properly about all matters concerning grammatical correctness. One only needs to think of the recurrence of causal *doncs* and relative *quin* which are encountered so frequently even in the Barcelona press.

***

[36]   26/I/1924

It is very noticeable how readily accepted are certain derivatives whose source words would sound to us, by contrast, as being completely foreign to Catalan. The presence here of a Catalan suffix gives them a Catalan appearance which obscures their Castilian provenance, and one does not realise that the Catalan suffix is attached to an alien word. Numerous examples could be cited. The other day we read in a Barcelona newspaper the word *hondonada* [= hollow, dip: Cast. *hondonada*; cf. Cat. *fondalada/clotada*].
[...]

***

[37]   30/I/1924

Regarding the lexical purification of literary Catalan, beyond our frontiers it has often been said, no doubt in good faith, that modern Catalan is full of Gallicisms, that its vocabulary has been cleared of Castilian words thanks to substitution of

* "Converses filològiques" (1923). Rafel (1984).

the latter by non-Hispanic ones, especially from French. And the same thing has also been said inside our own frontiers, but obviously here in bad faith, by people who would discredit what has been achieved in the work of purification.

Certainly we do find employed in the work of one writer or another certain words taken from French or Italian. But most of the terms labelled as Gallicisms are perfectly proper Catalan words. They are not Gallicisms but archaisms: *blasmar* (French *blâmer*), *arrestar* (French *arrêter*), *agençar* (French *agencer*), *afranquir* (French *afranchir*), *forest* (French *forêt*), *bruna* (French *brune*), *templa* (French *temple*), *ahurtar* (French *aheurter*), *ostatge* (French *otage*), etc., etc. All of these words are perfectly admissible in Catalan, and we could cite numerous examples of each one of them drawn from our medieval authors.

What does happen with some of them, when their meaning in Catalan was not the same as that conveyed by the corresponding French words, is that we now find them often used with the meaning of the modern French cognates. This occurs, for example, in the case of *abillar* used as an equivalent of Castilian *ataviar* [= to dress up finely], which many people deploy as a synonym of French *habiller*, that is *vestir* in Catalan [= to dress]. This [latter confusion] is what is to be condemned, but not the resurrection of *abillar*.

***

[38] 2/II/1924

Although many Castilianisms have been progressively expelled from our language, it is still indisputable that various new ones are pushing their way in. The literary language has recovered long-abandoned Catalan constructions, and we even observe these coming back into the spoken language, but at the same time we see many Catalan constructions giving way to Castilian ones freshly introduced. From this column in *La Publicitat* we have pointed out many of these foreign expressions which threaten to take root definitively in our language: the verb *estar* invading the range of *ésser* [along the lines of the *estar/ser* distinction in Castilian] (e.g., *estan al teatre* for *són al teatre* [= they are at the theatre]; *l'aigua ja està calenta* [for *l'aigua ja és calenta* = the water is warm now]); the periphrasis *haver-hi que* [cf. Cast. *hay que*] threatening to kill off the [impersonal] verb *caldre* [= to be necessary]; *tenir que* to the detriment of *haver de* [= to have to], etc. [...]

***

[39] 5/II/1924

It does seem impossible, and yet we still find that our newspapers are published with innumerable spelling mistakes. Take any Catalan daily and here you will find, alongside articles and other items done by certain [regular and reliable] editors and contributors, the telegraphic section where errors begin to be found, then other contents, and especially advertisements, which are riddled with the grossest of spelling mistakes. The fact is that a newspaper will have only a few editors and a few typographers who know anything about orthography. For as long as there are not enough of these to check over all the original copy nor all the printers' proofs, there will always be sections of the paper which will come out marred with spelling mistakes. In a newspaper, all those involved in preparing it ought to have a good knowledge of spelling, at least of spelling.

[…]

***

[40] 15/II/1924

One of my readers, pointing out to me some errors committed by certain present-day authors, very rightly says that there is nothing as dangerous as handling words with which we are unfamiliar except through our reading. Before using a word which does not belong to their familiar range of spoken vocabulary, everybody should take great care to inform themselves of the word's real meaning, not being satisfied with an idea of this that might have been formed by reading a couple of passages where the word occurs. This kind of approach simply does not take into account, if the written materials are from a modern author, that the word in question might well be used there with a false meaning.

[…]

***

[41] 26/III/1924

The second edition of the Orthographical Dictionary of the Institute of Catalan Studies has just come out. This new edition contains a number of modifications which, in the main, are not precisely orthographical in character. As is made clear in the prologue, in a word-list containing almost forty thousand items there are only about twenty of these that appear with modified spelling. And among these the spelling change is merely the emendation of an obvious *lapsus* (*perifèria* corrected to *perifèrie*, for instance), or of a simple typographical error (as with *conseqüencia* corrected to *conseqüència*). One sees, then, how unfounded are the reproofs of those who accuse the Institute of incessantly introducing modifications to its spelling system.

[…]

***

[42] 4/V/1924

It is pleasing to note how there is an ever more widespread interest among Catalans about the work going on to purify our language. Day by day more people are writing in to this section [of *La Publicitat*]. And, furthermore, it is satisfying to observe the tone of what they write when expressing disagreement with some proposals made by us or by one writer or another. None among those who write to us with an objection uses any longer that aggressive tone which has hitherto been so much displayed in our arguments over linguistic questions. Take any communication addressed to us and you will find there, modestly expounded, the opinion that this word or that is not properly Catalan, together with a suggestion of how it could be substituted. You will find calmly stated the view that one or another recent proposal is not the best solution, and that a different one is to be preferred. You will never find any petulant outburst or any intention of upsetting the proponents of a case which they are arguing against. Their observations and suggestions cannot but be well received by those who work assiduously to cleanse our language of all imperfections. As we are always ready and willing to rectify our opinions, nothing can please us more than contributions from experts in matters that are continually being raised.
[…]

***

[43] 10/VII/1924

From time to time it is a good thing to stop and examine the extent to which positive use is made of the improvements which are constantly being introduced into literary Catalan. To judge by the news clips and especially the telegraph reports printed in the Catalan press, no one would suspect that any serious progress had been achieved in recent years towards purifying and stabilising our language.
[…]

***

[44] 13/VII/1924

To be undertaken shortly, under the direction of a group of scholars, is the publication of our classic authors in a form which will make them accessible to a wider public than that reached by the editions available to date. We need not ponder here on all the diverse benefits to be drawn from acquaintance with these classics. Our only interest here is to emphasise how reading our medieval authors will contribute to dissemination of the numerous gains accruing to modern literary

Catalan from its harmonisation with the old language. It is above all to the recovery of words, idioms and expressions from medieval Catalan that the language today owes its undoubted superiority over the shrivelled and provincial vernacular that was Catalan at the beginning of the nineteenth-century literary revival. Acquaintance with old Catalan has allowed us to rediscover a large part of the lexis that we had lost during the long centuries of literary decadence. And, especially, it has provided us with the means of setting to rights our syntax by enabling us to replace with authentic constructions the innumerable ones which Catalan had persistently borrowed from the Spanish language. Nowadays there are grammars and other didactic works in which most of the improvements introduced into formal Catalan can be studied and learned. But, obviously, the best way for the greatest number of Catalans to get to know these improvements is through reading the ancient authors from whose works the grammarians and [modern] writers drew models for their reforms. For this reason we should be very pleased that a group of competent persons have begun work on producing a popular edition of our classics.

And those of us who are involved in the teaching of Catalan should be especially pleased about this. We are in a very difficult situation, as things are at present, whenever we wish to refer our students to any medieval author. Laying hands at a given moment on twenty or thirty copies of an old text is currently something difficult if not impossible. And this serious handicap will soon disappear with the publication of *Els Nostres Clàssics*.[89]

***

[45]   5/VIII/1924

Our daily newspapers could do an incalculable amount of good if they were to come out correctly written, in a Catalan free from Castilian forms and grammatical faults, and from inelegant inversions and pleonasms. The diffusion of good Catalan is in the hands of those who put together our daily newspapers. Thus it is such a pity that certain sections of the press should be constantly marred with mistakes of every kind: mistakes of spelling, of syntax and of lexis. Most of their readers have not learned Catalan at school, have had no opportunity to study Catalan grammar in depth and can only by reading refine and enrich their vocabulary. What benefit will they derive from a daily dose of a few pages written in a Catalan which is worse then the one they hear spoken, where the most outlandish Castilianisms alternate

---

89. The collection was originally published, under the direction of the philologist Josep Maria Casacuberta (1897–1985) by his Editorial Barcino, from 1924 to 1930. Publication was resumed in 1946 and continues to the present, with over 120 titles in its list.

with misused archaic forms, where the most slipshod imperfections of vulgar usage are admitted, where at every end and turn there appear incorrect constructions like those noted in our previous Conversation,[90] where not even proper spelling is consistently observed? Day after day we draw attention here to how deplorable is the Catalan found in parts of our press, and this is because we are distressed that the daily newspapers, which could contribute so positively to the diffusion of good Catalan, contribute rather to the perpetuation and even to the introduction of a whole host of defective spellings, forms, words and constructions.
[…]

∗∗∗

[46]   26/VIII/1924

[…] Given the present state of Catalan, if our writers were to decide to establish a rigorous distinction between a *qui* as subject [pronoun] and a *que* as direct object pronoun, it would be only with great difficulty that this innovation would make its way [back] into the spoken language, if indeed it were ever to be accepted there at all. This is because it is not a matter here, as it was in the case of [possessive] *llur*, of reintroducing an archaic word but rather of changing the meaning of a living word.

The desire to move the modern language closer to that of our medieval writers, the wish to establish a distinction that offers significant advantages for modern Catalan, these may lead our writers to admit an unstressed *qui* which can refer to things as well as to persons (as do our medieval unstressed *qui* and *qui* in French). In this case, the furthest that the *grammarian* can go is to allow the optional use of this *qui*, that is to say, to allow as correct and as *grammatical* use of both pronouns *qui* and *que* representing the subject of a verb.

It is up to the writers themselves to decide in favour of one or the other of these pronouns. They could give preference to the first of them, and systematic or at least frequent use of *qui* might have the effect of softening the association currently made between this pronoun and the idea of reference to a person or persons. This might occur to the extent that a *qui* referring to a thing or things (*la paret qui ha caigut* [for … *que ha caigut* = the wall which has fallen down]) would not strike us as unusual in the way that it does now, and to the extent that it might thus even take hold in the spoken language. Only then could the *grammarian* attempt to proscribe *que* in this function by declaring it *ungrammatical*. But this day seems very far away to us: and, for the time being, we would venture

---

90. 1/VII/1924, not included in the present selection.

to advise that, while admitting the above use of either pronoun, *qui* should be used in some moderation. This is because we need to take into account that this unstressed *qui*, applied to things as well as to persons, is offensive to our current linguistic sensitivities.

***

[47]   10/IX/1924

Our friend Josep Ferran i Mayoral[91] has said: "Obviously, in grammar as in every-thing else, habit – which can often be the perpetuation of a vice or simply of an act of negligence – is not sufficient to justify a rule. While it is right and necessary to pay Aristotelian attention to the facts, one should not forget the Platonic assess-ment, the possibility that *facts may be emended* in line with an ideal of perfection. Alongside the claims made on behalf of habit, it is also necessary in matters of grammar to pay attention to the claims of reason, of taste, of beauty, of culture."

Agreed. But the means of emending facts – and Ferran i Mayoral surely recognises this much – have to be supplied to us by the language itself. If Ferran i Mayoral is thinking about the implantation of a grammatical rule by which the relative [pronoun] would be *qui* or *que* depending on whether it were subject or direct object, this is because Catalan used to possess and still does conserve, more or less securely, an unstressed *qui* with nominative function. However, would Ferran i Mayoral be so bold as to introduce into his own Catalan a possessive relative, corresponding to Spanish *cuyo*, to French *dont* and to English *whose*? The language would certainly gain from this, but Catalan does not provide him with any word with this meaning which would be suitable for adoption. And so he has to renounce having a possessive relative, unless he falls into the error of arbitrarily using, as an equivalent of *cuyo*, relative *qual* or interrogative *quin*.

Catalan has two third-person possessives: *seu* and *llur*. *Llur* has become al-most completely unused in the spoken language, although it is still widely em-ployed in the literary idiom. And we think that Ferran i Mayoral – just as we our-selves do in our own writing – must establish between *llur* and *seu* the same strict distinction that French makes between *leur* and *sien*. This is artificial in itself, but it does rest on the actual existence, in Catalan, of the relatively archaic word *llur*: *llur* is not an invention. Now, it is clear that English, with its four third-person possessives (*his*, *her*, *its*, *their*), on this point stands superior to our language, and, if it were possible, we would all desire for literary Catalan the richness of English.

---

91. 1883–1955. Essayist and translator. The first surname is usually written as Farran.

To achieve this richness, however, we would have to *invent* the [necessary] words, and we wonder whether Ferran i Mayoral would do this?

And then, moreover, the viability of any proposed innovation must be taken into account. We are not at all opposed systematically to innovations, but our proviso is that we must think they can sooner or later be assimilated by the living language. A writer, at his own risk, may rigorously adopt a particular rule if he believes that through it some improvement is introduced into the literary language. The grammarian, however, must be more circumspect, and the most that he can do, in cases like *que* and *qui* or like *seu* and *llur*, is to recommend use of *qui* or *llur*, without ever condemning *que* and *seu*. He can do nothing else.

***

[48]   13/IX/1924

One editor of *La Publicitat*, Antoni Rovira i Virgili[92] as we are inclined to think, declares that he favours as we do optional *qui* over Antoni Bulbena's obligatory *qui*. At the same time, though, he concedes that the *que/qui* solution is *theoretically* superior to the solution involving *que* alone. He is right, if by *theoretically* he means that a language like French which possesses a nominative *qui* and an accusative *que* has advantages on this point over another language (Spanish) which possesses only *que*, to refer both to a grammatical subject and to a direct object. But let us suppose that, in Catalan, the *que/qui* solution proves to be, for one reason or another, unviable. In this case – since no theory is valid if it does not take into account all the circumstances affecting an issue – we cannot say that the above solution is *theoretically* superior to the other. Let us imagine a grammarian who arbitrarily took interrogative *quin* and applied it to mean the same as Spanish *cuyo* (not mere hypothesis, this, because, as is well known, *quin* has been widely used as a possessive relative). Could we ever say that this *quin* is *theoretically* superior to the periphrasis *el… del qual* to which we have to resort [in Catalan], since we lack a word equivalent to *cuyo*.

Even less appropriate is it to say, as has been occasionally insinuated, that the use of respective forms for the subject and the direct object (*qui/que*) is more *grammatical* than the use of a single pronoun (*que*) [for both cases]. If we were all to agree that Catalan should adopt the French rule, then if our good writers stuck to this rule and a large number of Catalans managed to banish *que* as subject

---

92. 1882–1949. Journalist, historian, essayist and politician. He was a founder-member of the Acció Catalana party and the main manager of the *La Publicitat*'s re-launching (1922) as a radical Catalanist publication. After his political and intellectual prominence through the 1920s and 1930s, he was exiled in 1939 and died in France.

from the way they spoke and wrote, then one could say, not that nominative *que* is *less grammatical* than *qui*, but that it is *anti-grammatical*. *Anti-grammatical* in Catalan in the same way that it is in French. But *que* used as subject would always be perfectly grammatical in Spanish, just like nominative *che* in Italian.

This is why we said that grammar has nothing to do with actually resolving the question that Bulbena has recently raised once again. It is true that in itself it is a grammatical issue, insofar as however it is resolved it will affect our grammar, and this will be turned into a grammatical rule. In establishing such a rule we can invoke many considerations: usage in old Catalan, the advantages of formally differentiating between subject and direct object in relative clauses, the wish to be freed from some confusion attributable perhaps to Spanish influence. But what we cannot invoke is grammar. Once the rule became established, and only then, grammar could be invoked to challenge any infraction of the agreed norm.

[49]   The task of purifying Catalan*

Two lectures

On the subject of my title I delivered, some years ago in this same establishment, two apparently contradictory lectures.

In the first of these, aimed at promoting intensification of the endeavour to purify [and to set straight] our language, I described the state of Castilianisation into which Catalan, especially literary Catalan, had declined. I called attention to the risk we were running of ending up in a virtual identification of our vocabulary and of our syntax with the vocabulary and syntax of the hegemonic language. And, ascribing to the term *dialect* one of the senses in which it was at that time employed in opposition to the term *language*, I expressed the fear that, if we did not put a stop to the damaging influence of Spanish, Catalan in its formal guise would become in some ways a *dialect* of the other language.

In the second lecture (given some years later), I responded to Ramón Menéndez Pidal[93] and took issue with his advice to Catalans to adopt Spanish decisively as their language of culture, instead of struggling to set back on its feet a Catalan language that was in terminal decline and profoundly Castilianised. Here I drew attention to the deep differences between the two Hispanic languages, the outcome

---

* "L'obra de depuració del català" (1924). Presidential address delivered at the Ateneu Barcelonès for the inaugural session of the academic year 1924–1925. Reprinted in Vallverdú (1980: 149–166).

93. 1869–1968. Spanish historian and philologist.

of the fact that the development from vulgar Latin had taken place, in our territory and in the Castilian-speaking lands, in two entirely independent ways. Catalan and Spanish differed, because of this, in a large number of morphological features: Spanish was closer to Portuguese than to Catalan, while Catalan was closer to Provençal than to Spanish. The morphological differences between Catalan and Spanish conferred on the two tongues such contrasting physiognomies that, despite the very marked Castilianisation of modern Catalan, the latter would always have to be considered, in any comparison, as an independent language and not as a *dialect*. The case can be likened, in another sphere, to that of English. Despite the deep imprint of French, affecting enormously its vocabulary and even to a considerable degree its sentence structure, English continued to be a Germanic language, and no one would ever dare to consider that it is a Romance one.

My use of the term *dialect* in two different senses might have made it seem that my two lectures contradicted each other. In the first I described the extent of Catalan's subjection to Castilian influences in the modern period. In the second one I argued that the survival of written Catalan meant the continuity of something more than a dialect that had been stricken by decadence before it could become a fully-fledged language. This would have equated our Catalan language with the Leonese dialect, which was the comparison enjoyed by Menéndez Pidal. My argument was that the endeavour under way to restore Catalan to its rightful condition and status [as a fully developed modern language], while it was challenging, was attainable. This was because most words that we might have thought were lost are to be found, marvellously preserved, in the different local modes of speaking that endure to this day. Furthermore, the evolution of Catalan since the Middle Ages had been relatively conservative, so that it was still possible to base the revived literary language upon that of our medieval authors, with no fear of falling into excessively archaic expression too far removed from spoken Catalan. Two obligations that the love for our mother-tongue placed upon us – its preservation as a written language and restoration of its stability and dignity – were neither exorbitant, the one, nor unattainable, the other.

In those two lectures the full scope of the task ahead was outlined: examination of every word in the vocabulary, the meaning of each one, all the constructions and idioms of the language that had come down to us, with the aim of identifying all the Castilianisms and incorrect forms; study in depth of old Catalan and of present-day spoken variants, which would be the source of means to remedy those imperfections; concentration all the time, though, on the fact that "the ideal which we pursue is not the resurrection of a medieval language, but rather the formation of the modern language that would have emerged out of old Catalan were it not for the long centuries of literary decadence and of subordination to a foreign language."

The task of purification had begun for sure in the earliest stages of our nine-teenth-century literary revival movement [renaixença], but it was not carried through systematically or intensively until recent years. Work had to be put under way on compiling the Orthographical Dictionary in order for all the words of our language to be studied one by one, with the concomitant discovery of numerous items with previously unsuspected Castilian origins. Likewise it was necessary to continue the work begun by Marian Aguiló, making a methodical investigation of our old texts and of the present-day dialects, in order to have available the resources necessary to rectify imperfections in the modern language. It was for these reasons that Enric Prat de la Riba founded the Philological Section of the Institute of Cata-lan Studies, because the huge enterprise being undertaken could not be completed except with the full-time participation of a group of specialists in linguistics.

Seeking out Castilianisms

This operation, even if applied only to vocabulary, is rife with difficulties. The fact is that there are some words whose structure immediately identifies them as Castilianisms, but then there are others which look like perfectly proper Catalan words until they are shown, only through very close lexicographical study, to be taken from Spanish. In the first category are most of the masculine nouns end-ing in -o, of which there is an extraordinary number [...]. Sometimes it is the presence of a rising diphthong (*vuelta, espuela, duenya, antiqüela*) or of a final -*n* (*plan, faisan, buçon, volcan*) that discloses Castilian origins. But there are also very numerous cases where this provenance is not shown by any external feature: thus it is with *espuma, sombra, prenda, garganta, isla, iglésia, hetxura* and so many other feminine nouns with final -*a* which is a common ending for both Catalan and Spanish. So it is too with many verbs with the infinitive in -*ar* – *empenyar, en-tregar, apoiar* [...] – another feature common to both languages. To these Spanish words which look like Catalan ones without having undergone any modification there are to be added others which, on being incorporated into our vocabulary, took on Catalan forms: those [Spanish] masculine nouns whose ending in -*o* or -*e* has been suppressed (*desahuci, hermòs, quebrat, alcanç, estutx, atràs*), or those [Spanish] verbs with the infinitive in -*ecer*, where this ending has been changed into -*èixer* (*adolèixer, favorèixer, permanèixer, pertenèixer*).[94]

Among the loan-words which from their appearance could pass for perfectly proper Catalan ones there are some which are not difficult to detect, like those deriving from Spanish words that clearly do not belong in our vocabulary or are

---

94. The Spanish forms and the correct Catalan equivalents for each of these examples are, re-spectively: *adolecer/patir, favorecer/afavorir, permanecer/romandre, pertenecer/pertànyer*.

Castilianisms in the same category as *espuma*, etc., or *empenyar*, etc., mentioned above: thus, *ganància, tonelada, vendatge, corassa, silleria, adelantar, estribar, aquilatar, arrodillar-se*. There are others whose detection requires a knowledge of the phonetic evolution of Catalan. A good example is *hermós*: a word like *formosus*, from which Spanish *hermoso* is derived, could not give *hermós* in Catalan, because our language conserves the initial Latin *f*. The absence of this *f* betrays *hermós* as a Castilianism, based on *hermoso* with just the suppression of the final *-o*. But then there are so very many Castilianisms which do not make themselves obvious to us by any specific phonetic or morphological feature, and which only thorough study of our early vocabulary can lead us to discover. Thus, if we do not find in old Catalan a word in present-day use, and if we find instead in early texts the idea it expresses denoted by a different word, then we can be almost certain that the first word in question is taken from Spanish. Such is the case with *entregar* [= to deliver, in Spanish] used instead of [the genuinely Catalan] *lliurar*.

The damaging effects of Spanish influence

To Castilian influence we owe the introduction of so many words and, thence, even the acquisition of a new sound, [χ][95] as represented by Castilian *j*, found in a considerable number of words in common use (*ojalà, traje, eje, rejilla, çanja, ajedreç*, etc.). It has also been the cause of disturbances in the structure and the pronunciation of numerous Catalan words. Many Latinisms have come into modern Catalan in a form which discloses that we have taken them not directly from Latin but through the mediation of Spanish. A very large number of these importations have been written and pronounced incorrectly in Catalan, with double *s* instead of single *s* or vice-versa, and this is due to the fact that they were taken from the Spanish. Both the single and the double Latin *s* are transcribed in Spanish as the same single *s*, and when we came to adopt the words in question into Catalan we did not recognise how to give them the correct spelling with *s* or *ss* according to their [true] Latin etymology. Whence we had, with double *ss* instead of single *s*, *explossió, adhessió, centèssim, infinitessimal, entussiasme*, etc., while single *s* appeared instead of double *ss* in words like *glosari, presió, discusió, agresió, premisa*, etc.

The sound [θ] represented by *z* [or *-ce-/-ci-*] in Spanish corresponds generally to the unvoiced sibilant [s] in Catalan. This accounts for the way in which [this principle has been erroneously extended so that] words like *zona, trapecio, topacio, amazona, piezómetro* have been given the Catalan equivalences of *çona, trapeci, topaci, amaçona, pieçòmetre*, instead of the appropriate forms *zona, trapezi,*

---

95. All phonetic transcriptions in this text are supplied by the translator.

topazi, amazona, piezòmetre [with the *z* here representing the voiced sibilant sound, as for English *z*]. To the similarly disruptive influence of Spanish we owe *apoplegia* for *apoplexia*, *cirugia* for *cirgurgia*, *olfat* for *olfacte*... The same cause is behind the adoption of Spanish suffixes, like the -*ès* found in words such as *avidès*, *candidès*, *senzillès* [for authentic Catalan *avidesa*, *candidesa*, *senzillesa*]. This is true also of the substitution of many second-conjugation verbs by third-conjugation ones, so that we often find *combatir, emitir, discurrir, excluir, concebir*, etc., instead of *combatre, emetre, discórrer, excloure, concebre*, etc. Then too, at the level of morphology, the same explanation applies to *complasc* or *provist*, instead of *complac* and *proveït*, and to changes in accentuation like *canvia, estudia, anuncia* instead of *canvia, estudia, anuncia* [with stress on the *i*].

Spanish influence has also produced modifications in the meaning of many Catalan words, perturbations much more difficult to detect and to remedy than those affecting just word structure. Coming as they do from one original language, Catalan and Spanish present a great number of words with a common source. Two words which in each language are respectively descendants from the same Latin root can quite frequently have a different meaning or different meanings. [With the Catalan term first in each case,] it is sufficient to compare *muller* [= wife] and *mujer* [= woman, wife]; *dona* [= woman, wife] and *dueña* [= proprietress, landlady, housewife]; *taula* [= table] and *tabla* [= board, plank]; *aguller* [= needle-case] and *agujero* [= hole]. Our *collir* [= to harvest, collect, pick up] has a smaller range than *coger* [= to take, get hold of], the latter corresponding generally to Catalan *agafar*. Catalan *venir* [= to come, basically as in English] has a wider range than *venir* in Spanish, so that in many cases where we use *venir* Castilians say *ir* [= to go]. So, what one sees happening is for the Catalan word, under the influence of the other language, to be given the same range of meaning as that covered by the corresponding word in Spanish. And if their meanings diverge, the Catalan word tends to be invested with the meaning of the Spanish one. Thus we see *ésser* being displaced by *estar* in those cases where Spanish has *estar* in place of *ser*: in Catalan *estar en un indret* [properly] means "to stay or to live in a place", but nowadays this verb is beginning to be used with the [general] meaning of "to be in a place", as when one hears *les meves germanes estaven al concert* [instead of *les meves germanes eren al concert*: = my sisters were at the concert]. [The attraction of Spanish accounts for the fact that] *lliurar* [= to deliver, hand over] is commonly used these days with the sense of *deslliurar* or *alliberar* [= to free, liberate: Cast. *librar*]; *garra* [= leg] is taking on the sense of *urpa* [= claw], *curar* [= to take care of, pay heed to] that of *guarir* [= to cure], *enconar* [= to put to the breast] that of *irritar* [= to annoy] or *enverinar* [= to poison].

The task of compiling our Dictionary entails study of each and every word in the language, comparing their meanings in early Catalan and in the modern language with corresponding terms in Spanish, Italian and French. This enables one to see the extent to which our vocabulary has been distorted by Castilian influence, so that, however far we progress in the work of purification, we shall never be able to eliminate entirely from our language the imprint of Spanish. It must be said, even so, that this is not a necessary requirement, for there is not a single language of culture that does not contain loan-words. Spanish, for example, has a large number of items taken from French, like *reproche, flecha, sargento, coronel, comandante, jefe, chimenea, marea...* The fact is, nevertheless, that just to attain for Catalan the same level in this regard as that observable in other languages with literary status – and this must indeed be our desire – represents an immense undertaking. This is especially so if one takes into account how Catalan is still in a state of subordination. The inevitable consequence is that, while some long-standing Castilianisms are being eradicated thanks to what grammarians and men of letters have achieved in purifying our language, we find new intrusions coming in day after day.

The vocabulary of Catalan and of Spanish

Catalan has undergone a gradual process by which its vocabulary has come to match ever more closely that of Spanish, either through the adoption of specific words or by giving to Catalan terms the same meaning as the corresponding Spanish words. A concept designated by a particular word in Spanish must be similarly designated in Catalan. Or if two ideas are expressed by a single Spanish word, then we will find a natural way of doing the same with a single term. Even when we have two available words we will probably abandon one of them, making the other cover the two meanings in question so that it becomes the exact equivalent of the Spanish word. If, on the other hand, it is Spanish that has two words to express two ideas which Catalan conveys with a single word, then one of the former is inevitably imported into our language, reducing the scope of the Catalan word so that it is turned into the exact equivalent of the second Spanish one. This is why, when we propose that a Spanish word should be abandoned, people ask us to supply one Catalan word which will be its exact equivalent and which can replace it in every context. They are not satisfied unless they are given a one-for-one equivalence in every case, but they fail to see that, even if we did manage to eradicate all the loan-words, our vocabulary would still be profoundly marked by Castilian.

When I have been asked to give an exact substitute for one Castilianism or another, it has not troubled me to have to say in some cases that there is no such thing. This is because, for sure, it is often right and proper that such word-for-word transfer cannot be done, in order that Catalan vocabulary does not become just a servile replica of the Spanish one. Just as there are things that cannot be said in French in the same way as they are expressed in Spanish, or vice-versa, there have to be things that cannot be said in Catalan in just the same way as they are expressed in Spanish. We have to sacrifice certain shades of meaning available in Spanish, while endeavouring to retain those inherent in our own language. Where Spanish says *los otros* [= the others] and *los demás* [= the rest], echoed in present-day Catalan *els altres* and *els demés*, we must get used to saying only *els altres* [covering both nuances]. On the other hand, we must strive to keep the pronoun *altri* [= somebody else, other people], which is tending to fall into disuse for the simple reason that Spanish has no word which corresponds exactly to it.

This identification of meanings between Catalan and Spanish vocabulary is particularly deplorable when it affects words with grammatical functions. The word-for-word transfer often affects the way a clause is structured, constituting a syntactical Castilianism. Spanish *bajo* can be a noun or adjective [= underside, hem, ground floor / short, low], an adverb [= softly, quietly] and a preposition [= under, beneath]. In the first two cases Catalan *baix* corresponds in meaning, while the third sense is conveyed by *sota*. But modern Catalan now uses *baix* as a preposition, because the correspondences *un hombre bajo / un home baix* [= a small man], *hablar bajo / parlar baix* [= to speak quietly] have lead to the translation of *bajo la presidencia* by *baix la presidència*, instead of by *sota la presidència* [= under the presidency]. The fact that Spanish *nada* is both pronoun and adverb, combining the meanings of two Catalan words *res* [= nothing] and *gens* [= not at all, by no means], makes some people now begin to use *res* as an adverb, saying *no menja res* instead of *no menja gens* [= he/she does not eat at all]. The fact that the Spanish conjunction *pues* is used with both a consecutive [= then] and a causal function [= as, because] has confused attempts to combat the improper use of *pues* in Catalan. Some people have taken the Catalan conjunction *doncs* (which is exclusively consecutive) and have used it as a substitute not just for consecutive *pues* but also for this word in its causal function: *no pots dir que l'hagis vist, doncs no ha arribat*, instead of *no pots dir que l'hagis vist, puix/perquè no ha arribat* [= you can't say that you have seen him, because he hasn't arrived yet].

The two prepositions *a* and *en* are common to Catalan and to Spanish. The latter language, in expressions of place, establishes a distinction between the two words, with *a* serving to denote the place towards which movement occurs, and *en* indicating the place where something is or where something happens: *ir a un sitio* [= to go to a place], *estar en un sitio* [= to be in a place]. This distinction is alien to Catalan, as it is to French. It is not unusual, however, to encounter in written Catalan numerous constructions attributable to application of the Castilian rule. The Catalan of the Renaixença displays a strong tendency for the two locative prepositions to be used in line with the Spanish norm. This tendency has subsequently been fought against with some success, but there are still many who cannot get used to the idea that *en* can signify the place towards which movement occurs and who look upon as incorrect and illogical a phrase like *pujar en aquella ermita* [= to go up to that hermitage].

Syntactical Castilianisms

There are countless syntactical Castilianisms in modern Catalan. The influence of Spanish has made itself felt in how verb tenses are used; it has brought about changes in the gender of nouns; it has produced substitution of all the phrases found in early Catalan referring to a neuter antecedent, replacing them with set phrases based on a neuter article other than the masculine one;[96] it has favoured suppression of expletive *no* in numerous contexts [where its use would be natural], and it has destabilised the positive value of the particles *res* [=anything], *gens* [= any at all], *mai* [= ever] and their analogues, to the extent of making us consider incorrect a sentence like, for example: *si res desapareix, serà que ell s'ho haurà emportat* [= if anything disappears, it will be because he has taken it away]. But perhaps the most serious of these syntactical Castilianisms has been the destruction of our system of conjunctions, which has been completely replaced by the Spanish system. Catalan has adopted all the conjunctive phrases of the other language, bringing about the disappearance of countless ones of its own. In some of these importations the form of one or more component word immediately betrays their origin, and this means that they are generally avoided in the written language (*sin embargo, con tal que, a medida que*). But the majority of cases like these go unnoticed, such as *en quant a, ademés*, and *tota vegada que* with causal value rather than the conditional one it had in early Catalan, and so too with relative *el que* made synonymous with *el qual*. This calquing of conjunctions and conjunctive phrases is attended by identical reproduction of Castilian practices in subordination and coordination. The sentence patterns of Catalan have become slavish imitations of Castilian ones. Thus the long propositions found in [formal] Spanish, amplified with all kinds of subordinate clauses, adverbial phrases and merely copulative gerunds, have become the normal sentence pattern in present-day Catalan. The abuse of subordination to the detriment of coordination is something which now afflicts in equal measure Spanish and Catalan.

---

96. Fabra refers here to the widespread use of *lo* as a neuter article in a variety of constructions all mimicking the behaviour of Castilian *lo*, principally as antecedent of a relative clause or as an adverbial, and in numerous idioms. Some of these functions are covered by the Catalan article *el*, but the language possesses a diversity of alternative constructions that are deemed more authentic. See also below, note 100 and p. 205.

Early Catalan

Those who initiated the task of restoring Catalan to its rightful condition and status could not have had a true idea of the degree to which Catalan had become Castilianised during the centuries of literary decadence. If they had been fully aware of this, they would perhaps have been less inclined to embark on the mission. Only during the continuing efforts to cleanse our language have we come to recognise the extent of the malady that had to be remedied. Much progress has now been made, however; what has been achieved is considerable; the effort invested has not been in vain, and we cannot feel discouraged by the size of the task still to be carried out. What we now know is that, however great the damage suffered, we are able to put it right.

And we must ask ourselves this question – Where did we find and where do we continue to find the means of carrying out the restoration of Catalan, the means to put a stop to the linguistic impoverishment and bring about the elimination of so many inadmissible words and phrases, the extirpation of so many defective components that are presented by the Catalan of the period of decadence? We find them, first of all, in the early language.

[Between the twelfth and the fifteenth centuries] Catalan had reached such a high degree of development that it still offers us in abundance invaluable materials for repairing our vocabulary and our syntax. Study of our medieval authors has made us aware of a great many words which enable us to do without numerous [more recent] importations from Castilian, ostensibly beyond remedy. It has likewise revealed to us a set of conjunctive terms, subordinating procedures and adverbial expressions, all of which allow us to construct sentences without relying on patterns imposed by the imitation of Spanish. Reading our early writers, we are presented repeatedly with a word used in the same sense for which we nowadays use a foreign one: it might be *assabentar-se* [= to find out, realise], which allows us to dispense with Castilian *enterar-se*; then it is *abillament* [= attire, finery] to translate *atavío*; or *aplatat* [= flattened] with which we can eliminate *aixatat*; or *amesurat* [= moderate, well-meaning, obliging] for *comedido*. But this knowledge of early Catalan is especially useful to us for removing Castilian-based features from our syntax. It has enabled us, for example, to correct the numerous mistakes we used to fall into in constructing relative clauses. It has shown us the neuter expressions with which we could replace the ones based upon the Spanish neuter article *lo*, and it has given us a whole set of conjunctive phrases with which to replace those which modern Catalan has borrowed under pressure from Castilian... The first stage was simply taking in an old word to substitute an alien one. Nowadays, though, literary Catalan presents, alongside these recovered lexical items, distinctive features of syntax reintroduced from the early language. We still have not freed ourselves from the Spanish manner of combining clauses, but this is not something to be brought about by the efforts of grammarians. It can be achieved only through assiduous reading of our medieval authors.

It must however be said that familiarisation with these writers does carry some risks, in view of the fact that not all the old words and expressions are now serviceable or appropriate. We need to avoid the exaggerations of those *arcaïtzants* who give blinkered priority to the language of the past, systematically preferring, where an alternative exists, the old word over a perfectly proper modern one, and favouring medieval intricacy in sentence structure. Then we must be careful not to make improper use of reintroduced elements. It is a good thing that words like *abillar* [= to array, adorn] or *freturar* [= to want for, lack] have been reinstated in modern Catalan, but it is lamentable to find them being used often as synonyms for *vestir* [= to dress] and *anhelar* [= to yearn for, crave]. Nothing would be gained by resurrection of the phrases *per tal com* [= because, especially as] and *per tal que* [= so that, in order that] if we were to use them without differentiating between their respective causal and final functions.

Dialect contributions and new words

The enrichment of our vocabulary is enhanced also by the input from dialects. We are all well aware of what literary Catalan owes to Jacint Verdaguer, the writer who creatively instilled into it a great stock of words that were unknown in urban speech. Also to be recalled are the contributions made by Majorcan writers and those from the Girona area. The monthly questionnaires sent by the Institute of Catalan Studies to its regional correspondents bring to light some very interesting words still not recorded in any dictionary. However, if elements from the early language have to be utilised with great care, no less tact is called for in making use of dialect materials. We must guard against accepting them without careful sorting and selection. And we must also guard particularly against taking in mere phonetic variants of the same word, as if these were lexical items in their own right. To be avoided at all costs is the error committed by the person who, having noticed the multiple forms – *nosatres, nosantres, nosatros, natros*, etc. – taken by the pronoun *nosaltres* [= we], expressed great delight at the incomparable richness of our language.

There is yet another means we have of enriching our vocabulary. Beyond the input from dialects and from early Catalan, we can resort to the creation of new words. Josep Carner once said: "We are still lacking in words which cannot be supplied to us by old Catalan or by languages from beyond our boundaries. So we shall have to invent them." But obviously we must do this by having recourse

to those means which all languages have for the formation of new words: derivation and composition. Words created on these patterns even have an advantage
over most archaic and dialect items, in that they can be immediately understood
by everybody. The first time I heard the noun *gatosar*, said by a man out hunting,
I knew at once that he meant a place where gorse-bushes [= *gatoses*] grew. On
hearing the adjective *apreuat* used, referring to *virtut* [= virtue], I realised that I
had discovered an equivalent [authentically derived from Catalan *preu* (= price)]
of the Spanish word *aquilatado* [= assayed, proven].

Derivatives and composites are what languages widely resort to when they
need to find denominations for new things [or concepts]. However, when a particular language exists in a condition of subservience to another, there is a constant preference to take from the dominant tongue ready-made terms for those
innovations, rather than to have recourse to its own systems for generating derivatives and composites. The consequence of this is a loss of vitality in its own
derivative suffixes. In urban Catalan of the mid-nineteenth century many [of our
indigenous] suffixes had become completely unproductive. Nowadays, thanks to
contributions from early Catalan and especially from our dialects, it is undeniable
that some of them have acquired new vitality, such as -*ívol* (*baronívol* [= manly],
forcívol = [tough, brawny], *llisquívol* [= slippery]), -*ol* and -*ell* (*estanyol* [= small
pool], *pujol* = [hillock], *fontinyol* [= small fountain]; *altell* [= hillock], *agudell*
[= rock pinnacle], *planell* [= plateau]) and -*all* (*aturall* [= hindrance], *fermall*
[= tether, fastener], *aclucalls* [= blinkers]). And in particular we have acquired a
certain aptitude for putting them into play, so that we know how to distinguish,
for example, between a Spanish deverbal noun in -*o* (*abono*) and its Catalan
equivalence in -*ment* (*abonament* [= season ticket, subscription: from *abonar* =
to pay for, subscribe]), or how to use a derivative in -*esa* (*bonesa* [= goodness])
where Spanish does not have a corresponding -*eza*.

Borrowings from Latin

A further means of enriching vocabulary is the taking of words from classical Latin. All the neo-Latin languages have resorted widely to this. All of them display,
alongside their hereditary vocabulary, an even greater number of words taken
from written Latin. So, where there is a gap in our lexis we can always turn to the
mother language for a loan-word to fill it. However, if we do not have an indig-
enous word going all the way back to a root in vulgar Latin, it is not permissible to
create a Catalan word by taking the relevant root-word and giving to it artificially
the form that it would have taken if it had come down to us through oral trans-
mission from generation to generation, like any historically evolved word. What

we can do, on the other hand, is to take a word from classical Latin and, adapting it slightly on philological principles, to incorporate it into our vocabulary so that it will be one more loan-word alongside countless Catalan words of learned origin. We can illustrate the point thus: *apoyo*, *appoggio* and *appui* [= support] are prolongations in Spanish, Italian and French respectively of a vulgar Latin *appodiu*, whereas it is not known that Catalan ever had any prolongation of the same word, which would have given *apuig*. Now, while ever there is no documentation of this *apuig* in early Catalan or in one of our dialects, we cannot substitute the Castilianism *apoio* with *apuig* on the grounds that this would have been the form taken by the prolongation of *appodiu* if it had persisted in Catalan. If, however, a writer is looking for an equivalent of the Spanish *ajeno* [= somebody else's, extraneous], which is a prolongation of *alienus*, he can recall that *alienus* is a word from classical Latin. So he is perfectly entitled to take this word and from it form *aliè* in Catalan, a solution far superior, it must be said, to the *agè* adopted by those who do not mind using a Castilianism, as long as it does not look like one, and who are satisfied just to knock off the *-o* in words like *apoio*, *plaço* or *anticipo*.[97]

The de-Castilianisers and the extreme archaists

Through utilisation of the methods we that have indicated, the process of rectifying our vocabulary and syntax has already made great advances. It is true that not all of the proposed reforms have yet secured general assent: many of them are still the subject of debate while others are even bitterly contested. We should not be distressed, however, that the innovations are encountering a certain resistance to their being admitted. Not all of them will be totally appropriate, and criticism is necessary in order that approbation is bestowed only on the ones which imply not real improvements alone but improvements that will be viable. We must not forget that in the task of purification of our language some big mistakes have been made.

There was a time when, between two words or two idioms whose meaning coincided, it was held that preference should systematically be given to the one which was furthest removed from Spanish. In every case of coincidence between Spanish and Catalan a Castilianism was detected, and it was sufficient that a Catalan word resembled too closely its Spanish counterpart for a substitute to be sought more or less arbitrarily. This was the time when the infinitive forms *valdre*, *vindre* and *tindre* were preferred over *valer*, *venir* and *tenir*, and it was even insinuated

---

97.   See above p. 125. The words *apoio/apoi*, *plaço/plaç* and *anticipo/anticip*, are flagrant Castilianisms in either guise, for which genuine Catalan words, respectively, are *recolzament* or *suport*, *termini*, *anticipació* or *avenç*.

that *sebre* should replace *saber*.[98] Then it was that forms like *etat, metallúrgia, ambent* and *greuíssim* were born,[99] and when *quin* – that *quin* [for *qual*] which we now have so much difficulty in banishing from the written language – became generalised to replace the relative adjective[/pronoun] *qual* (*la filla del teu amic amb la quina* [for *la qual*] *parlàvem* [= the daughter of your friend with whom we were speaking]).

There was also a time when some people claimed that any divergence between modern and medieval Catalan was unacceptable. Without close examination of whether a particular modern feature was in reality attributable to an imitation of Spanish or whether it had come about spontaneously outside this influence, adoption of the historical exemplar was systematically proposed, often with ex-aggeration in order to reinforce the contrast with Spanish. Then it was that, for example, the attempt was made to institute the rule that the past participle of a transitive verb should always agree with its direct object, with no account being taken of the frequency of invariable participles in early Catalan, and ignoring that non-agreement of the participle was a general feature in all the neo-Latin languages. The rule was: one could not say *havia escrit dues cartes* [= I had written two letters]; one had to say *havia escrites dues cartes*.

These days it is less likely that we shall fall into this kind of error brought about by the diehard opponents to Castilian influence and the extreme *arcaïtzants*, and one now desists from propping up innovations with arguments of a sentimental order. Nowadays we know full well that *valer* is superior to *valdre*, and that [rela-tive] *quin* is wrong and *qual* is correct. Likewise it is acknowledged that the article *el*, which some have pretended is a non-Catalan word, is one among so many cas-es of reinforcement of unstressed forms (*em, ens, et, els*, etc.), something by which Catalan is notably distinguished from Spanish. We are now better equipped to detect Castilianisms, and we are aware that, often, solutions which look as though they imply the correcting of a Castilian influence come, basically, from that very origin. Thus the causal use of *doncs* – an unimpeachably Catalan word, nothing like *pues* which our [causal] *puix* does resemble – is a Castilianism through and through. Those who opposed the use of *el* as definite article, mistakenly branding it as un-Catalan, were unaware that what was a real Castilianism was invariable

---

98. Preference for the infinitives in *-dre* was based on observation that the future and con-ditional tenses of these verbs contain the *-dr-* element (*valdré/valdria, vindré/vindria, tindré/tindria*, etc.), like the corresponding parts of *valer, venir* and *tenir* in Spanish. *Sebre* (for *saber*: cf. Cast. *saber*) is a dialectal variant (as too are the infinitve forms *valdre, vindre* and *tindre*).

99. See above pp. 125–126.

lo used as the neuter article.[100] The supporters of relative *quin*, so unlike Spanish *cual*, did not realise that, in using this word as the equivalent of [the Spanish possessive relative] *cuyo*, they were committing a most regrettable syntactical mimicry of Castilian.

The literary language and the spoken language

These days we have to be responsive to objections other than those raised by people who see everywhere corrupt forms and Castilianisms. We refer here especially to protests arising from the fear that acceptance of so many improvements might produce too pronounced a separation between written Catalan and the spoken language. There is a belief that, if we attempt to clear Catalan of all the defects that disfigure it, we shall necessarily move to the formation of a language that is too artificial, bristling with difficulties and virtually unintelligible. The holders of such views, however, need to be reminded of the surprising aptitude of spoken Catalan to assimilate the innovations effected in the written language. Nowadays we can observe in how people speak all kinds of words and idioms that were previously introduced artificially into written Catalan, elements which have so taken root in spoken Catalan that no one would now say that just thirty years ago they were completely unknown in colloquial registers. Through long experience we are well aware, then, that spoken Catalan is far from being an entity that is impermeable to advances made in the literary language. If the aptitude for renovation at the colloquial level continues to be ever stronger, we can well expect that the most recent improvements will enjoy the same success as previous ones. So too for the discovery of further defects and Castilianisms, at least to the indispensable extent that between the spoken and the written modes there does not appear a gulf any wider than that which invariably exists between the two levels in every context where a literary language has taken shape.

Then, moreover, attention should be drawn to the discretionary, not obligatory character with which very many of the reforms affecting grammar are presented. We must observe that, in the majority of cases, it is not prescribed to substitute a common construction with an archaic one. What is involved is the recovery of lost constructions or of grammatical words now no longer in common use, so that they, alongside existing options, increase the expressive resources of the language. Perhaps some writers, with more zeal than competence, will make excessive or

---

100. The existence in some dialects of *lo* as a masculine definite article was used to justify this form (instead of *el*) for the neuter article, mimicking Spanish structure. This became one of the big shibboleths in the regulation of modern Catalan, where *lo*, nonetheless, remains deeply rooted. See above, note 96.

inappropriate use of these older syntactical options. However, at a time when we are endeavouring to restore and to enrich our language, we cannot but try to recover as many as possible of the fine turns of expression which we admire in our medieval authors and which had been progressively lost to us through the long centuries of literary decadence.

It would certainly be absurd to intend to establish rigid norms for our syntax. But this is not a charge that can be directed against grammarians who recommend the use of those syntactical structures from early Catalan. "What!" some will say, "Are we to be prevented from using the reflexive form to designate an impersonal subject (*es venen llibres* [= books for sale]) and obliged to replace it systematically with the archaic pronoun *hom* [= one: cf. French *on*] and put *hom ven llibres*?" No grammarian has ever condemned the former construction, widespread in old Catalan. It has merely been pointed out how, alongside the construction with reflexive *es*, there is another one available with *hom* + singular verb, also abundantly used by our medieval authors. Whether the latter prospers depends upon our writers, and they, for the time being, ought certainly to use it in moderation. Possibly it will not take root and it will end up by being abandoned, but it will have been worthwhile to have essayed its recovery. If this old construction were to be put back into circulation and if it did in time become even the predominant one, our language would obviously have lost nothing. On the contrary, it would have at its disposal a construction which Spanish and modern Catalan can rightly look at with envy in the French language. And what we say about *hom* could also be said about every reform which does not behave specifically as a means of correcting an inadmissible Castilian-based solecism or a serious grammatical fault, but which is a source of enrichment for the language, emphasising those distinctive syntactical characteristics which have been so enfeebled in the modern era.

Thus, gentlemen, we need have no fear as long as our writers are capable of making wise use of all the means of expression placed at their disposal by an ever expanding familiarity with early Catalan, no fear of literary Catalan becoming a stilted organism, too far removed from the living tongue, nor any fear that we are moving, as some people are afraid, towards the establishment of rigid norms that could even impede the future development of the language.

There are still many difficulties to overcome, but the experience of many years shows us that they are not insuperable. Much progress has been made already, undoubtedly, in the work of purification not only of the written language but also of the spoken language, and these achievements allow us to be hopeful that present efforts being made will not be without fruit. We must not give in to weariness, to impatience nor to defeatism. We well know the arguments that are invoked: "The purification achieved thus far, is it not sufficient, even excessive, taking us too far away from the Catalan written by our nineteenth-century authors? If we do not halt these efforts, will we not reach a point where the language is unintelligible or where we are stifling it by subjecting it to over-rigid norms? If we are stubborn in striving towards an ever greater purification, do we not postpone for too long the day when we have a firmly fixed language, because we never leave behind the period of transition, which perhaps now is the time to bring to a close? And, if it is true that we shall never manage to free the language of all Castilianisms, is it now not time to sift through them in order to decide once and for all which ones we must resign ourselves to admitting definitively?" We who have witnessed the upwards march of the language cannot give in to such dispiriting insinuations. On the contrary, what has been achieved so far encourages us to continue in our task. Convinced that only in this way shall we be worthy successors of the men of the Renaixença, and that we shall deserve the gratitude of those who come after us, let us then continue working to purify the language, some by seeking new degrees of perfection, others by assessing and disseminating them, with every one of us devoting to this noble task all our knowledge and all our will-power.

[50]   A conversation with Pompeu Fabra*

[…]

A significant event

It seems incredible that a man of Pompeu Fabra's maturity and subtlety could have been born in a period of transition. The fact is that the grammarian's childhood and adolescence unfolded in a setting and atmosphere that reeked of provincialism: Barcelona in the years leading up to the Universal Exhibition of 1888. [I ask him,] "How many people wrote in Catalan at that time?"

At home, – Fabra explains, – although we were Barcelona people through and through, there was a closed compartment into which Catalan did not penetrate. I mean letter-writing. Letters, in accordance with what custom and practice demanded, were written only in Castilian. Well, it was I, a mere lad, who in our household was bold enough to break with this habitual behaviour. I must have been about 12 or 13 years old. My nephews, the Galí boys lived with us.[101] Between us there was not a very big age difference. They had to go away to Camprodon and

* "Conversa amb Pompeu Fabra". *Revista de Catalunya*, no. 23(?) (May 1926), 485–494. The interviewer was Tomàs Garcés (1901–1993), poet, critic and translator.

101. One of these was the educationalist and historian Alexandre Galí i Coll (1886–1969).

I, naturally, wrote to them there. But no sooner had I set down the traditional formula *Queridos sobrinos* [= Dear nephews, in Castilian] than a strong reaction stirred inside me. I found my words to be artificial. I could not put my affection into them. And so I was led irresistibly to write my first letter in Catalan.

I explained to my father what had happened, and so strong was his approval of the decision I had taken that I made my first convert.

The hunger for knowledge

At that time I did not have the slightest idea that such a thing as Catalan literature existed. And when I did become aware of its existence and came to understand the hidden reasons that moved me to write in my native language, I took the serious decision to begin studying it. I was hungry to know more. Looking through my parents' small collection of books, I came across Pere Labèrnia's Dictionary and the Grammar [Gramática de la lengua catalana, 1867] by Adolf Blanch and Antoni de Bofarull. I do not know how they had come to be there. These were my first two teachers. But not for long. Blanch's Grammar[102] was chaotic and inadequate. Having given the verbal paradigms, for example, he then says that if they show some forms that prove to be unviable, the reader can replace them according to his own fancy. I thought that this puerile evasion of the issue was contrary to the essential rules of proper Grammar, and it revealed to me that the condition of our language was very far from being normal.

This view was strengthened through my contact with a young Cuban, a neighbour of ours. More cultivated than I was, he knew various languages. Things thus combined to inspire in me the dream of creating a set of grammatical rules that Catalan was painfully lacking. My position was defined, then, as the defence of the Norm against anarchy.

[...]

A revival without a Grammar

If the cause of linguistic reform[103] encountered obstacles, this was not without reasons. In reality, we [the group of *L'Avenç*] were not the first ones to tackle

---

102. Blanch did not write any grammar alone. It must be an error of the transcription of this interview. Fabra must be referring to Bofarull and Blanch's grammar, as he often does in his texts.

103. In the preceding sections Fabra explains the aims and reception of his *Ensayo de gramática del catalán moderno* (1891) going on to summarise his contacts with the group of *L'Avenç* and

linguistic issues. On the contrary, – and this is why we met with such opposition – since the beginning of the Renaixença, the need to reshape the language had been so strongly felt that every individual writer became a sort of grammarian. And yet they all felt a mistrust of grammar, as of something dangerous, affecting not just literary production but also the language itself. There had been a Manuel Milà i Fontanals, and there had been a Marian Aguiló. Had they exercised much influence on how their contemporaries wrote? The first was an illustrious philologist, while the other was tirelessly dedicated to scrutiny of early Catalan and of the living dialects. It was they who cleared the ground and showed the way. But nobody followed them. Individuals went off in the directions that suited them best: none of them recognised the authority of a master. All of them were masters. Each one of them had drawn up, with varying degrees of adequacy, his own system. This was when the lamentable arguments about final -*as* and final -*es* in feminine plurals took place, and when the members of a certain Academy could not come to an agreement over whether one should say *alfabet* or *beceroles*.[104]

The work of our early nineteenth-century writers, then, was inevitably going to be fragmentary, from the philological point of view. It lacked unity, and it was riddled with errors. New blemishes – the more embarrassing because they were deliberate – were added to the ones acquired by Catalan during the centuries of literary decadence. The language became encumbered with irksome archaic words or forms and with ungainly neologisms. The resulting mix, however, was set within purely Castilian systems of syllabication and of sentence construction, which everybody accepted as authentic.

But what now causes most surprise and concern is the multiform irregularity that the written language took on. There were very few points of uncertainty that did not receive two or more different solutions, and it would be hard indeed to find two writers from that era who were in absolute agreement on every language issue. Supporters of the same solution for a particular question were irreconcilable antagonists on another. There were the advocates of feminine plurals in -*as* and those who supported -*es*, while between one and the other of these factions there were those who stood up for use of the *ç*. Then, from the four camps formed by writers who were separated by just these two issues, there were further divisions: some who stood for keeping geminate *ll* [*l·l* in the modern language] and others who would have suppressed it; those who wrote *v* according to the Castilian etymological rule, and those who wrote it in line more or less with usage in

---

participation in the campaign for the modernisation of Catalan. See our Introductory study (§2.5.4, p. 11).

104. See "Writers and grammarians", above p. 126.

early Catalan, etc. There have been in use at the same time eight different forms for the adverb *on* [= where].

The evolution of the new grammar

Once we had won the first battles against this chaos, we developed along the line of respecting the influence of early Catalan. One of the masters of the nineteenth-century linguistic renaissance, Marian Aguiló, a pure and isolated figure, was the vehicle for that influence. Contrary to what many might have thought, he looked with satisfaction on the stir that we were creating. I recall him saying to me, on more than one occasion: "When I saw a grammar book written by a young man, I expected that it would be dogmatic, intransigent and unreasonable. But I now see that its foundations are set in reality."

It could appear that we were contradicting ourselves through our concern to draw the modern literary language closer to early Catalan. Nothing of the kind. In the old language we found elements for purifying our vocabulary and particularly our syntax. And we aimed to dove-tail the modern language with its forbear, on the basis not of superficial components but of essential ones. We believed that our objective could be achieved, since there had not been a really differentiating break between old Catalan and the modern language. And now it has to be acknowledged that our project has become a more solid reality than that obtaining in the times of neuter article *lo*, of [spurious conjugated forms like] *mòria* [for present subjunctive *mori*] and *parlam* [for *parlem*].

The evolution of my own principles has settled and solidified, finally, in the present-day approach to problems of purifying our language: this is based on proper study of the living language and on proper study of old Catalan. The working materials for root-and-branch improvement arise out of that two-fold application.

Dialect forms and archaisms

Both the living language and the early one do present, however, hidden pitfalls. Dialect forms and archaic ones have to be deployed with good sense and cautiously, always with the aim of their being incorporated into the literary language. This applies even to the mimetic representation of actual speech. The writer is exposed in this case to the danger that dialectal features will infiltrate his prose. A harmfully cloying effect then occurs, as an over-resonant folkloric note. And, anyway, why should there be such insistence on reproduction of these spoken modes?

As if a dialogue between country folk in the Empordà[105] could not be elegantly represented without recourse to dialect modes.

As regards the deployment of words from early Catalan, an indispensable condition for this is the ability to understand their true meaning and to work them properly into normal discourse. This is not just a statement of the obvious. Unfortunately, we have had in very recent times the deplorable case of *freturar*, which has been so inappropriately used. The writer, as well as resisting the adoption of archaic terms just for the sake of it, has to put them into play in a way which is both adroit and opportune. He must not take them in en masse. Slowly does it. There is no doubt that some words or expressions which ten years ago seemed archaic have ceased to be so judged, thanks to how they have been reincorporated into the language.

When the writer opts to put in an archaic word, a dialect word or a neologism, he must be fully aware that he is performing an act of transcendent importance, and he must assume responsibility for what he is doing. He is making a long-term, a life-long, commitment to the word in question. However, when the word or expression introduced is not grafted into the living growth of the language, the same writer who ambitiously launched the item must himself remove it, in order to save the literary patrimony from interferences and pitfalls. He must have the courage to recognise his own mistakes. Our language is going through a period of convalescence. Thus every innovation must be provisional, *sub judice*, until such time as its efficacy is demonstrated.

Democratic theory of the linguistic norm

The test just referred to cannot be evaded, least of all by the grammarian. The specialist in this discipline has no individual authority to lay down the law *a priori*. From the study or the office it is impossible to anticipate and to cover every practical case. Sometimes the solution provided for a particular issue proves to be painfully uncomfortable in its application. When this occurs, the grammarian must not barricade himself tenaciously behind his theory, like some infallible superhuman authority. On the contrary, his duty is to attenuate any friction, looking to resolve conflict [between normative principles and colloquial usage] if this is necessary.

---

105. A sea-board and mountainous natural region in the north-east of the principality of Catalonia, often present in literature and in the popular imagination as the archetypal focus of traditional values associated with rural and sea-going life.

It must be recognised that the linguistic improvements currently being made are ones of detail and nuance, almost exclusively. For this reason they are to be prospected experimentally, with extreme care. For my own part I could never lay down a norm before having submitted it to that test of efficacy mentioned earlier. I always leave it for our writers to try out and to decide, ultimately, on its viability. Not all writers, however, can help me in this. I find that they are divided into three groups, of which only the third can serve my needs. In the first group are those last remnants of nineteenth-century anarchy, who stand against everything alien to their ingrained habits, and who passively obey the reflex action of jumping to the defence of their own defects. Then there is another group, perhaps more pernicious than the first one, containing those writers who espouse an expression or a word that they think improves the language, without stopping to consider whether or not it is viable, whether or not it fits into the tradition of Catalan's line of evolution. Finally, in a third group – admirable and indispensable collaborators of mine – are those prudent writers, who are at the same time both creative and beneficially influential, always aware of their own responsibility. It is to these writers that I entrust, tacitly, the testing of usages that I would wish to be normative. Without such testing, then, and only when its results are positive, my position is – I repeat – that the grammarian has no authority to impose anything. I am not a dictator: I favour democratic procedures.

Now, the assay process, after four or five years of positive outcome, should result in a strict rule. Then we ought to be able to say that whoever does not do such and such a thing or whoever does not do something in this way or that, is quite simply committing a grammatical error. My ideal would be that, thanks to this mechanism, we could arrive at the position reached, without an Academy, by England. At least in this way we would be spared from and immune against the blunderings of would-be grammarians.

Progress achieved and work still to be done

It is not for me to extol the progress that has been achieved. It is there for all to see. The most encouraging thing to be taken from this progress, though, is the discipline it signifies: a discipline which twenty years ago no one could have expected to see. On top of this, [we observe that] our vocabulary has improved. What lags furthest behind, without doubt, is syntax, and everything that is intimately related with thought processes: semantics, for example. But backwardness in these areas is understandable if we think of how far Catalan had previously declined, and if we take into account present-day bilingualism. This is the real enemy: bilingualism.

Ours is an uphill struggle. The task of purification in which we are engaged is an onerous one, because the causes of linguistic impurity still subsist.

This notwithstanding, Catalan now has general lines which are soundly structured. And we can have a vision of what our beautiful language will be like when a final stage of refinement has been completed.

Meanwhile, the work must go on. And the efforts are certainly being made. The translation of the ancient classics,[106] for example, will doubtless be a milestone on our upwards journey. Translations always signify lexical enrichment, an enrichment that is ever more necessary when a strict clearing-out has created many gaps.

Many beneficial things can be done. I would propose one straight away: revision of "stock phrases". How many of these in Catalan have a foreign cast! They need, then, to be taken apart and refashioned, to be given new life. In this way we would remove from the vital flow of our language the carcasses that are rotting in it. The revision I am proposing needs to be thoroughgoing. It is not just a matter of tinkering here and there with individual cases, but rather of creating new patterns and of inventing, where necessary, neologisms. In this area, more than in others, we see very starkly the need for our right-minded authors to collaborate in the work of purification.

Catalan literature

Progress on the language front has had repercussions, obviously, on our literature. If the nineteenth-century Catalan writers moved inside the bounds of a meek and mild version of Romanticism, the modern generations are oriented towards familiarity with the literatures of other countries, and I hope that we shall very soon see also the invigorating influence of the ancient classics.

The fact is that Catalan literature in our own day – without having an archetypal poet with the resounding presence of Jacint Verdaguer nor a powerful "genius" like Àngel Guimerà – has attained a unprecedented degree of maturity. I see Josep Carner as the representative personality of this second renaissance, in the same way that Molière and Lafontaine are symbols of France's golden age. [...]

---

106. This was the function of the Fundació Bernat Metge, set up in 1922 (in the context described in our Introductory study, §2.5.5, pp. 14–16). The work of the Foundation was re-started in 1946, and to date its list comprises well over two-hundred scrupulous translations into Catalan of Greek and Roman classic texts.

(Philological Conversations 1926)*

[51]   17/VI/1926

When a new word or a new turn of phrase appears in a writer's text, when some
archaic form or neologism is recommended, it is curious how the innovation introduced or proposed finds proselytes immediately, whether or not it is appropriate. And it is curious too how people rush to use the novelty, even without having
an exact idea of its meaning. It is a good thing that we are disposed to admit anything which tends to enrich and purify our language. But this should not mean
accepting any novelty whatsoever. Beforehand we should make certain that what
is involved is a real improvement (we should look carefully at exactly who is making the proposal!). And then we should not adopt anything until we have an exact
idea of its true meaning and scope. We should remember, if nothing else, the case
of causal *doncs*, of relative *quin*, of adversative *no res menys*.

It is better to renounce a word than to use it incorrectly. If the unfamiliar word
comes in to substitute for a correct term habitually used, the best thing is to do
without the former. If *desitjar, anhelar*, [= to want, desire] etc., are perfectly good,
why use instead of them a new word: *freturar*? The risk is often run, unnecessarily,
of a mistaken meaning being introduced as is the case with *freturar* which means
"to want for, be in need of ". And in the event that replacement of a habitual word
by a new one is unavoidable, because the former is absolutely inadmissible, then
you must ascertain carefully what the substitute is to be *in each separate case*. If
recolzar [= to lean, to prop up] can replace [the Castilianism] *apoiar* in one case or
another, this does not mean that it can be so used in every context: *apoiar* meaning "to support, give support to", for instance, cannot be substituted by *recolzar*.

***

[52]   12/IX/1926

The presence of a construction in early Catalan – and we are not thinking of
documents from before the thirteenth century, where the syntax vacillates, but of
samples from the later period of maturity – does not mean of itself that the construction in question has to be considered authentic for the Catalan of our times.
For example, the verb *haver* used impersonally is now always accompanied by
adverbial *hi*, in the language of the principality of Catalonia [*hi ha* = there is/are:
cf. French *il y a*], except in a few stereotyped phrases. We say *hi ha/hi havia/hi ha*

---

* "Converses filològiques". Fabra (1919–1928).

hagut/ha d'haver-hi un home [= there is/ there was/ there has been/there must be a man].

In old Catalan, impersonal *haver* did not normally take *hi*. Now, what would we say of the person who, basing himself on this feature of the early language, would sanction constructions like *ha un home, havia dos homes*, etc.?

When these days, in any translation from the Spanish, we find an impersonal *haver* without *hi*, this is evidently to be attributed to an imitation of Castilian. It would be pointless to pretend, citing the old usage, that this *haver* without *hi* can be justified as an archaism. The modern writer has obviously used it not out of imitation of old practice, but by copying directly from Castilian.

But it would be even worse if, putting forth examples (of which there would be no shortage) from old texts, some over-zealous advocate of archaic forms were to vindicate the construction we have been discussing and then to protest about the excessive rigidity of the modern rule which makes *hi* the obligatory accompaniment of impersonal *haver*.

(Philological Conversations 1927)*

[53]   17/VI/1927

Whenever it is proposed that some imported mode of expression should be proscribed, people often complain about having to renounce it. They think it is almost impossible to do without it and its absence implies, so they hold, a grievous lacuna in the language, without considering that very often the expression in question is also quite alien to languages like Italian or French. On the other hand, we find many who will not make good use of expressive possibilities belonging to their own language when these are foreign to Spanish. Then they replace them almost systematically with the periphrases that Spanish is obliged to resort to for want of the same idioms. Somebody will complain about the lack in Catalan of a neuter article that is differentiated from the masculine definite article. Somebody else is incapable of making proper use of adverbial *hi* and so substitutes it with *a ell, en ell* or *en el mateix*, etc, all of which are translations of the periphrases to which Spanish must have recourse since it does not possess an adverb equivalent to our *hi* and to French *y*.

Here is one example: *El Passeig de Gràcia comença a guanyar la seva popularitat mercès als llocs d'esbarjo que* **en ell** *varen anar establint-se...* [= The Passeig de Gràcia started to gain its popularity thanks to the places of entertainment that began to be established in it]. Why do we find here *en ell* and not *hi* [*establint-s'hi*]?

---

* "Converses filològiques". Fabra (1919–1928).

(Philological Conversations 1928)*

[54] 12/VI/1928

Without doubt syntactical Castilianisms are among the most difficult ones to extirpate. If it is a matter of proscribing a single alien word for which an adequate substitute has been found, it is sufficient to denounce the offending item and to indicate what is to replace it. Then immediately one sees a reduction in the use of the alien word, often with it being soon expelled for good. Even in the case where substitution presents the difficulty of not being achievable through a single replacement word (as in the case of *apoiar*, for example), not only is the intruder soon evicted but, after a certain period when erroneous substitutes are in play, the replacement words end up being correctly used.

But, when a syntactical Castilianism is involved, how very slowly does the process of elimination operate! And how frequent are the relapses it suffers! We must remember the cases of causal *doncs*, of the adjective *demés*, of the compound relative *el que*. They have been denounced over many years (their substitutes being *puix que*, *altres*, *el qual*); they have been talked about insistently, in condemnatory terms, on dozens of occasions. And yet, even nowadays, it is not unusual to finds instances of them even in the Barcelona press, even in books!

The need, then, is for attention to continue to be paid to them, once again, and again and again. It is not enough that many people no longer mistakenly use these words. No one at all ought to use them. And while ever there are writers who are incapable of avoiding them, it will be fully justified to keep returning to the matter, in order to see if finally their total eradication can be achieved.

So, readers should not be surprised if in these pages we bring up again the subject of causal *doncs*, of relative *el que*, of the adjective *demés*, of incorrect use of the word *quin* and of the neuter article… It is a shame that Catalan, at this moment in time, should still not yet be completely free of such defects.

[55] On the purification of the literary language*

The diffusion of written Catalan

In our times there has been a development which should be kept very much in view by those who are engaged in the task of restoring our language to its proper condition and status: the enormous increase in the number of Catalans who now

---

* "De la depuració de la llengua literària". *La Nova Revista* (1929), 1, 4–10. Reprinted in Vallverdú (1980: 167–176).

use the language in written communication. For every individual who fifty years ago wrote in Catalan, there are now hundreds. Back then the use of written Catalan was almost exclusively confined to a few men of letters: nowadays it is a majority of Catalan-speakers who write it. The effort to reinstate the written language could not be limited now just to the literary domain – to the exclusion of technical registers, etc. – and, furthermore, this effort must entail avoiding any kind of unnaturalness which might impede wide diffusion.

If written Catalan had not moved outside of the area assigned to it by Manuel Milà i Fontanals – who considered it to be appropriate only for the cultivation of certain literary genres – it might then have been able to adopt more freely any innovatory reform, beyond all consideration of viability in common use of the language. But if Catalan is to be used by everybody and on all occasions, one must proceed with very special care so that contact is not lost with the spoken language, prudently assessing the viability of every proposed innovation and even phasing in gradually, as appropriate, the introduction of innovations which are viable. The problem of purifying our language thus becomes particularly difficult. This is because, on the one hand, we are confronted with a language in need of reformation and restoration, into which numerous modifications positively must be introduced. But then, on the other hand, there is the danger that these modifications will lead us towards a language which is too distanced from spoken Catalan and which is, thus, unfit for adoption by everybody. And, furthermore, the consideration that it has to be not just the language of a group of writers, but the language to be used by all Catalans, imposes upon every writer of Catalan the duty to work towards making it completely uniform. People must be presented with a language that is accessible and uniform.

The unification of orthography

It is in the area of orthography where one sees very clearly the influence of the fact that a large proportion of Catalan-speakers have finally adopted Catalan as their preferred written medium. While written Catalan was only the language used by a small number of poets and men of letters, the existence of a single spelling system was of scant importance. From the moment written use becomes widespread, the issue of orthography acquires capital importance. Previously it was, one might say, a matter of indifference that every writer had his own spelling system. It is now essential that there should one single system: people have to be presented with words written always in the same way. The public is in no position to make choices in the matter. They do not want to have to decide for themselves, at every end and turn, on one spelling or another: they want to be given just one way of writing every single word. Only in this way will they be able to learn how to write according to an established set of rules. Knowing how to spell is a question of memory: through our reading we cumulatively associate every word with its visual image. And only when we have all these images engraved in our memory do we write with completely correct spelling. But this storing of visual images is made impossible if a large number of words appear sometimes with one spelling and sometimes with another. Even the person who knows very well, for example, that the word *dansa* is to be written with *s*, might have the idea of writing *dança* if he has frequently come across this form with *ç* in his reading. The existence of more than one orthographical system brings the inevitable consequence of people not knowing any system at all.

The Catalan of the Renaixença did not have a uniform orthography. With the need to renovate and to give a national unity to spelling as it was in the period of decadence, reforms were introduced by one writer and another, with the majority of such reforms failing to obtain universal consent. Some respected the written tradition of the golden age of Catalan and rejected plural forms in *-as* (*cosas, taulas*), while others would not accept plurals in *-es* (*cases, taules*) finding this spelling to be incompatible with modern pronunciation. Some, for use of the letters *b* and *v*, stuck by etymological principles (*caball, gobern*), while others were guided by those dialects which do not confuse *b* and *v* (*cavall, govern*). It was natural that things like this should happen, and, during the early stages of the literary renaissance, it was not even a serious handicap for cultivation of the language. However, when virtually everybody takes to writing in Catalan, the need is for a spelling system that is uniform and settled. And the duty of all who write in Catalan is to put aside any intransigence if the time comes when a set of rules meets readily with majority support and observance.

The need to sacrifice personal views

What we have just described entailed sacrifices on the part of all of us who had *our own* system for writing. But we have had to make these sacrifices for the benefit of the diffusion, and the decorum too, of our written language. The truth is that we have attached excessive importance to whether our orthography should be this one or that one, when the really important thing is that there should be a single [unified] system of some kind. Perfectly defensible criteria allowed variously the spellings *set* and *fret* (Adolf Blanch-Manuel de Bofarull), *sed* and *fred* (Ferrer Dictionary,[107] *L'Avenç* 1892), or *set* and *fred* (Institut d'Estudis Catalans):

---

107. Fabra must be referring to the *Diccionario castellano-catalán* and *Diccionario catalán-castellano* (1836), by Magí Ferrer (1792–1862).

all three criteria had their supporters during the nineteenth century. However, when the task was undertaken to make Catalan spelling uniform, it was necessary for one of them to be adopted and for the other two to be abandoned. If at any point one spelling solution is readily adopted by a large majority, and if this entails writing *set* and *fred*, let us obediently write *set* and *fred*, even though we might prefer *set* and *fret*[108] or *sed* and *fred*, because what is needed above all, in the present circumstances, is that there should be just one set of rules for spelling.

On a personal note, I wish just to recall that I had been a firm advocate for suppression of etymological *h*, which the Institute of Catalan Studies [eventually] maintained (*L'Avenç* 1892, International Congress on the Catalan Language 1906). I am well aware, then, how hard it is to renounce a spelling solution that one has favoured for a long time. But I have to say that, ever since the system of the IEC has been generally accepted, the fact that this set of rules has been widely adopted by writers in Catalan has overturned any regret I might have felt at renouncing some of my own proposals which were not incorporated there. Whichever system had been [officially] adopted, it would have gone against, in one detail or another, the spelling habits of contemporary writers. Nor would the few who opposed what the Institute accepted and promulgated have been able to come up with a system that pleased everybody, and it is even most unlikely that they could have agreed completely among themselves over what this [model] should be. Consideration of this ought to induce them to set aside their intransigence. Their attitude, while it could never shake support for the system of the IEC, certainly makes it harder for people to absorb it.

With the diversity of spelling systems operating in the Catalan of the Renaixença, when it came to fixing a single, unified set of rules it was obviously impossible to satisfy everybody who wrote in the language. If some used *ai* or *blanc*, while others wrote *ay* or *blanch*, etc., it was impossible not to contradict one faction or another. On every point there were going to be winners and losers. What was imperative, however, was that no convention should be adopted which went against any important natural feature of the language. Catalan presents a considerable diversity of pronunciation, and the spelling to be adopted had not to be incompatible with any of the major dialect modes. The difficulties presented by dialectal diversity are not, however, difficult to resolve orthographically. A word like *flor* is pronounced in some places with open *o* [ɔ][109] and elsewhere with close *o* [o]; in some regions the final *r* is sounded, in others it is not; but the spelling *flor* fits every pronunciation, whether the sign *o* is read as [ɔ] or as [o] and whether

---

108. The original here has *fred*, but context and meaning both demand that this should be *fret*.

109. Phonetic transcriptions supplied by the translator.

or not the silent -r applies. While patterns for reading aloud vary according to regional speech habits, a single spelling still matches the different dialect pronunciations of the same word. And it must be agreed that, as regards respect for this diversity in speech, the spelling system promulgated by the Institute of Catalan Studies is very hard to improve on. Indeed, when it was drawn up, very special attention was paid to avoiding the countless dialectal spellings (dialectal in the sense that they corresponded to only a single regional variant) that infested the Catalan of the Renaixença (*cosas* [for *coses*], *començan* [for *comencen*], *caball* [for *cavall*], *vuidar* [for *buidar*], etc.).

Morphological diversity

In morphology it is much more difficult to achieve uniformity, not just difficult but impossible. If one dialect says *pateix* [from *patir* = to suffer] and another *patix*, if in one dialect it is *canto* [from *cantar* = to sing] while in another it is *cante* and in yet another *cant*, if the written language adopts one single form [for each case like the foregoing], it can only be with the sacrifice of one or other of these dialect variants. Fortunately, though, Catalan is a language of sufficient homogeneity for acceptance of different dialect forms not to compromise seriously the unity of the written language. Forms taken from the central dialect, which benefit anyway from having the widest geographical extent, are the ones which are generally adopted, even when they differ (*pensem* [not *pensam*], *pensés* [not *pensàs*]) from how they appear in early texts. But writers who in their normal speech use other forms are at liberty to use these in what they write, when they are important features of their own dialect and especially when they are forms belonging to the old written language (like *pens, cant, deim* in Majorcan Catalan, [compared with present-day central inflections *penso, canto, diem* from *pensar, cantar, dir*]). It is the writers themselves who must weigh up whether they ought to favour particular features of their own dialect over corresponding forms from central Catalan. It would be quite a different thing for somebody, out of mere fondness for the old language, to take to using forms that are now completely superseded, like *cantist* instead of *cantares* [= you sang] or *dir li he* instead of *li diré* [= I shall tell him/her]. It is not intolerable for the written language to reveal, in attenuated form, dialect differences, which are an acknowledged fact. But it would not be legitimate for it to be speckled with the private whims of a writer who chooses to forget the real nature of that social institution which we call a language.

There will surely be very few writers who are happy with the [first-person singular] verb-ending in -o (*canto* [from *cantar* = to sing], *penso* [from *pensar* = to think, etc.]), which is unknown in early Catalan and is still alien to the speech of the Balearics and Valencia. Many would doubtless wish to see the modern literary language freed of it. However, we are held up from adopting decisively the old uninflected forms (*cant, pens*) by consideration of the enormous, perhaps invincible, resistance to their re-establishment that would be offered by the spoken language of Catalonia [i.e., Barcelona and the other eastern-central zones]. For it would not be only a question of effecting the omission of a final -*o*: it would be necessary, with many verbs, to modify also the stem, and the new form with no desinence often looks very different from the form in -*o* currently used and from other parts of the same verb. Should the uninflected forms be renounced? Or should they be put to the test? I dare not answers these questions. I am, though, inclined to think that, at least for a long time to come, we need not contemplate the possibility of eliminating from [normative] Catalan those verb-endings in -*o*.

Syntax and lexis

The improvements still to be made will be more numerous in the areas of syntax and of lexis than in morphology. In the latter, the only thing that might move us to introduce change is the desire to attenuate dialectal differences or, in the one single matter discussed above, to free Catalan of verb-endings in -*o*, which we find to be mismatched with the morphological physiognomy of our language. Our syntax and vocabulary, on the other hand, have been so profoundly disrupted that the necessary reforms are here innumerable. Fortunately, however, most of these rectifications do not present anything like the difficulties created by the morphological ones. Just as easily as our syntax and our lexis suffered numerous changes under the damaging influence of an alien language, so now they are readily susceptible to renovating action. We have experience of this: most of the reforms introduced into written Catalan have been, or are on their way to being, incorporated into the spoken language. Capacity for renewal on this front surpasses without doubt the most optimistic expectations. Now, this ductility of the spoken language does mean that the writers' responsibility is so much the greater: they must be very careful about not making mistakes, since any errors they commit can have repercussions just like the things they do that are well-judged, so that the language can be disfigured by the very people whose mission it is to purify it. It is sufficient to recall how difficult it is to remove now from the language defective forms and turns of phrase that were introduced in the past by the extreme opponents of Castilian influence (causal *doncs*, relative *quin*, etc.).

A writer should not commit himself to using a word or an expression taken either from early Catalan or from one of the dialects without being quite sure about its meaning. Let him not be guilty, for example, of establishing an association between the word *freturar* [= to want for, lack] and the concept of *anhelar* [= to yearn for, crave], or of grafting on to the adverbial phrase *no res menys* [= in addition] the function of adversative conjunction. Then, when he is quite clear about the meaning of a particular word or expression, he should not be deterred from using it just through the consideration that it is ancient or dialectal, but he must think out very carefully whether the item in question makes a real contribution to the language. With already so many things crying out for reform, the fact is that it is dangerous to make innovations for their own sake, like, for example, in my view, adoption of the [antiquated] words *assats*, *ops*, *hoc*, or separating out the inflected future tense into the infinitive plus auxiliary (*dir li he* instead of *li diré*).

We may come across a serious flaw in the modern language, and this is when, in order to be rid of it, we should resort to finding an alternative, be it an archaic or dialect form, or even a neologism. And only then, even encountering strong resistance to incorporation of the innovation, should we persevere in maintaining its use in the written language. And we should renounce it only if and when we become convinced that the resistance is invincible. How viable an improvement might be is something always to be taken into account. However, when equal resistance is encountered, our insistence on continuing to support an innovation must depend on the advantage that it signifies for the language. It is quite right to go on testing in use something that can correct a serious defect in our language, but if this does not work it will be better to withdraw it quickly, because what is most to be avoided is the creation of too big a schism between the written language and its spoken form.

Acceptance of an innovatory reform by a large proportion of the Catalan-speaking public is something of supreme importance. Such acceptance can authenticate even a remedial change that is completely arbitrary. On the other hand, a venerable expression that has fallen into disuse and is then restored cannot strictly be considered as authentic if it does not have that acceptance. Any trialling of material aimed at improvement is to be commended, but it would not be commendable for the proponent of an innovation to insist on maintaining it for a long time in the face of its rejection by the speaking public. And a good indicator of this rejection is when most good writers do not give it their support.

In syntax, fortunately, if we introduce expression A with the intention of replacing expression B which we deem defective, adoption of A does not imply *ipso facto* the condemnation and abandonment of B. Here the case is not as in orthography, where acceptance of a particular spelling signifies the proscription of any other ways of writing the same word. The word *braç* [= arm] was written this way and also as *bras* during the nineteenth century. As soon as an orthographical system is accepted according to which *braç* is the correct form, *bras* is condemned to disappear, and it becomes a spelling mistake. In syntax, by contrast, A and B can co-exist alongside one another. Item A can thus be subjected to a period of testing: if it fails to gain general acceptance it is then a matter of not insisting on maintaining it; it will be abandoned, and the experiment will have had no adverse effect on the use of B. But if A is viable and if it obtains preference among good writers, to the extent that none of them use expression B any longer, we shall then be able to proscribe the latter. Item B will have been eliminated from the literary language, and use of it will constitute a grammatical error.

There are obviously instances where it has been possible to condemn as erroneous and ungrammatical a habitual expression, without waiting for writers to come into line with this position. But in such cases the obviousness of the defective form (*els hi* for [dative plus accusative object pronouns] *els ho*, *el que* for [relative] *el qual*) allowed one to be sure in advance that good writers would give their consent. In general, however, it is necessary to wait for them to give their support for a proposed reform, which is a guarantee that it is appropriate, well-judged not only because of its intrinsic rightness but also as regards its potential viability in the communal language.

The writers' collaboration

Of inestimable importance is the existence of a community of writers who are ready and willing to collaborate in the endeavour to restore the condition and status of Catalan. Thanks to this, it is possible to be more decisive in putting to the test any proposed linguistic improvement, because in the event of it being mistaken the error is quickly noticed. Verification of any innovation is thus immediately obtained, and the person who has suggested it will quickly see whether it is to be renounced or whether, on the contrary, it can be set up as a rule for usage.

When it comes to checking the viability of a new emendation, a single person can more easily make a mistake than can a number of people together. The proposal to use *qui* as [relative] subject to the complete exclusion of *que* [*la pluja qui cau* = the rain which falls], although so simple to apply in the act of writing – it being merely a matter of changing every subject *que* for *qui* – has not enjoyed among writers the good reception given, for example, to the exercise of eliminating from Catalan the use of the neuter article *lo*. The suppression of *lo* was relatively difficult to bring about, since the substitution for this word differs in every case that one encounters in the act of writing, involving variously *el*, *al*, *allò*, *el que és*, *el que té de*, *com*, etc. Now, this divergence in the writers' attitudes towards these two innovations accords perfectly with the different potential for viability of each solution within the spoken language. While suppression of neuter *lo* does not lead to any unnatural expression in Catalan, the implantation of relative subject *qui*, to the exclusion of *que*, entails breaking an association between the word *qui* and the idea of a personal [as opposed to an inanimate] subject, an association which is deeply rooted in the minds of very many Catalan-speakers.

Thus we see how advisable it is that we should all be moved by a very strong spirit of cooperation. Let us suggest initiatives, but let us always be ready to change our minds, staying attentive to the reception that our thinking might have among those companions with whom we share a responsibility towards the language. We must try always to reach a consensus, and it is because there already exists a good number of writers inspired by this spirit of collaboration that we can now be sure of being able eventually to deliver to the Catalan people a language which is both restored to a pure condition and accessible for all to use.

[56] The normalisation of grammar*

We can today be pleased and proud to possess an important set of grammatical rules that are generally accepted. Naturally, this would not have been possible if Catalan writers had not abandoned that former spirit of intransigence which made some of them stick stubbornly to their own opinion even when the opposing view had gained the approval of all the other writers. We do not believe that there is anybody nowadays who disputes that a literary language must have a fixed grammatical system which is observed by all. But, in order for Catalan to achieve this, it is obviously necessary, when divergences arise, that each individual should be prepared at all times to abandon his own particular solution if it is not the one favoured by support from the main body of writers. If this were not so, the only outcome would be pointless delaying of the progress towards having a settled grammar, something we are all working for. The solution which enjoys majority support is the one which, by virtue of this alone, has effectively won the day, and nothing would be gained by placing obstacles in the way of its definitive adoption. In this way, we can be sure that achievement of majority approval among writers is a guarantee of the intrinsic appropriateness of the usage in question. And so, by supporting it ourselves, we need not fear that we might be contributing to the implantation of a quite erroneous norm.

Because our writers have understood that a grammatical system has to be established and that, to achieve this, they must be prepared to accept majority decisions, we have reached the position of having a set of unanimously accepted grammatical rules. For this reason we must proceed with great caution, in cases

---

* "La normalització de la gramàtica". *La Revista* (VII–XII/1929), 3–4. Reprinted in Vallverdú (1980: 177–180).

still unresolved, so that there is no sudden recurrence of that spirit of intransigence which was the cause, among other banes, of the orthographical anarchy that we can all remember: that bigoted attitude which made people stick with extremist obstinacy to their own ways of doing things and which, when they could not force their solutions on others, made them even deny that there was any advantage in having a fixed system. We can recall how very many times we have heard it said that the norms, as they gained ever more authority, would impede the free development of the language, that they would put it in a straitjacket, etc., etc.!

It must be said that we have no reason to believe that the unyielding spirit referred to will break out again. And thus we hope that all the disagreements which remain will soon disappear. If we were to have any doubt at all that we must strive to settle these controversies, a single consideration would suffice to dispel all uncertainty: while ever there continue to be disagreements, we must ask which grammar can we teach to the Catalan-speaking public? We might say to them that such a construction or such a form is to be avoided, and then they will find them being used by one writer or another. We must always remember what happened with our orthography. People are able to learn it now, something which was previously impossible. Nowadays it makes sense to perform spelling correction on a text: previously, nobody knew what correct spelling was. We must try hard to achieve in morphology and syntax the same state of fixed regularity that we have reached in orthography. It is true that for some years now a good number of publications are appearing with a certain grammatical uniformity, thanks to the labours of a few proof-readers who have revised works submitted to them, correcting them in line with the grammatical system advocated by the Institute of Catalan Studies. How much easier and more efficient will be the beneficial work of these proof-readers, as soon as they are in a position to operate without so many optional rules and without so many unresolved points of grammar! Emili Guanyavents,[110] for example, has achieved much on this front, despite having had to work with a still unstable system and despite being constantly impeded by vetoes from one writer or the other. We who are familiar with what he has done can appreciate how quickly grammatical correctness would be spread abroad as soon as a body of good proof-readers could revise the grammar of texts with the same certainty that they nowadays have when revising spelling.

The cooperation between writers and grammarians – so frequently recommended by Josep Maria López-Picó[111] in the pages of *La Revista* – is of

---

110. 1860–1941. Writer and translator. He was associated with the group of *L 'Avenç*, later becoming an official proof-reader for the IEC and language consultant for several major publishers.

111. 1886–1959. Writer and publisher. He was fully identified with the artistic and intellectual spirit of Noucentisme.

inestimable value, because it is a guarantee of sound judgement in the drawing up of the normative system to be established. It would be dangerous, however, if those collaborating in this endeavour were not prepared to respect the solutions which, in competition with alternative proposals, gain the support of an imposing majority. It is right that everybody's opinions should be taken into account, but on the condition of being sure that we must end up in agreement, thus to arrive at unanimous acceptance of a single set of norms.

Only then, when we are in possession of a fixed grammatical code, will it be possible to spread correct usage among the Catalan-speaking public. And only then will we be able to count on having an appropriate number of proof-readers to whom we can entrust the grammatical correction of texts, in the same way that we now entrust to them spelling correction.

[57] **Preface to the first edition of the *Diccionari general de la llengua Catalana* (1932)***

In 1923, when the Military Directorate took power in Spain, the work of compiling the [complete and definitive] Dictionary of the Institut d'Estudis Catalans was well advanced and the collected materials were extremely abundant. Composition and checking of entries had been started on by members of the Institute's Historico-archaeological, Philological and Scientific sections. In view of the time invested in the undertaking, however, it should certainly have been further advanced by that date. Difficulties of all kinds, especially in the first years of activity of the Lexicographical Offices, had hindered progress in the work of collecting, ordering and deploying the material. And, at that date, it was anticipated that, even if new difficulties did not arise, there would still be a long delay in completion of the enormous task of compiling and printing the future Dictionary.

However, with the coming of the Dictatorship, immediately seen to be antagonistic to all things Catalan, it was clear that preparation of the complete Dictionary would encounter new and greater difficulties. It was then that colleagues in the Philological Section thought it appropriate to set about putting together a [concise] General Dictionary of the Catalan Language with the dimensions and characteristics of the present volume. The idea was that this would make up for the lack of the full Dictionary still in preparation, for as long as it would take for the latter to be published. All that was necessary for us was to continue in the work assigned to us in the putting together of the full Dictionary of the IEC. This

---

* Pròleg al *Diccionari general de la llengua catalana*. (1932). Barcelona: Llibreria Catalònia. Reprinted in Mir/Solà (2007: 147–1961).

comprised the writing-up of entries, working with the previously classified collected material. The difference was, now, that it was not a question of filling out the data with textual quotations, nor or of including in the word-list collected items that were archaic or dialectal. Preparation of the General Dictionary did not have to imply any delay to the main Dictionary of the IEC, as the first was an indispensable part of the second. The task we were charged with – producing the work which is now put at the public's disposal – can truly be considered to be the *ground-plan* for the Institute's future Dictionary.

The present Dictionary does not claim to contain all the words that went into the main inventory: this is the function reserved for the big Dictionary still to come. There the entry-words will be distributed in two separate alphabetical lists (as, for example, in the English Webster, or in the Italian Petrocchi). Separated from words in general use in the [modern] language, space will be given to entries for items which range from the ancient word now fallen into total disuse through to the most insignificant dialect word and even to Castilianisms and any other words, today considered unacceptable, to be found in the writings of nineteenth-century authors. All such items can be included there, and it is also quite right that they should be included. But this is not the case in a Dictionary like the present one, for which the aim is that it should be normative and where their inclusion might seem like encouragement to use them. The other approach would be very dangerous at the present moment when many people, desirous of improving their Catalan, go in search of the unusual word with which to replace the one used habitually, correct or not.

There will certainly be those who object to not finding in this General Dictionary one word or another which is peculiar to their own region. They need to understand, though, that if an item of this kind is to figure one day in [future editions of] this General Dictionary of the literary language, it has to be because a local writer fully familiar with the word in question has elevated it to the category of a literary word. Otherwise, we would run the risk of loading our literary vocabulary with words which, inappropriately absorbed by people at large, would tend to encumber the work of giving written Catalan a pure and fixed form. The non-inclusion of such words might be criticised also by certain linguists who are seeking information about them. But these people have to be aware that the present Dictionary is compiled out of concern not for their research but for the improvement of written Catalan and its diffusion among the general body of Catalan-speakers. This is why, on the one hand, we omit words which have an undoubted interest for the linguist, while on the other hand we consign technical terms of Greco-Latin formation, international words, these, of meagre lexicographical interest, but which have to be included in a normative dictionary because many people will doubtless care to know their Catalan form.

In the compilation of this Dictionary use has been made of many dictionaries of Catalan and of other languages (principally that of the Spanish Academy, [the French one of] Hatzfeld and Darmesteter, and Webster's English Dictionary), of published lexicographical collections (the Marià Aguiló Dictionary, the Bulletin of Catalan Dialectology, etc.) and collections held in the Lexicographical Offices (including the ones compiled by Manuel de Montoliu and Carles Riba,[112] together with the botanical files by Miquel de Garganta).[113] Many specialists have been consulted, and assessment by the Philological Section has been called for in the frequent cases of uncertainty over the true meaning or the proper definition of a particular word. Every precaution has been taken to avoid inaccurate definitions. Even so, it will not have been possible to avoid unwitting inclusion of some which are inexact, deficient or unclear, although the risk of this will have been attenuated by complementing the definition with a brief sample to exemplify use of the word in question and to make its use clear, whenever it is an important item or one whose meaning is hard to pin down.

[…]

[58] Deviations in the concepts of language and Homeland*

I

With the first centenary of our literary renaissance and as we enter a new century in its evolution, we feel the urge to engage in a conscientious meditation upon the progress made by Catalanism and upon what still needs to be done. We observe, on the one hand, how patriotic feeling has spread considerably and how the activities of several generations have taken solid shape in cultural and political attainments. On the other hand, however, it is necessary to bring light to bear upon certain current deviations which imply serious dangers. There are two such errors or deviations which we aim to rectify with the present lines: first, the concept of our Homeland as being formed exclusively by the territory of the present-day Generalitat, that is, the reduction to its constituent regions which has

---

112. 1893–1959. Poet, translator, critic. His reputation and influence, closely identified with *noucentista* values, were established in the 1920s, and he is acknowledged to be one of the most outstanding literary and intellectual figures of twentieth-century Catalonia.

113. 1903–1988. Pharmacologist and botanist. After 1939 he pursued his scientific work in Colombia.

* «Desviacions en els conceptes de llengua i Pàtria». *Oc* 16–17: 76–80 (January–April 1934). Reprinted in: Lamuela & Murgades (1984: 283–289).

come about through a weakening of national consciousness; secondly, the notion which confers upon our Homeland an excessive extent, one which it has never had, arising from a confusion of Catalanism with Occitanism.[114]

II

Our Homeland, for us, is the territory where the Catalan language is spoken. It stretches, then, from the Corbières range in the north to the fertile ground of Oriola in the south, and from the eastern parts of Aragon across to the Mediterranean. It comprises four major regions – the Principality of Catalonia, Valencia, the Balearic Islands and the Roussillon – each one of these having its own particular and interesting characteristics, and their personality must be preserved at every level, as it endows us with such a great richness of aspects. There is no danger of absorption of one region by the others, nor any desire at all for such a thing. This would contradict the historical tradition and the liberal spirit of our people. Respectful of this diversity, it also behoves us to acquire full awareness of our collective unity and to strengthen it accordingly, above all in the cultural aspect. Unity does not signify submission of some people to others, nor does it mean external uniformity. Unity means the creation of common ideals and the joy of possessing a culture which we all call our own. Where this unity must show itself most energetically is face to face with other countries: in the contrast between what is national and what is foreign is where we must strengthen the sense of belonging to a mother country, over and above regional differences. With these words we are not expounding any new theory: they correspond to the traditional, orthodox conception of conscious and responsible Catalanism. This is not to say, of course, that we would stand in the way of any possible aspect of Catalan expansion which might arise at any given time and which might be viable.

III

Of the two errors we are combating, there is no doubt that more extensive and inveterate is the first one, which limits our homeland to the territory of what were

---

114. The historical territory of Occitania (or the Languedoc) covers most of southern France. Its language, variously designated as Gascon or Limousin or Provençal, is a close relative of Catalan. It enjoyed a revival in the nineteenth century, the Félibrige movement, parallel with but weaker than the Catalan Renaixença. Reference in the text is to confusion between the two languages, in the late nineteenth-century context, and to certain projects for a common front in political self-affirmation. The implications are dealt with in Section IV of the present text. See Kremnitz, Prologue, pp. XXIX–XXX and Introduction, §2.4.

four Spanish provinces [Barcelona, Girona, Lleida and Tarragona].[115] Manifestations of national consciousness during the Middle Ages (of which the chronicler Ramon Muntaner[116] and King Pere III[117] are the outstanding exponents) respond to an integral sense of a home country. The weakening and then the disappearance of the sense of unity coincides with the period of political and cultural decadence [between the sixteenth and the eighteenth centuries], and it goes without saying that the nation which governs us from beyond our own frontiers has endeavoured – and still endeavours – by every means to foster and accentuate divergence between the Catalan-speaking lands. Fortunately, the effects of our modern revival movement are restoring, gradually, the former spirit of totality. We have travelled a long way forwards, but it must be acknowledged that we still have not reached the stage of full collective consciousness. The best fruit from commemoration of the centenary of the Renaixença must be the extirpation of everything which stands in the way of immediate attainment of this ideal. And we believe, sincerely, that the second deviation to which we have alluded – although it springs from a noble and fervent patriotic intent – constitutes a most serious obstacle to this goal.

IV

In the question pertaining to Occitanism, we find nowadays, among ourselves, fluctuating perspectives: on occasions Occitania is the sum of various regions forming a single nationality (as it was defined by Josep Aladern[118] at the beginning of the twentieth century); at other times it is a compound of different nationalities with their own personalities which vaguely constitute a "super-nation".

---

115. Fabra here says literally "four ex-provinces". This is because the Republican Generalitat brought in its own territorial division, based on historical and natural regions, the *comarques*, to replace the system of provincial Diputacions introduced for the whole of Spain in 1833. The division into provinces was reinstated after the Civil War and was retained in the new Spanish Constitution of 1978.

116. 1265–1336. Chronicler. As a soldier he was actively involved in Catalan campaigns in Minorca, Sicily and the eastern Mediterranean. His Chronicle (written between 1325 and 1328) is the most important, in literary and historical terms, of the four great medieval Catalan chronicles. See §2.5.1.

117. 1319–1387. King of Catalonia-Aragon 1336–1387. He intervened in the composition of the Chronicle covering his reign.

118. Pen-name of Cosme Vidal i Rosich, 1869–1918. Writer, publisher, journalist.

Within these two conceptions there is the very widespread opinion that all the territories included between the Limoges area and the south of Valencia, and between the Alps and the Atlantic, speak a single language with various nuances, dialects in effect, which, it is supposed, display little divergence. This leads to the conclusion, naturally, that within the supposed Occitanian language one finds on an equal footing the Catalan of Catalonia (and of Valencia and Majorca), Limousin, Gascon and Provençal, etc.

One ought to reflect seriously on the danger for consciousness of language unity entailed in something which at first sight could seem to represent no such risk. Instead of the geographical area of our language being expanded – as some might see it – Catalan is in fact diluted within this superior linguistic unity and fragmented into diverse languages or dialects. Occitanism thus conceived tends, indirectly, to set up against the one Catalan language a *Valencian language* and a *Majorcan language* on the same grounds that there would be for a *Minorcan language* or a *language* identified with Lleida or with Castelló, etc.

Furthermore, there is a scientific argument which stands against these theories based on the idea of the big Occitanian language family. Modern-day linguistics affirms that Catalan and the tongue of the Languedoc – known among all Romance philologists by the name of Provençal – are two different languages. They constitute two quite separate language groups, despite the various resemblances to be found between them, resemblances no more important than those encountered between Castilian and Portuguese. Some varieties of Provençal are, certainly, easily understood by an averagely educated Catalan, but this does not signify that the two languages share an identity. It would occur to no one to say that Catalan and Italian form part of the same linguistic unit just on the grounds that a Catalan audience can follow with relative ease a play put on in Italian, not a difficult language if one compares it with some of the Occitanian varieties, like Auvergnois or Gascon, intelligible only to someone who has specialised in studying them.

In order to make a comparison between any two languages, we must take particularly into account the period from which compared texts come and the dialects to which these belong. The present-day versions of the two languages in question must, naturally, be referred to, and the terms of comparison should not be dialects from language-frontier zones but ones which have become consolidated as literary languages. (Two writers whose respective idioms could serve this purpose would be Frederic Mistral[119] and Jacint Verdaguer.) If we were to compare some early Catalan texts with contemporary Provençal ones, we would

---

119. 1830–1914. Writer and most prominent figure in the revival of nineteenth-century Occitanian language and culture, the Félibrige. He won the Nobel Prize in 1908. See Kremnitz, Prologue, p. XXX.

encounter instances of similarities in both sets shared with texts in other Romance languages. The troubadour-style poetry written by medieval Catalan poets has to be left aside. This genre makes exclusive use of Provençal, just like the Italian troubadours also adopt the same medium, like Alfonso X of Castile writes in Galician, and like the very early writers in England use French. We should also discount certain prose texts which abound in forms derived from Provençal, a feature which can be compared to the linguistic influence of Castilian on Catalan writers from the period of literary decadence.

The position we take on this matter does not prevent us from appreciating fully the strong reasons (geographical proximity, the parallelism between the Occitanian and the Catalan revival movements, good relations currently in evidence between sporting teams from the two countries) for us to study with interest the language, the literature and the history of the Occitanian lands (Gascony, the Limousin, the Auvergne, Languedoc and Provence) and to intensify exchanges with all of them (in literary, artistic and other cultural spheres), exchanges which now more than ever it is appropriate to encourage. And we wish very specially to express our sympathetic solidarity with the practitioners of the arts, letters and sciences in the Occitanian lands who have displayed affectionate interest for our country and its culture.

V

We emphasise the supreme importance related, in present times, to all the confusion and vacillation over the concept of Homeland.

We must remember the debilitating effect we suffered from use of the name Aragon to designate the Catalan-Aragonese confederation.[120] Abroad, the confederation was known by the title of "kingdom of Aragon", and the name of Catalonia unjustly lost international recognition precisely from the moment when national integration was achieved through the conquests of Ramon Berenguer IV and Jaume I.[121] Today there would be a similar danger if the Catalan-speaking territories were considered to be included under the denomination of Occitania.

---

120. Ramon Berenguer IV, Count of Barcelona (1113–1162), acquired through marriage the throne of Aragon in 1137. From that time onwards, the title of King(dom) had formal priority over that of Count(y), and Aragon was the term commonly used to refer to the Catalan-Aragonese confederation. The political and cultural attainments of the confederation, however, from the twelfth until the fifteenth century, were protagonised mainly by the Catalans, and their language was also dominant. See §2.5.1.

121. The reign of Jaume I of Catalonia-Aragon (1208–1276), together with that of Ramon Berenguer IV (see note 120), are looked upon as the most glorious epochs of medieval Catalan history: consolidation of the Peninsular domains and expansion in the Mediterranean.

Let us also remember, furthermore, how orthographical and grammatical in-
stability delayed, during the nineteenth century, the consolidation of our national
language and how they have notoriously impeded its modern-day expansion. It
is necessary, then, to prevent similar vacillations from damaging and delaying
consolidation among our people of a full national consciousness.

Barcelona, May 1934
Pompeu Fabra, Ramon d'Alòs-Moner, Ramon Aramon i Serra,
Pere Bohigas, Josep Maria Capdevila, Josep Maria de Casacuberta,
Pere Corominas, Joan Corominas, Francesc Martorell,
Jaume Massó i Torrents, Manuel de Montoliu, Lluís Nicolau d'Olwer,
Marçal Olivar, Antoni Rovira i Virgili, Jordi Rubió, Pau Vila.[122]

[59]   Presidential address to the Barcelona Jocs Florals (1934)*

Something we have been delighted to see has been the recognition of the official
status of the Catalan language.[123] Little did Manuel Milà i Fontanals imagine the
possibility of this coming about when, in his presidential address of 1859, referring to Catalan, he spoke these words: "With an enthusiasm tinged with a little
sadness, we confer here on this language a celebration, we dedicate to it a filial re-
membrance, and we reserve for it at least a safe refuge." The idea of a Catalan language fit to be the official language of Catalonia, at that time, did not even exist.
It had to be created. But those men of letters who re-established the Jocs Florals
opened up the route which was to lead us, one day, to witness just that: Catalan
declared to be the official language of Catalonia.

---

122. The signatories were all distinguished intellectuals and philologists and participants in the
cultural dimension of Catalan politics during the period of the second Spanish Republic. Some
survived until well after the Spanish Civil War (Aramon, Casacuberta, J. Corominas, Rubió,
Vila) and played important roles in the defence and recovery of Catalan through the active
repression of the first decades of the Franco regime. It is noticeable that all are listed alphabeti-
cally except Fabra, a detail which would indicate that he was responsible for drafting the text.

* "Discurs del President". *Jocs Florals de Barcelona*. ([1934]: no publication details given), 19–
29. Reprinted in: Lamuela & Murgades (1984: 199–206).

123. Under the second Spanish Republic (1931–1936) the Statute of Autonomy for Catalonia,
drafted in 1931, was approved by the central government in 1932. Among various (limited)
dispensations for self-rule, the Statute made Catalan the official language, alongside Spanish, in
the territories administered by the Generalitat de Catalunya.

Over the panoply of the Catalan dialects, our medieval writers had formed a *single* written language, a literary language in which regional differences in speech barely showed through. The Catalan which was written in the early phase of our nineteenth-century revival was not the modern language which would have emerged from that early one but for the disruptive effects of literary decadence. Nevertheless it was still necessary for us to use Catalan in writing, even in the poor, damaged form of it that came out of the period of decadence, in order for us to shape a new something that could properly be called a *Catalan language*, a literary medium that could be the worthy succession to our glorious medieval language. And it was thanks to the restoration of the Jocs Florals that the scarce few who formally cultivated Catalan increased in number, and that continuity in this cultivation became assured. Otherwise, the endeavour to set the language back on its feet, now an accomplished fact, could never have been fulfilled.

It is true that the systematic work of purifying and fixing Catalan has been carried out beyond the bounds of the Jocs Florals. But it was indubitably the men of this institution who set the process in motion by recognising that the language had to be cleared of the blemishes contracted during the centuries of decadence, and by anticipating that this could be achieved only through knowledge of the early language and of all its modern spoken varieties. An effort to come into line with the language of our great medieval writers while utilising material provided by present-day dialects: this was the work begun by those worthy figures, with Marian Aguiló outstanding among them. It was necessary to form, on top of the dialect level, a single written language, the same one for all Catalans. And it was not long before a voice was raised, within the Jocs Florals, calling for the creation of such an instrument. It came from another Majorcan, Jeroni Rosselló[124] who, in his presidential address of 1873, recalling the existence of a unified language in the middle ages, declared that it was "quite imprudent to allow so many corruptions by which different communities disfigured it". And he pointed the way to getting over this defect: "We must all be selective, with clear vision and good judgement," he said, "and aim to take in all items of value, as long as they are authentic, from wherever they come, rejecting anything that blurs the clear mirror in which the comely figure of the beloved one can be contemplated." The way ahead was clearly signposted: but the work required could not be done by the Jocs Florals. For this institution to fulfil the task, it would have been necessary, at least, for the permanent commission of the Jocs Florals to have been turned

---

124. 1827–1902. Poet. He wrote in the troubadour manner cultivated under the aegis of the Jocs Florals, and he also initiated publication of the complete works of the great Majorcan polymath Ramon Llull.

into a kind of academy, as was proposed in 1879 by another president, Gonçal Serraclara.[125] Only in this way could they have carried out, systematically, the study of the defects in need of emendation plus the work of selection and unification advocated by Jeroni Rosselló. The Jocs Florals, as they were then and as they have continued to be, could not have accomplished this.

Only a long time after the restoration of the Jocs Florals was a body set up which has been able to work in an organised way on the job of purifying and giving settled form to written Catalan. But the enterprise had its origins in the earliest phase of the literary Renaixença, and there is no question that the Jocs Florals of Barcelona contributed greatly to it. Each new writer became a new collaborator in the task, all of them concerned about the "melioration of the Catalan language", and it was in the poetry festivals of the Jocs Florals that people like Aguiló or Rosselló pointed the way to achieving this. What is more, the work of purifying and fixing the language called for the collaboration of philologists and grammarians, and it is a fact that the first of our nineteenth-century philologists and grammarians figure among the founders and the regular jurors of the Jocs Florals: we are thinking of an Antoni de Bofarull, an Adolf Blanch, a Manuel Milà and, pre-eminently, of a Marian Aguiló, the man who undertook the giant work of assembling the lexicographical data necessary for the remaking of our dictionary.

The thing is that, in the absence of an authority recognised by everybody concerned, work on the improvement of Catalan generated all kinds of disagreements among the writers. In the early years of the revival movement, the grammatical system adopted was that of Catalan as it ended up during the period of literary decadence. According to Bofarull, who fixed completely on that system, improvement of the language was to be reduced to a clearing out of the lexis. Marian Aguiló, however, quickly objected to that system itself and set his mind to correcting the defects in it. Thereafter, improvements proposed by this Majorcan philologist and poet, which some accepted and others disapproved of, gave rise to competition between two systems. And the differences between them were accentuated when the followers of Marian Aguiló, beyond the confines of the Jocs Florals, still working along the lines of drawing modern Catalan closer to its medieval forbear, went about the modernisation of Catalan morphology and orthography. Faced with two conflicting sets of rules, the majority of writers adopted, for any point at issue, the solution that took their fancy more, whichever system it happened to belong to. And the permanent commission of the Jocs Florals, lacking the authority which they might have had if they had been quick enough to turn themselves into an academy – as Gonçal Serraclara would have wished – were powerless

---

125. 1841–1885. Politician. He was active in federalist and republican movements, from 1868 through the 1870s.

to remedy this state of affairs: grammatical questions, especially orthographical ones, stirred passions to such an extent that, in order to avoid imperilling the very survival of the Jocs Florals, the permanent commission agreed to respect written forms and usages as decided by each writer for himself. When, in 1894, Eberhard Vogel presided over the ceremonies of the Jocs Florals, he could declare with good reason: "There is a parasite which is gnawing at the inwards of modern Catalan literature: anarchy." And when the German philologist complained that we still had not managed to create a unified written language, he was obliged to remark that, within the Jocs Florals, an atmosphere had been created which was if anything unfavourable towards the creation of that instrument of expression; it was more a case of keen approval being given there to the freedom for every writer to compose his work in his own dialect, whose differential features he could accentuate; and then, on the other hand, the imposition of a unified written language, it being necessarily a product of [disciplined] artifice, could only displease those who had made of spontaneity an instrument with which to justify their using written Catalan as opposed to a language from outside.

The anarchy about which Eberhard Vogel complained in his presidential address lasted until the publication of the Orthographical Norms of the Institute of Catalan Studies [1913] and until that body's adoption of the grammatical system proposed in my 1912 Grammar. The Institute, aiming through its publications to have Catalan read by scholars of every country, clearly saw the advantage of their appearing with a uniform orthography. So the internal decision was taken to draw up a set of rules for spelling to be observed by members of that academic body and other contributors to its publications. Once the Norms were drawn up, with participation from writers of all tendencies, a call was made by Enric Prat de la Riba inviting everybody to adopt them in order to put an end to the orthographical anarchy that so interfered with the diffusion of written Catalan, making it obviously unsuitable to occupy its rightful place in [the life of] Catalonia. Prat de la Riba's appeal was heeded: the Orthographical Norms were immediately accepted by the great majority of writers and of Catalan publications. The only ones to oppose them were many of those who, inside and outside the ambit of the Jocs Florals, had remained faithful to Bofarull's grammatical system. Despite this opposition, however, the orthographical anarchy came to an end thanks to a particular turn of events. This came about through the fact that the [Reial] Acadèmia de Bones Lletres, to challenge the Norms of the IEC, was putting together an alternative set of rules, and these were supported by opponents of the ones promulgated by the Institute.

It was easy to understand why that opposition continued: to adopt the Norms of the IEC would have meant, for them, renouncing certain orthographical conventions which they deemed to be inviolable and which they had defended persistently, sometimes passionately, against attacks from the modernisers. The *antinormistes*, our antagonists, could perhaps be criticised for being incapable of sacrificing their own preferences in the interests of orthographical unification, which is what the members of the Institute of Catalan Studies had done. But the *antinormistes* were not in exactly the same position as the other side, the modernisers, who had committed themselves in advance to be bound by the results of a voting system and who had participated in the long discussions held before the votes. If the others thought that some of the Institute's Norms were wrong, one can understand that they should have striven to maintain their own preferences. Nevertheless, their attitude did hinder the wider use of written Catalan, and this was regrettable, which is why we modernisers took strong issue with them on many occasions. But I declare here and now, most sincerely, that I do not recall being overly aggressive towards them, and, if this ever happened, I should be sorry about it, because they were motivated by the same ardent desire as we were: the urge to achieve the highest degree of perfection for our written language. I had always been confident that the *antinormistes* would patriotically give up their stance of resistance, as soon as our language was declared official and was thereby called to be learned and used by all Catalans. And thus it has been: in its latest bulletin, the Acadèmia de Bones Lletres has published the following declaration of support for the Orthographical Norms of the IEC: "Another thing that the Academy has renounced has been the orthographical system which it developed when philological studies were sparse and which it defended in persistent and energetic campaigns. But the unyielding constancy of this defence, which in a free literary arena could have been a virtue, would have been fatal if it had been continued at a time when Catalan, now the official language of Catalonia, required an external unity to make it suitable to meet all the people's needs, in the present circumstances of newly constituted political autonomy. For this reason the Academy has adopted the Orthographical Norms of the Institut d'Estudis Catalans."

Seeing this renunciation by the Acadèmia de Bones Lletres, we should not think to speak of winners and losers. In order to arrive at a unified orthography it has been necessary, at this point in time, for the *antinormistes* to relinquish some of the solutions they stood by. But then, who has not had to do the same, at one time or another, during the lengthy process of regulating our spelling? We must remember that what we had come to call the system of the Institute is one which was eventually born out of intense discussions involving participation by writers of every tendency, in the process of which not one of these individuals did not have to sacrifice one or another of their most cherished solutions. From those of us who intervened in drawing up the Norms of the IEC through to the last people to adopt them, we have all been both winners and losers: winners on certain points, losers on others. And we must all be satisfied that we were capable of sacrificing, some sooner than others, certain of *our own* positions, if this has meant arriving at the orthographical unity so necessary for the diffusion of written Catalan.

Today we can rejoice at having achieved not only this unity at the level of spelling but also unity on the wider linguistic plane, which has made it possible for Catalan to be elevated to the status of the official language of Catalonia. We were called on to normalise its morphology and its syntax, to purify and to re-shape its lexis. In this endeavour we also have had to fight our battles: sometimes to make people understand the need to create a unified written language transcending dialectal varieties at the spoken level; at other times to convince those who defended archaic solutions that we were involved in something more than just a restoration of the medieval language; and then, finally, to eliminate the divergences which would inevitably arise in the procedures of rigorous selection demanded for the fashioning of a literary language. Fortunately, in recent years, those struggles became gradually less intense: people came to understand more and more how a collective enterprise demanded that inflexible attitudes be abandoned. And in this atmosphere of cooperation, a grammatical system – the one previously adopted by the Institute of Catalan Studies, improved with modifications suggested by the fuller understanding of problems – has steadily gained acceptance until it now enjoys the support of all practising writers. With this kind of harmony abroad, it was uncomfortable to encounter still the conflict between two orthographical systems, something which, from the start, had seriously compromised calm debate of pros and cons in proposals for improvement of the language. And it is for this reason, emphatically, that we should be pleased at the decision taken by the Acadèmia de Bones Lletres.

Indeed: we must celebrate having put an end to dissension among ourselves, because this is the guarantee of a more efficient collaboration in the efforts demanded of us, still, by the task of setting to rights and widening the use of written Catalan. We can, without any doubt, be delighted at what has been achieved: we have only to compare the impoverished language of the period of literary decadence with the purified and normalised Catalan of today. Let us recall that, at the time of the restoration of the Jocs Florals, Milà i Fontanals could say, with good reason, referring to our language that we had to "reserve for it a safe refuge", and now its official status is recognised. We can be delighted with the distance we have travelled, but there is still a long way to go.

Regarding the work of reconsolidation, it would be mistaken to think that all that remains to be done are some minor improvements to the grammatical system, some definitive adjustments to our syntax, the incorporation of just a few archaic or dialect words. Now that Catalan is making its way into ambits from which it had been hitherto banished, one is made more aware that the job of putting the lexis in perfect order is still unfinished: technical vocabularies must be thoroughly revised; countless things to do with trades and professions, with the arts and with industry are designated with Castilian words. We are flooded with enquiries, like "What is the Catalan for such-and-such a thing?", enquiries which need often to be changed into "What should the Catalan be for such-and-such a thing?"...

And, regarding the work of making the use of Catalan more widespread, we can say that it is only just beginning. This is something which requires our maximum efforts, because – it must be stressed – it is not just a matter of widening the use of Catalan in the sense of people getting used to writing preferentially in the language instead of making exclusive use of Castilian. Rather is it to do with making people more familiar with literary Catalan, this purified and normalised idiom that we have worked so hard to fashion, and which is not the impoverished language as it is spoken by the majority of our people and as it is written for the most part, full of Castilianisms and embarrassingly vulgar expressions. The teaching of Catalan is to be fostered, especially in the sectors best equipped to spread knowledge of it among the bulk of the Catalan-speaking population: [that is to say], those who write for public consumption and also, as of now, school-teachers.

The number of people whose reading is in Catalan is increasing by the day, but what about the kind of Catalan supplied to them by our publications? Is it *consistently* correct? Our language will soon be taught – it is to be believed – in all the schools of Catalonia. But do *all* the school-teachers know Catalan? We have to be aware that if we do not move quickly on making the use of Catalan more consistently widespread, there is the risk that all the progress towards restoring our language to its proper condition and status will have been in vain. There is the danger, now more than ever, that Catalan will become a calque of the Castilian language. Within a bilingual regime, the only means of resisting the pernicious influence of the alien language is perfect knowledge of the mother tongue. Without this, there will be an inevitable continuation of the process of Castilianisation which began during the period of decadence and which the modern revival movement has not put a stop to.

We still have in front of us, then, a huge task to complete. This must not be forgotten, since it would be disastrous for us to believe, on the evidence of results already achieved, that the time has come to rejoice triumphantly, and for self-satisfaction to make us think that our work is at an end. It is a matter now of consolidating what has been achieved, bringing it to completion and making it known among the entire body of Catalan-speakers. An arduous undertaking, to which I hope that we shall all apply our best efforts so that differences do not reappear among those who have the responsibility to carry it out.

Index of names and concepts

Presentation of the index of names and subjects

An index of names and subjects is mainly conceived as a means to look for a specific item. However, it can also be useful to determine which names and subjects are related to the general topic of the book and, since the Editor believes that this secondary function might be of use in a work relating to Fabra, an extensive set of concept entries has been included in the index.

Included under some important headings (notably, *Renaixença* and *redreçament*) are instances where these terms are glossed or given explicative renderings in the translation: See §4.2.2.

The Catalan definite articles (*el, la, l', els, les*) are not included in the alphabetical ordering. Bold type indicates a major reference to an indexed name or concept.

As Fabra does not use always the same terms to refer to a meaning and since his texts are presented here in translation, some entries include all the words sharing the same lexical base so that the reader may have access to all the fragments in which Fabra deals with the same subject. Ex.: *artifice/artificial/artificially*.

A

Acadèmia de Bones Lletres de Barcelona *See Reial Acadèmia de Bones Lletres de Barcelona*

Academia de Buenas Letras de Barcelona *See Reial Acadèmia de Bones Lletres de Barcelona*

Academia, Real – Española *See Real Academia Española de la Lengua*

accents   78, 114, 112, 115, 116, 118–120, **139**, 142, 176

acceptability *See codification, criteria for*

acceptance   XXVI, XXVIII, **41**, **54**, 60, 65, 74, 132, 136, 147, 150, **202–203**, 206, 218 *See also codification, criteria for, acceptability*

accessible   167, 197, 204 *See also codification, criteria for, prospective functionality*

Acció Catalana   155, 171

acquisition   158, 175 *See also loan-words*

adoption   49, 123, 170, 176–177, **202**, 204, 216 *See also loan-words*

advantage for language   **45**, **54–55**, **123**, 149, 158–159, **162–163**, 169, 171–172, 182, 202, 205, 216 *See also melioration for language*

Aguiló, Marià/Marian   87, 88, 101, **119**, 131, 135–136, 139, 142, 174, 189, 190, 208, 214, **215**

Aladern, Josep (pseud. Cosme Vidal i Rosich)   210

Albanian   3

Albert i Paradís, Caterina *See Català, Víctor*

Alcover, Antoni Maria   XVIII, **15–16**, 26, **34**, 56, 88, 120–121, 142

Alfonso X   212

Alfonso XIII   18–19

Alghero (Sardinia)   XXXI, 3, 6 *See also Alguer, l'*

Alguer, l'   3 *See also Alghero*

Aliança Obrera   31

Alibèrt, Loïs   XXXI

Alighieri, Dante *See Dante*

Alòs-Moner, Ramon d'   213

analogy with other languages *See codification, criteria for*

Andalusian dialect   **66–67**, 151
Andorra   XXX, 3, 32
Anglicisms *See English words; and also loan-
  words and terms, sporting*
anti-centralism
  against Barcelona   43
  against Madrid   31 *See also Catalanism
    and nationalism, Catalan*
anti-grammatical   172
antinormisme/antinormistes   XXIV, **34**, 75,
  217 *See also sacrifice of personal views, Jocs
  Florals, orthographical anarchy and Reial
  Acadèmia de Bones Lletres*
appropriateness
  grammatical – *See codification, criteria for*
  structural – *See codification, criteria for*
approval   204 *See also democratic theory of
  linguistic norm*
Arabic   7, 33
Aragon   XXX–XXXI, 3, 8, 20, 209–210, 212
Aramon i Serra, Ramon   **XXXII, 213**
arbitrary   XXIII, 41, 117, 125, 150, 170–171,
  183, **202**
archaisms   41, 59, 69, 126, 132, **146–147**,
  151, 165, **190–191**, 195 *See also codification,
  criteria for, historicity; innovation; learned
  word; medieval Catalan; novelty and
  neologism*
archaists/*arcaïtzants*   181, **183–185**
Aribau, Bonaventura Carles   XXX, 10
Arteaga, Josep Maria d'   55
artifice/artificial/artificially   170, 182, **185**,
  216 *See also democratic theory of linguistic
  norm and norm, prescriptive*
assessment of reform measures   46, 73, 123,
  170, 187, **197, 208** *See also evaluation of
  tests on usage, evaluation of tests on usage
  of appropriate uses and evaluation of tests
  on usage of the implanted element*
Associació Protectora de l'Ensenyança
  Catalana   35, 93
Asturian *bable*   **66–67**, 151
asyllabic   **137, 140** *See also orthography and
  orthoepy*
Ateneu Barcelonès   XIII, **32**, 35, 37, 55, 120,
  172

author   136, 140, 145, 153, 165–168, 173, 180–
  181, 186, 193, 207 *See also writer*
authority   11, 13, 17, 23, **40, 51**, 115, **118**, 131–
  132, 136, 189, **191–192**, 205, 215
autonomy
  (codification criterion) *See codification,
    criteria for*
  political – *See Statute of Catalan Autonomy*
Avenç, L'   **13**, 30, 32, 89, 115, 117, **119, 188**,
  198–199 *See also campaign, linguistic;
  modernise; and reform, linguistic*

B
bable of Asturias *See Asturian bable*
Badia, Alfred   34
Badia i Margarit, Antoni Maria   XXVII,
  27–28, 97
Balaguer, Víctor   XXX
Balari i Jovany, Josep   133
Balearic Islands   XVIII, XXX, 3, 6, 11, 23,
  148, 201, 209 *See also Balearic variety of
  Catalan*
Balearic variety of Catalan   8, 23–24,
  68, 142, **147**, 151–152, 202, 211 *See also
  Balearic Islands; codification, criteria
  for, diasystematicity; Majorcan dialect;
  Minorcan dialect; parastantard variants;
  and texts of Fabra (commented), Task of
  the Valencian and Balearic Writers…*
Bally, Charles   55, 63, 98
Barcelona
  Counts of   6
  University of – *See University of Barcelona*
Barcelonese dialect   38, **42–43, 124** *See
  also Eastern Catalan and Eastern Central
  Catalan*
Barcino (publishing house)   168 *See also
  Nostres Clàssics, Els; and Casacuberta,
  Josep Maria*
Basque   XXVII
Baudelaire, Charles   90
Berrendonner, Alain   65
bilingual/bilingualism   **61, 192, 219**
bisyllabic   145 *See also orthography and
  orthoepy*
Blanch, Adolf   **114**, 135, 139, **188**, 198–199, 215

Bofarull, Antoni de   114–116, 119, 135, 139,
    188, 198–199, 215–216
Bohigas, Pere   213
Bopp, Franz   55
borrowing   50, 73, 137–138, 148–149, 151, 168,
    180, 182 See also loan-words
Bosch-Gimpera, Pere   XIII
Bréal, Michel   56
Brossa, Jaume   12
Bulbena, Antoni   119, 121, 141, 171–172

C
Calmette, Joseph   15
calque   50–52, 59, 63, 73, 80, 125, 153–154,
    199, 161, 179, 219 See also Castilianism,
    syntactical; interference; loan-words and
    meanings, identification of
Calveras, Josep   34, 99 See also
    antinormisme
campaign, linguistic   13, 30, 32, 119, 189 See
    also Avenç, L'
Capdevila, Josep Maria   213
Carner, Josep   14–15, 181, 193
Carxe, el   3
Casacuberta, Josep Maria   168, 213
Casas i Carbó, Joaquim See Casas-Carbó,
    Joaquim; and Cases-Carbó, Joaquim
Casas-Carbó, Joaquim   13, 82, 89 See also
    Cases-Carbó, Joaquim
case See semantic role
Cases-Carbó, Joaquim   119 See also Casas-
    Carbó, Joaquim
Cases i Rubiol, Melcior   120
Castile   8, 212
Castilian   XXIX, XXXII, 9, 12, 21, 39, 44–45,
    47–51, 54–55, 59–63, 66, 79–82, 113–117,
    120–122, 124–126, 126–130, 144–145, 151–
    153, 158, 161, 164, 173, 189, 211, 219 See also
    Castilianisms and Spanish
Castilianisms   39, 50–51, 59–60, 69, 79–80,
    88, 143, 148–149, 165, 172–179, 183–187
    See also calque, Castilian, interference,
    loan-words and Spanish
    identification of meanings See meanings,
    identification of –
    lexical –   127, 129, 148–149, 160, 164

syntactical –   51, 59–60, 120, 143, 148,
    158, 178–179, 196 See also calque and
    meanings, identification of –
Català, Víctor (pseud. Caterina Albert i
    Paradís)   13
Catalan
    – lands   3–6 See also Països Catalans
    speaking-Catalan domain   XXVI, 3–6
        See also Catalonia; Catalònia, Greater;
        and Països Catalans
    speaking-Catalan lands   XXV, 3–6 See
        also Catalonia; Catalònia, Greater; and
        Països Catalans
    speaking-Catalan territories   XXVI,
        XXX, 3–6, 38, 124, 147–148, 210, 212 See
        also Catalonia; Catalònia, Greater; and
        Països Catalans
    medieval – See medieval Catalan
Catalan Grammar (1918–1933) (Gramàtica
    catalana)   XXVI, 31, 37, 56, 82
Catalanism
    (ideology)   11–12, 14, 18–19, 35, 155,
        208–209 See also nationalism, Catalan
    (Catalan interference in Castilian)   62
Catalonia
    Principality of –   XVII, 3–6, 23
    Greater – (Catalunya Gran)   3–6, 38, 124
        See also Catalan, Catalònia and Països
        Catalans
    New –   6
    Northern –   3, 8
    Old –   6
Catalònia
    (homeland)   3–6, 38, 66 See also Catalan;
        Catalonia, Greater; and Països Catalans
    (journal)   35
censorship   18–19, 21, 23
centralism
    Barcelonese –   43, 147–148
    French – See also France and nationalism,
        French
    Spanish –   8–9, 24, 31 See also Madrid
        and nationalism, Spanish
Cervantes, Miguel de   8, 76, 80
Chancelry, Royal   6

change *See also flexibility of language, innovation, interference, Labov and variant*
  linguistic – 41, **46–47**, **60–62**
    causes of – **61**
    – from above 39
    – from below 60
    consequences of – **61**
    direction of – **62**
    emerging variant *See emerging variant*
    external factors of – **61**
    external and psycholinguistic factors of – **61**
    internal factors of – **61**
    origins of – **60–61**
    process of – **60–61**
    relation of – with norm of habitual use 62
    resistance to – **62** *See also innovation, linguistic, resistance to*
    types of – **62**
checking of reform measures 50, 203 *See also evaluation of tests on usage, evaluation of tests on usage of appropriate uses and evaluation of tests on usage of the implanted element*
Chinese 33
Civil War, Spanish (1936–1939) XXV, XXIX, XXXI, 21–22, 32, 34–35, 89, 155, 210, 213
clarity 53, 141 *See also codification, criteria for, intelligibility*
classification
    – in neo-Latin languages *See neo-Latin languages, classification of Catalan among –*
    – in Romance languages *See Romance languages, classification of Catalan among –*
clause 60, 126–128, 156, 172, **178–181** *See also proposition and sentence*
codification *See also lexis, morphology, normative standard language, orthoepy, orthography, syntax, uniform language / (language) uniformity and united language*
    criteria for –

acceptability 43, **48–49**, 54, 58, 64–65, 74, 129, 132, 146, 159 *See also acceptance*
analogy with other languages 50, 52–54, 61, 63–64, 72 *See also de-Castilianisation, diversity, inter-linguistic; and Romance languages*
autonomy **49**, 52, 63, **68–69**, 72 *See also cultivation, de-Castilianisation, purification of language and subordinated language*
confirmed functionality 48, 58 *See also norm, objective*
diasystemacity 44, 71 *See also dialect, selection and texts of Fabra (commented), Task of the Valencian and Balearic Writers...*
distinctiveness 45, 52–55, 62, 163, 169–170, 178 *See also differentiation*
etymological suitability **45–46** *See also etymological/etymology and Latin*
evaluation of tests on usage **50–53**, 65, 70, 72–73, **202** *See also assessment of reform measures, checking of reform measures and testing of reform measures*
evaluation of tests on usage of appropriate uses 52 *See also assessment of reform measures, checking of reform measures and testing of reform measures*
evaluation of tests on usage of the implanted element 50 *See also assessment of reform measures, checking of reform measures and testing of reform measures*
genuineness 50, 54, 64, 71, 73 *See also purification of language; and sensitivity, linguistic*
grammatical appropriateness 47, 53–54, 63
guarantee of pertinent use **49** *See also development of language; innovation; norm, objective; and system*
historicity 44, 52, 54, **64**, 72–73 *See also archaisms and medieval Catalan*

implantation   **48, 54, 58, 63–65, 71**, 203
  See also norm, objective
intelligibility   **48, 58, 65, 74, 185**, 187
  See also clarity
paradigmatic homogeneity   **45**
prospective functionality   **48, 58–59,
  64–65, 70, 73–74** See also accessible
  and viability
regularity   **45**, 117, 205
simplicity   **48, 58**
specificity   **50, 74**
structural appropriateness   **45, 52**
suitability to a linguistic
  conception   47
suitability to a stylistic conception   47,
  71 See also formal
Collected Lessons for the Higher Catalan
  Course (1933–1934) (Recull de les lliçons
  del curs de català superior 1933–1934
  pel mestre En Pompeu Fabra) See texts of
  Fabra (commented)
Companys, Lluís   20, **31–32**
completion of language   **44, 53, 58**
composition / composite words   **182** See also
  neologism and new word
conception
  suitability to a linguistic – See codification,
    criteria for
  suitability to a stylistic – See codification,
    criteria for
confirmed functionality See codification,
  criteria for
Congress, I International – on the Catalan
  Language   **15**, 30, 32, 56, 87, 199
consciousness
  – of language   30, **60–61**, 211
  national –   **209–210**, 213 See also
    nationalism, Catalan
consensus   **40, 204** See democratic theory of
  linguistic norm
Constitution
  French –   8
  Spanish – of 1978   XXIX, 6, 23, 210
"Conversa amb Pompeu Fabra" See texts of
  Fabra (commented), Conversation with
  Pompeu Fabra, A

"Conversa filològica" See texts of Fabra
  (commented), Philological Conversation
Conversation with Pompeu Fabra, A
  ("Conversa amb Pompeu Fabra") See texts
  of Fabra (commented)
Corominas, Pere   213
Corominas/Coromines, Joan   83, **85**, 95, 213
correct/correction   71, 120, **141, 161–162,
  169**, 202, **205–206**, 219 See also
  codification, fault; grammar, normative;
  and grammatical
Coseriu, Eugenio   **59, 73** See also norm,
  objective; system; and use
cultivation of / to cultivate language   38,
  58, 72, **197–198**, 214 See also codification,
  criteria for, guarantee for pertinent use;
  development of language; elaboration,
  functional; enrichment; flexibility of
  language; innovation; lexis, reshape of;
  melioration; perfect; purification; refine
  language, to; and stylistic distribution of
  forms
Curs superior de català professat pel
  mestre Pompeu Fabra a la Universitat
  Autònoma de Barcelona See texts of Fabra
  (commented), Higher Catalan Course,
  1936–1937
Curtius, Georg   56

D
Dalmau, Delfí   **36**, 61
Danish   3 See also Dano-Norwegian
Dano-Norwegian   33 See also Danish and
  Norwegian
Dante   XVII, 7
Darmesteter See Dictionnaire général … and
  Hatzfeld
Decadence   **7–9, 68, 75, 134–136, 146–148,
  151, 168, 173, 180, 189**, 198, 210, 212, **214–215,
  218–219**
de-Castilianisation/de-Castilianisers
  (descastellanitzadors a ultrança)   **38–39,
  41, 69, 71, 78–79, 124–126, 183–185** See also
  codification, criteria for, analogy with other
  languages and autonomy; and purification
  of language

defect, linguistic   40, 48–49, 50–51, 74, 116–117, 129, 132, 138, 143, 146, 154–155, 159, 162, 164, 169, 185, 201–203, 214–215 *See also error, fault and mistake*

democratic theory of linguistic norm   40, 63, 191–192 *See also consensus, fault, grammarian, philologist and writer*

derivation/derivative   61, 79, 137, 141, 145, 149–150, 157, 163–164, 174–175, 182, 212 *See also neologism, new word and suffixes*

descastellanització/descastellanitzador See de-Castilianisation

"Desviacions en els conceptes de llengua i Pàtria" *See texts of Fabra (commented), Deviations in the Concepts of Language and Homeland*

development of language   XXX, 22, 61, 63, 140, 173, 180, 186, 205 *See also codification, criteria for, guarantee for pertinent use; elaboration, functional; enrichment; expressive; flexibility of language; lexis, reshape of; melioration; purification; refine language, to; and stylistic distribution of forms*

Deviations in the Concepts of Language and Homeland ("Desviacions en els conceptes de llengua i Pàtria") *See texts of Fabra (commented)*

dialect   38, 41–44, 59, 63, 66, 68, 70–71, 73–74, 84, 88, 117, 119, 121, 123–124, 128, 131, 136, 144–152, 158, 181–183, 190–191, 199–202, 207–208, 211, 214, 216, 218 *See also codification, criteria for, diasystematicity; language; patois; spoken language; subordinated language*

Andalusian –   *See Andalusian dialect*

Asturian *bable See Asturian* bable

bable of Asturias *See Asturian* bable

definition of –   172–173, 184 *See also autonomy; diversity, inter-linguistic; dominant tongue; impoverished language; language; literary language; national language; patois; provincial language; subordinated language; and vernacular*

Balearic – *See Balearic variety of Catalan*

Eastern Catalan *See Eastern Catalan*

Eastern Central Catalan *See Eastern Central Catalan*

Leonese – *See Leonese dialect*

Majorcan – *See Majorcan dialect*

Minorcan – *See Minorcan dialect*

Valencian – *See Valencian variety of Catalan*

Western Catalan   5, 211

diasystemacity *See codification, criteria for; and also dialect*

diatopy   68–69 *See also dialect; and diversity, geographical*

Diccionari català-valencià-balear (Catalan-Valencian-Balearic Dictionary)   15, 88

Diccionari general de la llengua catalana See General Dictionary of the Catalan Language

Diccionari ortogràfic See Orthographical Dictionary

Diccionario de la Real Academia Española   88

Dictatorship   206 *See also Franco, Francisco; and Primo de Rivera, Miguel*

Dictionnaire général de la langue française   88, 89 *See Hatzfeld …*

Diez, Friedrich   56

differentiation   45, 50,163, 172, 181 *See also codification, criteria for, distinctiveness*

diffusion of norms   58, 168–169, 196–198, 218 *See also codification, criteria for, evaluation of tests on usage / evaluation of tests on usage of appropriate uses / evaluation of tests on usage of the implanted element; proof-correction; printers; publications; schools; spread of norms; teachers; testing of reform measures; vehiculation of norms; and writers*

Diputació de Barcelona (provincial government)   16–17, 210 *See also Prat de la Riba, Enric*

discourse
   Fabra's –   17, 65

discretionary norms   39, 185 *See also flexiblity of language, not recommendable form, preferred form, rigid norms and tolerable form*

"Discurs del President" *See texts of Fabra (commented), Presidential Address to the Barcelona Jocs Florals* [1934]
distinction/distinctive/distinctiveness *See codification, criteria for*
diversity
    functional –   52 *See also codification, criteria for, guarantee for pertinent use; development of language; elaboration, functional; enrichment; lexis, reshape of; melioration; purification; refine language, to; and stylistic distribution of forms*
    geographical –   61, **199–200**, 209 *See also dialect, diasystematicity and diversity, interlinguistic*
    historical – *See archaism, Decadence, medieval catalan and* Renaixença
    inter-linguistic – *See codification, criteria for, analogy with other languages; dialect, definition of; and language; Romance languages*
    social – *See language professional*
domain, linguistic   38, **67** *See also Catalan, Catalònia, Greater Catalònia and Països Catalans*
dominant tongue   **XXIX**, 81, 182 *See also official language and subordinated language*
Don Quijote   8

E
early Catalan   42, 176, **179–182**, 186, **190–191**, 194, 201 *See also medieval Catalan*
Eastern Catalan   5, 84, **88**, 117 *See also Barcelonese dialect and Eastern Central Catalan*
Eastern Central Catalan   **163**, **200** *See also Barcelonese dialect and Eastern Catalan*
elaboration, functional / elaborate, to   **53** *See also cultivation / cultivate, to; development of language; enrichment; melioration; modernise; purification; and refine language, to*
    stylistic distribution of forms *See stylistic distribution of forms*

emerging variant   **62**, **64**, **66**, 146, **158**, 173, 214 *See also change*
Empordà, l'   191
England   40, 52, 192, 212 *See also English*
English   33, **41**, 116, 156, 170, 173, 207–208 *See also England*
English words   **158–159** *See also loan-words and terms, sporting*
enrichment of language / increase of the expressive resources   **38–39**, 46, **58**, **64–65**, 71, 117, **124**, **146–148**, **181–183**, 186 *See also cultivation / cultivate, to; development of language; elaboration, functional; expressive; melioration; refine language, to; richness; and stylistic distribution of forms*
error   **40**, 52, 122, **170**, 192, 201, 203 *See also defect, fault and mistake*
Espriu, Salvador   22
Estorch, Pau   **120**
etymological/etymology   78, **118–119**, 121, 136, 138, **140–141**, 175, 189, **198–199** *See also codification, criteria for, etymological suitability*
etymological suitability *See codification, criteria for; and also etymological/ etymology*
evaluation of tests on usage *See codification, criteria for*
evaluation of tests on usage of appropriate uses *See codification, criteria for*
evaluation of tests on usage of the implanted element *See codification, criteria for*
evolution, linguistic   45, **53**, **56**, **60–61**, 63, 67, 71, **129**, 131, 140, 145, **151**, **163**, 173, 175, **192** *See also change*
expression of thougt   42 *See also proposition, clause and sentence*
expressive
    – need   **53–54**, 71, 73
    – resources   **39**, 45, **50**, **65**, 185, 195 *See also development of language, enrichment, melioration and refine language, to*

F

Farran i Mayoral, Josep   170
fault   143, 168, 186 *See also correct; defect; democratic theory of norm; error; grammar, normative; imperfection; incorrect; mistake; norm; rule; solecism; and ungrammatical*
Febrer, Andreu   7
Félibrige   XXX, 209
Felipe IV (of Spain)   8
Felipe V (of Spain)   XXV, 9
Ferran i Mayoral, Josep   *See Farran i Mayoral, Josep*
Ferrer, Magí   198
"Filòlegs i poetes" *See texts of Fabra (commented), Philologists and Poets*
Finnish   3
Fishman, Joshua   15
fixation of language   42, 58, 72–73, 121, 132–133, 147,187, 204–207, 215 *See also codification; normalisation; perfection; purification of language; stabilisation of literary language; uniform language / (language) uniformity; and united language*
flexibility
– of language   63, 144 *See also change; cultivate, to; development of language; elaboration, functional; enrichment of language; melioration; refine language, to; and stylistic distribution of forms*
– of norms   XXIII, 40, 43, 63 *See also discretionary norms, flexiblity of language, formal, not recommendable form, preferred form, rigid norms and tolerable form*
formal/formality   38, 43, 47, 53, 69–71, 76, 131, 168 *See also codification, critera for, suitability to a stylistic conception; and flexibility of norms*
Forteza, Tomàs   56
Fraga   XXXI
France   XXX, 8, 193
Franco, Francisco   31
Franja de Ponent, la   3
French   33, 37, 45, 51, 53–54, 80–81, 84, 90, 115–117 *See also France and Gal·licisms*
functional elaboration *See elaboration, functional*

functionality
confirmed – *See codification, criteria for*
prospective – *See codification, criteria for*
Fundació Bernat Metge   193
Fuster, Joan   17

G

gain for language   127, 136, 161, 167, **181** *See also melioration for language*
Galí, Alexandre   187
Galician   212
Gallicisms   164–165 *See also French, interference and loan-words*
Gallo-romance   6 *See also Romance languages, classification of Catalan among –*
Garcés, Tomàs   35, 187
Garganta, Miquel de   208
Gaudí, Antoni   12
General Dictionary of the Catalan Language (*Diccionari general de la llengua catalana*)   20, 31
Generalitat de Catalunya   20, **23**, 208, 210, 213
genuineness *See codification, criteria for*
German   33
Girona   88, 181
golden age, Catalan   6, 10, 19, 198 *See also medieval Catalan*
good Catalan   126, 168–169 *See also correct/ correction and grammar, normative*
grammar
descriptive –   84 *See also norm. objective; normal; and use*
normative –   36, 40, 51, 65, 72, 82, 86, **192**, 206 *See also correct; fault; grammarian; norm, prescriptive; and purification*
prescriptive –   65, 74, 86, 115, 143 *See also grammarian; and norm, prescriptive*
Grammar, Catalan (1918–1933) *See Catalan Grammar (1918–1933)*
grammarian   40, 50–52, 63, 126–134, 162, 169, 171, **191–192**, 205 *See also grammar, normative; norm; and philologist*
grammatical   169, 171–172 *See also correct*
– appropriateness *See codification, criteria for; and also norm, objective*

grammaticalisation   58 *See also fixation*

Greater Catalonia   5, 38, 124 *See also Catalan and Països Catalans*

greco-latin terms   137–138, 207 *See also Greek, Hellenisms, Latinisms and learned words*

Greek   33, 137–138, 141 *See also greco-latin terms, Hellenisms and learned words*

Grimm, Jacob   56

Gröber, Gustav   56

groups in Romance languages *See Romance languages, classification of Catalan among –*

Guanyavents, Emili   75, 205

guarantee of pertinent use *See codification, criteria for; and also cultivation and norm, objective*

Guardamar   XXXI

Guéret   XXXI

Guimerà, Àngel   11, 193

H

Hassy, Paul   85

Hatzfeld and Darmesteter (French) dictionary   89, 209

Hellenisms   137 *See also greco-latin terms, Greek and learned words*

Herder, Johann Gottfried   15

Higher Catalan Course, 1936–1937 (Curs superior de català professat pel mestre Pompeu Fabra a la Universitat Autònoma de Barcelona) See texts of Fabra (commented)

historicity *See codification, criteria for; and also archaisms and medieval Catalan*

Historico-archaeological Section   206 *See also Institute of Catalan Studies*

Homeland   208–213 *See also Catalan, Catalònia, nation and Països Catalans*

homogeneity

paradigmatic – *See codification, criteria for*

hybrid word   155 *See also calque, Castilianisms and loan-words*

hypercorrection   61, 63, 73 *See also interference*

I

Ibero-romance *See Romance languages, classification of Catalan among –*

Ibsen, Henrik   12, 89–90

identification of meanings *See calque; Castilianism, syntactical; change, types of; and meaning, identification of*

imperfection   124, 154–155, 163, 167, 169 *See also fault*

implantation *See codification, criteria for*

importation / imported word   39, 50, 62, 117, 146, 148–149, 175, 177–180, 195 *See also loan-words*

impoverished language / impoverishment of language   61, 75, 122, 127, 130, 218–219 *See also inferiority of a language, patois and subordinated language*

improvement for language   46, 55, 123, 136, 162, 167–168, 171, 183, 185, 192, 194, 201–203, 215, 218 *See also melioration for language*

inadmissible form   43, 46, 49, 162, 194 *See also incorrect, not recommendable form, preferred form and tolerable form*

incorrect/incorrection   46, 48, 164, 179, 194 *See also correct/correction, fault, solecism and ungrammatical*

inferiority of a language   53, 130, 133 *See also dialect, cultivation of language, impoverished language and superiority of a language*

innovation, linguistic   22, 39, 41, 46–49, 52, 65, 80, 136, 140–141, 157, 160, 162, 169, 171, 182–185, 191, 194, 197, 202–203 *See also archaism; change; codification, criteria of; grammatical appropriateness; cultivation of language; Latinisms; learned words; neologism; new word; and novelty*

resistance to –   141, 162, 183, 191, 201–202, 217, 219 *See also change, resistance to –*

Institut d'Estudis Catalans (Institute of Catalan Studies)   XVIII, XXV-XXVI, 15, 17, 21, 23–24, 36, 133–134, 136, 166, 174, 181, 199–200, 216–218

Institut Escola   ("School Institute")   20

Institute of Catalan Studies *See Institut d'Estudis Catalans*

intelligibility *See codification, criteria for*

interference   37, 48, 56, 59, 61–65, 72–73, 191 *See also calque, change, Castilianism, de-Castilianisation, fault, Gallicism and hypercorrection*

   secondary moment –   64 *See also norm, objective; sensitivity, linguistic; and system*

Italian   33, 50, 53, 84, 115–116, 122, 128, 156, 165, 172, 177, 183, 195, 211

J

Jaume I   212

Jespersen, Otto   56, 67, 84–85

Jocs Florals   10–11, 34, 35, 37, 116, 128, 132, 133, 134, 137, 146, 215, 216–218 *See also* antinormisme, *metrics, orthographical anarchy, poetry,* Renaixença *and writer*

journals   XXIII, 13, 19, 83, 113–114, 159 *See also publications*

K

Kremnitz, Georg   8, 18, 30, 36, 38, 58, 67, 124, 209, 211

L

Labèrnia, Pere   88, 114, 120, 122, 141, 188

Labov, William   60, 64 *See also change*

Lafontaine, Jean de   193

Lamuela, Xavier   XXVII, 37, 43

language

   completion of – *See completion of language*

   cultivation of – *See cultivation of language*

   development of – *See development of language*

   impoverished – *See impoverished language*

   – as social institution   XXVII–XXVIII, 48, 68–71, 91, 200

   – definition   42 *See also dialect, definition; and diversity, inter-linguistic*

   – professional   40–41, 69, 72 *See also diversity, social; proof-correction; printers; publications; and writers*

   – uniformity / unity *See uniformity, language; and unity of language*

   literary – *See literary language*

   medieval – *See medieval Catalan*

   melioration for – *See melioration for language*

   minority – *See minority language*

   modern – *See modern language*

   national – *See national language*

   normalised – *See normalised language*

   official – *See official language*

   patois *See patois*

   perfect – *See perfect language*

   provincial – *See provincial language*

   purified – *See purified language*

   referential – *See referential language*

   spoken – *See spoken language*

   standard – *See standard language*

   subordinated – / subordination of – / subservience of – *See subordinated language / subordination of language / subservience of language*

   technical – *See vocabulary, technical*

   written – *See written language*

langue d'Oc   XXIX, 211 *See also Occitan*

Languedoc   209, 211–212 *See also Occitania*

Latin   33, 45–46, 114–116, 121, **129**, 138–139, 141, **149**, 175–176, 182–183, 207 *See also codification, criteria for, etymological suitability; and learned words*

   greco-latin terms *See greco-latin terms*

   – languages   131 *See also neo-Latin languages and Romance languages*

   vulgar –   6, 156, 173, 182–183 *See also codification, criteria for, etymological suitability*

Latinisms   120–122, 137, 175–176, 182–183 *See also greco-latin terms and learned words*

learned word   39, 121–122, 137–138, 141, 150, 183 *See also Greek, innovation, Latinisms, neologism, novelty and popular word*

Leibnitz, Gottfried   15

Leonese dialect   173

letter dated 13/IX/1910 *See texts of Fabra (commented), letter dated 13/IX/1910*

level *See also register*

   formal – *See formal/formality*

vernacular – *See vernacular level*
Lexicographical Offices   206, 208 *See also Institute of Catalan Studies*
lexis   86–89, 145, 150, 182–183, 201–203 *See also vocabulary and word*
    reshape of –   218 *See also cultivation of language; elaboration, functional; enrichment; melioration; purification of language; refine language; and richness*
Linguaphone Institute   36
Lliga Regionalista   16, 18
Limousin   XXIX, 209, 211–212 *See also llemosí*
linguistic
    emerging – variant *See emerging linguistic variant*
    – campaign *See campaign, linguistic*
    – change *See change, linguistic*
    – conception, suitability to a *See codification, criteria for, suitability to a linguistic conception*
    – defect *See defect, linguistic*
    – domain *See domain, linguistic*
    – evolution *See evolution, linguistic*
    – impoverishment *See impoverished language*
    – innovation *See innovation, linguistic*
    – norm, democratic theory of *See democratic theory of linguistic norm*
    – reform *See reform, linguistic*
    – sensitivity *See sensitivity, linguistic*
literary *See also national language, redreçament, referential language, subordinated language and standard language*
    – language   XXVIII, 86, 116–117, 122–124, 128, 130–134, 144, 147–148, 170–171, 185–187, 190, 204, 211–217, 219
    – register   XXIII, XXVIII
    – status   50, 71–72, 129–130, 133, 144, 148, 173, 177, 219
Lithuanian   3
llemosí   XXIX–XXX, 10 *See also Limousin*
Llull, Ramon   7, 126, 129, 214
loan-words   138, 141, 150, 159, 174, 177, 182–183 *See also acquisition, adoption, Anglicisms, borrowings, Castilianims,*
Gallicisms, importation, neologism and new word
López-Picó, Josep Maria   205
Louis XIV   8
Luther, Martin   XVII

M
Macià, Francesc   20
Madrid   12, 20, 31 *See also centralism; Spain; and nationalism, Spanish*
Maeterlinck, Maurice   89–90
Mancomunitat de Catalunya   XXVI, 16, 18–19, 36, 90
Maó   XXXI
Majorca/Majorcans   9, 70, 143, 181, 183, 211, 213 *See also Balearic Islands and Majorcan dialect*
Majorcan dialect   88, 142, 148, 200, 211 *See also Balearic variety of Catalan and Majorca/Majorcans*
Maragall, Joan   13, 15, 35, 123
March, Ausiàs   7
Martorell, Joanot   8
Massó i Torrents, Jaume   13, 82, 213
meaning *See also semantic and word*
    identification of –   60, 178 *See also Castilianism, syntactical; and calque*
medieval Catalan   52–54, 63–66, 135, 138, 140–141, 146–147, 158, 159, 168–169, 171, 173, 175, 176, 178, 181–184, 218 *See also archaisms; codification, criteria for, historicity; early catalan; golden age; and medieval/classic Catalan writers*
medieval/classic Catalan writers   19, 70, 126, 173, 180–181, 212, 214 *See also archaisms; early catalan; codification, criteria for, historicity; golden age; medieval Catalan; and old Catalan*
Melanchton, Phillip   XVII
melioration for language   215 *See also advantage for language; cultivation / cultivate, to; development of language; elaboration, functional; enrichment; flexibility of language; gain for language; improvement for language; purification; refine language, to, and stylistic distribution of forms*

memory   153, **198**

Menéndez Pidal, Ramón   15, **172–173**

Metge, Bernat   7–8, 126, 129

metrics   132, 145 *See also Jocs Florals, poetry and writer*

Meyer-Lübke, Wilhelm   XXI, XXVII, 56, 67

Milà i Fontanals, Manuel   41, **131**, 133, 135, 144, 189, 197, 213, 218

Military Directorate *See Primo de Rivera, Miguel*

Minorca   XXXI, 210 *See also Balearic Islands*

Minorcan dialect   **211** *See also Balearic variety of Catalan*

minority language   3 *See also dialect, impoverished language, patois and subordinated language*

Miquel i Planes, Ramon   **35**

mistake   51, **63**, **65**, 155, 166, 191, 203 *See also defect and fault*

Mistral, Frederic   XXX, **42**, **211**

Modernisme/modernista   14, 17, 30, 34–35, 89–90, 127 *See also Avenç, L'*

modernisation of / to modernise language   XXVI, 11, **74–82**, 135–136, **215–217** *See also Avenç, L'; codification; elaboration, functional; Modernisme; Noucentisme; redreçament*

Molière   193

Moll, Francesc de B.   15, **88**

monosyllable   129, 145 *See also orthography and orthoepy*

Montoliu, Manuel de   87, 208, 213

Morel-Fatio, Alfred   56

morphology/morphological   37, 39, 55–56, 58, **66**, 69, **74**, 79, 83–85, 114, 116, **118–123**, **128–129**, 140, 147–148, 151, **162**, 173, 175–176, **200–201**, 205, 215

"*mot qui*, El" *See texts of Fabra (commented),* "*word* qui, *The*"

Muntaner, Ramon   **210**

Murcia   3

Muret, battle of   **XXX**

Murgades, Josep   XXVII, 32

N

nacionalitat catalana, La   15–16

nation   5, **210** *See also Catalan, Catalonia, Homeland, national, nationalism, nationality and Països Catalans*

national   9, 209

– community   XXV, 212 *See also Catalan, Catalonia, Homeland, national, nationalism, nationality and Països Catalans*

– consciousness   **209–210**, 213 *See also nationalism*

– language   3, **66–67**, 133, **144**, 147, **158**, 198, 213 *See also literary, official language,* redreçament, *referential language, standard language, and subordinated language*

– status of language *See status of language, national*

nationalism   **XXIX**, 90 *See also patriotic*

Catalan –   **XXIX**, XXXI, 9, **14–15**, 18, 20, 23 *See also Catalanism; and consciousness, national*

French –   **8** *See also France*

Occitanism *See Occitanism*

Spanish –   **XXIX**, 210 *See also centralism, Madrid and Spain*

Nationalist Federal Republican Union   35

nationality   38, 210 *See also Països Catalans and* Catalònia

nationhood   9, 12, 15, 38, 124 *See also nationalism and nationality*

natural feature / naturalness   38, 53, **61**, 67, 114, **124**, 129, **161**, 177, **197**, **199**, 203 *See also norm, objective; normal; spontaneity; and use*

need

expressive – *See expressive need and expressive resource*

neogrammatical   67

neo-grammarians   XXVII, **74**, **83–84**

neo-Latin languages   128, 135, 138, 140, 182 *See also Romance languages*

Classification of Catalan among –   **66**, **152** *See also Romance language, Classification of Catalan among*

neologism   41, **45**, 87, **131–132**, 189, **191**, 193, **194**, 202 *See also archaism, composition, derivation, innovation, learned words, loan-words and new word*

new word   46–47, 160, 181–182, 194 *See also
composition, derivation, innovation, loan-
words and neologism*

newspapers   61, 113, 152, 159, 164–166, 168–
169 *See also publications*

Nonell i Mas, Jaume   119

norm   23, 40–41, 51, 73, 117, 133, 172, 186,
188, 192, 205 *See also fault and rule*

democratic theory of linguistic – *See
democratic theory of linguistic norm*

diffusion of – *See diffusion of norms*

discretionary – *See discretionary norms*

objective –   59, 62–63, 73 *See also
codification, criteria for, confirmed
functionality / guarantee for pertinent
use; Coseriu; natural feature /
naturalness; normal; spontaneity;
system; and use*

prescriptive –   62–63, 73–74, 172, 186 *See
also grammar, normative/prescriptive*

rigid – *See rigid norms*

normal   41, 54, 188, 191, 200 *See also
Coseriu; natural feature / naturalness;
norm, objective; norm, prescriptive;
spontaneity; system; and use*

normalise, to / normalisation of
language   12, 22, 55, 58, 90, 134, 218–219
*See also codification; fixation of language;
grammar, normative/prescriptive;
perfection; and purification of language*

normative
– discourse *See discourse, Fabra's*
– grammar *See grammar, normative/
prescriptive*
– standard language / normativisation
XXIII, XXVIII, 5, 13, 16–18, 23, 29, 34, 40,
51, 55, 64–65, 72, 83, 85, 91, 191–192, 206
*See also codification, redreçament and
standard language*

Normes de Castelló de la Plana   XVIII,
XXVI

"normes de l'Institut, Les" *See texts of Fabra
(commented), Norms of the Institut
d'Estudis Catalans, The*

*Normes Ortogràfiques See Orthographical
Norms*

Norms of the Institut d'Estudis Catalans, The
("Les normes de l'Institut") *See texts of
Fabra (commented)*

Northern Catalonia *See Catalonia, Northern*

Norwegian   3, 90 *See also Dano-Norwegian*

Nostres Clàssics, Els   19, 168 *See also Barcino
(publishing house); and Casacuberta, Josep
Maria*

not recommendable form   164 *See also
discretionary norms, flexibility of norms,
inadmissible form, preferred form, stylistic
distribution of forms and tolerable form*

Noucentisme/noucentista   35, 75, 90

Nova Cançó, La   22

Nova Planta decrees   XXV, 9

novelty   46, 194 *See also archaism,
innovation, learned word and neologism*

O

"obra de depuració del català, L'" *See texts
of Fabra (commented), Task of Purifying
Catalan, The*

Occitan/Occitania/Occitanian   XXIV,
XXVII, XXVIII, 42, 210–215 *See also
Homeland; language; texts of Fabra
(commented), Deviations in the Concepts of
Language Homeland; and Provençal*

Occitanism (ideology)   209–211

official language   XVIII, XXVII, 3, 8, 17,
20–21, 32, 125, 133, 151, 213, 217–218 *See also
dominant tongue and national language*

old Catalan   7, 39, 44, 46, 54, 80, 131,
142–144, 146–151, 172–173, 175, 190 *See also
medieval Catalan*

Oliba, Bishop   17

Oller, Narcís   11, 74–82

*On Linguistic and Orthographical
Reform* ("Sobre la reforma lingüística
y ortográfica") *See texts of Fabra
(commented)*

*On Various Unresolved Issues in Present-
day Literary Catalan* ("Sobre diferents
problemes pendents en l'actual català
literari") *See texts of Fabra (commented)*

Ors, Eugeni d' (*Xènius*)   14, 17 *See also
Noucentisme*

orthoepy   74, 162–163 *See also asyllabic,*
   bisyllable, codification, metrics,
   monosyllable and phonetics
orthographical anarchy   132–133,
   135–136, 145, 205, 213, 215–216 *See also*
   antinormisme, *Blanch, Bofarull, Jocs*
   Florals, Reial Acadèmia de Bones Lletres de
   Barcelona, Renaixença, *sacrifice of personal*
   views and writers
Orthographical Dictionary (*Diccionari*
   ortogràfic)   87, 166, 174 *See also texts of*
   Fabra (commented), Norms of the Institut
   d'Estudis Catalans, The ("Les normes de
   l'Institut")
Orthographical Norms   35, 87, 133–134,
   141–142, 216–217 *See also texts of Fabra*
   (commented), Norms of the Institut
   d'Estudis Catalans, The ("Les normes de
   l'Institut")
orthographical reform *See campaign,*
   linguistic; and reform, linguistic
orthography   39, 58, 69, 73, 85, 91, 118–121,
   129, 135–142, 153, 156, 163, 197–199, 202,
   205, 215–218 *See also asyllabic, bisyllable,*
   codification, memory, monosyllable,
   spelling and written accents

P
Països Catalans   XXVI, **XXXI**, 5–6, 15, 38,
   124 *See also Catalan; Catalònia; domain,*
   linguistic; Greater Catalonia; Homeland;
   and nation
Palestra   35
paradigmatic homogeneity *See codification,*
   criteria for
parastandard variants   23 *See also*
   codification, criteria for, diasystematicity;
   literary language; selection; and texts of
   Fabra (commented), Task of the Valencian
   and Balearic Writers…
Passy, Paul   56
patois/*patuès*   8, 22, **68**, 72 *See also dialect,*
   impoverished language, provincial
   language, subordinated language and
   vernacle

patriotic/patriotical/patriotically   35, 40, 117,
   130–131, 208, 210, 217 *See also Homeland*
   and nationalism
Pere III   129, 210
perfect / perfection of language   46, 73, 145,
   170, 187, 217 *See also cultivation, fixation,*
   normalisation and purification of language
personal views, sacrifice of *See sacrifice of*
   personal views
Petrocchi Italian dictionary   207
Philological Conversation ("Conversa
   filològica") *See texts of Fabra (commented)*
Philological Conversations   XXIII, XXVIII,
   33, 37, 62, 67
Philological Section *See also Institute of*
   Catalan Studies)   15, 17, 31–32, 87, **90**,
   141–142, 174, 206, **208**
philologist/philological   XXVIII, 11, 39, 124,
   126, 131, 146, 159, 183, 189, 211, 213, 215, 217
   See also grammarian
Philologists and Poets ("Filòlegs i poetes") *See*
   texts of Fabra (commented)
phonetics   37, 55–56, 69, 74, 83–84 *See*
   also orthoepy, phoneme, phonology and
   pronunciation
phoneme   121, 137 *See also phonetics and*
   phonology
phonology   XXI, 5, 78 *See also phoneme*
phrase   44, 46, 49, 52, 148, 152, **156**, 179–181,
   193–194 *See also proposition*
Pla, Josep   34, 36
Poe, Edgar A.   90
poetry   126, 144–145, 212, 215 *See also*
   metrics, Jocs Florals and writer
political autonomy *See Statute of Catalan*
   Autonomy
poor language   214 *See also impoverished*
   language and patois
popular, words of – origin   137–138, 141 *See*
   also learned word; and norm, objective
Portuguese   33, 53, 115–116, 122, 173, 211
Prague School   67
Prat de la Riba, Enric   15–18, 31, 34, **174**, 216
preferred form   42–43, 53, 125, 129, 161 *See*
   also discretionary norms of language,
   flexiblity of norms, inadmissible form, not

recommendable form, tolerable form and
stylistic distribution of forms
prescriptive
– discourse *See discourse, Fabra's*
– grammar *See grammar, normative/*
prescriptive
– norm *See norm, prescriptive*
Presidential Address to the Barcelona Jocs
Florals [1934] ("Discurs del President")
See texts of Fabra (commented)
Primo de Rivera, Miguel   XXVI–XXVII, 31,
33, 35, 87
printers / printing houses   153, 159, 164,
166–167 *See also language professional,*
proof-correction, publications, teachers and
writers
pronunciation   79, 87, 116, 136, 138, 142, 145,
148, 151, 158–160, 162–163, 175, 198–200
See also orthoepy and phonetics
proof-correction   40, 72, 166, 167, 205–206
See also language professional, printers,
publications, teachers and writers
proposal/propose, to   39–41, 46, 49–53,
64–65, 72, 86, 91, 162, 167, 171, 183, 194,
197, 203, 218 *See also democratic theory of*
linguistic norm, discretionary norms and
flexibility of norms
proposition   57, 59, 86, 156, 179 *See also*
clause and sentence
prospective functionality *See codification,*
criteria for
Provençal   XXIX–XXX, 33, 42, 173, 209,
211–212 *See also Félibrige, langue d'Oc*
Mistral and Occitanian
provincial language   66, 136, 158, 168 *See*
also dialect, impoverished language, patois
and subordinated language
publications   127, 129, 141, 153, 159, 205,
216, 219 *See also language professional,*
newspapers, printers, proof-correction,
teachers and writers
Publicidad, La / Publicitat, La   19, 33, 155,
165, 167, 171
Puig i Cadafalch, Josep   18
purification of language / purified Catalan /
purifying language   144–149, 154–155,
157–159, 162, 164–165, 167, 174, 183–187,

190, 214, 218–219 *See also codification,*
criteria for, autonomy; cultivation; de-
Castilianisation; elaboration, functional;
enrichment; fixation of language; grammar,
normative/prescriptive; lexis, resahape
of; melioration for language; perfection;
purism; and refine language, to
purism/purist/purity   XXIX, XXXII, 22,
39–40, 46, 50–51, 58, 63, 70, 117, 123–124
See also purification of language
Pyrenees (Treaty of)   8
Pyrénées-Orientales   3 *See also Roussillon*

Q
Queipo de Llano, Gonzalo   35

R
Racine, Jean   XVII
Rafanell, August   XXIX–XXX
Ramon Berenguer IV   212
Real Academia Española   35, 88
Recull de les lliçons del curs de català superior
1933–1934 pel mestre En Pompeu Fabra
See texts of Fabra (commented), Collected
Lessons for the Higher Catalan Course
(1933–1934)
redreçament/redreçar   18, 38, 41, 58, 63,
70, 73, 76 *See also literary language;*
modernise; normative standard language;
reform, linguistic; restoration; uniform
language / (language) uniformity; and
united language
referential language   XXVII, 18, 36, 73
See also literary, national language,
redreçament *and standard language*
refine, to / refinement of language   38,
41–42, 58, 66–67, 72, 123–124, 168, 193 *See*
also cultivation; development of language;
elaboration, functional; enrichment;
flexibility of language; melioration;
perfection; purification; redreçament; *and*
stylistic distribution of forms
reform/reformation
linguistic –   11, 13, 16–19, 30, 32, 34–35,
39, 41, 54, 70, 78, 89, 115, 117, 119, 128,
134–136, 168, 183, 185–186, 188, 197,
201–203 *See also* antinormisme;

Avenç, L'; Casas-Carbó; codification; elaboration, functional; Institut d'Estudis Catalans; Modernisme; Noucentisme; orthographical anarchy; redreçament; and Renaixença

register *See also level of language*
  formal – *See formal/formality*
  literary – *See literary language*
  technical – **41**, 197 *See also vocabulary, technical*

regularity *See codification, criteria for*

Reial Acadèmia de Bones Lletres de Barcelona 11, 34, 115–116, 133, **216–219** *See also* antinormisme *and orthographical anarchy*

Renaissance
  Catalan – 133, 140, 144–145, 190, 193, 198, 209 *See also* Renaixença
  European – 7

Renaissènça See Félibrige

Renaixença (nineteenth-century revival movement) XXX, **12**, **17**, 34, **48**, **54**, 68, 75–76, **118**, 120, 121, 130–132, 134, 144–145, 151, 174, 178, 187, 198–200, 210, 215 *See also Jocs Florals; Renaissance, Catalan; orthographical anarchy; Romantic; and writers*

Republic,
  Spanish first – (1873–74), XXV, XXX
  Spanish second – (1931–36) **XXVI**, XXXI, 19, 31, 213

resistance
  to change *See change, resistance to –*
  to innovation *See innovation, resistance to –*

resource, expressive *See expressive resource*

restoration of / restore language to 18, **39**, 41, 44, 48, 50, **64**, 71, 129–131, 134, 147–148, 173, **180**, 186, **202–203**, 218 *See also* redreçament

Revista de Catalunya 19, 35

Revue Hispanique 56

Riba, Carles 87, **208**

richness 45, 71, 150, **170–171**, 181 *See also cultivation of language; development of language; elaboration, functional;*

enrichment; melioration; poor language; and refine language, to

rigid/rigidity of norms 73, **186–187**, 195 *See also discretionary norms and flexibility*

Romance languages 3, 6, 60, 63, 69, 115, 123, 126, **129**, 173, 212 *See also codification, criteria for, analogy with other languages; dialect, definition of; diversity, inter-linguistic; language; and neo-Latin languages*
  Classification of Catalan among – 42, **66**, 152

Romanian 33, 48, 83, 122, 128, 140

Romantic/Romanticism XVIII, XXV, XXX, **9–10**, 13, 15, 114, 193 *See also* Renaixença

Rosselló, Jeroni **214–215**

Roussillon XXX, 3, 8, 15, **209** *See also Pyrénées-Orientales*

Rovira i Virgili, Antoni **171**, 213

rule 40–41, 46, 48, 52, 54–55, 65, 73, 114–117, 120, **129**, 136, 143, 153, 170–172, 188, **192**, 198–199, 203–205, **215–216** *See also fault and norm*

Russian 33

Ruyra, Joaquim **15**

S

sacrifice of personal views 133, 198–200, 217 *See also* antinormisme *and orthographical anarchy*

Sagarra, Josep Maria de 20

Salses XXXI

Sandfield, Kristian 61

Sardinian 33

Saroïhandy, Jean-Joseph 56

Saussure, Ferdinand de XXVII, 41, 56, 66–67

Schädel, Bernhard **15**, 56

schools 23, 37, 81, 83, 85, 113, 133, 168, 219 *See also diffusion of norms*

Scientific Section of Institute of Catalan Studies 206

selection 58, 70, 73, 146–147, 181, 215, 218 *See also codification, criteria for, diasystematicity; parastantard variants; redreçament; and texts of Fabra*

(commented), *Task of the Valencian and Balearic Writers…*
semantic   57–58, **145**, 151, 157, **192** *See also word; and meaning, identification of*
semantic calque   158 *See also calque; Castilianism, syntactical; and meaning, identification of*
semantic role   57
sensitivity, linguistic   55, 170 *See also codification, criteria for, genuineness; interference, secondary moment; norm, objective; and system*
sentence   53, **57**, **86**, **179–181**, 189 *See also clause and proposition*
Serbo-Croatian   33
Serraclara, Gonçal   **215**
Serra Húnter, Jaume   XIII
Shakespeare, William   XVII
simplicity *See codification, criteria for*
"Sobre diferents problemes pendents en l'actual català literari" *See texts of Fabra (commented), On Various Unresolved Issues in Present-day Literary Catalan*
"Sobre la reforma lingüística y ortográfica" *See texts of Fabra (commented), On Linguistic and Orthographical Reform*
social
    institution, language as social – *See language as social institution*
    – diversity *See diversity, social*
Societat Catalana d'Estudis Històrics   XIV
solecism   **128–129**, 186 *See also fault, incorrect and ungrammatical*
Spain   XXIX–XXX, **6**, 151, 206 *See also centralism, Madrid and nationalism, Spanish*
Spanish
    – civil War *See civil War, Spanish*
    – Academy *See Real Academia Española*
    – language   XXIX, XXXII, 21, 23, 33, 35, 52–53, **60**, 64, **66–67**, 71–72, 113, 152, 156–159, 173–179, 183 *See also Castilian and Castilianism*
    – nationalism *See nationalism, Spanish*
    – Succession War   9
specificity *See codification, criteria for*

spelling   35, 78–79, **87**, **113–117**, 119, 121, 133, **135–142**, 148, 153, 156, **158–160**, 162, 166, **197–200**, 206, **216–218** *See also orthography*
spoken language   22, 34, 41, 44, 49, 53–55, 61, **69**, 71, 74, 76, 83, 114, **117–118**, **122–125**, 143–148, 163, 168–169, 173, **185–187**, 191–192, 197, **201–203**, 214, 218 *See also dialect; diversity, geographical; spontaneity; and written language*
spontaneity   13, 52, **60**, 64–65, 127, 159, **216** *See also Coseriu; natural feature / naturalness; norm, objective; normal; spoken language; and use*
sporting terms *See terms, sporting; and also Anglicisms*
spread of norms *See diffusion of norms*
stabilisation of literary language   17, **58**, 63, 118, **128–129**, 131, **133–135**, 155, **162**, 173, **179**, 205, **213** *See also fixation of language and redreçament*
standard/standardisation of
    language   XXIII, XXVI–XXXII, 5–6, 13, 18, 22–24, 34, 36, 38, 41, 84 *See also literary language, normative standard language, redreçament and referential language*
status
    literary – *See literary status*
    national – of language   129 *See also national language and redreçament*
Statute
    of Balearic Autonomy (1983)   23
    of Catalan Autonomy *See also political autonomy*
        – (1932)   20, 31–32, 213
        – (1979)   23
    of Valencian Autonomy (1982)   23
stock phrases   193
Storm, John   85
structural appropriateness *See codification, criteria for*
stylistic
    – conception, suitability to a *See codification, criteria for*
    – distribution of forms   39, 53, 59, 71 *See also cultivation of language; development of language; elaboration,*

functional; enrichment; melioration;
  not recommended form; preferred form;
  refine language, to; and tolerable form
subordinated / subordination / subservience
  of language   7, **68**, **125**, **146**, **148**, **173**, **177**
  See also codification, criteria of, autonomy;
  dialect; dominant tongue; impoverished
  language; language; literary language;
  national language; patois; provincial
  language; and vernacle
suitability to a linguistic conception *See*
  codification, criteria for
suitability to a stylistic conception *See*
  codification, criteria for
superiority of a language   123, **168**, **170**–**171**,
  183–184 *See also inferiority of a language*
Sweet, Henry   56, 85
suffixes   145, **150**, **164**, **176**, 182 *See also*
  derivation
syllabic/syllable   115, 129, 134, **145**, 189 *See*
  also orthography and orthoepy
syntactical *See syntax*
  – change *See change, syntactical*
  – codification *See codification, syntactical*
  – diversity *See diversity, syntactical*
  – Castilianism *See Castilianism, syntactical*
syntax   45, 50, 116–118, 120–122, 147, **154**, 157,
  162, 168, 180, 186, 192–193, 201–203, 205
  See also codification and syntactical
system   58–59, 61, 64–65, 74, 83, 112, 115–117,
  119, 179, 204 *See also codification, criteria*
  for, guarantee for pertinent use; Coseriu;
  and norm, objective

T
Tagliavini, Carlo   XXIII
"tasca dels escriptors valencians i balears, La"
  See texts of Fabra (commented), Task of the
  Valencian and Balearic Writers, The
Task of Purifying Catalan, The ("L'obra de
  depuració del català") *See texts of Fabra*
  (commented)
Task of the Valencian and Balearic Writers,
  The ("La tasca dels escriptors valencians i
  balears") *See texts of Fabra (commented)*
teachers/teaching of Catalan   20, 34, **42**–**43**,
  82–**86**, **126**, **168**, 205, **219** *See also diffusion*

of norms, proof-correction, printers,
  publications and writers
technical
  – register *See register, technical*
  – vocabulary *See vocabulary, technical*
terminology *See terms, sporting; and*
  vocabulary, technical
terms
  greco-latin – *See greco-latin terms*
  sporting –   **160** *See also Anglicisms*
testing of reform measures   **191**–**192**,
  201–**203** *See also codification, criteria for,*
  evaluation of tests on usage / evaluation
  of tests on usage of appropriate uses
  / evaluation of tests on usage of the
  implanted element; and diffusion of norms
texts of Fabra (commented)
  Collected Lessons for the Higher Catalan
    Course (1933–1934) (Recull de les
    lliçons del curs de català superior
    1933–1934 pel mestre En Pompeu
    Fabra)   **45**, **48**
  Conversation with Pompeu Fabra, A
    ("Conversa amb Pompeu Fabra")   **52**
  Deviations in the Concepts of Language
    and Homeland ("Desviacions en els
    conceptes de llengua i Pàtria")   **XXXI**,
    107
  Higher Catalan Course, 1936–1937
    (Curs superior de català professat pel
    mestre Pompeu Fabra a la Universitat
    Autònoma de Barcelona)   **53**
  letter dated 13/IX/1910   **49**
  Norms of the Institut d'Estudis Catalans,
    The ("Les normes de l'Institut")   133–
    134, 216–217
  On Linguistic and Orthographical Reform
    ("Sobre la reforma lingüística y
    ortográfica")   **XV**, **37**
  On Various Unresolved Issues in Present-
    day Literary Catalan ("Sobre diferents
    problemes pendents en l'actual català
    literari")   **32**, **37**, **44**, **67**, 107,
  Philological Conversation ("Conversa
    filològica"): 18/XI/1919: **44**, **50**;
    30/XII/1919: **48**; 31/XII/1919: **48**; 24/
    I/1920: **46**; 4/II/1920: **49**; 25/V/1920:

66, 68–69; 8/XII/1922: **45**; 13/XII/1922: **50**, **69**; 17/XII/1922: **53**; 30/XII/1922: **50**; 23/I/1923: **48**; 1/IV/1923: **66**; 24/IV/1923: **47**; 24/V/1923: **51**; 13/XII/1923: **45**; 10/IX/1924: **46**; 13/IX/1924: **45**; 17/VI/1926: **46**; 12/IX/1926: **68**; 25/II/1927: **49**; 17/III/1927: **52**; 17/VI/1927: **50**; 20/VII/1927: **47**; 12/VI/1928: **51**

Philologists and Poets ("Filòlegs i poetes") **7**

Presidential Address to the Barcelona Jocs Florals [1934] ("Discurs del President") **44**

Task of Purifying Catalan, The ("L'obra de depuració del català") **37**, **44**

Task of the Valencian and Balearic Writers, The ("La tasca dels escriptors valencians i balears") XV, **8**, **37** *See also codification, criteria for, diasystematicity; and parastandard variants*

"word *qui*, The" ("El mot *qui*") **53–55**

Tirant lo Blanc **7**, 126, 129

tolerable form **43**, **48**, 129, **200** *See also discretionary norms, flexiblity of norms, inadmissible form, not recommendable form, preferred form and stylistic distribution of forms*

Tortosa **XXIX**

translation 46, **60–61**, **69**, 126, **153**, **157–158**, **193** *See also change, external and psycholinguistic factors of; and change, process of*

word-for-word –/transfer **60**, **178**

Trobes en llaors de la Verge Maria **7**

troubadours **XXIX**, 10, **130**, **135**, **212** *See also Jocs Florals*

U

ungrammatical **64**, **169**, 203 *See also fault, incorrect and solecism*

uniform language / language uniformity **38**, **115**, **123**, **197–200**, **209** *See also codification, fixation of language, redreçament and united language*

united/unity language XIX, **XXX**, 68, **122**, **146**, 200, **209–211**, **217–218** *See also codification; fixation of language; redreçament; and uniform language / (language) uniformity*

University

– of Toulouse XIII, 34

– of Barcelona XIII, 17, **31–34**, **55–56**

use/usual **42**, **127**, 163 *See also Coseriu; natural feature / naturalness; norm, objective; normal; and spontaneity*

guarantee of pertinent – *See codification, criteria for*

V

Valencia **XXVI**, **XXIX–XXX**

Valencian variety of Catalan 3, **6–9**, 11, **23–24**, 68, 88, 201, 209, **211** *See also codification, criteria for, diasystematicity; dialect; parastandard variants; and texts of Fabra (commented), Task of the Valencian and Balearic Writers…*

Vallverdú, Francesc **XXVII**

variant **39**, **42**, **61–62**, **70**, **72–74**, **173**, **181**, 200 *See also change, process of*

emerging linguistic – *See emerging linguistic variant*

parastandard – *See parastandard variant*

variation *See diversity*

vehiculation of norms **49**, **52**, **58**, **64** *See also codification, criteria for, evaluation of tests on usage / evaluation of tests on usage of appropriate uses / evaluation of tests on usage of the implanted element; diffusion of norms; proof-correction; printers; publications; teachers; and writers*

Verdaguer, Jacint 11, **42**, **150**, **181**, 193, 211

verification of reform measures **203** *See also codification, criteria for, evaluation of tests on usage / evaluation of tests on usage of appropriate uses / evaluation of tests on usage of the implanted element*

vernacle / vernacular level **XXVI**, 13, **22**, **43**, 68, **70**, **72**, **168** *See also dialect, patois and subordinated language*

Veu de Catalunya, La 16

viable/viabilility   40–41, 49, 51, 54, 171,
183, 192, 197, 202–203 *See also accessible;
and codification, criteria for, prospective
functionality*
Vic   150
Vidal de Besalú, Ramon   XXVIX
Vidal i Rosich, Cosme *See Aladern, Josep*
Viëtor Wilhelm   56, 85
view, sacrifice of personal – *See sacrifice of
personal view*
vocabulary   24, 60, 87–88, 117, 120–122, 125,
127, 173, 181, 207 *See also lexis and word*
technical –   218 *See also register, technical*
Vogel, Eberhard   216
Volkgeist   12
vowel   78, 121, 145 *See also orthography and
orthoepy*
vulgar Latin   *See Latin, vulgar*

W
War, Spanish civil *See civil War, Spanish*
Wartburg, Walter von   XXI
Webster's New International Dictionary   88,
207–208
word *See lexis, meaning, neologism, semantic,
and vocabulary*
Anglicism *See Anglicism*
archaism *See archaism*
Castilianism *See Castilianism*
composite – *See composition*
derivative – *See derivative*
dialectal – *See dialect; diasystematicity;
and diversity, geographical*
distinctiveness *See codification, criteria for
distinctiveness*
Gallicism *See Gallicism*
Greek – *See Greek word*
hybrid – *See hybrid word*

Latinism – *See Latinism*
learned – *See learned word*
new – *See neologism*
popular – *See popular, word of – origin*
sporting terms *See terms, sporting; and
also Anglicisms*
stylistic distribution of forms *See stylistic
distribution of forms*
terminology *See terms; and vocabulary,
technical*
"word *qui*, The" ("El mot *qui*") *See texts of
Fabra (commented)*
word-for-word transfer/translation *See
translation, word-for-word –/transfer*
written accents   78, 115, 118, 139, 142 *See also
orthoepy and orthography*
written language   24, 41, 47, 50, 61, 64, 69,
116, 119, 136, 143–144, 148, 150, 196–197,
202, 214–218 *See also codification;
cultivation of language; fixation of
language; normalisation; perfection;
purification of language; spoken language;
stabilisation of literary language; uniform
language / (language) uniformity; and
united language*
writers / literary people   40, 51, 86, 144,
191–193, 196–197, 203–204 *See also author,
language professional, metrics, poetry,
proof-correction, printers, publications and
teachers*
medieval – *See medieval writers and also
medieval Catalan*
nineteenth century – *See Jocs Florals,
Modernisme and Renaixença*

X
Xènius See Ors, Eugeni d'